COLONELS IN BLUE

COLONELS IN BLUE
Union Army Colonels of the Civil War

THE MID-ATLANTIC STATES:
*Pennsylvania, New Jersey, Maryland, Delaware,
and the District of Columbia*

ROGER D. HUNT

STACKPOLE
BOOKS

Copyright © 2007 by Roger D. Hunt

Published by
STACKPOLE BOOKS
5067 Ritter Road
Mechanicsburg, PA 17055
www.stackpolebooks.com

Printed in China

10 9 8 7 6 5 4 3 2 1

FIRST EDITION

Library of Congress Cataloging-in-Publication Data

Hunt, Roger D.
  Colonels in blue : Union Army colonels of the Civil War : the mid-Atlantic states :
Pennsylvania, New Jersey, Maryland, Delaware, and the District of Columbia /
Roger D. Hunt. — 1st ed.
     p. cm.
  Includes bibliographical references.
  ISBN-13: 978-0-8117-0253-9
  ISBN-10: 0-8117-0253-7
  1. United States—History—Civil War, 1861-1865—Biography. 2. United States.
Army—Officers—Biography. 3. Middle Atlantic States—Biography. 4. United
States—History—Civil War, 1861–1865—Registers. 5. Registers of births, etc.—
United States. 6. Registers of births, etc.—Middle Atlantic States. I. Title.

E467.H895 2007
973.7'45—dc22
  [B]
                                                      2007008108

In Memory of

DAVID W. CHARLES, JR.
(1925–2004)

Civil War Photo Historian

TABLE OF CONTENTS

INTRODUCTION

At the beginning of the Civil War, the Regular army of the United States numbered only 1,098 officers and 15,304 enlisted men. Faced with this shortage of manpower in suppressing the escalating rebellion, President Abraham Lincoln issued a call for 75,000 militia for three months service on April 15, 1861, and then a call for 500,000 volunteers for three years service on July 22, 1861. These calls for troops and others issued later in the war specified that the various state governors would appoint the commanding officers of the regiments raised in their states.

Patriotic fervor throughout the Northern states resulted in spirited competition to complete the organization of regiments to meet the state quotas. In most cases the prospective commanders of these regiments were prominent citizens whose military background (if any) consisted of service in a local militia organization. In general the early-war Union Army colonels were known more for their patriotic enthusiasm than for their military competence. Many of them were more successful in convincing their fellow townsmen to enlist than they were in actually leading them into battle. Fortunately for the Union cause, the colonels who stayed in the service soon acquired the necessary military skills or were replaced by subordinates who proved their capabilities on the field of battle.

This book is the third in a series of books containing biographical sketches and photographs of that diverse group of motivated citizens who attained the rank of colonel in the Union Army but failed to win promotion to brigadier general or brevet brigadier general. This volume presents the colonels who commanded regiments from the Mid-Atlantic states of Pennsylvania, New Jersey, Maryland, and Delaware plus the District of Columbia. At the beginning of each chapter is a breakdown by regiment of all the colonels who commanded regiments from that state, with the name of each colonel being followed by the dates of his service. Included in this breakdown are the colonels who were promoted beyond the rank of colonel, with their final rank indicated in bold letters. Those indicated as attaining the rank of brigadier general are covered in the book *Generals in Blue* by Ezra J. Warner, while those attaining the rank of brevet brigadier general are covered in the book *Brevet Brigadier Generals in Blue* by Roger D. Hunt and Jack R. Brown.

Some explanatory notes are necessary concerning the content of the biographical sketches:

1. The date associated with each rank is generally the date when the colonel was commissioned or appointed rather than the date when he was mustered at that rank. However, the date of muster was used whenever the date of commission or appointment was not available. The reader should be aware that these dates were constantly being revised by the War Department, so that any hope of providing completely accurate dates is virtually impossible.

2. When the word "Colonel" is italicized, this indicates that the colonel was commissioned as colonel but never mustered as such.

3. The following abbreviations are used in the text:

AAG	Assistant Adjutant General
ACM	Assistant Commissary of Musters
ACP	Appointment, Commission, and Personal
ADC	Aide-de-Camp
AIG	Assistant Inspector General
AQM	Assistant Quartermaster
Brig.	Brigadier
Bvt.	Brevet
Capt.	Captain
CB	Commission Branch
Co.	County or Company
Col.	Colonel
CSA	Confederate States Army
DOW	Died of Wounds
GAR	Grand Army of the Republic
Gen.	General
GSW	Gun Shot Wound

KIA	Killed in Action		USA	United States Army
Lt.	Lieutenant		USAMHI	United States Army Military History Institute
MOLLUS	Military Order of the Loyal Legion of the United States		USCT	United States Colored Troops
NHDVS	National Home for Disabled Volunteer Soldiers		USMA	United States Military Academy
			USV	United States Volunteers
RQM	Regimental Quartermaster		VRC	Veteran Reserve Corps
Twp.	Township		Vol.	Volume
US	United States		VS	Volunteer Service

ACKNOWLEDGMENTS

Although I appreciate the contributions of all of the individuals in the following list, I want to mention a few individuals whose contributions to this volume have been especially noteworthy. Rick Carlile, Henry Deeks, Perry Frohne, Thomas Harris, Mike McAfee, Steve Meadow, Alan Sessarego, and Dave Zullo have been especially diligent in locating elusive photographs and providing valuable information. Dr. Richard Sommers and Randy Hackenburg have provided ready access to the unparalleled photo archives of the US Army Military History Institute. Alan Aimone has been equally hospitable in providing access to the outstanding collections at the US Military Academy Library. Ronn Palm and Ken Turner have been especially generous in allowing access to their fine collections of Pennsylvania images. Similarly, John Kuhl in New Jersey and Gil Barrett in Maryland have contributed numerous images from their outstanding collections. Finally, Andy McKay has been instrumental in locating images and information in Delaware.

Jill M. Abraham, National Archives, Washington, DC
Alan C. Aimone, US Military Academy Library, West Point, NY
Michael Albanese, Kendall, NY
Ted Alexander, Greencastle, PA
Dennis Babbitt, Florissant, MO
Anthony J. Balzarano, Pearl River, NY
Gil Barrett, New Bern, NC
Catherine Baty, Historical Society of Carroll County, Westminster, MD
Everitt Bowles, Woodstock, GA
Mike Brackin, Manchester, CT
George C. Bradley, Carlisle, PA
Paul J. Brzozowski, Fairfield, CT
David L. Callihan, Dryden, NY
Robert Cammaroto, Alexandria, VA
Richard F. Carlile, Dayton, OH
John L. Carnprobst, Pittsburgh, PA
Alex. Chamberlain, Bloomsburg, PA

Diane L. Cooter, Syracuse University Library, Syracuse, NY
Henry Deeks, Ashburnham, MA
Bill Dekker, Caldwell, NJ
Robert L. Diem, Coatesville, PA
Russell P. Dodge, Warren, NJ
Early American History Auctions, Rancho Santa Fe, CA
Don Enders, Harrisburg, PA
James Enos, Carlisle, PA
Ruel Eskelsen, Historical Society of Washington, DC
Jacqueline T. Eubanks, Stuart, FL
Jerry Everts, Lambertville, MI
Charles Faust, Shillington, PA
David D. Finney, Howell, MI
James C. Frasca, Croton, OH
Perry M. Frohne, Oshkosh, WI
Larry K. Fryer, Columbia, MD
Rev. Richard E. Gardiner, Huntingdon, PA
Paula Gidjunis, Philadelphia, PA
William Gladstone, West Palm Beach, FL
Randy Hackenburg, US Army Military History Institute, Carlisle, PA
James O. Hall, McLean, VA
Sue Hannegan, Mill Hall, PA
Thomas Harris, New York, NY
Gary T. Hawbaker, Elizabethtown, PA
Virginia M. Hiatt, Union City, IN
Ian Janssen, University of Delaware Archives, Newark, DE
Craig T. Johnson, Towson, MD
Alan Jutzi, The Huntington Library, San Marino, CA
Doug Kauffmann, Greenwood, SC
Jeff Kowalis, Orland Park, IL
Michael Kraus, Pittsburgh, PA
John W. Kuhl, Pittstown, NJ
Mary E. Linne', National Archives, Washington, DC
James M. Madden, King of Prussia, PA

Charles Manuel, Bakershill, CA
Benedict R. Maryniak, Lancaster, NY
Edward Max, Honey Brook, PA
Michael J. McAfee, Newburgh, NY
Robert F. MacAvoy, Clark, NJ
John F. McCormack, Jr., West Chester, PA
Edward McGuire, New York State Library, Albany, NY
Andy McKay, Newark, DE
Sally McKee, Cecil County Historical Society, Elkton, MD
Steven J. Meadow, Midland, MI
Mike Medhurst, Kansas City, MO
Marie Melchiori, Vienna, VA
Tom Molocea, North Lima, OH
David M. Neville, Export, PA
Howard L. Norton, Vilonia, AR
Olaf, Berkeley, CA
Peter Osborne, Minisink Valley Historical Society, Port Jervis, NY
Carolyn E. Owsley, Monroe, NC
Ronn Palm, Kittanning, PA
William A. Phillis, Livonia, MI
Nicholas P. Picerno, Bridgewater, VA
Walter Plunkett, Tucson, AZ
Henry Pomerantz, Deerfield, IL
Russ A. Pritchard, Jr., Holly Springs, MS
James Quinlan, Alexandria, VA
Edmund J. Raus, Jr., Manassas, VA
Randy B. Rauscher, Colts Neck, NJ
Brett Reigh, Pennsylvania State Archives, Harrisburg, PA
David L. Richards, Gettysburg, PA
Stephen B. Rogers, Ithaca, NY
Paul Russinoff, Washington, DC
Donald K. Ryberg, Westfield, NY
James Schoonmaker, Naples, FL
Patrick A. Schroeder, Daleville, VA
Alan J. Sessarego, Gettysburg, PA
Sam Small, Gettysburg, PA
Barry A. Smith, Greensboro, NC
Timothy H. Smith, Gettysburg, PA
Dr. Richard J. Sommers, US Army Military History Institute, Carlisle, PA
Larry M. Strayer, Dayton, OH
William B. Styple, Kearny, NJ
Karl E. Sundstrom, North Riverside, IL
David Taylor, Sylvania, OH
Dee Dee Thompson, Maryland Historical Society, Baltimore, MD
Daniel C. Toomey, Linthicum, MD

Ken C. Turner, Ellwood City, PA
Tim Van Scoyoc, Blair County Historical Society, Altoona, PA
Marie H. Washburn, Frederick County Historical Society, Frederick, MD
Michael W. Waskul, Ypsilanti, MI
Wes Williams, Uniontown, PA
Michael J. Winey, Mechanicsburg, PA
Robert J. Younger, Morningside Bookshop, Dayton, OH
Bonnie Yuhas, Mohnton, PA
Buck Zaidel, Cromwell, CT
Dave Zullo, Lake Monticello, VA

I am also indebted to the staffs of the following libraries for their capable assistance:

Adams County Historical Society, Gettysburg, PA
Albright Memorial Library, Scranton, PA
Berks County Historical Society, Reading, PA
Broome County Historical Society, Binghamton, NY
Burlington County Library, Mount Holly, NJ
Cadiz Public Library, Cadiz, OH
Carnegie Free Library, Connellsville, PA
Centre County Library & Historical Museum, Bellefonte, PA
Chester County Historical Society, West Chester, PA
Civil War Library & Museum, Philadelphia, PA
Connecticut State Library, Hartford, CT
Coshocton Public Library, Coshocton, OH
Delaware Bureau of Museums & Historic Properties, Dover, DE
Delaware Public Archives, Dover, DE
Family History Library, Salt Lake City, UT
The Historical Society of Delaware, Wilmington, DE
Historical Society of Frederick County, Frederick, MD
The Historical Society of Pennsylvania, Philadelphia, PA
The Historical Society of Washington, DC
The Huntington Library, San Marino, CA
James V. Brown Library, Williamsport, PA
Kansas City Public Library, Kansas City, MO
Lancaster County Library, Lancaster, PA
Library of Congress, Washington, DC
Maryland Historical Society, Baltimore, MD
McKeesport Heritage Center, McKeesport, PA
Meadville Public Library, Meadville, PA

Minisink Valley Historical Society, Port Jervis, NY
Minnesota Historical Society, St. Paul, MN
National Archives, Washington, DC
National Society Daughters of the American Revo-
    lution, Washington, DC
New Castle Public Library, New Castle, PA
New England Historic Genealogical Society,
    Boston, MA
New Jersey Historical Society, Newark, NJ
New Jersey State Archives, Trenton, NJ
New York Genealogical and Biographical Society,
    New York, NY
The New-York Historical Society, New York, NY
New York State Library, Albany, NY
Ohio Historical Society, Columbus, OH
Pennsylvania State Archives, Harrisburg, PA
Pennsylvania State Library, Harrisburg, PA
Philadelphia City Archives, Philadelphia, PA
Plainfield Free Public Library, Plainfield, NJ
Port Jervis Free Library, Port Jervis, NY

Reading Public Library, Reading, PA
Schuylkill County Historical Society, Pottsville, PA
Shenango Valley Community Library, Sharon, PA
Soldiers and Sailors National Military Museum
    and Memorial, Pittsburgh, PA
Special Collections and University Archives, Rut-
    gers University Libraries, New Brunswick, NJ
State Historical Society of Iowa, Des Moines, IA
Union City Public Library, Union City, IN
Uniontown Public Library, Uniontown, PA
US Army Military History Institute, Carlisle, PA
US Military Academy Library, West Point, NY
University of Delaware Archives, Newark, DE
Vigo County Public Library, Terre Haute, IN
Washington County Free Library, Hagerstown,
    MD
Wayne County Public Library, Honesdale, PA
West Virginia State Library, Charleston, WV
Wyoming Historical & Geological Society,
    Wilkes-Barre, PA

PENNSYLVANIA

1st Cavalry

George D. Bayard	Sept. 14, 1861	Promoted **Brig. Gen., USV**, April 28, 1862
Owen Jones	May 5, 1862	Resigned Jan. 29, 1863
John P. Taylor	Jan. 30, 1863	Mustered out Sept. 9, 1864, **Bvt. Brig. Gen.**
Hampton S. Thomas	Jan. 4, 1865	To 2nd PA Provisional Cavalry, June 17, 1865

1st Provisional Cavalry

William W. Sanders	June 17, 1865	Mustered out July 13, 1865

2nd Cavalry

Richard B. Price	Sept. 7, 1861	Mustered out Jan. 31, 1865, **Bvt. Brig. Gen.**
William W. Sanders	March 26, 1865	To 1st PA Provisional Cavalry, June 17, 1865

2nd Provisional Cavalry

Charles L. Leiper	June 17, 1865	Mustered out Aug. 7, 1865, **Bvt. Brig. Gen.**

3rd Cavalry

William H. Young	July 10, 1861	Resigned Oct. 31, 1861
William W. Averell	Oct. 12, 1861	Promoted **Brig. Gen., USV**, Sept. 26, 1862
John B. McIntosh	Sept. 26, 1862	Promoted **Brig. Gen., USV**, July 21, 1864
Edward S. Jones	Aug. 16, 1864	Mustered out Aug. 24, 1864

3rd Provisional Cavalry

Theophilus F. Rodenbough	June 24, 1865	Mustered out Oct. 31, 1865, **Bvt. Brig. Gen.**

4th Cavalry

David Campbell	Sept. 20, 1861	To 5th PA Cavalry, March 12, 1862
James H. Childs	March 12, 1862	KIA Sept. 17, 1862
James K. Kerr	Sept. 18, 1862	Resigned May 17, 1863
George H. Covode	May 1, 1864	DOW June 25, 1864
Samuel B. M. Young	June 25, 1864	Mustered out July 1, 1865, **Bvt. Brig. Gen.**

5th Cavalry

Max Friedman	Aug. 3, 1861	Resigned March 9, 1862
David Campbell	March 12, 1862	Resigned Oct. 13, 1862
Robert M. West	April 29, 1864	Mustered out Aug. 7, 1865, **Bvt. Brig. Gen.**

6th Cavalry (organization failed)

William W. McNulty	Sept. 6, 1861	Discharged Oct. 12, 1861

6th Cavalry

Richard H. Rush	July 27, 1861	Resigned Sept. 29, 1863
Charles Ross Smith	Sept. 30, 1863	Mustered out Sept. 19, 1864
Charles L. Leiper	March 20, 1865	To 2nd PA Provisional Cavalry, June 17, 1865, **Bvt. Brig. Gen.**

7th Cavalry

George C. Wynkoop	Aug. 21, 1861	Discharged June 25, 1863
William B. Sipes	June 25, 1863	Resigned Nov. 30, 1864
Charles C. McCormick	Jan. 10, 1865	Mustered out Aug. 23, 1865, **Bvt. Brig. Gen.**

8th Cavalry

Ernest G. Chormann	Sept. 18, 1861	Discharged Dec. 31, 1861
David M. Gregg	Jan. 17, 1862	Promoted **Brig. Gen., USV**, Nov. 29, 1862
Ernest G. Chormann	June 1, 1863	Revoked June 9, 1863
Pennock Huey	June 25, 1863	Mustered out Jan. 23, 1865, **Bvt. Brig. Gen.**
William A. Corrie	July 1, 1865	Resigned Aug. 3, 1865

9th Cavalry

Edward C. Williams	Oct. 20, 1861	Resigned Oct. 9, 1862
Thomas C. James	Oct. 14, 1862	Died Jan. 13, 1863
Thomas J. Jordan	Jan. 13, 1863	Mustered out July 18, 1865, **Bvt. Brig. Gen.**

11th Cavalry

Josiah Harlan	July 23, 1861	Discharged Aug. 19, 1862
Samuel P. Spear	Aug. 20, 1862	Resigned May 9, 1865, **Bvt. Brig. Gen.**
Franklin A. Stratton	May 10, 1865	Mustered out Aug. 13, 1865, **Bvt. Brig. Gen.**

12th Cavalry

William Frishmuth	Nov. 7, 1861	Resigned April 20, 1862
Lewis B. Pierce	April 21, 1862	Discharged Dec. 15, 1864
Marcus A. Reno	Jan. 1, 1865	Mustered out July 20, 1865, **Bvt. Brig. Gen.**

13th Cavalry

James A. Galligher	July 1, 1862	Discharged Oct. 6, 1863
Michael Kerwin	April 22, 1864	Mustered out July 14, 1865

14th Cavalry

James M. Schoonmaker	Nov. 24, 1862	Discharged July 31, 1865

15th Cavalry

William J. Palmer	Sept. 8, 1862	Mustered out June 21, 1865, **Bvt. Brig. Gen.**

16th Cavalry

John Irvin Gregg	Oct. 18, 1862	Mustered out Aug. 11, 1865, **Bvt. Brig. Gen.**

17th Cavalry

Josiah H. Kellogg	Nov. 19, 1862	Discharged Dec. 17, 1864
James Q. Anderson	Dec. 18, 1864	Mustered out June 20, 1865

18th Cavalry

Timothy M. Bryan, Jr.	Dec. 24, 1862	Discharged Dec. 29, 1864
Theophilus F. Rodenbough	Jan. 1, 1865	To 3rd PA Provisional Cavalry, June 24, 1865, **Bvt. Brig. Gen.**

19th Cavalry

Alexander Cummings	Oct. 24, 1863	Discharged Feb. 6, 1865, **Bvt. Brig. Gen.**

20th Cavalry (6 months)

John E. Wynkoop	July 7, 1863	Mustered out Jan. 7, 1864

20th Cavalry (3 years)

John E. Wynkoop	Feb. 16, 1864	Dismissed Jan. 18, 1865
Gabriel Middleton	March 1, 1865	Mustered out June 20, 1865

21st Cavalry (6 months)

William H. Boyd	Aug. 20, 1863	Mustered out Feb. 20, 1864

21st Cavalry (3 years)

William H. Boyd	Feb. 20, 1864	Discharged Nov. 4, 1864
Oliver B. Knowles	Nov. 5, 1864	Mustered out July 8, 1865, **Bvt. Brig. Gen.**

22nd Cavalry

Jacob Higgins	March 5, 1864	Mustered out July 21, 1865

1st Light Artillery

Charles T. Campbell	Sept. 13, 1861	Resigned Feb. 8, 1862, Later **Brig. Gen., USV**
Robert M. West	July 28, 1862	To 5th PA Cavalry, April 29, 1864, **Bvt. Brig. Gen.**
Robert B. Ricketts	March 15, 1865	Discharged July 3, 1865

2nd Heavy Artillery

Charles Angeroth	Feb. 8, 1862	Discharged June 21, 1862
Augustus A. Gibson	June 24, 1862	Discharged July 22, 1864
James L. Anderson	July 23, 1864	KIA Sept. 29, 1864
William M. McClure	Sept. 30, 1864	Resigned March 7, 1865
Samuel D. Strawbridge	April 4, 1865	Mustered out Jan. 29, 1866

2nd Provisional Heavy Artillery

Thomas Wilhelm	April 20, 1864	To 2nd PA Heavy Artillery, Aug. 26, 1864, **Bvt. Brig. Gen.**

3rd Heavy Artillery

Joseph Roberts	March 19, 1863	Mustered out Nov. 13, 1865, **Bvt. Brig. Gen.**

4th Heavy Artillery

See 2nd Provisional Heavy Artillery

William M. McClure	April 30, 1864	Not mustered

5th Heavy Artillery

George S. Gallupe	Sept. 10, 1864	Mustered out June 30, 1865

6th Heavy Artillery
Charles Barnes   Sept. 13, 1864   Mustered out June 13, 1865, **Bvt. Brig. Gen.**

Erie Regiment Infantry
John W. McLane   April 27, 1861   Mustered out July 20, 1861

1st Infantry
Samuel Yohe   April 20, 1861   Mustered out July 27, 1861

1st Reserve Infantry
See 30th Infantry

1st Militia
Henry McCormick   Sept. 11, 1862   Discharged Sept. 25, 1862

1st Chasseurs
Charles Lespes   June 16, 1863   Authority revoked Aug. 30, 1863

2nd Infantry
Frederick S. Stumbaugh   April 20, 1861   Mustered out July 27, 1861, Later **Brig. Gen., USV**

2nd Reserve Infantry
See 31st Infantry

2nd Militia
John L. Wright   Sept. 13, 1862   Discharged Sept. 25, 1862

3rd Infantry
Francis P. Minier   April 20, 1861   Mustered out July 29, 1861

3rd Reserve Infantry
See 32nd Infantry

3rd Militia
William Dorris, Jr.   Sept. 14, 1862   Discharged Sept. 24, 1862

4th Infantry
John F. Hartranft   April 20, 1861   Mustered out July 27, 1861, Later **Brig. Gen., USV**

4th Reserve Infantry
See 33rd Infantry

4th Militia
Robert Litzinger   Sept. 15, 1862   Discharged Sept. 25, 1862

5th Infantry
Robert P. McDowell   April 21, 1861   Mustered out July 24, 1861

5th Reserve Infantry
See 34th Infantry

5th Militia
Henry C. Longnecker   Sept. 11, 1862   Discharged Sept. 27, 1862

6th Infantry
James Nagle   April 22, 1861   Mustered out July 26, 1861, Later **Brig. Gen., USV**

6th Reserve Infantry
See 35th Infantry

6th Militia
James Armstrong   Sept. 15, 1862   Discharged Sept. 28, 1862

7th Infantry
William H. Irwin   April 23, 1861   Mustered out July 23, 1861, **Bvt. Brig. Gen.**

7th Reserve Infantry
See 36th Infantry

7th Militia
Napoleon B. Kneass   Sept. 12, 1862   Discharged Sept. 26, 1862

8th Infantry
Anthony H. Emley   April 23, 1861   Mustered out July 29, 1861

8th Reserve Infantry
See 37th Infantry

8th Militia
Alfred Day   Sept. 11, 1862   Discharged Sept. 25, 1862

9th Infantry
Henry C. Longnecker   April 24, 1861   Mustered out July 29, 1861

9th Reserve Infantry
See 38th Infantry

9th Militia
John Newkumet   Sept. 12, 1862   Discharged Sept. 27, 1862

10th Infantry
Sullivan A. Meredith   April 26, 1861   Mustered out Aug. 1, 1861, Later **Brig. Gen., USV**

10th Reserve Infantry
See 39th Infantry

10th Militia
Richard M. Frame   Sept. 16, 1862   Discharged Sept. 26, 1862

11th Infantry (3 months)
Phaon Jarrett   April 26, 1861   Mustered out Aug. 1, 1861

11th Infantry (3 years)
Richard Coulter	Nov. 27, 1861	Mustered out July 1, 1865, **Bvt. Brig. Gen.**

11th Reserve Infantry
See 40th Infantry

11th Militia
Charles A. Knoderer	Sept. 12, 1862	Discharged Sept. 25, 1862

12th Infantry
David Campbell	April 25, 1861	Mustered out Aug. 5, 1861

12th Reserve Infantry
See 41st Infantry

12th Militia
Oliver J. Dickey	Sept. 16, 1862	Discharged Sept. 27, 1862

13th Infantry
Thomas A. Rowley	April 25, 1861	Mustered out Aug. 6, 1861, Later **Brig. Gen., USV**

13th Reserve Infantry
See 42nd Infantry

13th Militia
James Johnson	Sept. 17, 1862	Discharged Sept. 26, 1862

14th Infantry
John W. Johnston	April 30, 1861	Mustered out Aug. 7, 1861

14th Militia
Robert B. McComb	Sept. 16, 1862	Discharged Sept. 28, 1862

15th Infantry
Richard A. Oakford	April 27, 1861	Mustered out Aug. 8, 1861

15th Militia
Robert Galway, Jr.	Sept. 15, 1862	Discharged Sept. 28, 1862

16th Infantry
Thomas A. Ziegle	May 3, 1861	Mustered out Aug. 1, 1861

16th Militia
Joseph Willcox	Sept. 17, 1862	Discharged Sept. 27, 1862

17th Infantry
Francis E. Patterson	April 25, 1861	Mustered out Aug. 2, 1861, Later **Brig. Gen., USV**

17th Militia
James Gilkyson	Sept. 17, 1862	Discharged Sept. 27, 1862

18th Infantry
William D. Lewis, Jr.   April 24, 1861   Mustered out Aug. 6, 1861, **Bvt. Brig. Gen.**

18th Militia
Ralph L. Maclay   Sept. 12, 1862   Discharged Sept. 27, 1862

19th Infantry
Peter Lyle   April 27, 1861   Mustered out Aug. 29, 1861, **Bvt. Brig. Gen.**

19th Militia
Robert Klotz   Sept. 15, 1862   Discharged Sept. 27, 1862

20th Infantry
William H. Gray   April 30, 1861   Mustered out Aug. 3, 1861

20th Militia
William B. Thomas   Sept. 18, 1862   Discharged Sept. 28, 1862

20th Emergency Troops
William B. Thomas   June 17, 1863   Mustered out Aug. 10, 1863

21st Infantry
John F. Ballier   April 29, 1861   Mustered out Aug. 9, 1861, **Bvt. Brig. Gen.**

21st Militia
Alexander Murphy   Sept. 15, 1862   Discharged Sept. 26, 1862

22nd Infantry
Turner G. Morehead   April 23, 1861   Mustered out Aug. 5, 1861, **Bvt. Brig. Gen.**

22nd Militia
Samuel M. Wickersham   Sept. 16, 1862   Discharged Oct. 1, 1862

23rd Infantry (3 months)
Charles P. Dare   April 21, 1861   Mustered out July 31, 1861

23rd Infantry (3 years)
David B. Birney   Aug. 31, 1861   Promoted **Brig. Gen., USV**, Feb. 17, 1862
Thomas H. Neill   Feb. 17, 1862   Promoted **Brig. Gen., USV**, Nov. 29, 1862
John Ely   Dec. 13, 1862   Resigned Dec. 6, 1863, **Bvt. Brig. Gen.**
John F. Glenn   Jan. 19, 1864   Mustered out Sept. 8, 1864

23rd Militia
George B. Wiestling   Sept. 21, 1862   Discharged Oct. 1, 1862

24th Infantry
Joshua T. Owen   May 8, 1861   Mustered out Aug. 10, 1861, Later **Brig. Gen., USV**

24th Militia
Russell F. Lord, Jr.   Sept. 20, 1862   Discharged Sept. 22, 1862

25th Infantry

Henry L. Cake | April 18, 1861 | Mustered out Aug. 1, 1861

25th Militia

Constant M. Eakin | Sept. 15, 1862 | Discharged Oct. 1, 1862

26th Infantry

William F. Small | May 5, 1861 | Discharged June 30, 1862
Benjamin C. Tilghman | March 1, 1863 | To 3rd USCT, July 28, 1863, **Bvt. Brig. Gen.**

26th Emergency Troops

William W. Jennings | June 22, 1863 | Mustered out July 30, 1863

27th Infantry

Max Einstein | May 31, 1861 | Discharged Oct. 2, 1861
Adolph E. Buschbeck | Nov. 1, 1861 | Mustered out June 11, 1864

27th Emergency Troops

Jacob G. Frick | June 22, 1863 | Mustered out July 31, 1863

28th Infantry

John W. Geary | June 28, 1861 | Promoted **Brig. Gen., USV**, April 25, 1862
Gabriel DeKorponay | April 25, 1862 | Discharged March 26, 1863
Thomas J. Ahl | Nov. 15, 1863 | Resigned March 18, 1864
John Flynn | June 9, 1864 | Mustered out Nov. 6, 1865, **Bvt. Brig. Gen.**

28th Emergency Troops

James Chamberlin | June 23, 1863 | Mustered out July 28, 1863

29th Infantry

John K. Murphy | July 1, 1861 | Discharged April 23, 1863, **Bvt. Brig. Gen.**
William Rickards, Jr. | April 24, 1863 | Discharged Nov. 2, 1864
Samuel M. Zulick | March 25, 1865 | Mustered out July 17, 1865, **Bvt. Brig. Gen.**

29th Emergency Troops

Joseph W. Hawley | June 23, 1863 | Mustered out Aug. 1, 1863

30th Infantry (1st Reserve Infantry)

Richard Biddle Roberts | June 9, 1861 | Resigned Nov. 1, 1862
William Cooper Talley | March 1, 1863 | Mustered out June 13, 1864, **Bvt. Brig. Gen.**

30th Emergency Troops

William N. Monies | June 25, 1863 | Mustered out July 27, 1863

31st Infantry (2nd Reserve Infantry)

William B. Mann | June 21, 1861 | Resigned Oct. 30, 1861
William McCandless | Nov. 1, 1861 | Mustered out June 16, 1864

31st Emergency Troops

John Newkumet | June 30, 1863 | Mustered out Aug. 8, 1863

32nd Infantry (3rd Reserve Infantry)
Horatio G. Sickel | July 28, 1861 | Mustered out June 17, 1864, **Bvt. Brig. Gen.**

32nd Militia
Charles S. Smith | June 26, 1863 | Mustered out Aug. 1, 1863

33rd Infantry (4th Reserve Infantry)
Robert G. March | May 9, 1861 | Resigned Oct. 1, 1861
Albert L. Magilton | Oct. 4, 1861 | Resigned Dec. 23, 1862
Richard H. Woolworth | Dec. 24, 1862 | KIA May 9, 1864
Thomas F. B. Tapper | May 10, 1864 | Mustered out June 17, 1864

33rd Emergency Troops
William W. Taylor | June 26, 1863 | Mustered out Aug. 4, 1863

34th Infantry (5th Reserve Infantry)
Seneca G. Simmons | June 21, 1861 | DOW July 1, 1862
Joseph W. Fisher | July 1, 1862 | Mustered out June 11, 1864, **Bvt. Brig. Gen.**

34th Militia
Charles Albright | July 3, 1863 | Mustered out Aug. 24, 1863, **Bvt. Brig. Gen.**

35th Infantry (6th Reserve Infantry)
William W. Ricketts | June 22, 1861 | Discharged Feb. 27, 1862
William Sinclair | April 1, 1862 | Resigned June 6, 1863
Wellington H. Ent | July 1, 1863 | Mustered out June 11, 1864, **Bvt. Brig. Gen.**

35th Militia
Henry B. McKean | July 4, 1863 | Mustered out Aug. 7, 1863

36th Infantry (7th Reserve Infantry)
Elisha B. Harvey | June 26, 1861 | Resigned July 4, 1862
Henry C. Bolinger | Aug. 1, 1862 | Discharged Aug. 19, 1864, **Bvt. Brig. Gen.**

36th Militia
Hiram C. Alleman | July 4, 1863 | Mustered out Aug. 11, 1863

37th Infantry (8th Reserve Infantry)
George S. Hays | June 22, 1861 | Resigned July 11, 1862
Silas M. Baily | March 1, 1863 | Mustered out May 24, 1864, **Bvt. Brig. Gen.**

37th Militia
John Trout | July 4, 1863 | Mustered out Aug. 4, 1863

38th Infantry (9th Reserve Infantry)
Conrad F. Jackson | July 27, 1861 | Promoted **Brig. Gen., USV**, July 17, 1862
Robert Anderson | July 17, 1862 | Resigned June 12, 1863

38th Militia
Melchior H. Horn | July 3, 1863 | Mustered out Aug. 7, 1863

39th Infantry (10th Reserve Infantry)

John S. McCalmont	June 29, 1861	Resigned May 9, 1862
James T. Kirk	May 13, 1862	Resigned Oct. 18, 1862
Adoniram J. Warner	April 25, 1863	To 17th VRC, Nov. 15, 1863, **Bvt. Brig. Gen.**

39th Militia

James Nagle	July 1, 1863	Mustered out Aug. 2, 1863, **Brig. Gen., USV**

40th Infantry (11th Reserve Infantry)

Thomas F. Gallagher	July 1, 1861	Resigned Dec. 17, 1862, **Bvt. Brig. Gen.**
Samuel M. Jackson	April 9, 1863	Mustered out June 13, 1864, **Bvt. Brig. Gen.**

40th Militia

Alfred Day	July 2, 1863	Mustered out Aug. 16, 1863

41st Infantry (12th Reserve Infantry)

John H. Taggart	July 25, 1861	Resigned July 8, 1862
John H. Taggart	Aug. 19, 1862	Mustered out Sept. 23, 1862
Martin D. Hardin	Sept. 1, 1862	Mustered out June 11, 1864, Later **Brig. Gen., USV**

41st Militia

Edward R. Mayer	July 5, 1863	Mustered out Aug. 4, 1863

42nd Infantry (13th Reserve Infantry)

Thomas L. Kane	June 12, 1861	Resigned June 13, 1861, Later **Brig. Gen., USV**
Charles J. Biddle	June 13, 1861	Resigned Dec. 11, 1861
Hugh W. McNeil	Jan. 22, 1862	KIA Sept. 16, 1862
Charles F. Taylor	Sept. 17, 1862	KIA July 2, 1863

42nd Militia

Charles H. Hunter	July 6, 1863	Mustered out Aug. 12, 1863

43rd Infantry

See 1st Light Artillery

43rd Militia

William W. Stott	July 6, 1863	Mustered out Aug. 13, 1863

44th Infantry

See 1st Cavalry

44th Militia

Enos Woodward	July 6, 1863	Mustered out Aug. 27, 1863

45th Infantry

Thomas Welsh	Oct. 21, 1861	Promoted **Brig. Gen., USV**, Nov. 29, 1862
John I. Curtin	April 13, 1863	Mustered out July 17, 1865, **Bvt. Brig. Gen.**

45th Militia

James T. Clancy	Aug. 13, 1863	Mustered out Aug. 29, 1863

46th Infantry

Joseph F. Knipe	Oct. 31, 1861	Promoted **Brig. Gen., USV**, Nov. 29, 1862
James L. Selfridge	May 10, 1863	Mustered out July 16, 1865, **Bvt. Brig. Gen.**

46th Militia

John J. Lawrence	July 8, 1863	Mustered out Aug. 19, 1863

47th Infantry

Tilghman H. Good	Aug. 5, 1861	Mustered out Sept. 24, 1864
John P. S. Gobin	Jan. 3, 1865	Mustered out Dec. 25, 1865, **Bvt. Brig. Gen.**

47th Militia

James P. Wickersham	July 9, 1863	Mustered out Aug. 14, 1863

48th Infantry

James Nagle	Oct. 1, 1861	Promoted **Brig. Gen., USV**, Sept. 10, 1862
Joshua K. Sigfried	Sept. 20, 1862	Mustered out Sept. 30, 1864, **Bvt. Brig. Gen.**
Henry Pleasants	Oct. 1, 1864	Mustered out Dec. 18, 1864, **Bvt. Brig. Gen.**
George W. Gowen	March 1, 1865	KIA April 2, 1865, **Bvt. Brig. Gen.**
Isaac F. Brannon	April 3, 1865	Mustered out July 17, 1865

48th Militia

John B. Embich	July 8, 1863	Mustered out Aug. 26, 1863

49th Infantry

William H. Irwin	Feb. 28, 1862	Resigned Oct. 24, 1863, **Bvt. Brig. Gen.**
Thomas M. Hulings	March 26, 1864	KIA May 10, 1864
Baynton J. Hickman	June 29, 1865	Resigned June 28, 1865
Amor W. Wakefield	July 14, 1865	Mustered out July 15, 1865

49th Militia

Alexander Murphy	July 14, 1863	Mustered out Sept. 3, 1863

50th Infantry

Benjamin C. Christ	Sept. 30, 1861	Mustered out Sept. 30, 1864, **Bvt. Brig. Gen.**
William H. Telford	May 1, 1865	Mustered out July 30, 1865

50th Militia

Emlen Franklin	July 1, 1863	Mustered out Aug. 15, 1863

51st Infantry

John F. Hartranft	Nov. 16, 1861	Promoted **Brig. Gen., USV**, May 12, 1864
Edwin Schall	May 13, 1864	KIA June 3, 1864
William J. Bolton	June 26, 1864	Mustered out July 17, 1865, **Bvt. Brig. Gen.**

51st Militia

Oliver Hopkinson	July 10, 1863	Mustered out Sept. 2, 1863

52nd Infantry

John C. Dodge, Jr.	Nov. 5, 1861	Discharged Nov. 5, 1863
Henry M. Hoyt	Nov. 6, 1863	Mustered out Nov. 3, 1864, **Bvt. Brig. Gen.**
John B. Conyngham	March 1, 1865	Mustered out July 12, 1865

52nd Militia

William A. Gray	July 9, 1863	Mustered out Sept. 1, 1863

53rd Infantry

John R. Brooke	Nov. 7, 1861	Promoted **Brig. Gen., USV**, May 12, 1864
S. Octavius Bull	Sept. 18, 1864	Mustered out Oct. 31, 1864
William M. Mintzer	Nov. 2, 1864	Mustered out June 30, 1865, **Bvt. Brig. Gen.**

53rd Militia

Henry Royer	July 13, 1863	Mustered out Aug. 20, 1863

54th Infantry

Jacob M. Campbell	Feb. 27, 1862	Discharged Sept. 3, 1864, **Bvt. Brig. Gen.**
Albert P. Moulton	April 3, 1865	Discharged May 30, 1865

54th Militia

Thomas F. Gallagher	July 4, 1863	Mustered out Aug. 17, 1863, **Bvt. Brig. Gen.**

55th Infantry

Richard White	Aug. 2, 1861	Mustered out March 24, 1865
John H. Filler	March 25, 1865	Mustered out March 15, 1865

55th Militia

Robert B. McComb	July 3, 1863	Mustered out Aug. 26, 1863

56th Infantry

Sullivan A. Meredith	March 6, 1862	Promoted **Brig. Gen., USV**, Nov. 29, 1862
J. William Hofmann	Jan. 8, 1863	Mustered out March 7, 1865, **Bvt. Brig. Gen.**
Henry A. Laycock	March 17, 1865	Mustered out July 1, 1865

56th Militia

Samuel B. Dick	July 5, 1863	Mustered out Aug. 13, 1863

57th Infantry

William Maxwell	Aug. 24, 1861	Resigned Feb. 27, 1862
Charles T. Campbell	March 4, 1862	Promoted **Brig. Gen., USV**, Nov. 29, 1862
Peter Sides	March 12, 1863	Discharged Nov. 28, 1864
George Zinn	March 19, 1865	Mustered out June 29, 1865, **Bvt. Brig. Gen.**

57th Militia

James R. Porter	July 8, 1863	Mustered out Aug. 17, 1863

58th Infantry

J. Richter Jones	Feb. 13, 1862	KIA May 23, 1863
Carlton B. Curtis	May 23, 1863	Resigned July 2, 1863
Cecil Clay	Nov. 20, 1864	Mustered out Jan. 24, 1866, **Bvt. Brig. Gen.**

58th Militia

George H. Bemus	July 1, 1863	Mustered out Aug. 15, 1863

59th Infantry
See 2nd Cavalry

59th Militia

George P. McLean	June 27, 1863	Mustered out Sept. 9, 1863

60th Infantry
See 3rd Cavalry

60th Militia

William F. Small	June 19, 1863	Mustered out Sept. 8, 1863

61st Infantry

Oliver H. Rippey	July 24, 1861	KIA May 31, 1862
George C. Spear	June 1, 1862	KIA May 3, 1863
George F. Smith	May 4, 1863	Mustered out Sept. 7, 1864
George F. Smith	Sept. 29, 1864	Resigned April 26, 1865
Robert L. Orr	April 27, 1865	Mustered out June 28, 1865

62nd Infantry

Samuel W. Black	July 4, 1861	KIA June 27, 1862
Jacob B. Sweitzer	June 27, 1862	Mustered out July 13, 1864, **Bvt. Brig. Gen.**

63rd Infantry

Alexander Hays	Oct. 9, 1861	Promoted **Brig. Gen., USV**, Sept. 29, 1862
Algernon S. M. Morgan	Sept. 29, 1862	Discharged April 18, 1863
William S. Kirkwood	April 18, 1863	DOW June 25, 1863
John A. Danks	July 1, 1863	Mustered out Aug. 5, 1864

64th Infantry
See 4th Cavalry

65th Infantry
See 5th Cavalry

66th Infantry

Alfred W. Chantry	June 21, 1861	Superseded
John Patrick	Jan. 20, 1862	Resigned Feb. 6, 1862

67th Infantry

John F. Staunton	July 24, 1861	Dismissed Sept. 1, 1864
Harry White	Jan. 18, 1865	Mustered out Feb. 22, 1865, **Bvt. Brig. Gen.**
John C. Carpenter	June 1, 1865	Mustered out July 14, 1865

68th Infantry

Andrew H. Tippin	June 26, 1862	Mustered out June 9, 1865

69th Infantry
Joshua T. Owen	Aug. 18, 1861	Promoted **Brig. Gen., USV**, Nov. 29, 1862
Dennis O'Kane	Dec. 1, 1862	DOW July 4, 1863
William Davis	Jan. 1, 1865	Mustered out July 1, 1865

70th Infantry
See 6th Cavalry

71st Infantry
Edward D. Baker	June 22, 1861	KIA Oct. 21, 1861, **Brig. Gen., USV**
Isaac J. Wistar	Nov. 11, 1861	Promoted **Brig. Gen., USV**, Nov. 29, 1862
Richard Penn Smith	Feb. 1, 1863	Mustered out July 2, 1864

72nd Infantry
DeWitt C. Baxter	Aug. 10, 1861	Mustered out Aug. 24, 1864, **Bvt. Brig. Gen.**

73rd Infantry
John A. Koltes	Aug. 2, 1861	KIA Aug. 30, 1862
George A. Muhleck	Aug. 30, 1862	Resigned Jan. 27, 1863
William Moore	Jan. 28, 1863	Resigned Feb. 8, 1864
Charles C. Cresson	May 1, 1865	Mustered out Aug. 24, 1865

74th Infantry
Alexander Schimmelfennig	Sept. 30, 1861	Promoted **Brig. Gen., USV**, Nov. 29, 1862
John A. Hamm	Dec. 8, 1862	Mustered out March 2, 1863
Adolph Von Hartung	April 4, 1863	Resigned July 11, 1864
Gottlieb Hoburg	April 1, 1865	Mustered out Aug. 29, 1865

75th Infantry
Henry Bohlen	Sept. 30, 1861	Promoted **Brig. Gen., USV**, April 28, 1862
Philip J. Schopp	Sept. 14, 1862	Discharged Nov. 7, 1862
Francis Mahler	July 30, 1862	DOW July 4, 1863

76th Infantry
John M. Power	Aug. 10, 1861	Resigned Aug. 7, 1862
DeWitt C. Strawbridge	Aug. 9, 1862	Resigned Nov. 20, 1863
John C. Campbell	Jan. 11, 1864	Resigned Aug. 16, 1864
John S. Littell	Oct. 29, 1864	Mustered out July 18, 1865, **Bvt. Brig. Gen.**

77th Infantry
Frederick S. Stumbaugh	Oct. 26, 1861	Promoted **Brig. Gen., USV**, Nov. 29, 1862
Thomas E. Rose	Feb. 1, 1863	Mustered out Dec. 6, 1865, **Bvt. Brig. Gen.**

78th Infantry
William Sirwell	Aug. 26, 1861	Discharged Nov. 17, 1863
William Sirwell	March 9, 1864	Mustered out Nov. 4, 1864
Augustus B. Bonnaffon	March 11, 1865	Mustered out Dec. 14, 1865

79th Infantry
Henry A. Hambright	Oct. 18, 1861	Mustered out July 20, 1865, **Bvt. Brig. Gen.**

80th Infantry
See 7th Cavalry

81st Infantry

James Miller	Aug. 8, 1861	KIA June 1, 1862
Charles F. Johnson	June 1, 1862	Resigned Nov. 24, 1862
Henry Boyd McKeen	Nov. 24, 1862	KIA June 3, 1864
William Wilson	Oct. 30, 1864	Mustered out June 29, 1865

82nd Infantry

David H. Williams	July 23, 1861	Promoted **Brig. Gen., USV**, Nov. 29, 1862
Isaac C. Bassett	May 3, 1863	Mustered out July 20, 1865, **Bvt. Brig. Gen.**

83rd Infantry

John W. McLane	July 24, 1861	KIA June 27, 1862
Strong Vincent	June 27, 1862	Promoted **Brig. Gen., USV**, July 3, 1863
Orpheus S. Woodward	March 28, 1864	Mustered out Sept. 20, 1864, **Bvt. Brig. Gen.**
Chauncey P. Rogers	March 7, 1865	Mustered out June 28, 1865

84th Infantry

William G. Murray	Aug. 30, 1861	KIA March 23, 1862
Samuel M. Bowman	June 21, 1862	Mustered out May 15, 1865, **Bvt. Brig. Gen.**

85th Infantry

Joshua B. Howell	Nov. 12, 1861	Promoted **Brig. Gen., USV**, Sept. 12, 1864

87th Infantry

George Hay	Sept. 25, 1861	Discharged May 8, 1863
John W. Schall	May 9, 1863	Mustered out Oct. 13, 1864
Walter S. Franklin	Jan. 31, 1865	Not mustered
James Tearney	May 10, 1865	Mustered out June 29, 1865

88th Infantry

George P. McLean	Aug. 9, 1861	Resigned Dec. 1, 1862
George W. Gile	Jan. 24, 1863	Discharged March 2, 1863, **Bvt. Brig. Gen.**
Louis Wagner	March 3, 1863	Mustered out June 30, 1865, **Bvt. Brig. Gen.**

89th Infantry
See 8th Cavalry

90th Infantry

Peter Lyle	March 10, 1862	Mustered out Nov. 26, 1864, **Bvt. Brig. Gen.**

91st Infantry

Edgar M. Gregory	Aug. 2, 1861	Discharged Nov. 30, 1867, **Bvt. Brig. Gen.**

92nd Infantry
See 9th Cavalry

93rd Infantry

James M. McCarter	Oct. 28, 1861	Dismissed Nov. 27, 1862
John M. Mark	Nov. 27, 1862	Resigned March 12, 1863
James M. McCarter	April 13, 1863	Resigned Aug. 19, 1863
Charles W. Eckman	Dec. 16, 1864	Mustered out June 27, 1865

95th Infantry

John M. Gosline	Oct. 12, 1861	DOW June 29, 1862
Gustavus W. Town	June 28, 1862	KIA May 3, 1863
Thomas J. Town	May 3, 1863	Resigned Aug. 5, 1863
John Harper	April 3, 1865	Mustered out July 17, 1865

96th Infantry

Henry L. Cake	Sept. 23, 1861	Resigned March 12, 1863
William H. Lessig	March 13, 1863	Mustered out Oct. 21, 1864

97th Infantry

Henry R. Guss	Oct. 29, 1861	Resigned June 22, 1864, **Bvt. Brig. Gen.**
Galusha Pennypacker	Aug. 15, 1864	Promoted **Brig. Gen., USV**, Feb. 18, 1865
John Wainwright	June 1, 1865	Mustered out Aug. 28, 1865

98th Infantry

John F. Ballier	Sept. 30, 1861	Discharged Nov. 26, 1862
Adolph Mehler	Nov. 26, 1862	Discharged March 12, 1863
John F. Ballier	April 24, 1863	Mustered out June 29, 1865, **Bvt. Brig. Gen.**

99th Infantry

Romain Lujeane	July 22, 1861	Resigned Nov. 7, 1861
Thomas W. Sweney	Nov. 7, 1861	Resigned Jan. 24, 1862
Peter Fritz	Feb. 25, 1862	Resigned June 10, 1862
Asher S. Leidy	June 11, 1862	Discharged April 9, 1864
Edwin R. Biles	Aug. 23, 1864	Mustered out July 1, 1865, **Bvt. Brig. Gen.**

100th Infantry

Daniel Leasure	Aug. 31, 1861	Mustered out Aug. 30, 1864
Norman J. Maxwell	April 18, 1865	Mustered out July 24, 1865, **Bvt. Brig. Gen.**

101st Infantry

Joseph H. Wilson	Oct. 4, 1861	Died May 30, 1862
David B. Morris	July 21, 1862	Mustered out Jan. 24, 1865
James Sheafer	May 31, 1865	Mustered out June 25, 1865

102nd Infantry

Thomas A. Rowley	Aug. 6, 1861	Promoted **Brig. Gen., USV**, Nov. 29, 1862
Joseph M. Kinkead	Jan. 15, 1863	Resigned May 27, 1863
John W. Patterson	May 27, 1863	KIA May 5, 1864
James Patchell	April 18, 1865	Mustered out June 28, 1865

103rd Infantry

John B. Finlay	Sept. 7, 1861	Not mustered
Theodore F. Lehmann	Oct. 30, 1861	Mustered out June 25, 1865

104th Infantry

William W. H. Davis	Sept. 5, 1861	Mustered out Sept. 30, 1864, **Bvt. Brig. Gen.**
Theophilus G. Kephart	May 2, 1865	Mustered out Aug. 25, 1865

105th Infantry

Amor A. McKnight	Aug. 28, 1861	Resigned July 29, 1862
William W. Corbet	July 30, 1862	Resigned Sept. 10, 1862
Amor A. McKnight	Sept. 20, 1862	KIA May 3, 1863
Calvin A. Craig	May 4, 1863	DOW Aug. 17, 1864
James Miller	April 25, 1865	Mustered out July 11, 1865

106th Infantry

Turner G. Morehead	Aug. 28, 1861	Discharged April 4, 1864, **Bvt. Brig. Gen.**
William L. Curry	April 5, 1864	DOW July 7, 1864
John H. Gallager	June 23, 1865	Mustered out June 30, 1865

107th Infantry

Thomas A. Ziegle	March 6, 1862	Died July 15, 1862
Thomas F. McCoy	Aug. 6, 1862	Mustered out July 13, 1865, **Bvt. Brig. Gen.**

108th Infantry
See 11th Cavalry

109th Infantry

Henry J. Stainrook	Nov. 8, 1861	KIA May 3, 1863
Lewis W. Ralston	May 4, 1863	Discharged April 12, 1864

110th Infantry

William D. Lewis, Jr.	Jan. 2, 1862	Resigned Dec. 20, 1862, **Bvt. Brig. Gen.**
James Crowther	Dec. 21, 1862	KIA May 3, 1863
Isaac Rogers	April 23, 1864	DOW May 23, 1864
Franklin B. Stewart	June 19, 1865	Mustered out June 28, 1865

111th Infantry

Matthew Schlaudecker	Jan. 24, 1862	Resigned Nov. 6, 1862
George A. Cobham, Jr.	Nov. 7, 1862	KIA July 20, 1864, **Bvt. Brig. Gen.**
Thomas M. Walker	April 23, 1865	Mustered out July 19, 1865, **Bvt. Brig. Gen.**

112th Infantry
See 2nd Heavy Artillery

113th Infantry
See 12th Cavalry

114th Infantry

Charles H. T. Collis	Sept. 1, 1862	Mustered out May 29, 1865, **Bvt. Brig. Gen.**

115th Infantry

Robert E. Patterson	June 25, 1862	Resigned Dec. 2, 1862, **Bvt. Brig. Gen.**
Francis A. Lancaster	Dec. 2, 1862	KIA May 3, 1863
William C. Ward	June 19, 1864	Not mustered

116th Infantry

Dennis Heenan	Sept. 1, 1862	Discharged Jan. 26, 1863
St. Clair A. Mulholland	May 3, 1864	Mustered out June 3, 1865, **Bvt. Brig. Gen.**
David W. Megraw	June 4, 1865	Mustered out July 14, 1865

117th Infantry

See 13th Cavalry

118th Infantry

Charles M. Prevost	Aug. 28, 1862	To 16th VRC, Sept. 29, 1863, **Bvt. Brig. Gen.**
James Gwyn	Dec. 5, 1863	Mustered out June 1, 1865, **Bvt. Brig. Gen.**

119th Infantry

Peter C. Ellmaker	Aug. 2, 1862	Resigned Jan. 12, 1864
Gideon Clark	Jan. 13, 1864	Mustered out June 19, 1865, **Bvt. Brig. Gen.**

121st Infantry

Chapman Biddle	Aug. 1, 1862	Resigned Dec. 10, 1863
Alexander W. Biddle	Dec. 11, 1863	Resigned Jan. 9, 1864
James Ashworth	Jan. 10, 1864	Discharged Feb. 10, 1864

122nd Infantry

Emlen Franklin	Aug. 14, 1862	Mustered out May 16, 1863

123rd Infantry

John B. Clark	Aug. 21, 1862	Mustered out May 13, 1863

124th Infantry

Joseph W. Hawley	Aug. 18, 1862	Mustered out May 17, 1863

125th Infantry

Jacob Higgins	Aug. 16, 1862	Mustered out May 18, 1863

126th Infantry

James G. Elder	Aug. 13, 1862	Mustered out May 20, 1863

127th Infantry

William W. Jennings	Aug. 16, 1862	Mustered out May 29, 1863

128th Infantry

Samuel Croasdale	Aug. 25, 1862	KIA Sept. 17, 1862
Joseph A. Mathews	Nov. 1, 1862	Mustered out May 19, 1863, **Bvt. Brig. Gen.**

129th Infantry

Jacob G. Frick	Aug. 15, 1862	Dismissed Jan. 25, 1863
Jacob G. Frick	April 10, 1863	Mustered out May 18, 1863

130th Infantry

Henry I. Zinn	Aug. 17, 1862	KIA Dec. 13, 1862
Levi Maish	Dec. 14, 1862	Mustered out May 21, 1863

131st Infantry

Peter H. Allabach	Aug. 18, 1862	Mustered out May 23, 1863

132nd Infantry

Richard A. Oakford	Aug. 22, 1862	KIA Sept. 17, 1862
Vincent M. Wilcox	Sept. 18, 1862	Resigned Jan. 21, 1863
Charles Albright	Jan. 24, 1863	Mustered out May 24, 1863, **Bvt. Brig. Gen.**

133rd Infantry

Franklin B. Speakman	Aug. 21, 1862	Mustered out May 26, 1863

134th Infantry

Matthew S. Quay	Aug. 23, 1862	Resigned Dec. 7, 1862
Edward O'Brien	Dec. 8, 1862	Mustered out May 26, 1863

135th Infantry

James R. Porter	Aug. 19, 1862	Mustered out May 24, 1863

136th Infantry

Thomas M. Bayne	Aug. 23, 1862	Resigned Jan. 30, 1863
Thomas M. Bayne	March 18, 1863	Mustered out May 29, 1863

137th Infantry

Henry M. Bossert	Aug. 25, 1862	Resigned March 14, 1863
Joseph B. Kiddoo	March 15, 1863	Mustered out June 1, 1863, **Bvt. Brig. Gen.**

138th Infantry

Charles L. K. Sumwalt	Aug. 30, 1862	Dismissed March 30, 1863
Matthew R. McClennan	May 2, 1863	Mustered out June 23, 1865, **Bvt. Brig. Gen.**

139th Infantry

Frederick H. Collier	Sept. 1, 1862	Mustered out Nov. 27, 1865, **Bvt. Brig. Gen.**

140th Infantry

Richard P. Roberts	Sept. 8, 1862	KIA July 2, 1863
John Fraser	July 4, 1863	Mustered out May 31, 1865, **Bvt. Brig. Gen.**

141st Infantry

Henry J. Madill	Sept. 5, 1862	Mustered out May 28, 1865, **Bvt. Brig. Gen.**

142nd Infantry

Robert P. Cummins	Sept. 1, 1862	DOW July 2, 1863
Alfred B. McCalmont	July 4, 1863	To 208th PA Infantry, Sept. 12, 1864, **Bvt. Brig. Gen.**
Horatio N. Warren	June 3, 1865	Mustered out May 29, 1865

143rd Infantry

Edmund L. Dana	Nov. 18, 1862	Mustered out Aug. 4, 1865, **Bvt. Brig. Gen.**

144th Infantry

George Crookes	Sept. 3, 1862	Organization failed

145th Infantry
Hiram L. Brown	Sept. 5, 1862	Resigned Feb. 1, 1865, **Bvt. Brig. Gen.**
David B. McCreary	Jan. 17, 1865	Mustered out May 31, 1865, **Bvt. Brig. Gen.**

146th Infantry
John D. C. Johnson	July 1862	Organization failed

147th Infantry
Ario Pardee, Jr.	March 19, 1864	Resigned June 13, 1865, **Bvt. Brig. Gen.**
John Craig	June 14, 1865	Mustered out July 15, 1865

148th Infantry
James A. Beaver	Sept. 8, 1862	Discharged Dec. 22, 1864, **Bvt. Brig. Gen.**
James F. Weaver	June 1, 1865	Mustered out June 1, 1865

149th Infantry
Roy Stone	Aug. 30, 1862	Resigned Jan. 27, 1865, **Bvt. Brig. Gen.**
John Irvin	Jan. 28, 1865	Mustered out Aug. 4, 1865

150th Infantry
Langhorne Wister	Sept. 4, 1862	Resigned Feb. 22, 1864, **Bvt. Brig. Gen.**
Henry S. Huidekoper	Feb. 23, 1864	Resigned March 5, 1864
George W. Jones	June 15, 1865	Mustered out June 23, 1865

151st Infantry
Harrison Allen	Nov. 11, 1862	Mustered out July 31, 1863, **Bvt. Brig. Gen.**

152nd Infantry
See 3rd Heavy Artillery

153rd Infantry
Charles F. W. Glanz	Oct. 11, 1862	Mustered out July 24, 1863

154th Infantry
Benjamin C. Brooker	Oct. 29, 1862	Organization failed

155th Infantry
Edward J. Allen	Sept. 5, 1862	Discharged July 21, 1863
John H. Cain	July 22, 1863	Resigned Aug. 30, 1863
Alfred L. Pearson	July 1, 1864	Mustered out June 2, 1865, **Bvt. Brig. Gen.**

156th Infantry
Charles Ernenwein	Sept. 18, 1862	Organization failed

157th Infantry
William A. Gray	Oct. 21, 1862	Organization failed

158th Infantry
David B. McKibbin	Nov. 24, 1862	Mustered out Aug. 12, 1863, **Bvt. Brig. Gen.**

159th Infantry
See 14th Cavalry

160th Infantry
See 15th Cavalry

161st Infantry
See 16th Cavalry

162nd Infantry
See 17th Cavalry

163rd Infantry
See 18th Cavalry

165th Infantry

Charles H. Buehler	Dec. 16, 1862	Mustered out July 28, 1863

166th Infantry

Andrew J. Fulton	Nov. 25, 1862	Mustered out July 28, 1863

167th Infantry

Charles A. Knoderer	Nov. 6, 1862	DOW Feb. 15, 1863
Joseph DePuy Davis	March 19, 1863	Mustered out Aug. 12, 1863

168th Infantry

Joseph Jack	Dec. 1, 1862	Mustered out July 25, 1863

169th Infantry

Lewis W. Smith	Nov. 28, 1862	Mustered out July 27, 1863

171st Infantry

Everard Bierer	Nov. 18, 1862	Discharged Aug. 8, 1863

172nd Infantry

Charles Kleckner	Nov. 19, 1862	Mustered out Aug. 1, 1863

173rd Infantry

Daniel Nagle	Nov. 17, 1862	Mustered out Aug. 17, 1863

174th Infantry

John Nyce	Nov. 19, 1862	Mustered out Aug. 7, 1863

175th Infantry

Samuel A. Dyer	Nov. 22, 1862	Mustered out Aug. 7, 1863

176th Infantry

Ambrose A. Lechler	Nov. 28, 1862	Mustered out Sept. 17, 1863

177th Infantry

George B. Wiestling	Nov. 28, 1862	Mustered out Aug. 7, 1863

178th Infantry

James Johnson	Dec. 2, 1862	Mustered out July 27, 1863

179th Infantry

William H. Blair	Dec. 8, 1862	Mustered out July 27, 1863, **Bvt. Brig. Gen.**

180th Infantry
See 19th Cavalry

181st Infantry
See 20th Cavalry

182nd Infantry
See 21st Cavalry

183rd Infantry

George P. McLean	March 8, 1864	Resigned May 3, 1864
John F. McCullough	May 28, 1864	KIA May 31, 1864
James C. Lynch	July 19, 1864	Mustered out Oct. 5, 1864, **Bvt. Brig. Gen.**
George T. Egbert	Oct. 7, 1864	Mustered out July 13, 1865

184th Infantry

John H. Stover	April 4, 1864	Mustered out July 14, 1865

185th Infantry
See 22nd Cavalry

186th Infantry

Henry A. Frink	May 30, 1864	Mustered out Aug. 15, 1865, **Bvt. Brig. Gen.**

187th Infantry

John S. Schultze	April 1, 1864	Declined
John E. Parsons	May 1, 1865	Mustered out Aug. 3, 1865

188th Infantry

George K. Bowen	April 12, 1864	Discharged Nov. 2, 1864
George K. Bowen	Nov. 12, 1864	Discharged March 27, 1865
John G. Gregg	May 1, 1865	Resigned July 1, 1865
Joseph C. Briscoe	June 28, 1865	Dismissed Nov. 3, 1865, **Bvt. Brig. Gen.**
Samuel I. Givin	Nov. 26, 1865	Mustered out Dec. 14, 1865

189th Infantry
See 2nd Provisional Heavy Artillery

190th Infantry

William R. Hartshorne	July 23, 1864	Mustered out June 28, 1865, **Bvt. Brig. Gen.**

191st Infantry

James Carle	June 6, 1864	Mustered out June 28, 1865, **Bvt. Brig. Gen.**

192nd Infantry (100 days)

William B. Thomas	July 15, 1864	Mustered out Nov. 11, 1864

192nd Infantry (1 year)
William W. Stewart   March 26, 1865   Mustered out Aug. 24, 1865 **Bvt. Brig. Gen.**

193rd Infantry
John B. Clark   July 19, 1864   Mustered out Nov. 9, 1864

194th Infantry
James Nagle   July 24, 1864   Mustered out Nov. 5, 1864, **Brig. Gen., USV**

195th Infantry (100 days)
Joseph W. Fisher   July 24, 1864   Mustered out Nov. 4, 1864, **Bvt. Brig. Gen.**

195th Infantry (1 year)
Joseph W. Fisher   March 12, 1865   Mustered out Jan. 31, 1866, **Bvt. Brig. Gen.**

196th Infantry
Harmanus Neff   July 9, 1864   Mustered out Nov. 22, 1864

197th Infantry
John R. Haslett   July 22, 1864   Mustered out Nov. 11, 1864

198th Infantry
Horatio G. Sickel   Sept. 15, 1864   Mustered out June 4, 1865, **Bvt. Brig. Gen.**

199th Infantry
Joseph C. Briscoe   Oct. 3, 1864   To 188th PA Infantry, June 28, 1865, **Bvt. Brig. Gen.**

200th Infantry
Charles W. Diven   Sept. 3, 1864   Mustered out May 18, 1865, **Bvt. Brig. Gen.**

201st Infantry
Francis Asbury Awl   Aug. 29, 1864   Mustered out June 21, 1865

202nd Infantry
Charles Albright   Sept. 4, 1864   Mustered out Aug. 3, 1865, **Bvt. Brig. Gen.**

203rd Infantry
John W. Moore   Sept. 10, 1864   KIA Jan. 15, 1865
Oliver P. Harding   Jan. 16, 1865   Dismissed May 2, 1865
Amos W. Bachman   May 3, 1865   Mustered out June 22, 1865

204th Infantry
See 5th Heavy Artillery

205th Infantry
Joseph A. Mathews   Sept. 2, 1864   Mustered out June 2, 1865, **Bvt. Brig. Gen.**

206th Infantry
Hugh J. Brady   Sept. 8, 1864   Mustered out June 26, 1865

207th Infantry

Robert C. Cox	Sept. 9, 1864	Mustered out May 31, 1865, **Bvt. Brig. Gen.**

208th Infantry

Alfred B. McCalmont	Sept. 12, 1864	Mustered out June 1, 1865, **Bvt. Brig. Gen.**

209th Infantry

Tobias B. Kaufman	Sept. 16, 1864	Mustered out May 31, 1865

210th Infantry

William Sergeant	Sept. 24, 1864	DOW April 11, 1865
Edward L. Witman	April 12, 1865	Mustered out May 30, 1865

211th Infantry

James H. Trimble	Sept. 16, 1864	Resigned March 18, 1865
Levi A. Dodd	April 4, 1865	Discharged Aug. 4, 1865, **Bvt. Brig. Gen.**

212th Infantry

See 6th Heavy Artillery

213th Infantry

John A. Gorgas	March 4, 1865	Mustered out Nov. 18, 1865

214th Infantry

David B. McKibbin	April 5, 1865	Mustered out April 30, 1866, **Bvt. Brig. Gen.**

215th Infantry

Francis Wister	April 21, 1865	Mustered out July 31, 1865

Thomas Jefferson Ahl

THOMAS JEFFERSON AHL

Captain, Co. H, 28 PA Infantry, July 11, 1861. Ambulance Officer, 12 Army Corps, Army of the Potomac, Sept. 28, 1862. Provost Marshal, 12 Army Corps, Aug. 4, 1863. Colonel, 28 PA Infantry, Nov. 15, 1863. Commanded 1 Brigade, 2 Division, 12 Army Corps, Army of the Cumberland, Nov. 27–Dec. 1, 1863. Resigned March 18, 1864, "on account of some dispute in my muster in as colonel" and also because of "a complaint at Department Headquarters of my making a false statement in getting the order to proceed home with my regiment."

Born: April 2, 1839 York Co., PA
Died: April 1, 1887 Kirksville, MO
Occupation: Traveling lumber dealer in Arkansas before war. Commercial salesman after war.
Miscellaneous: Resided Pittsburgh, PA; New York City, NY; Boston, MA; Cincinnati, OH; and Kirksville, Adair Co., MO
Buried: Forest Cemetery, Kirksville, MO (Section B, Lot 85)
References: Pension File and Military Service File, National Archives. Obituary, *Pittsburgh Dispatch*, April 3, 1887. Letters Received, Volunteer Service Branch, Adjutant General's Office, File P170(VS)1864, National Archives.

PETER HOLLINGSHEAD ALLABACH

Colonel, 131 PA Infantry, Aug. 18, 1862. Commanded 2 Brigade, 3 Division, 5 Army Corps, Army of the Potomac, Sept. 12, 1862–Feb. 15, 1863 and March 7–May 23, 1863. Honorably mustered out, May 23, 1863.

Peter Hollingshead Allabach

Born: Sept. 9, 1824 Forty Fort, Luzerne Co., PA
Died: Feb. 11, 1892 Washington, DC
Other Wars: Mexican War (Sergeant, Co. E, 3 US Infantry)
Occupation: Practiced dentistry and held a position in US mail service before war. Captain, US Capitol Police, 1879–92.
Miscellaneous: Resided Pittston, Luzerne Co., PA; Harrisburg, Dauphin Co., PA; and Washington, DC
Buried: Arlington National Cemetery, Arlington, VA (Section 1, Lot 253)
References: Joseph R. Orwig. *History of the 131st Pennsylvania Volunteers.* Williamsport, PA, 1902. Pension File, National Archives. Obituary, *Washington Evening Star,* Feb. 12, 1892. *Under the Maltese Cross Antietam to Appomattox: Campaigns 155th Pennsylvania Regiment.* Pittsburgh, PA, 1910. William H. Egle and James M. Lamberton. *History of Perseverance Lodge, No. 21, F. & A. M., Pennsylvania, at Harrisburg.* Harrisburg, PA, 1901.

HIRAM CLAY ALLEMAN

1 Lieutenant, Co. E, 15 PA Infantry, May 1, 1861. Honorably mustered out, Aug. 7, 1861. Captain, Co. D, 127 PA Infantry, Aug. 5, 1862. Lieutenant Colonel, 127 PA Infantry, Aug. 16, 1862. Shell wound right knee, Fredericksburg, VA, Dec. 13, 1862. Shell wound Chancellorsville, VA, May 3, 1863. Honorably mustered out, May 29, 1863. Colonel, 36 PA Militia, July 4, 1863. Honorably mustered out, Aug. 11, 1863.

Born: Sept. 15, 1831 Highspire, Dauphin Co., PA
Died: Oct. 22, 1906 New York City, NY
Occupation: Lawyer
Offices/Honors: PA House of Representatives, 1864–65. US District Attorney, Territory of Colorado, 1873–75.
Miscellaneous: Resided Harrisburg, Dauphin Co., PA, to 1866; Philadelphia, PA, 1866–73; Denver, CO, 1873–75; Washington, DC, 1875–79; London, England, 1879–87; New York City, NY, after 1887
Buried: Oak Hill Cemetery, Washington, DC (Lot 925)
References: Pension File, National Archives. Samuel P. Bates. *Martial Deeds of Pennsylvania.* Philadelphia, PA, 1875. *A Biographical Album of Prominent Pennsylvanians.* Second Series. Philadelphia, PA, 1889. *History of the 127th Regiment Pennsylvania Volunteers.* Lebanon, PA, 1902.

Hiram Clay Alleman
ROGER D. HUNT COLLECTION, USAMHI.
A. G. KEET, HARRISBURG, PA.

EDWARD JAY ALLEN

Volunteer ADC, Staff of Major Gen. John C. Fremont, April–June 1862. Colonel, 155 PA Infantry, Sept. 5, 1862. Discharged for disability, July 21, 1863, having been absent from duty over five months due to chronic rheumatism.

Born: April 27, 1830 New York City, NY
Died: Dec. 26, 1915 Pittsburgh, PA
Education: Attended Duquesne College, Pittsburgh, PA
Occupation: Early in life a pioneer in Oregon Territory, he engaged in various civil engineering projects including the preliminary survey of the route of the Northern Pacific Railroad. Returning to Pittsburgh in 1855, he built a section of the aqueduct which supplied the City of Washington, DC, with water, and was constructing a portion of the Virginia Central Railroad when the war began. After the war he was one of the organizers of the Pacific and Atlantic Telegraph Co., and served as its secretary until it was purchased by Western Union.

Miscellaneous: Resided Pittsburgh, PA

Buried: Homewood Cemetery, Pittsburgh, PA (Section 10, Lot 145)

References: *National Cyclopedia of American Biography.* Obituary Circular, Whole No. 836, Pennsylvania MOLLUS. *Under the Maltese Cross: Antietam to Appomattox: Campaigns 155th Pennsylvania Regiment.* Pittsburgh, PA, 1910. Military Service File, National Archives. Obituary, *Pittsburgh Dispatch,* Dec. 27, 1915. William H. Powell, editor. *Officers of the Army and Navy (Volunteer) Who Served in the Civil War.* Philadelphia, PA, 1893. Samuel P. Bates. *Martial Deeds of Pennsylvania.* Philadelphia, PA, 1875. Letters Received, Volunteer Service Branch, Adjutant General's Office, File P980(VS)1863, National Archives.

JAMES L. ANDERSON

Captain, Battery G, 2 PA Heavy Artillery, Dec. 10, 1861. Major, 2 PA Heavy Artillery, March 1, 1862. *Colonel,* 2 PA Heavy Artillery, July 23, 1864. GSW head, Chapin's Farm, VA, Sept. 29, 1864.

Born: 1825? MD

Died: Sept. 29, 1864 KIA Chapin's Farm, VA

Occupation: Jeweler

Miscellaneous: Resided Philadelphia, PA

Buried: Chapin's Farm, VA (Body never recovered)

References: Pension File and Military Service File, National Archives. George W. Ward. *History of the 2nd Pennsylvania Veteran Heavy Artillery From 1861 to 1866.* Philadelphia, PA, 1904. Letters Received, Volunteer Service Branch, Adjutant General's Office, File W516(VS)1866, National Archives.

Edward Jay Allen

FROM *UNDER THE MALTESE CROSS: ANTIETAM TO APPOMATTOX: CAMPAIGNS 155TH PENNSYLVANIA REGIMENT.*

James Quigley Anderson

JAMES QUIGLEY ANDERSON

1 Lieutenant, Co. A, 17 PA Cavalry, Sept. 6, 1862. Captain, Co. A, 17 PA Cavalry, Dec. 11, 1862. Major, 17 PA Cavalry, Jan. 11, 1863. Lieutenant Colonel, 17 PA Cavalry, June 13, 1863. Dismissed Feb. 18, 1864, for "having, in violation of existing orders and the customs of war, crossed the line of pickets, delivering and receiving letters from persons outside the lines." Restored to his command, March 22, 1864. Colonel, 17 PA Cavalry, Dec. 18, 1864. Honorably mustered out, June 20, 1865, upon consolidation of the regiment.

Born: July 5, 1831 Brighton, Beaver Co., PA
Died: Oct. 10, 1865 Beaver, PA
Education: Attended Beaver (PA) Academy
Occupation: Civil engineer engaged in laying out government lands in Missouri
Miscellaneous: Resided Beaver, Beaver Co., PA; and Kansas City, MO
Buried: Beaver Cemetery, Beaver, PA

References: Samuel P. Bates. *Martial Deeds of Pennsylvania.* Philadelphia, PA, 1875. Henry P. Moyer. *History of the 17th Regiment Pennsylvania Cavalry.* Lebanon, PA, 1911. Military Service File, National Archives. Letters Received, Volunteer Service Branch, Adjutant General's Office, File A981(VS)1864, National Archives.

ROBERT ANDERSON

Lieutenant Colonel, 9 PA Reserves, May 3, 1861. Colonel, 9 PA Reserves, July 17, 1862. Commanded 3 Brigade, 3 Division, 3 Army Corps, Army of Virginia, Aug. 30–Sept. 1, 1862. Commanded 3 Brigade, 3 Division, 1 Army Corps, Army of the Potomac, Sept. 14–Oct. 2, 1862 and Dec. 13–30, 1862. Dismissed March 3,

Robert Anderson

1863, to date Feb. 10, 1863, for "drunkenness in the street whilst stopping in the City (Washington) for medical treatment." Backed by almost unanimous support of his regiment and influential civilians, his dismissal was revoked and he was restored to his command, June 8, 1863. Resigned June 12, 1863.

Born: May 17, 1817 NY
Died: June 17, 1876 Pittsburgh, PA
Other Wars: Mexican War (2 Lieutenant, Co. K, 1 PA Infantry)
Occupation: Post office clerk
Offices/Honors: Postmaster, Pittsburgh, PA, 1853–58
Miscellaneous: Resided Pittsburgh, PA
Buried: St. Mary's Cemetery, Pittsburgh, PA (Section G, Lot 5)
References: Military Service File, National Archives. Anderson family archives, courtesy of John L. Carnprobst. Obituary, *Pittsburgh Gazette*, June 19, 1876. Josiah R. Sypher. *History of the Pennsylvania Reserve Corps.* Lancaster, PA, 1865. Letters Received, Volunteer Service Branch, Adjutant General's Office, File W450(VS)1863, National Archives. Albert J. Edwards. *Souvenir Pittsburgh Post Office.* Pittsburgh, PA, 1891.

CHARLES ANGEROTH

Lieutenant Colonel, 27 PA Infantry, May 31, 1861. Resigned Sept. 7, 1861, in order to "find an appointment as artillery officer in one of the newly raised artillery regiments." Colonel, 2 PA Heavy Artillery, Feb. 8, 1862. Discharged upon adverse report of a Board of Examination, June 21, 1862.

Born: Aug. 23, 1810 Prussia
Died: Jan. 23, 1882 Camden, NJ
Other Wars: Several years in the artillery service of the Prussian army. Mexican War (1 Sergeant, Co. E, 1 PA Infantry).
Occupation: Upholsterer
Miscellaneous: Resided Camden, Camden Co., NJ
Buried: Evergreen Cemetery, Camden, NJ
References: Obituary, *Philadelphia Public Ledger*, Jan. 24, 1882. Obituary, *Camden Post*, Jan. 30, 1882. Letters Received, Volunteer Service Branch, Adjutant General's Office, File A67(VS)1862, National Archives. George W. Ward. *History of the 2nd Pennsylvania Veteran Heavy Artillery from 1861 to 1866.* Philadelphia, PA, 1904. Military Service File, National Archives.

JAMES ARMSTRONG

Captain, Co. E, 12 PA Infantry, April 25, 1861. Honorably mustered out, Aug. 5, 1861. Captain, Co. A, 100 PA Infantry, Aug. 26, 1861. Major, 100 PA Infantry, Sept. 10, 1861. Lieutenant Colonel, 100 PA Infantry, Oct. 9, 1861. Resigned July 12, 1862, "in consequence of more than six months continued ill health, unfitting me entirely for the proper discharge of the duties of my position." Colonel, 6 PA Militia, Sept. 15, 1862. Honorably discharged, Sept. 28, 1862.

Born: 1819 North Huntington Twp., Westmoreland Co., PA
Died: April 16, 1891 Greensburg, PA
Education: Attended Jefferson College, Canonsburg, PA
Other Wars: Mexican War (1 Lieutenant, Co. E, 2 PA Infantry)
Occupation: Printer and newspaper editor in early life. Later practiced law.
Miscellaneous: Resided Pittsburgh, PA, 1850–58; Washington, PA, 1858–68; and Greensburg, Westmoreland Co., PA, 1868–91
Buried: St. Clair Cemetery, Greensburg, PA (Section T, Lots 114–115)
References: Pension File and Military Service File, National Archives. William G. Gavin. *Campaigning with the Roundheads: The History of the 100th Pennsylvania Veteran Volunteer Infantry Regiment in the American Civil War.* Dayton, OH, 1989. George D. Albert, editor. *History of the County of Westmoreland.* Philadelphia, PA, 1882. Obituary, *Greensburg Daily Tribune*, April 16, 1891.

JAMES ASHWORTH

Captain, Co. I, 121 PA Infantry, Aug. 22, 1862. Major, 121 PA Infantry, April 21, 1863. GSW breast, right arm and right knee, Gettysburg, PA, July 1, 1863. Lieutenant Colonel, 121 PA Infantry, Dec. 11, 1863. *Colonel*, 121 PA Infantry, Jan. 10, 1864. Discharged for disability, Feb. 10, 1864, on account of wounds received in action. Captain, 146 Co., 2 Battalion, VRC, Jan. 16, 1865. Captain, Co. G, 20 VRC, Sept. 23, 1865. Honorably mustered out, June 30, 1866.

Born: Sept. 11, 1836 Bury, Lancashire, England
Died: March 21, 1882 Gainesville, FL
Education: Attended Philadelphia (PA) Central High School

James Ashworth (postwar)
FROM *HISTORY OF THE 121ST REGIMENT PENNSYLVANIA VOLUNTEERS.*

Occupation: Superintendent of a shipping firm and US Internal Revenue official
Offices/Honors: Resigned position as Collector of Internal Revenue, Jan. 31, 1882
Miscellaneous: Resided Frankford, Philadelphia Co., PA
Buried: Cedar Hill Cemetery, Philadelphia, PA (Section V, Lot 52)
References: William W. Strong. *History of the 121st Regiment Pennsylvania Volunteers.* Philadelphia, PA, 1906. Pension File, National Archives. Obituary, *Philadelphia Public Ledger,* March 22, 1882. Letters Received, Volunteer Service Branch, Adjutant General's Office, Files A36(VS)1864 and T398(VS)1865, National Archives. *Papers Read Before the Historical Society of Frankford,* Vol. 1, No. 1, 1906.

FRANCIS ASBURY AWL

1 Lieutenant, Co. D, 11 PA Infantry, April 23, 1861. 1 Lieutenant, Adjutant, 11 PA Infantry, April 26, 1861. Honorably mustered out, Aug. 1, 1861. Captain, Co. A, 127 PA Infantry, Aug. 1, 1862. Honorably mustered out, May 8, 1863. Colonel, 201 PA Infantry, Aug. 29, 1864. Honorably mustered out, June 21, 1865.

Born: April 8, 1837 Harrisburg, PA
Died: March 25, 1904 Harrisburg, PA
Education: Attended Dickinson College, Carlisle, PA
Occupation: Bank cashier
Miscellaneous: Resided Harrisburg, Dauphin Co., PA
Buried: Harrisburg Cemetery, Harrisburg, PA (Section E-2, Lot 35)
References: *Commemorative Biographical Encyclopedia of Dauphin County, PA.* Chambersburg, PA, 1896. Pension File, National Archives. Obituary, *Harrisburg Patriot,* March 26, 1904. *History of the 127th Regiment Pennsylvania Volunteers.* Lebanon, PA, 1902. William H. Egle. *Pennsylvania Genealogies.* Harrisburg, PA, 1896. Charles P. Meck, compiler. *First City Zouaves and City Grays: History of Harrisburg's Leading Military Organization, 1861–1913.* Harrisburg, PA, 1914.

Francis Asbury Awl
COURTESY OF PERRY M. FROHNE.
WOLFF'S GALLERY, No. 10 ROYAL ST., ALEXANDRIA, VA.
OPPERMAN, PHOTOGRAPHER.

AMOS W. BACHMAN

Sergeant, Co. C, 99 PA Infantry, Aug. 8, 1861. 1 Sergeant, Co. C, 99 PA Infantry, Dec. 1, 1862. 2 Lieutenant, Co. C, 99 PA Infantry, Feb. 3, 1863. GSW, Wilderness, VA, May 6, 1864. 1 Lieutenant, Co. C, 99 PA Infantry, May 17, 1864. Captain, Co. C, 99 PA Infantry, Aug. 8, 1864. Captain, Co. A, 203 PA Infantry, Sept. 20, 1864. Lieutenant Colonel, 203 PA Infantry, Jan. 16, 1865. Colonel, 203 PA Infantry, May 3, 1865. Honorably mustered out, June 22, 1865.

Born: May 30, 1839 Pequea Twp., Lancaster Co., PA
Died: Oct. 28, 1888 Willow Street, Lancaster Co., PA
Education: Attended Millersville (PA) State Normal School

Occupation: School teacher before war. Carpenter and gas inspector in the Philadelphia Gas Department after war.
Miscellaneous: Resided Philadelphia, PA; and Willow Street, Lancaster Co., PA
Buried: Fernwood Cemetery, Philadelphia, PA (Section 20, Lot 331)
References: DeForest L. Bachman. *After Twenty-Five Years of Peaceful Repose.* Philadelphia, PA, 1913. Obituary, *Lancaster Daily Intelligencer,* Oct. 29, 1888. Obituary, *Philadelphia Public Ledger,* Oct. 30, 1888. Pension File and Military Service File, National Archives. *Biographical Annals of Lancaster County, PA.* Spartanburg, SC, 1985.

THOMAS McKEE BAYNE

Captain, Co. H, 136 PA Infantry, Aug. 9, 1862. Colonel, 136 PA Infantry, Aug. 23, 1862. Resigned and discharged for disability, Jan. 30, 1863, due to "chronic diarrhea since Dec. 14, 1862, and a gonorrheal disease of seven months standing." Upon request of nine officers of the 136 PA Infantry, acceptance of his resignation was canceled, March 3, 1863. Remustered as Colonel, 136 PA Infantry, April 8, 1863, to date from March 18, 1863. Honorably mustered out, May 29, 1863.

Amos W. Bachman
MICHAEL J. McAFEE COLLECTION.
J. E. McCLEES, ARTIST, 910 CHESTNUT STREET, PHILADELPHIA, PA.

Thomas McKee Bayne
RONN PALM COLLECTION.
A. G. KEET, HARRISBURG, PA.

Born: June 14, 1836 Bellevue, Allegheny Co., PA
Died: June 16, 1894 Washington, DC (committed suicide by pistol shot)
Education: Attended Westminster College, New Wilmington, PA
Occupation: Lawyer
Offices/Honors: District Attorney, Allegheny Co., PA, 1870–73. US House of Representatives, 1877–91.
Miscellaneous: Resided Pittsburgh, PA; and Washington, DC
Buried: Union Dale Cemetery, Pittsburgh, PA (Division 2, Section B, Lot 19)
References: *Biographical Directory of the American Congress.* Letters Received, Volunteer Service Branch, Adjutant General's Office, File B1294(VS)1862, National Archives. Military Service File, National Archives. Obituary, *Washington Evening Star*, June 16, 1894. Obituary, *Pittsburgh Dispatch*, June 17, 1894.

GEORGE HAMLIN BEMUS

1 Lieutenant, Co. F, 9 PA Reserves, April 26, 1861. Acting ADC, Staff of Brig. Gen. Conrad F. Jackson, May 17, 1862–Dec. 13, 1862. Discharged for disability, Feb. 17, 1863, due to injuries received at Fredericksburg, VA, Dec. 13, 1862, when his horse fell on him. Colonel, 58 PA Militia, July 1, 1863. Honorably mustered out, Aug. 15, 1863.

Born: May 1, 1831 Pine Grove, PA
Died: Dec. 28, 1896 Corry, PA
Education: Attended Fredonia (NY) Academy
Occupation: Lawyer
Offices/Honors: PA House of Representatives, 1865–66
Miscellaneous: Resided Meadville, Crawford Co., PA; Petrolia, Butler Co., PA; and Corry, Erie Co., PA
Buried: Greendale Cemetery, Meadville, PA (Section 1, Lot 23)
References: Thomas Waln-Morgan Draper. *The Bemis History and Genealogy.* San Francisco, CA, 1900. Obituary, *Crawford Journal, Meadville, PA*, Dec. 31, 1896. Pension File, National Archives.

ALEXANDER WILLIAMS BIDDLE

Major, 121 PA Infantry, Sept. 1, 1862. Lieutenant Colonel, 121 PA Infantry, April 20, 1863. *Colonel*, 121 PA Infantry, Dec. 11, 1863. Resigned Jan. 9, 1864, due to the reduced strength of the regiment, "considering my position neither beneficial to the Army nor to myself, with repeated entreaties from my relatives to use every effort to return home on account of my family affairs."

Born: April 29, 1819 Philadelphia, PA
Died: May 2, 1899 Philadelphia, PA
Education: Graduated University of Pennsylvania, Philadelphia, PA, 1838
Occupation: Banker
Offices/Honors: President of the Board of Directors of City Trusts, 1882–84. Director of the Pennsylvania Railroad Company, 1874–99.
Miscellaneous: Resided Philadelphia, PA. First cousin of Bvt. Brig. Gen. James Biddle and Colonel Chapman Biddle.
Buried: Laurel Hill Cemetery, Philadelphia, PA (Section X, Lots 151–154)
References: *Col. Alexander Biddle, 1819–1899. Memorial Services in Girard College Chapel.* Philadelphia, PA, 1899. *Men of America: A Biographical Album of the City Government of Philadelphia in the Bi-Centennial Year.* Philadelphia, PA, 1883. John W. Jordan, editor. *Colonial Families of Philadelphia.* New York and Chicago, 1911. William W. Strong. *History of the 121st Regiment Pennsylvania Volunteers.* Philadelphia, PA, 1906. Military Service File, National Archives. Obituary Circular, Whole No. 374, Pennsylvania MOLLUS. Obituary, *Philadelphia Public Ledger*, May 3, 1899. Moses King. *Philadelphia and Notable Philadelphians.* New York City, NY, 1902.

CHAPMAN BIDDLE

Colonel, 121 PA Infantry, Aug. 1, 1862. GSW head, Gettysburg, PA, July 1, 1863. Commanded 1 Brigade, 3 Division, 1 Army Corps, Army of the Potomac, June 30–July 2, 1863, July 10–Sept. 14, 1863, and Oct. 14–Dec. 10, 1863. Resigned Dec. 10, 1863, since "my regiment for several months past has numbered for duty scarcely more than a company, a force altogether too small to act efficiently as a battalion or to require the services of a field officer."

Alexander Williams Biddle (on horseback)
FROM *HISTORY OF THE 121ST REGIMENT PENNSYLVANIA VOLUNTEERS.*

Chapman Biddle (postwar)
FROM *HISTORY OF THE 121ST REGIMENT PENNSYLVANIA VOLUNTEERS.*

Born: Jan. 22, 1822 Philadelphia, PA
Died: Dec. 9, 1880 Philadelphia, PA
Education: Attended St. Mary's College, Baltimore, MD
Occupation: Real estate lawyer
Miscellaneous: Resided Philadelphia, PA. First cousin of Bvt. Brig. Gen. James Biddle and Colonel Alexander Biddle.
Buried: Churchyard of St. James the Less, Philadelphia, PA (Lots 167–168)
References: Charles Godfrey Leland. *A Memoir of Chapman Biddle.* Philadelphia, PA, 1882. William W. Strong. *History of the 121st Regiment Pennsylvania Volunteers.* Philadelphia, PA, 1906. Military Service File, National Archives. Obituary, *Philadelphia Public Ledger,* Dec. 10, 1880.

CHARLES JOHN BIDDLE

Colonel, 13 PA Reserves, June 13, 1861. Commanded 1 Brigade, Banks' Division, Army of the Potomac, Aug. 28–Sept. 25, 1861. Appointed Brig. Gen., USV, Aug. 31, 1861, but declined the appointment. Resigned Dec. 11, 1861, to take his seat in Congress.

Born: April 30, 1819 Philadelphia, PA
Died: Sept. 28, 1873 Philadelphia, PA
Education: Graduated Princeton (NJ) University, 1837
Other Wars: Mexican War (Captain, US Voltigeurs)
Occupation: Lawyer before war. Newspaper editor after war.
Offices/Honors: US House of Representatives, 1861–63
Miscellaneous: Resided Philadelphia, PA
Buried: St. Peter's Episcopal Churchyard, Philadelphia, PA

Charles John Biddle
NATIONAL ARCHIVES.

References: Frank W. Leach. *Biddle Family*. Philadelphia, PA, 1932. Josiah R. Sypher. *History of the Pennsylvania Reserve Corps*. Lancaster, PA, 1865. *Proceedings of a Meeting of the Bar of Philadelphia Relative to the Death of Charles J. Biddle; and a Memoir of the Deceased by the Hon. John Cadwalader*. Philadelphia, PA, 1874. Letters Received, Volunteer Service Branch, Adjutant General's Office, File B102(VS)1861, National Archives. Obituary, *Philadelphia Public Ledger*, Sept. 29, 1873. *Biographical Directory of the American Congress.*

EVERARD BIERER

Captain, Co. F, 11 PA Reserves, June 20, 1861. Taken prisoner, Gaines' Mill, VA, June 27, 1862. Confined Libby Prison, Richmond, VA. Exchanged Aug. 14, 1862. GSW left arm, South Mountain, MD, Sept. 14, 1862. Colonel, 171 PA Infantry, Nov. 18, 1862. Commanded 1 Brigade, 5 Division, 18 Army Corps, Department of North Carolina. Commanded District of the Pamlico, 18 Army Corps, Department of North Carolina, June 1863. Dishonorably discharged, upon the expiration of his term of service, for having "illegally removed and shipped from Washington, NC, a large mirror valued at $300.00 and other valuable property, with the view of appropriating the same to his private use." His dishonorable discharge was revoked, Sept. 26, 1863, and he was honorably discharged to date, Aug. 8, 1863. Captain, 127 Co., 2 Battalion, VRC, Feb. 6, 1864. Resigned March 12, 1864.

Born: Jan. 9, 1827 Uniontown, PA
Died: Dec. 26, 1910 Hiawatha, KS
Education: Attended Madison College, Uniontown, PA
Occupation: Lawyer
Offices/Honors: District Attorney, Fayette Co., PA, 1850–53. KS House of Representatives, 1868.
Miscellaneous: Resided Uniontown, Fayette Co., PA, to 1865; and Hiawatha, Brown Co., KS, after 1865
Buried: Mount Hope Cemetery, Hiawatha, KS (Block 11, Lot 33)
References: George W. Martin, editor. *Transactions of the Kansas State Historical Society, 1907–08*. Topeka, KS, 1908. *The United States Biographical Dictionary*. Kansas Volume. Chicago and Kansas City, 1879. Pension File and Military Service File, National Archives. Samuel T. Wiley, editor. *Biographical and Portrait Cyclopedia of Fayette County, PA*. Chicago, IL, 1889. Letters Received, Volunteer Service Branch, Adjutant General's Office,

Everard Bierer (postwar)
FROM *HISTORY OF THE STATE OF KANSAS.*

Files B247(VS)1862 and B1129(VS)1863, National Archives. Joseph Gibbs. *Three Years in the Bloody Eleventh: The Campaigns of a Pennsylvania Reserves Regiment*. University Park, PA, 2002. Alfred T. Andreas. *History of the State of Kansas*. Chicago, IL, 1883.

SAMUEL WYLIE BLACK

Colonel, 62 PA Infantry, July 4, 1861. GSW head, Gaines' Mill, VA, June 27, 1862.

Born: Sept. 3, 1816 Pittsburgh, PA
Died: June 27, 1862 KIA Gaines' Mill, VA
Other Wars: Mexican War (Lieutenant Colonel, 1 PA Infantry)
Occupation: Lawyer
Offices/Honors: Associate Justice, Nebraska Territory Supreme Court, 1857–59. Governor of Nebraska Territory, 1859–61.

Samuel Wylie Black
RONN PALM COLLECTION.
PUBLISHED BY E. & H. T. ANTHONY, 501 BROADWAY, NEW YORK,
FROM PHOTOGRAPHIC NEGATIVE IN
BRADY'S NATIONAL PORTRAIT GALLERY.

Miscellaneous: Resided Pittsburgh, PA; and Nebraska City, Otoe Co., NE

Buried: Allegheny Cemetery, Pittsburgh, PA (Section 4, Lot 18)

References: J. Sterling Morton. *Illustrated History of Nebraska.* Lincoln, NE, 1905. Samuel P. Bates. *Martial Deeds of Pennsylvania.* Philadelphia, PA, 1875. Thomas A. McMullin and David Walker. *Biographical Directory of American Territorial Governors.* Westport, CT, 1984. *The 62nd Pennsylvania Volunteers in the War for the Union. Dedicatory Exercises at Gettysburg.* Pittsburgh, PA, 1889.

AUGUSTUS BENTON BONNAFFON

Sergeant, Co. K, 12 PA Infantry, April 25, 1861. Honorably mustered out, Aug. 5, 1861. Major, 78 PA Infantry, Sept. 17, 1861. Lieutenant Colonel, 78 PA Infantry, July 25, 1864. Colonel, 78 PA Infantry, March 11, 1865. Honorably mustered out, Dec. 14, 1865.

Born: 1837 Pittsburgh, PA

Died: July 12, 1867 Indianola, TX (yellow fever)

Occupation: Railroad freight agent and steamship clerk before war. Regular Army (1 Lieutenant, 35 US Infantry) after war.

Miscellaneous: Resided Pittsburgh, PA

Buried: Laurel Hill Cemetery, Philadelphia, PA (Section 17, Lot 70)

References: Letters Received, Commission Branch, Adjutant General's Office, File W763(CB)1867, National Archives. Joseph T. Gibson, editor. *History of the 78th Pennsylvania Volunteer Infantry.* Pitts-

Augustus Benton Bonnaffon
ROGER D. HUNT COLLECTION, USAMHI.
F. GUTEKUNST, 704 & 706 ARCH STREET, PHILADELPHIA, PA.

burgh, PA, 1905. Pension File and Military Service File, National Archives. Letters Received, Volunteer Service Branch, Adjutant General's Office, File B3337(VS)1864, National Archives.

HENRY MILLER BOSSERT

Captain, Co. C, 11 PA Infantry, April 25, 1861. Honorably mustered out, Aug. 1, 1861. Colonel, 137 PA Infantry, Aug. 25, 1862. Commanded 1 Brigade, 2 Division, 6 Army Corps, Army of the Potomac, Nov.–Dec. 1862. Commanded 3 Brigade, 1 Division, 1 Army Corps, Army of the Potomac, Feb. 17–March 9, 1863. Resigned March 14, 1863, since "my business (for which I gave bail to the amount of $15,000) . . . is in a dilapidated condition" so as "to destroy my comfort . . . and unfit me for the proper discharge of my duties."

Born: Jan. 15, 1825 Northampton Co., PA
Died: Jan. 23, 1892 Westport, PA
Education: Attended Lafayette College, Easton, PA
Occupation: School teacher and sales agent for several book firms
Offices/Honors: Register and Recorder, Clinton Co., PA, 1861–64
Miscellaneous: Resided Reading, Berks Co., PA; Northumberland Co., PA; Bald Eagle Twp. and Westport, Clinton Co., PA
Buried: Noyes Cemetery, Westport, PA
References: Obituary, *Lock Haven Evening Express*, Jan. 25, 1892. Floyd G. Hoenstine. *Soldiers of Blair County, PA.* Hollidaysburg, PA, 1940. Samuel P. Bates. *Martial Deeds of Pennsylvania.* Philadelphia, PA, 1875. *Commemorative Biographical Record of Central Pennsylvania, Including the Counties of Centre, Clinton, Union and Snyder.* Chicago, IL, 1898. Military Service File, National Archives.

GEORGE KIRTLEY BOWEN

Private, Co. F, 17 PA Infantry, April 25, 1861. Honorably mustered out, Aug. 2, 1861. Captain, Battery C, 3 PA Heavy Artillery, Nov. 13, 1862. Lieutenant Colonel, 188 PA Infantry, April 1, 1864. *Colonel*, 188 PA Infantry, April 12, 1864. Discharged for disability, Nov. 2, 1864, due to chronic diarrhea. Restored to his command, Nov. 12, 1864. Dismissed March 27, 1865, for "intoxication, gross ignorance of his duties, and allowing a total want of discipline to exist in his regiment." Dismissal revoked by Act of Congress, April 4, 1902, and he was honorably discharged to date, March 27, 1865.

Henry M. Bossert
COURTESY OF SUE HANNEGAN.

Born: May 12, 1835 Manchester, England
Died: Oct. 23, 1902 Palmyra, Burlington Co., NJ
Education: Attended University of Pennsylvania, Philadelphia, PA (Class of 1855)
Occupation: Civil engineer for Philadelphia and Reading Railroad before war. Engaged in civil engineering and farming after war.
Offices/Honors: Postmaster, Camden, Seward Co., NE, 1882–84
Miscellaneous: Resided Philadelphia, PA; Camden, Seward Co., NE; and Bertrand, Phelps Co., NE
Buried: Morgan Cemetery, Cinnaminson, Burlington Co., NJ

George Kirtley Bowen
ROGER D. HUNT COLLECTION, USAMHI.
W. L. GERMON'S ATELIER, NO. 702 CHESTNUT STREET,
PHILADELPHIA, PA.

References: Arthur G. Freeland, editor. *Delta Phi Centennial Catalogue, 1827–1927.* N.p., 1927. *University of Pennsylvania: Biographical Catalogue of the Matriculates of the College.* Philadelphia, PA, 1894. Military Service File, National Archives. William S. Settle. *History of the 3rd Pennsylvania Heavy Artillery and 188th Pennsylvania Volunteer Infantry.* Lewistown, PA, 1886. Death notice, *Philadelphia Public Ledger,* Oct. 25, 1902. Letters Received, Volunteer Service Branch, Adjutant General's Office, File G425(VS)1865, National Archives.

WILLIAM HENRY BOYD

Captain, Co. C, 1 NY Cavalry, July 19, 1861. Major, 1 NY Cavalry, April 3, 1863. GSW right side of neck, Bethesda Church, VA, June 3, 1864. Colonel, 21 PA Cavalry (6 months), Aug. 20, 1863. Colonel, 21 PA Cavalry (3 years), Feb. 20, 1864. Discharged for disability, Nov. 4, 1864, due to wounds received in action.

Born: July 14, 1825 Quebec, Canada
Died: Oct. 7, 1887 Washington, DC
Occupation: Publisher of Boyd's Washington, DC, Directories
Miscellaneous: Resided Chambersburg, Franklin Co., PA; and Washington, DC
Buried: Glenwood Cemetery, Washington, DC (Section C, Lot 111)
References: Pension File and Military Service File, National Archives. Letters Received, Volunteer Service Branch, Adjutant General's Office, File B1472(VS)1863, National Archives. William H. Beach. *The 1st New York (Lincoln) Cavalry.* New York City, NY, 1902. Obituary, *Washington Post,* Oct. 8, 1887. William H. Powell, editor. *Officers of the Army and Navy (Volunteer) Who Served in the Civil War.* Philadelphia, PA, 1893. Obituary, *Washington Evening Star,* Oct. 8, 1887. Samuel P. Bates. *Martial Deeds of Pennsylvania.* Philadelphia, PA, 1875.

William Henry Boyd
TED ALEXANDER COLLECTION, USAMHI.

HUGH JAMES BRADY

Major, 23 PA Militia, Sept. 21, 1862. Honorably discharged, Sept. 30, 1862. Lieutenant Colonel, 177 PA Infantry, Nov. 20, 1862. Honorably mustered out, Aug. 7, 1863. Colonel, 206 PA Infantry, Sept. 8, 1864. Honorably mustered out, June 26, 1865.

Born: Nov. 11, 1824 Greensburg, PA
Died: Jan. 7, 1903 Meade, TN
Other Wars: Mexican War (Private, Co. E, 2 PA Infantry)
Occupation: Merchant and miller before war. Merchant and farmer after war.
Offices/Honors: Storekeeper and Gauger in US Customs service
Miscellaneous: Resided Greensburg, Westmoreland Co., PA, to 1849; Indiana, PA, 1849–69; McMinnville, Warren Co., TN, 1869–74; Cummingsville and Meade, Van Buren Co., TN, after 1874. Father of 13 children by two wives.
Buried: Hodges Cemetery, near Cummingsville, Van Buren Co., TN
References: Landon D. Medley. *History of Van Buren County, TN.* N.p., 1987. *Memorial and Biographical Record of the Cumberland Region.* Chicago, IL, 1898. Pension File and Military Service File, National Archives.

ISAAC F. BRANNON

Corporal, Co. D, 6 PA Infantry, April 22, 1861. Honorably mustered out, July 26, 1861. 1 Lieutenant, Co. K, 48 PA Infantry, Aug. 22, 1861. Captain, Co. K, 48 PA Infantry, Aug. 29, 1862. Acting ADC, 1 Brigade, 2 Division, 9 Army Corps, Army of the Potomac, June 21–Oct. 6, 1864. Major, 48 PA Infantry, Oct. 6, 1864. Lieutenant Colonel, 48 PA Infantry, Jan. 2, 1865. Colonel, 48 PA Infantry, April 3, 1865. Commanded 1 Brigade, 2 Division, 9 Army Corps, Army of the Potomac, June 18–July 8, 1865. Honorably mustered out, July 17, 1865. Bvt. Colonel, USV, April 2, 1865, for conspicuous and gallant conduct before Petersburg, VA.

Born: 1833? Cumberland Co., PA
Died: June 18, 1896 Eastern State Penitentiary, Philadelphia, PA
Miscellaneous: Resided Cressona, Schuylkill Co., PA; and Philadelphia, PA
Buried: Body donated to science

Isaac F. Brannon
MASSACHUSETTS MOLLUS COLLECTION, USAMHI.
SEELEY & MURPHY, 69 KING STREET, ALEXANDRIA, VA.

References: Pension File and Military Service File, National Archives. Joseph Gould. *The Story of the Forty-Eighth.* Philadelphia, PA, 1908. Oliver C. Bosbyshell. *The 48th in the War.* Philadelphia, PA, 1895. Francis B. Wallace, compiler. *Memorial of the Patriotism of Schuylkill County in the American Slaveholder's Rebellion.* Pottsville, PA, 1865. Death Certificate.

BENJAMIN CLARKSON BROOKER

Colonel, 154 PA Infantry, Oct. 29, 1862. Regiment did not complete organization.

Born: 1812? England
Died: Jan. 29, 1883 Roxborough, Philadelphia Co., PA
Occupation: Engaged in the auction business
Miscellaneous: Resided Philadelphia, PA
Buried: Ronaldson Cemetery, Philadelphia, PA. Removed to a mass grave in Forest Hills Cemetery, Somerton, Philadelphia Co., PA, when Ronaldson Cemetery was discontinued in 1950.
References: Obituary, *Philadelphia Public Ledger*, Jan. 31, 1883. Letters Received, Volunteer Service Branch, Adjutant General's Office, Files B1675(VS)1862 and B187(VS)1863, National Archives.

Timothy Matlack Bryan, Jr.
ROGER D. HUNT COLLECTION, USAMHI.

TIMOTHY MATLACK BRYAN, JR.

Lieutenant Colonel, 12 MA Infantry, June 26, 1861. Resigned Oct. 7, 1862, because "at the death of Colonel Fletcher Webster, a captain of the regiment was promoted to the colonelcy over me." Colonel, 18 PA Cavalry, Dec. 24, 1862. Commanded 1 Brigade, 3 Division, Cavalry Corps, Army of the Potomac, April 16–May 6, 1864. Discharged for disability, Dec. 29, 1864, due to chronic diarrhea.

Born: March 9, 1832 Philadelphia, PA
Died: April 9, 1881 Vincentown, NJ
Education: Graduated US Military Academy, West Point, NY, 1855
Occupation: 2 Lieutenant, 10 US Infantry (resigned Jan. 1, 1857) and merchant before war. Geologist and scientist after war, making frequent contributions to the publications of the Philadelphia Academy of Natural Sciences.
Miscellaneous: Resided New York City, NY; Boston, MA; and Vincentown, Burlington Co., NJ

Buried: Laurel Hill Cemetery, Philadelphia, PA (Section H, Lots 103–104)
References: Pension File and Military Service File, National Archives. Obituary, *Mount Holly Herald*, April 16, 1881. *Annual Reunion*, Association of the Graduates of the US Military Academy, 1881. George W. Cullum. *Biographical Register of the Officers and Graduates of the US Military Academy.* Third Edition. Boston and New York, 1891. *History of the 18th Regiment of Cavalry Pennsylvania Volunteers.* New York City, NY, 1909.

Charles Henry Buehler
RONN PALM COLLECTION.
W. J. MILLER, PHOTOGRAPHER,
256 W. PRATT ST., NEAR SHARP, BALTIMORE, MD.

CHARLES HENRY BUEHLER

Captain, Co. E, 2 PA Infantry, April 20, 1861. Honorably mustered out, July 26, 1861. Major, 87 PA Infantry, Sept. 14, 1861. Colonel, 165 PA Infantry, Dec. 16, 1862. Honorably mustered out, July 28, 1863.

Born: Feb. 9, 1825 Gettysburg, PA
Died: March 24, 1896 Gettysburg, PA
Education: Attended Gettysburg (PA) College
Occupation: Printer and newspaper editor before war. Coal and lumber merchant and Adams Express Company agent after war.
Miscellaneous: Resided Gettysburg, Adams Co., PA
Buried: Evergreen Cemetery, Gettysburg, PA
References: H. Minot Pitman. *Fahnestock Genealogy: Ancestors and Descendants of Johann Diedrich Fahnestock.* Concord, NH, 1945. Pension File, National Archives. George R. Prowell. *History of the 87th Regiment Pennsylvania Volunteers.* York, PA, 1901. Samuel T. Wiley, editor. *Biographical and Portrait Cyclopedia of the Nineteenth Congressional District of Pennsylvania.* Philadelphia, PA, 1897. Samuel P. Bates. *Martial Deeds of Pennsylvania.* Philadelphia, PA, 1875. Obituary Circular, Whole No. 320, Pennsylvania MOLLUS. Obituary, *Gettysburg Star and Sentinel*, March 24, 1896.

SAMUEL OCTAVIUS BULL

Private, Co. C, 4 PA Infantry, April 20, 1861. Honorably mustered out, July 26, 1861. Captain, Co. A, 53 PA Infantry, Sept. 18, 1861. Major, 53 PA Infantry, June 2, 1862. Provost Marshal, 2 Army Corps, Army of the Potomac, March 19, 1863–Oct. 31, 1864. Lieutenant Colonel, 53 PA Infantry, May 17, 1864. *Colonel*, 53 PA Infantry, Sept. 18, 1864. Honorably mustered out, Oct. 31, 1864. Assistant Engineer, US Military Railroads in North Carolina, Nov. 1864–June 1865.

Samuel Octavius Bull (sixth from right) with Staff of Major Gen. Winfield S. Hancock
MASSACHUSETTS MOLLUS COLLECTION, USAMHI.

Born: Dec. 26, 1834 Elverson, Chester Co., PA
Died: Jan. 26, 1905 Marsh, Chester Co., PA
Occupation: Civil and mining engineer, engaged in "mining for gold and silver from Mexico to British Columbia." Also raised livestock and served as deputy marshal in Texas.
Miscellaneous: Resided Chester Co., PA; and Philadelphia, PA, until 1878. Then resided in West Virginia, Montana, Texas, Indian Territory, and Sudlerville, Queen Anne Co., MD, before returning to Chester Co., PA, late in life.
Buried: St. Mary's Episcopal Churchyard, Warwick, Chester Co., PA
References: Pension File and Military Service File, National Archives. Obituary, *West Chester Daily Local News*, Jan. 27, 1905. James H. Bull. *Record of the Descendants of John and Elizabeth Bull.* San Francisco, CA, 1919. Douglas R. Harper. *"If Thee Must Fight": A Civil War History of Chester County, Pennsylvania.* West Chester, PA, 1990. Irvin G. Myers. *We Might As Well Die Here: The 53rd Pennsylvania Veteran Volunteer Infantry.* Shippensburg, PA, 2004.

ADOLPH EBERHARD BUSCHBECK

Lieutenant Colonel, 27 PA Infantry, Sept. 8, 1861. Colonel, 27 PA Infantry, Nov. 1, 1861. Commanded 1 Brigade, 1 Division, 1 Army Corps, Army of Virginia, Aug. 30–Sept. 12, 1862. Commanded 1 Brigade, 2 Division, 11 Army Corps, Army of the Potomac, Oct. 27–Nov. 27, 1862, Dec. 1862–Feb. 22, 1863, March 5–28, 1863, April 12–June 10, 1863, July–Sept. 25, 1863. Commanded 2 Division, 11 Army Corps, Army of the Potomac, Feb. 22–March 5, 1863 and March 28–April 12, 1863. Commanded 1 Brigade, 2 Division, 11 Army Corps, Army of the Cumberland, Sept. 25–Nov. 28, 1863 and March 3–April 14, 1864. Commanded 2 Division, 11 Army Corps, Army of the Cumberland, Nov. 28, 1863–March 3, 1864. Commanded 2 Brigade, 2 Division, 20 Army Corps, Army of the Cumberland, April 14–May 22, 1864. Honorably mustered out, June 11, 1864.

Born: March 23, 1821 Coblentz, Prussia
Died: May 26, 1883 Florence, Italy

Adolph Eberhard Buschbeck (seated, second from left) and his staff, including Surgeon Henry Van Aernam (seated, right).
COURTESY OF DAVE TAYLOR.

Education: Attended Potsdam Military Academy, near Berlin, Germany

Occupation: Served as an officer in the Prussian army, 1838–53. In 1853 came to America, where he taught school, including a long term as Professor of Mathematics, Philadelphia Central High School.

Miscellaneous: Resided Philadelphia, PA, to 1873; later at Wiesbaden, Germany; and Florence, Italy

Buried: Cimitero agli Allori, Florence, Italy

References: Obituary Circular, Whole No. 126, Pennsylvania MOLLUS. Pension File, National Archives. Obituary, *New York Times*, May 30, 1883. Dispatches from US Consuls in Florence, Italy, National Archives. Wilhelm Kaufmann. *The Germans in the American Civil War.* Translated by Steven Rowan and edited by Don Heinrich Tolzmann with Werner D. Mueller and Robert E. Ward. Carlisle, PA, 1999. Joseph G. Rosengarten. *The German Soldier in the Wars of the United States.* Second edition, revised and enlarged. Philadelphia, PA, 1890. Ella Lonn. *Foreigners in the Union Army and Navy.* Baton Rouge, LA, 1951.

JOHN HERRON CAIN

Private, Co. K, 12 PA Infantry, April 25, 1861. Honorably mustered out, Aug. 5, 1861. Captain, Co. C, 155 PA Infantry, Aug. 29, 1862. Major, 155 PA Infantry, Sept. 2, 1862. Lieutenant Colonel, 155 PA Infantry, Dec. 31, 1862. Colonel, 155 PA Infantry, July 22, 1863. Resigned Aug. 30, 1863, at the urging of Brig. Gen. Kenner Garrard, who described him as "not competent to administer the officers of a regiment and properly command it."

Born: Nov. 18, 1838 Pittsburgh, PA

Died: April 29, 1903 Franklin, PA

Occupation: Bank teller before war. Oil producer and oil refiner after war.

Miscellaneous: Resided Pittsburgh, PA; St. Louis, MO; and Chattanooga, TN, before war; and Franklin, Venango Co., PA, after war

Buried: Franklin Cemetery, Franklin, PA

References: Obituary Circular, Whole No. 489, Pennsylvania MOLLUS. Obituary, *Pittsburgh Dispatch*, April 30, 1903. Herbert C. Bell, editor. *History of Venango County, PA; Its Past and Present.* Chicago, IL, 1890. Pension File and Military Service File, National Archives. *Under the Maltese Cross: Antietam to Appomattox: Campaigns 155th Pennsylvania Regiment.* Pittsburgh, PA, 1910. *Companions of the Military Order of the Loyal Legion of the United States.* New York City, NY, 1901.

John Herron Cain
FROM *UNDER THE MALTESE CROSS: ANTIETAM TO APPOMATTOX: CAMPAIGNS 155TH PENNSYLVANIA REGIMENT.*

HENRY LUTZ CAKE

Colonel, 25 PA Infantry, April 18, 1861. Honorably mustered out, Aug. 1, 1861. Colonel, 96 PA Infantry, Sept. 23, 1861. Resigned March 12, 1863, for "reasons to be assigned by His Excellency the Governor of this Commonwealth," having previously expressed his displeasure with state authorities for having "thrust upon me for my close association in the field, officers that I cannot recommend and in whom, knowing all about them, I have no confidence."

Born: Oct. 6, 1827 near Northumberland, PA

Died: Aug. 26, 1899 Northumberland, PA

Occupation: Printer and newspaper publisher before war. Engaged in the mining and shipping of coal after war.

Offices/Honors: US House of Representatives, 1867–71

Henry Lutz Cake
MASSACHUSETTS MOLLUS COLLECTION, USAMHI.

Miscellaneous: Resided Pottsville, Schuylkill Co., PA; Tamaqua, Schuylkill Co., PA; Philadelphia, PA; and Northumberland, Northumberland Co., PA

Buried: Riverview Cemetery, Northumberland, PA

References: Pension File, National Archives. Letters Received, Volunteer Service Branch, Adjutant General's Office, File C251(VS)1863, National Archives. Francis B. Wallace, compiler. *Memorial of the Patriotism of Schuylkill County in the American Slaveholder's Rebellion.* Pottsville, PA, 1865. *Biographical Directory of the American Congress. National Cyclopedia of American Biography.* David A. Ward. "Of Battlefields and Bitter Feuds: The 96th Pennsylvania Volunteers," *Civil War Regiments,* Vol. 3, No. 3 (1993). William W. H. Davis. *History of the Doylestown Guards.* Doylestown, PA, 1887. Obituary, *Pottsville Miners' Journal,* Aug. 28, 1899.

DAVID CAMPBELL

Colonel, 12 PA Infantry, April 25, 1861. Honorably mustered out, Aug. 5, 1861. Colonel, 4 PA Cavalry, Sept. 20, 1861. Colonel, 5 PA Cavalry, March 12, 1862. Commanded Post of Williamsburg, VA, June–Sept. 1862. Taken prisoner, Williamsburg, VA, Sept. 9, 1862. Exchanged Sept. 21, 1862. Dismissed Oct. 13, 1862, for "incompetency and gross neglect of duty" in the "disgraceful defeat" at Williamsburg. Dismissal revoked, Sept. 10, 1863, and his resignation accepted to date Oct. 13, 1862.

Born: Jan. 11, 1824 PA
Died: March 20, 1888 Sewickley, PA
Occupation: Wholesale dry goods merchant before war. Insurance agent after war.

David Campbell
COURTESY OF RICHARD F. CARLILE.
PUBLISHED BY E. ANTHONY, 501 BROADWAY, NEW YORK, FROM PHOTOGRAPHIC NEGATIVE IN BRADY'S NATIONAL PORTRAIT GALLERY.

Miscellaneous: Resided Pittsburgh, PA; and Sewickley, Allegheny Co., PA

Buried: Allegheny Cemetery, Pittsburgh, PA (Section 16, Lot 74)

References: Obituary, *Pittsburgh Press*, March 21, 1888. Military Service File, National Archives. Letters Received, Volunteer Service Branch, Adjutant General's Office, Files C366(VS)1862 and D768(VS)1862, National Archives.

JOHN C. CAMPBELL

Captain, Co. A, 76 PA Infantry, Oct. 1, 1861. Lieutenant Colonel, 76 PA Infantry, Aug. 20, 1862. Colonel, 76 PA Infantry, Jan. 11, 1864. Resigned Aug. 16, 1864, "owing to continued physical disability" from "an aggravated attack of chronic diarrhea."

Born: Aug. 10, 1824 Westmoreland Co., PA

Died: Feb. 5, 1908 Newark, OH

Occupation: Coal mine operator

Miscellaneous: Resided Coshocton, Coshocton Co., OH; and Newark, Licking Co., OH

Buried: Oak Ridge Cemetery, Coshocton, OH

References: Obituary, *Newark Daily Advocate*, Feb. 6, 1908. Obituary, *Coshocton Daily Age*, Feb. 6, 1908. *Memorial Record of Licking County, OH*. Chicago, IL, 1894. Pension File and Military Service File, National Archives.

JOHN CALVIN CARPENTER

2 Lieutenant, Co. E, 67 PA Infantry, April 17, 1862. Captain, Co. K, 67 PA Infantry, Dec. 26, 1862. Taken prisoner, Winchester, VA, June 15, 1863. Confined Libby Prison, Richmond, VA. Paroled March 14, 1864. Major, 67 PA Infantry, May 1, 1865. Lieutenant Colonel, 67 PA Infantry, May 15, 1865. Colonel, 67 PA Infantry, June 1, 1865. Honorably mustered out, July 14, 1865.

Born: Feb. 5, 1838 Indiana, PA

Died: May 21, 1921 Chanute, KS

Education: Attended Kenyon College, Gambier, OH

Occupation: Lawyer

Offices/Honors: KS Senate, 1868–70, 1876–78, and 1900–04. Collector of Internal Revenue, 1878–88.

Miscellaneous: Resided Indiana, PA, to 1866; Erie, Neosho Co., KS, 1866–70; Chanute, Neosho Co., KS, 1870–1921. Brother of Colonel Leonard W. Carpenter (4 OH Infantry).

Buried: Elmwood Cemetery, Chanute, KS

John Calvin Carpenter (postwar)
FROM *HISTORY OF NEOSHO AND WILSON COUNTIES, KS.*

References: William E. Connelley. *A Standard History of Kansas and Kansans.* Chicago and New York, 1918. *The United States Biographical Dictionary.* Kansas Volume. Chicago and Kansas City, 1879. Obituary, *Chanute Daily Tribune*, May 23, 1921. Pension File and Military Service File, National Archives. Letters Received, Volunteer Service Branch, Adjutant General's Office, File M1791(VS)1864, National Archives. L. Wallace Duncan. *History of Neosho and Wilson Counties, KS.* Fort Scott, KS, 1902.

JAMES CHAMBERLIN

1 Sergeant, Co. G, 4 PA Infantry, April 18, 1861. Honorably mustered out, July 26, 1861. Captain, Co. D, 52 PA Infantry, Aug. 28, 1861. GSW breast, Fair Oaks, VA, May 31, 1862. Having been entrusted with the settlement of his father's large estate, he resigned May 11, 1863, since "the coming of age of all the heirs absolutely requires a settlement." Colonel, 28 PA Emergency Troops, June 23, 1863. Honorably mustered out, July 28, 1863. Appointed to Governor Andrew G. Curtin's staff with the rank of colonel, he served as State Military Agent for the Southwest, with headquarters at Nashville, TN, from May 27, 1864 to April 1, 1866.

Born: June 27, 1836 near Lewisburg, PA
Died: July 26, 1909 Nashville, TN
Education: Graduated Harvard University Law School, Cambridge, MA, 1859. Graduated Bucknell University, Lewisburg, PA, 1860.
Occupation: Lawyer
Miscellaneous: Resided Lewisburg, Union Co., PA; and Nashville, TN
Buried: Mount Olivet Cemetery, Nashville, TN (Section 13, Lot 210)
References: Pension File and Military Service File, National Archives. Obituary, *Nashville American*, July 27, 1909. Smith B. Mott. *The Campaigns of the 52nd Regiment Pennsylvania Volunteer Infantry*. Philadelphia, PA, 1911. *Annual Report of the Adjutant General of Pennsylvania for the Year 1866*. Harrisburg, PA, 1867.

ALFRED WILSON CHANTRY

Colonel, 66 PA Infantry, June 21, 1861. Superseded by Colonel John Patrick, Jan. 16, 1862.

Born: 1816? Ireland
Died: Dec. 7, 1865 Philadelphia, PA
Occupation: Merchant tailor
Miscellaneous: Resided Philadelphia, PA
Buried: Old Cathedral Cemetery, Philadelphia, PA (Section B, Range 4, Lot 29, unmarked)
References: Pension File, National Archives. Death notice, *Philadelphia Public Ledger*, Dec. 11, 1865. Samuel P. Bates. *History of Pennsylvania Volunteers, 1861–65*. Harrisburg, PA, 1869–71. Death certificate.

JAMES HARVEY CHILDS

1 Lieutenant, Co. K, 12 PA Infantry, April 25, 1861. Honorably mustered out, Aug. 5, 1861. Lieutenant Colonel, 4 PA Cavalry, Oct. 18, 1861. Colonel, 4 PA Cavalry, March 12, 1862. Shell wound left hip, Antietam MD, Sept. 17, 1862.

Born: July 4, 1834 Pittsburgh, PA
Died: Sept. 17, 1862 KIA Antietam, MD
Education: Graduated Miami University, Oxford, OH, 1852
Occupation: Civil engineer, wholesale dry goods merchant and manufacturer of cotton goods
Miscellaneous: Resided Pittsburgh, PA
Buried: Allegheny Cemetery, Pittsburgh, PA (Section 20, Lot 1)

James Harvey Childs
LIBRARY OF CONGRESS.

References: Samuel P. Bates. *Martial Deeds of Pennsylvania*. Philadelphia, PA, 1875. *General Catalogue of the Graduates and Former Students of Miami University, 1809–1909*. Oxford, OH, 1910. Daniel Wait Howe. *Howe Genealogies*. Boston, MA, 1929. *A Brief History of the 4th Pennsylvania Veteran Cavalry*. Pittsburgh, PA, 1891.

ERNEST GEORGE CHORMANN

Colonel, 8 PA Cavalry, Sept. 18, 1861. Discharged Dec. 31, 1861, upon adverse report of a Board of Examination. Colonel, 8 PA Cavalry, June 1, 1863. His muster into service being "without authority from the War Department through imposition" on his part, "and in violation of the intention of the Governor of Pennsylvania," was revoked June 9, 1863, and he was dishonorably mustered out to date, June 1, 1863.

Born: Sept. 19, 1828 France
Died: Date and place of death unknown. He appears in the 1900 census living with his brother's family in Milford, DE.
Other Wars: Mexican War (Sergeant, Co. B, MD and DC Battalion Infantry)
Occupation: Artist, engraver, and inventor
Miscellaneous: Resided Philadelphia, PA; and Milford, Kent Co., DE
Buried: Burial place unknown
References: Pension File and Military Service File, National Archives. Letters Received, Volunteer Service Branch, Adjutant General's Office, File M45(VS)1862, National Archives.

JAMES T. CLANCY

Captain, Co. B, 1 NY Infantry, April 23, 1861. Major, 1 NY Infantry, Sept. 10, 1861. Dismissed Oct. 14, 1862, for "conduct unbecoming an officer and a gentleman" in disobeying an order of Colonel Dyckman concerning the use of a tent and poles. Dismissal revoked, Dec. 18, 1862, and he was honorably discharged to date Oct. 14, 1862. Colonel, 45 PA Militia, Aug. 13, 1863. Honorably mustered out, Aug. 29, 1863. Private, Co. C, 1 NJ Cavalry, Oct. 24, 1863. Sergeant, Co. C, 1 NJ Cavalry, Sept. 1, 1864. 2 Lieutenant, Co. F, 1 NJ Cavalry, Sept. 23, 1864. 1 Lieutenant, Adjutant, 1 NJ Cavalry, Dec. 20, 1864. Captain, Co. B, 1 NJ Cavalry, June 8, 1865. Honorably mustered out, July 24, 1865.

Born: 1833? Albany, NY
Died: Dec. 1870 Remedios, Cuba
Offices/Honors: Medal of Honor, Vaughan Road, VA, Oct. 1, 1864. "Shot the Confederate Brig. Gen. John Dunovant dead during a charge, thus confusing the enemy and greatly aiding in his repulse."
Miscellaneous: Died while serving as colonel of an American expeditionary force supporting Cuban revolution against Spanish rule
Buried: Burial place unknown
References: Military Service File, National Archives. Letters Received, Volunteer Service Branch, Adjutant General's Office, File M1976(VS)1862, National Archives. George Lang, Raymond L. Collins, and Gerard F. White, compilers. *Medal of Honor Recipients, 1863–1994*. New York City, NY, 1995. Death notice, *New York Herald*, Oct. 8, 1871. "A Volunteer in Cuba," *New York Times*, April 30, 1870.

JOHN BARR CLARK

Colonel, 123 PA Infantry, Aug. 21, 1862. Honorably mustered out, May 13, 1863. Colonel, 193 PA Infantry, July 19, 1864. Commanded Post of Wilmington, DE, Aug.–Sept. 1864. Honorably mustered out, Nov. 9, 1864.

Born: Oct. 9, 1827 near Cadiz, OH
Died: Jan. 13, 1872 Pittsburgh, PA
Education: Graduated Franklin College, New Athens, OH, 1848
Occupation: Presbyterian clergyman
Miscellaneous: Resided Canonsburg, Washington Co., PA; and Pittsburgh, PA
Buried: Union Cemetery, Cadiz, OH (Section 3, Lot 92)

John Barr Clark
RONN PALM COLLECTION.
R.M. GANO & CO., NOS. 90 & 92 FEDERAL ST., ALLEGHANY CITY, PA.

References: Obituary, *Cadiz Republican*, Jan. 18, 1872. *Franklin College Register. Biographical and Historical.* Wheeling, WV, 1908. Military Service File, National Archives. Scott B. Lang. *The Forgotten Charge: The 123rd Pennsylvania at Marye's Heights, Fredericksburg, VA.* Shippensburg, PA, 2002.

JOHN BUTLER CONYNGHAM

2 Lieutenant, Co. C, 8 PA Infantry, April 22, 1861. Honorably mustered out, July 29, 1861. Major, 52 PA Infantry, Sept. 28, 1861. Acting AIG, Davis' Brigade, US Forces Folly Island, SC, Department of the South, July–Aug. 1863. Lieutenant Colonel, 52 PA Infantry, Nov. 6, 1863. Taken prisoner, Fort Johnson, Charleston Harbor, SC, July 3, 1864. Confined Charleston, SC, and Columbia, SC. Paroled Dec. 10, 1864. Colonel, 52 PA Infantry, March 1, 1865. Commanded 1 Brigade, 2 Division, 23 Army Corps, Department of North Carolina, June 24–July 4, 1865. Honorably mustered out, July 12, 1865.

Born: Sept. 29, 1827 Wilkes-Barre, PA
Died: May 27, 1871 Wilkes-Barre, PA
Education: Graduated Yale University, New Haven, CT, 1846

Occupation: Lawyer before war. Regular Army (Captain, 24 US Infantry, Nov. 11, 1869).
Offices/Honors: One of the founders of the Delta Kappa Epsilon fraternity
Miscellaneous: Resided St. Louis, MO, 1852–56; and Wilkes-Barre, Luzerne Co., PA
Buried: Hollenback Cemetery, Wilkes-Barre, PA (Lot 217)
References: Smith B. Mott. *The Campaigns of the 52nd Regiment Pennsylvania Volunteer Infantry.* Philadelphia, PA, 1911. Oscar J. Harvey and Ernest G. Smith. *History of Wilkes-Barre.* Wilkes-Barre, PA, 1929. *Catalogue of the Delta Kappa Epsilon Fraternity. Biographical and Statistical.* New York City, NY, 1890. Military Service File, National Archives.

John Butler Conyngham
COURTESY OF ALAN J. SESSAREGO.

William Wakefield Corbet
RONN PALM COLLECTION.
R. W. ADDIS, PHOTOGRAPHER, MCCLEES' GALLERY,
308 PENNA. AVENUE, WASHINGTON, DC.

WILLIAM WAKEFIELD CORBET

Lieutenant Colonel, 105 PA Infantry, Aug. 31, 1861. Colonel, 105 PA Infantry, July 30, 1862. Resigned Sept. 10, 1862, on account of "continued ill health" due to "chronic diarrhea contracted in the swamps before Richmond."

Born: June 4, 1827 Coder, Jefferson Co., PA
Died: Sept. 4, 1904 Brookville, PA
Occupation: Store clerk and bookkeeper early in life. Later operated a grocery store and then entered the lumber business.
Offices/Honors: Prothonotary and Recorder, Jefferson Co., PA, 1857–60
Miscellaneous: Resided Ridgway, Elk Co., PA; and Brookville, Jefferson Co., PA
Buried: Brookville Cemetery, Brookville, PA
References: William J. McKnight. *Jefferson County, PA: Her Pioneers and People.* Chicago, IL, 1917. Pension File, National Archives. Obituary, *Brookville Jeffersonian Democrat,* Sept. 8, 1904. Kate M. Scott. *History of the 105th Regiment of Pennsylvania Volunteers.* Philadelphia, PA, 1877.

WILLIAM A. CORRIE

Captain, Co. F, 8 PA Cavalry, Aug. 19, 1861. Having been officially published as "Absent Without Leave," and failing to appear before the Military Commission within 15 days, he was dismissed to date Jan. 4, 1864. Restored to his command, Feb. 25, 1864, upon evidence that the charge was erroneous. Major, 8 PA Cavalry, March 11, 1864. GSW right arm, Deep Bottom, VA, Aug. 16, 1864. Lieutenant Colonel, 8 PA Cavalry, Dec. 30, 1864. *Colonel,* 8 PA Cavalry, July 1, 1865. Dismissed Aug. 3, 1865 for "conduct prejudicial to good order and military discipline, disobedience of orders, and conduct unbecoming an officer and a gentleman." Dismissal revoked Jan. 22, 1866, and his resignation accepted to date, Aug. 3, 1865.

Born: 1824? Boston, MA
Died: Dec. 7, 1896 Darby, Delaware Co., PA
Occupation: Organ builder
Miscellaneous: Resided Philadelphia, PA; Bordentown, Burlington Co., NJ; and Darby, Delaware Co., PA
Buried: Woodlands Cemetery, Philadelphia, PA (Section L, Lots 34–35)

References: Pension File and Military Service File, National Archives. Obituary, *Chester Times,* Dec. 10, 1896. Letters Received, Volunteer Service Branch, Adjutant General's Office, File C229(VS)1864, National Archives.

GEORGE HAY COVODE

1 Lieutenant, Co. D, 4 PA Cavalry, Sept. 16, 1861. Captain, Co. D, 4 PA Cavalry, Oct. 1, 1861. Major, 4 PA Cavalry, March 12, 1862. Lieutenant Colonel, 4 PA Cavalry, Dec. 8, 1863. Colonel, 4 PA Cavalry, May 1, 1864. GSW left arm and stomach, St. Mary's Church, VA, June 24, 1864.

Born: Aug. 19, 1835 Fairfield Twp., Westmoreland Co., PA
Died: June 25, 1864 DOW near St. Mary's Church, VA
Occupation: Merchant
Miscellaneous: Resided Lockport, Westmoreland Co., PA
Buried: Methodist Cemetery, West Fairfield, Westmoreland Co., PA

George Hay Covode
Ken Turner Collection.
Brady's National Photographic Portrait Galleries, Broadway and Tenth Streets, New York.

References: Military Service File, National Archives. George D. Albert, editor. *History of the County of Westmoreland.* Philadelphia, PA, 1882. *A Brief History of the 4th Pennsylvania Veteran Cavalry.* Pittsburgh, PA, 1891. Letters Received, Volunteer Service Branch, Adjutant General's Office, File W1536(VS)1864, National Archives.

CALVIN AUGUSTUS CRAIG

Corporal, Co. I, 8 PA Infantry, April 24, 1861. Honorably mustered out, July 29, 1861. Captain, Co. C, 105 PA Infantry, Aug. 28, 1861. Lieutenant Colonel, 105 PA Infantry, July 29, 1862. GSW ankle, 2nd Bull Run, VA, Aug. 29, 1862. Colonel, 105 PA Infantry, May 4, 1863. GSW foot, Gettysburg, PA, July 2, 1863. GSW lower jaw, Wilderness, VA, May 5, 1864. Commanded 2 Brigade, 3 Division, 2 Army Corps, Army of the Potomac, Aug. 11–16, 1864. GSW head, Deep Bottom, VA, Aug. 16, 1864.

Born: Dec. 7, 1833 Greenville, Clarion Co., PA
Died: Aug. 17, 1864 DOW City Point, VA

Education: Graduated Duff's Commercial College, Pittsburgh, PA, 1858
Occupation: Engaged in the lumber business and later in the mercantile business
Miscellaneous: Resided Greenville (now Limestone), Clarion Co., PA
Buried: Limestone Memorial Cemetery, Limestone, PA
References: Pension File and Military Service File, National Archives. Kate M. Scott. *History of the 105th Regiment of Pennsylvania Volunteers.* Philadelphia, PA, 1877. Samuel P. Bates. *Martial Deeds of Pennsylvania.* Philadelphia, PA, 1875. A. J. Davis, editor. *History of Clarion County, PA.* Syracuse, NY, 1887.

JOHN CRAIG

Captain, Co. I, 6 PA Infantry, April 22, 1861. Honorably mustered out, July 21, 1861. Captain, Co. N, 28 PA Infantry, Aug. 30, 1861. Major, 147 PA Infantry, Oct. 10, 1862. Lieutenant Colonel, 147 PA Infantry, Jan. 27, 1864. Colonel, 147 PA Infantry, June 14, 1865. Honorably mustered out, July 15, 1865.

Calvin Augustus Craig
MEADE ALBUM, CIVIL WAR LIBRARY & MUSEUM,
PHILADELPHIA, PA.

John Craig
WILLIAM H. LAMBERT ALBUM, USAMHI.
BRADY'S NATIONAL PHOTOGRAPHIC PORTRAIT GALLERIES,
352 PENNSYLVANIA AVE., WASHINGTON, DC.

Born: Oct. 23, 1830 Lehigh Gap, Carbon Co., PA
Died: Oct. 22, 1908 Lower Towamensing Twp., Carbon Co., PA
Occupation: Mail route operator before war. Pursued lumbering and general mercantile business after war.
Offices/Honors: PA House of Representatives, 1885–86
Miscellaneous: Resided Lehigh Gap, Carbon Co., PA. Brother-in-law of Brig. Gen. Charles A. Heckman.
Buried: Towamensing Cemetery, Palmerton, Carbon Co., PA
References: Pension File, National Archives. *Portrait and Biographical Record of Lehigh, Northampton, and Carbon Counties, PA.* Chicago, IL, 1894. Obituary Circular, Whole No. 653, Pennsylvania MOLLUS. Charles R. Roberts. *History of Lehigh County, PA.* Allentown, PA, 1914. Obituary, *Mauch Chunk Democrat,* Oct. 24, 1908. Alfred Mathews and Austin N. Hungerford. *History of the Counties of Lehigh and Carbon, in the Commonwealth of Pennsylvania.* Philadelphia, PA, 1884.

CHARLES CLEMENT CRESSON

2 Lieutenant, Co. D, 66 PA Infantry, Aug. 3, 1861. 1 Lieutenant, Co. E, 73 PA Infantry, March 13, 1862. GSW right arm, 2nd Bull Run, VA, Aug. 29, 1862. Captain, Co. E, 73 PA Infantry, Aug. 30, 1862. GSW left side and abdomen, Chancellorsville, VA, May 2, 1863. Acting AIG, Staff of Colonel Adolph Buschbeck, 1 Brigade, 2 Division, 11 Army Corps, Army of the Cumberland, Sept. 8–Dec. 25, 1863. Major, 73 PA Infantry, Jan. 1, 1864. GSW right shoulder and chest, Pine Knob, GA, June 15, 1864. Lieutenant Colonel, 73 PA Infantry, Aug. 21, 1864. *Colonel,* 73 PA Infantry, May 1, 1865. Honorably mustered out, Aug. 24, 1865.

Born: Feb. 24, 1844 Philadelphia, PA
Died: March 15, 1906 San Antonio, TX
Occupation: Regular Army (1 Lieutenant, 1 US Cavalry, retired April 4, 1879). Later engaged in mercantile business. Professor of Military Science and Tactics, West Texas Military Academy, San Antonio, TX, 1900–06.
Miscellaneous: Resided Philadelphia, PA; and San Antonio, Bexar Co., TX
Buried: San Antonio National Cemetery, San Antonio, TX (Section A, Lot 142)
References: Obituary Circular, Whole No. 831, California MOLLUS. Obituary, *San Antonio Daily Express,* March 16, 1906. Pension File and Military Service

Charles Clement Cresson
WILLIAM H. LAMBERT ALBUM, USAMHI.
J. E. McCLEES, ARTIST, 910 CHESTNUT STREET, PHILADELPHIA, PA.

File, National Archives. John W. Jordan, editor. *Colonial Families of Philadelphia.* Philadelphia, PA, 1911. Samuel P. Bates. *Martial Deeds of Pennsylvania.* Philadelphia, PA, 1875. Letters Received, Appointment, Commission and Personal Branch, Adjutant General's Office, File 5339(ACP)1871, National Archives. Letters Received, Volunteer Service Branch, Adjutant General's Office, File C736(VS)1865, National Archives.

SAMUEL CROASDALE

Private, Co. I, 25 PA Infantry, April 28, 1861. Honorably mustered out, July 26, 1861. Captain, Co. C, 128 PA Infantry, Aug. 14, 1862. Colonel, 128 PA Infantry, Aug. 25, 1862. GSW head, Antietam, MD, Sept. 17, 1862.

Born: Aug. 23, 1837 Hartsville, PA
Died: Sept. 17, 1862 KIA Antietam, MD
Occupation: Lawyer
Miscellaneous: Resided Doylestown, Bucks Co., PA
Buried: Doylestown Cemetery, Doylestown, PA

Samuel Croasdale
MEADE ALBUM, CIVIL WAR LIBRARY & MUSEUM,
PHILADELPHIA, PA.

References: Samuel P. Bates. *Martial Deeds of Pennsylvania.* Philadelphia, PA, 1875. William W. H. Davis. *History of the Doylestown Guards.* Doylestown, PA, 1887. J. H. Battle, editor. *History of Bucks County, PA.* Philadelphia, PA, 1887. Ingabee B. Minniear. *The Croasdale Family from Yorkshire, England, and Their Descendants.* N.p., 1965.

GEORGE CROOKES

Colonel, 144 PA Infantry, Sept. 3, 1862. Regiment did not complete organization.

Born: 1834? Ireland
Died: Dec. 30, 1879 Philadelphia, PA
Occupation: Smelter
Miscellaneous: Resided Philadelphia, PA
Buried: Mount Moriah Cemetery, Philadelphia, PA (Section 47, St. Paul's Church Ground (East Section), Lot 67)
References: Letters Received, Volunteer Service Branch, Adjutant General's Office, File C802(VS)1862, National Archives. Death Certificate. Death notice, *Philadelphia Public Ledger,* Jan. 1, 1880.

JAMES ELI CROWTHER

Captain, Co. I, 14 PA Infantry, April 26, 1861. Honorably mustered out, Aug. 7, 1861. Lieutenant Colonel, 110 PA Infantry, Oct. 1, 1861. Colonel, 110 PA Infantry, Dec. 21, 1862. GSW right breast, Chancellorsville, VA, May 3, 1863.

Born: Jan. 16, 1818 Centre Co., PA
Died: May 3, 1863 KIA Chancellorsville, VA
Occupation: Farmer, stage agent, and liveryman
Miscellaneous: Resided Curwensville, Clearfield Co., PA; and Tyrone, Blair Co., PA
Buried: Fredericksburg National Cemetery, Fredericksburg, VA (Grave 2897)
References: Samuel P. Bates. *Martial Deeds of Pennsylvania.* Philadelphia, PA, 1875. Pension File and Military Service File, National Archives. Bob Hileman, Jr. *The Crowther Letters: Family, Companions, and Rebels.* Second Edition. Tarentum, PA, 2004. Bob Hileman, Jr. *The Crowther Letters: Chasing Stonewall to Chancellorsville.* Tarentum, PA, 2004. Obituary, *Altoona Tribune,* May 19, 1863.

James Crowther
MEADE ALBUM, CIVIL WAR LIBRARY & MUSEUM,
PHILADELPHIA, PA.

ROBERT PARSON CUMMINS

Captain, Co. A, 10 PA Reserves, June 20, 1861. Having reluctantly accepted the position "with the understanding that I was to remain but three months," he resigned Jan. 8, 1862. Colonel, 142 PA Infantry, Sept. 1, 1862. Commanded 2 Brigade, 3 Division, 1 Army Corps, Army of the Potomac, Dec. 27, 1862–Feb. 16, 1863. GSW chest, Gettysburg, PA, July 1, 1863.

Born: 1827? Somerset Co., PA
Died: July 2, 1863 DOW Gettysburg, PA
Occupation: Apothecary operator and mail contractor
Offices/Honors: Sheriff of Somerset Co., PA, 1861–63
Miscellaneous: Resided Somerset, Somerset Co., PA
Buried: Union Cemetery, Somerset, PA
References: Samuel P. Bates. *Martial Deeds of Pennsylvania.* Philadelphia, PA, 1875. Pension File and Military Service File, National Archives. Horatio N. Warren. *The Declaration of Independence and War History. Bull Run to the Appomattox.* Buffalo, NY, 1894. Michael A. Dreese. *The Hospital on Seminary Ridge at the Battle of Gettysburg.* Jefferson, NC, 2002. William H. Koontz, editor. *History of Bedford and Somerset Counties, PA.* New York and Chicago, 1906.

Robert Parson Cummins
MEADE ALBUM, CIVIL WAR LIBRARY & MUSEUM, PHILADELPHIA, PA.
JOHN HOLYLAND, METROPOLITAN GALLERY,
250 PENNSYLVANIA AVENUE, WASHINGTON, DC.

William Lovering Curry
COURTESY OF EVERITT BOWLES.
F. GUTEKUNST, PHOTOGRAPHER,
704 & 706 ARCH STREET, PHILADELPHIA, PA.

WILLIAM LOVERING CURRY

Lieutenant Colonel, 22 PA Infantry, April 23, 1861. Honorably mustered out, Aug. 7, 1861. Lieutenant Colonel, 106 PA Infantry, Oct. 1, 1861. Taken prisoner, Fair Oaks, VA, June 9, 1862. Confined Salisbury, NC. Paroled Aug. 17, 1862. *Colonel,* 106 PA Infantry, April 5, 1864. GSW right thigh, Spotsylvania, VA, May 11, 1864.

Born: Jan. 29, 1833 Philadelphia, PA
Died: July 7, 1864 DOW Washington, DC
Education: Graduated Philadelphia (PA) Central High School, 1850
Occupation: Engaged in the manufacture of paper hangings
Miscellaneous: Resided Philadelphia, PA

Buried: Laurel Hill Cemetery, Philadelphia, PA (Section 15, Lot 58)

References: Joseph R. C. Ward. *History of the 106th Regiment Pennsylvania Volunteers.* Philadelphia, PA, 1906. Samuel P. Bates. *Martial Deeds of Pennsylvania.* Philadelphia, PA, 1875. Military Service File, National Archives. Death notice, *Philadelphia Public Ledger,* July 11, 1864.

CARLTON BRANDAGA CURTIS

Lieutenant Colonel, 58 PA Infantry, Sept. 1, 1861. Colonel, 58 PA Infantry, May 23, 1863. Resigned July 2, 1863, in response to the adverse report of a Board of Examination, which concluded that he "has not the requisite capacity nor qualifications for the position of colonel," but gave him credit "for a desire . . . to conscientiously perform his duties."

Born: Dec. 17, 1811 Madison Co., NY
Died: March 17, 1883 Erie, PA

Carlton Brandaga Curtis (postwar)
LIBRARY OF CONGRESS.

Occupation: Lawyer. Also interested in banking and oil production.

Offices/Honors: PA House of Representatives, 1836–38. US House of Representatives, 1851–55 and 1873–75.

Miscellaneous: Resided Warren, Warren Co., PA; and Erie, Erie Co., PA, after 1866

Buried: Oakland Cemetery, Warren, PA

References: *History of Erie County, PA.* Chicago, IL, 1884. J. S. Schenck, editor. *History of Warren County, PA.* Syracuse, NY, 1887. Samuel P. Bates. *Martial Deeds of Pennsylvania.* Philadelphia, PA, 1875. *Biographical Directory of the American Congress.* Military Service File, National Archives. Obituary, *Warren Mail,* March 20, 1883. William Horatio Barnes. *American Government. Biographies of Members of the House of Representatives of the Forty-Third Congress.* New York City, NY, 1874.

JOHN ANDERSON DANKS

Captain, Co. E, 63 PA Infantry, Sept. 9, 1861. GSW right leg, Fair Oaks, VA, May 31, 1862. Major, 63 PA Infantry, Sept. 29, 1862. GSW Chancellorsville, VA, May 3, 1863. Taken prisoner, Chancellorsville, VA, May 3, 1863. Confined Libby Prison, Richmond, VA. Paroled May 23, 1863. Lieutenant Colonel, 63 PA Infantry, June 26, 1863. Colonel, 63 PA Infantry, July 1, 1863. GSW left forearm and hand, Wilderness, VA, May 5, 1864. Honorably mustered out, Aug. 5, 1864.

Born: March 11, 1826 Venango Co., PA
Died: July 25, 1896 Glenfield, PA
Occupation: Iron worker before war. Grocer and Methodist clergyman after war.
Offices/Honors: PA House of Representatives, 1866. For nine years Chaplain-in-Chief, Union Veteran Legion.
Miscellaneous: Resided Etna, Allegheny Co., PA; Connellsville, Fayette Co., PA; and Glenfield, Allegheny Co., PA
Buried: Etna Cemetery, Etna, PA
References: Gilbert A. Hays. *Under the Red Patch: Story of the 63rd Regiment Pennsylvania Volunteers.* Pittsburgh, PA, 1908. Pension File and Military Service File, National Archives. Obituary, *Connellsville Courier,* July 31, 1896. Obituary, *Pittsburgh Press,* July 26, 1896. Letters Received, Volunteer Service Branch, Adjutant General's Office, File I466(VS)1863, National Archives.

John Anderson Danks
FROM *UNDER THE RED PATCH: STORY OF THE 63RD REGIMENT PENNSYLVANIA VOLUNTEERS.*

CHARLES P. DARE

Colonel, 23 PA Infantry, April 21, 1861. Honorably mustered out, July 31, 1861. Colonel, 2 Regiment, Philadelphia City Home Guard, Aug. 19, 1861.

Born: 1824? Philadelphia, PA
Died: Oct. 25, 1863 Philadelphia, PA
Occupation: Clerk in employ of Philadelphia, Wilmington, and Baltimore Railroad Company
Miscellaneous: Resided Philadelphia, PA
Buried: Laurel Hill Cemetery, Philadelphia, PA (Section W, Lot 209)
References: Pension File, National Archives. William J. Wray, compiler. *History of the 23rd Pennsylvania Volunteer Infantry.* Philadelphia, PA, 1904. Obituary, *Philadelphia Public Ledger,* Oct. 27, 1863. Commissions File, Records of the Department of Military and Veterans' Affairs, Pennsylvania State Archives.

JOSEPH DePUY DAVIS

Lieutenant Colonel, 167 PA Infantry, Nov. 6, 1862. Colonel, 167 PA Infantry, March 19, 1863. Honorably mustered out, Aug. 12, 1863.

Born: Oct. 10, 1825 Allentown, PA
Died: Aug. 4, 1907 Reading, PA
Education: Attended US Military Academy, West Point, NY (Class of 1846)
Other Wars: Mexican War (Private, Co. I, 3 KY Infantry; and 2 Lieutenant, 11 US Infantry)
Occupation: Lawyer
Offices/Honors: PA Senate, 1867–73
Miscellaneous: Resided Reading, Berks Co., PA; Chicago, IL; and Marshall, Harrison Co., TX
Buried: Charles Evans Cemetery, Reading, PA (Section I – Margin, Lot 52)
References: Pension File and Military Service File, National Archives. Obituary, *Reading Daily Eagle,* Aug. 5, 1907.

Charles P. Dare
FROM *HISTORY OF THE 23RD PENNSYLVANIA VOLUNTEER INFANTRY.*

WILLIAM DAVIS

Private, Co. H, 19 PA Infantry, May 18, 1861. Honorably mustered out, Aug. 29, 1861. Captain, Co. K, 69 PA Infantry, Sept. 11, 1861. Major, 69 PA Infantry, July 4, 1863. Lieutenant Colonel, 69 PA Infantry, July 4, 1864. GSW right knee, Reams' Station, VA, Aug. 25, 1864. *Colonel*, 69 PA Infantry, Jan. 1, 1865. Honorably mustered out, July 1, 1865.

Born: 1833? County Cork, Ireland
Died: Dec. 18, 1883 Philadelphia, PA
Occupation: Hatter
Offices/Honors: President of the Silk Hat Finishers' Association
Miscellaneous: Resided Philadelphia, PA
Buried: Mount Peace Cemetery, Philadelphia, PA (Section P, Lot 165, illegible government headstone)
References: Obituary, *Philadelphia Public Ledger*, Dec. 20, 1883. Pension File, National Archives. Letters Received, Volunteer Service Branch, Adjutant General's Office, File D936(VS)1862, National Archives. Anthony W. McDermott. *A Brief History of the 69th Regiment Pennsylvania Veteran Volunteers.*

William Davis
DON ENDERS COLLECTION, USAMHI.

Philadelphia, PA, 1889. Don Ernsberger. *Paddy Owen's Regulars: A History of the 69th Pennsylvania "Irish Volunteers."* N.p., 2004.

ALFRED DAY

Colonel, 8 PA Militia, Sept. 11, 1862. Honorably discharged, Sept. 25, 1862. Colonel, 40 PA Militia, July 2, 1863. Honorably mustered out, Aug. 16, 1863.

Born: June 23, 1823 Canton, NY
Died: May 18, 1873 Philadelphia, PA
Other Wars: Mexican War (Sergeant Major, 1 Battalion, MD and DC Infantry)
Occupation: Engaged in the coal business, first as a retailer and then as a wholesale shipper
Offices/Honors: Naval Officer, Port of Philadelphia, 1853
Miscellaneous: Resided Philadelphia, PA
Buried: Mount Moriah Cemetery, Philadelphia, PA (Section 37, Lot 64)
References: Obituary, *Philadelphia Public Ledger*, May 20, 1873. Pension File, National Archives.

GABRIEL DeKORPONAY

Lieutenant Colonel, 28 PA Infantry, June 28, 1861. Colonel, 28 PA Infantry, April 25, 1862. Discharged for disability, March 26, 1863, due to "varicocele of left testis, which prevents him from riding on horseback," and also "albuminuria, which unfits him for field duty."

Born: 1809? or 1819? Hinm, Aba-Tvarer, Hungary
Died: Feb. 10, 1866 Philadelphia, PA
Other Wars: Mexican War (Captain, Co. B, 3 MO Mounted Infantry)
Occupation: Dance instructor and fencing master early in life. Later became an interpreter for the Eastern District of the US Courts.
Miscellaneous: Resided St. Louis, MO; and Philadelphia, PA. While teaching dancing, he has been credited with introducing the polka to this country.
Buried: Mount Moriah Cemetery, Philadelphia, PA (Section 50, Lot 33, unmarked)
References: Pension File and Military Service File, National Archives. Letters Received, Volunteer Service Branch, Adjutant General's Office, File D267(VS)1863, National Archives. Edmund Vasvary. *Lincoln's Hungarian Heroes.* Washington, DC, 1939. Obituary, *Philadelphia Public Ledger*, Feb. 13, 1866.

Gabriel DeKorponay

SAMUEL BERNARD DICK

Captain, Co. F, 9 PA Reserves, July 27, 1861. GSW right thigh, Dranesville, VA, Dec. 20, 1861. Discharged for disability, Feb. 25, 1863, due to chronic diarrhea and bilious intermittent fever. Colonel, 56 PA Militia, July 5, 1863. Honorably mustered out, Aug. 13, 1863.

Born: Oct. 26, 1836 Meadville, PA
Died: May 10, 1907 Meadville, PA
Education: Attended Allegheny College, Meadville, PA
Occupation: Banker and railroad executive
Offices/Honors: US House of Representatives, 1879–81
Miscellaneous: Resided Meadville, Crawford Co., PA
Buried: Greendale Cemetery, Meadville, PA (Section 1, Lot 54)

Samuel Bernard Dick (postwar)
FROM *A BIOGRAPHICAL ALBUM OF PROMINENT PENNSYLVANIANS.*

References: Robert C. Brown. *History of Crawford County, PA.* Chicago, IL, 1885. Obituary, *Meadville Tribune Republican,* May 11, 1907. *A Biographical Album of Prominent Pennsylvanians.* First Series. Philadelphia, PA, 1888. Letters Received, Volunteer Service Branch, Adjutant General's Office, File W1277(VS)1862, National Archives. *Biographical Directory of the American Congress. Centennial Edition of the Daily Tribune-Republican of Saturday Morning, May 12th, 1888.* Meadville, PA, 1983. *Companions of the Military Order of the Loyal Legion of the United States.* New York City, NY, 1901.

OLIVER JESSE DICKEY

Lieutenant Colonel, 10 PA Infantry, April 26, 1861. Honorably mustered out, July 31, 1861. Colonel, 12 PA Militia, Sept. 16, 1862. Honorably discharged, Sept. 27, 1862.

Born: April 6, 1823 Old Brighton, Beaver Co., PA
Died: April 21, 1876 Lancaster, PA
Education: Attended Dickinson College, Carlisle, PA
Occupation: Lawyer
Offices/Honors: District Attorney, Lancaster County, PA, 1856–59. US House of Representatives, 1868–73.

Oliver Jesse Dickey
COURTESY OF NEW YORK STATE LIBRARY.
FREDERICK H. MESERVE. HISTORICAL PORTRAITS.

John Crawford Dodge, Jr.
ROGER D. HUNT COLLECTION, USAMHI.
C. H. WILLIAMSON'S PHOTOGRAPHIC PORTRAIT GALLERY,
"VIGNETTE SPECIALITY," 245 FULTON STREET, BROOKLYN, NY.

Miscellaneous: Resided Beaver, Beaver Co., PA; and Lancaster, Lancaster Co., PA

Buried: Woodward Hill Cemetery, Lancaster, PA (Section M, Lot 52)

References: Obituary, *Lancaster Daily Intelligencer*, April 21, 1876. *Biographical Directory of the American Congress*. William H. Barnes. *History of Congress: The Forty-First Congress of the United States, 1869–71*. New York City, NY, 1872. Franklin Ellis and Samuel Evans. *History of Lancaster County, PA*. Philadelphia, PA, 1883.

JOHN CRAWFORD DODGE, JR.

Captain, Co. A, 11 PA Infantry, April 24, 1861. Honorably mustered out, July 31, 1861. Colonel, 52 PA Infantry, Nov. 5, 1861. Resigned Nov. 5, 1863, due to rheumatism and "general debility, resulting from an attack of fever."

Born: Oct. 22, 1823 Dodgeville, MA

Died: Oct. 5, 1905 Dodgeville, MA

Education: Attended US Military Academy, West Point, NY (Class of 1845)

Occupation: Lumber dealer before war. Mercantile business after war.

Miscellaneous: Resided Williamsport, Lycoming Co., PA, before war; Brooklyn, NY, 1864–85; and Dodgeville, Bristol Co., MA, 1885–1905

Buried: Island Cemetery, Dodgeville, MA

References: Pension File and Military Service File, National Archives. Smith B. Mott. *The Campaigns of the 52nd Regiment Pennsylvania Volunteer Infantry*. Philadelphia, PA, 1911. Obituary, *Attleboro Sun*, Oct. 6, 1905.

WILLIAM DORRIS, JR.

Colonel, 3 PA Militia, Sept. 14, 1862. Honorably discharged, Sept. 24, 1862.

Born: Sept. 10, 1822 Huntingdon, PA
Died: Sept. 2, 1904 Huntingdon, PA
Education: Graduated Lafayette College, Easton, PA, 1840
Occupation: Lawyer
Miscellaneous: Resided Huntingdon, Huntingdon Co., PA
Buried: Riverview Cemetery, Huntingdon, PA
References: Obituary, *Huntingdon Monitor*, Sept. 8, 1904. John F. Stonecipher, compiler. *Biographical Catalogue of Lafayette College, 1832–1912.* Easton, PA, 1913. J. Simpson Africa. *History of Huntingdon and Blair Counties, PA.* Philadelphia, PA, 1883.

*William Dorris, Jr. (prewar)
with first wife Elizabeth (center) and
Margaret Dorris (widow of Zechariah Gemmill)*
COURTESY OF THE AUTHOR.

SAMUEL A. DYER

Captain, Co. C, 1 PA Reserves, May 31, 1861. Lieutenant Colonel, 175 PA Infantry, Nov. 12, 1862. Colonel, 175 PA Infantry, Nov. 22, 1862. Dishonorably discharged, upon the expiration of his term of service, for having "illegally removed and shipped from Washington, NC, a large mirror valued at $300.00 and other valuable property, with the view of appropriating the same to his private use." The charges having been found to be a "base fabrication," his dishonorable discharge was revoked, Oct. 8, 1863, and he was honorably mustered out to date, Aug. 7, 1863.

Born: Jan. 9, 1839 Chester, PA
Died: Nov. 25, 1894 Chester, PA
Occupation: His early success in the hotel and wholesale liquor businesses was followed by even greater success in the banking and railway businesses
Miscellaneous: Resided Chester, Delaware Co., PA
Buried: Rural Cemetery, Chester, PA (Section K, Lots 201/209)
References: Obituary, *Chester Times*, Nov. 26, 1894. Letters Received, Volunteer Service Branch, Adjutant General's Office, Files B1129(VS)1863 and D698(VS)1863, National Archives. Military Service File, National Archives.

CONSTANT MATHIEU EAKIN

Colonel, 25 PA Militia, Sept. 15, 1862. Honorably discharged, Oct. 1, 1862.

Born: 1799 France
Died: Oct. 2, 1869 West Philadelphia, PA
Education: Graduated US Military Academy, West Point, NY, 1817
Occupation: Regular Army (1 Lieutenant, 2 US Artillery, resigned Oct. 27, 1828). Assistant in the US Geodetic Survey, 1834–50. Civil engineer, 1850–69.
Miscellaneous: Resided West Philadelphia, PA
Buried: Woodlands Cemetery, Philadelphia, PA (Section E, Lot 195)
References: George W. Cullum. *Biographical Register of the Officers and Graduates of the US Military Academy.* Third Edition. Boston and New York, 1891. Death notice, *Philadelphia Public Ledger*, Oct. 4, 1869. US Military Academy Cadet Application Papers, National Archives.

Constant Mathieu Eakin
MASSACHUSETTS MOLLUS COLLECTION, USAMHI.

CHARLES WESLEY ECKMAN

Private, Co. H, 93 PA Infantry, Sept. 25, 1861. 2 Lieutenant, Co. H, 93 PA Infantry, Oct. 21, 1861. 1 Lieutenant, Co. H, 93 PA Infantry, July 25, 1862. Captain, Co. H, 93 PA Infantry, Oct. 21, 1862. GSW left foot, Wilderness, VA, May 5, 1864. Major, 93 PA Infantry, Sept. 24, 1864. Acting AIG, 1 Brigade, 2 Division, 6 Army Corps, Army of the Shenandoah, Sept. 21–Oct. 19, 1864. Shell wound left groin, Cedar Creek, VA, Oct. 19, 1864. Lieutenant Colonel, 93 PA Infantry, Nov. 11, 1864. Colonel, 93 PA Infantry, Dec. 16, 1864. Commanded 1 Brigade, 2 Division, 6 Army Corps, Army of the Potomac, April 22–May 2, 1865. Honorably mustered out, June 27, 1865. Bvt. Colonel, USV, Oct. 19, 1864, for gallant and meritorious services throughout the campaign before Richmond and in the Shenandoah Valley.

Born: June 27, 1837 Punxsutawney, PA
Died: May 3, 1906 Roaring Creek, PA

Occupation: Farmer and boatman before war. Engaged in general mercantile business and oil refining business after war. Steel mill superintendent in later life.
Offices/Honors: Postmaster, Danville, PA, 1869–85
Miscellaneous: Resided Danville, Montour Co., PA; Harrisburg, Dauphin Co., PA; and Roaring Creek, Montour Co., PA
Buried: Odd Fellows Cemetery, Danville, PA
References: *Historical and Biographical Annals of Columbia and Montour Counties, PA.* Chicago, IL, 1915. Pension File and Military Service File, National Archives. Penrose G. Mark. *Red: White: and Blue Badge Pennsylvania Veteran Volunteers. A History of the 93rd Regiment.* Harrisburg, PA, 1911. Robert T. Lyon. *A Photographic Supplement of the 93rd Regiment Pennsylvania Volunteers.* Muncy, PA, 1987. Obituary, *Danville Morning News*, May 4, 1906.

Charles Wesley Eckman and his wife, Sophia
RANDY HACKENBURG COLLECTION, USAMHI.
WENDEROTH, TAYLOR & BROWN,
912–914 CHESTNUT STREET, PHILADELPHIA, PA.

Charles Wesley Eckman
RANDY HACKENBURG COLLECTION, USAMHI.

GEORGE T. EGBERT

1 Lieutenant, Co. G, 106 PA Infantry, Aug. 27, 1861. Resigned Aug. 31, 1862, "my hearing having become impaired by disease so as to entirely unfit me for service." Captain, Co. A, 183 PA Infantry, Jan. 13, 1864. GSW left forearm, Todd's Tavern, VA, May 8, 1864. Major, 183 PA Infantry, May 24, 1864. Lieutenant Colonel, 183 PA Infantry, July 20, 1864. Colonel, 183 PA Infantry, Oct. 7, 1864. Commanded 4 Brigade, 1 Division, 2 Army Corps, Army of the Potomac, June 3–June 28, 1865. Honorably mustered out, July 13, 1865.

George T. Egbert
ROGER D. HUNT COLLECTION, USAMHI.
W. L. GERMON'S TEMPLE OF ART, 914 ARCH STREET,
PHILADELPHIA, PA.

Born: 1838? Montgomery Co., PA
Died: Aug. 13, 1898 Maywood, WV
Occupation: Merchant before war. Lawyer after war.
Miscellaneous: Resided Philadelphia, PA; Atlee, Hanover Co., VA; Catlettsburg, Boyd Co., KY; and Maywood, Fayette Co., WV
Buried: Burial place unknown
References: Pension File, National Archives. Obituary, *Charleston Daily Mail Tribune*, Aug. 20, 1898. Letters Received, Volunteer Service Branch, Adjutant General's Office, File E318(VS)1864, National Archives.

MAX EINSTEIN

Colonel, 27 PA Infantry, May 31, 1861. Honorably discharged, Oct. 2, 1861, upon the recommendation of Maj. Gen. George B. McClellan, who said, in a communication to Secretary of War Cameron, "From an examination of the charges preferred against him and an intimate personal knowledge of the condition of the regiment, I can simply state that the interests of the service demand Colonel Einstein's dismissal. He is in no respects fit to be a colonel."

Max Einstein
COURTESY OF OLAF.
FREDERICK GUTEKUNST, 706 ARCH STREET, PHILADELPHIA, PA.

Born: Oct. 10, 1822 Buchau, Wurtemberg, Germany
Died: April 1, 1906 Philadelphia, PA
Occupation: US Internal Revenue agent
Offices/Honors: Appointed US Consul, Nuremburg, Germany, Nov. 13, 1861. Appointment rejected by US Senate, March 19, 1862.
Miscellaneous: Resided Philadelphia, PA
Buried: Mount Sinai Cemetery, Philadelphia, PA (Section 2, Lot 200)
References: Simon Wolf. *The American Jew as Patriot, Soldier, and Citizen.* Philadelphia, PA, 1895. Obituary, *Philadelphia Public Ledger*, April 2, 1906. Pension File and Military Service File, National Archives. Letters Received, Volunteer Service Branch, Adjutant General's Office, File P17(VS)1861, National Archives.

James Gettys Elder
FROM *UNDER THE MALTESE CROSS: ANTIETAM TO APPOMATTOX: CAMPAIGNS 155TH PENNSYLVANIA REGIMENT.*

JAMES GETTYS ELDER

Captain, Co. C, 2 PA Infantry, April 20, 1861. Honorably mustered out, July 26, 1861. Colonel, 126 PA Infantry, Aug. 13, 1862. Two GSW left thigh, Fredericksburg, VA, Dec. 13, 1862. Honorably mustered out, May 20, 1863.

Born: Feb. 13, 1822 Markes, Franklin Co., PA
Died: Dec. 16, 1882 Chambersburg, PA
Occupation: Merchant (in partnership with Bvt. Brig. Gen. William D. Dixon) before war. Banker after war.
Offices/Honors: Treasurer of Franklin Co., PA, 1864–66
Miscellaneous: Resided St. Thomas, Franklin Co., PA; and Chambersburg, Franklin Co., PA.
Buried: Cedar Grove Cemetery, Chambersburg, PA

References: George O. Seilhamer. *Biographical Annals of Franklin County, PA.* Chicago, IL, 1905. Pension File, National Archives. Samuel P. Bates. *Martial Deeds of Pennsylvania.* Philadelphia, PA, 1875. Ted Alexander, compiler. *The 126th Pennsylvania.* Shippensburg, PA, 1984. *Under the Maltese Cross Antietam to Appomattox: Campaigns 155th Pennsylvania Regiment.* Pittsburgh, PA, 1910. Obituary, *Chambersburg Valley Spirit*, Dec. 20, 1882.

PETER CLARKSON ELLMAKER

Colonel, 1 Regiment Infantry, Gray Reserves, Reserve Brigade, 1 Division, PA Militia, April 29, 1861. Colonel, 119 PA Infantry, Aug. 2, 1862. Commanded 3 Brigade, 1 Division, 6 Army Corps, Army of the Potomac, Nov. 20–Dec. 5, 1863. Resigned Jan. 12, 1864, due to the continued effects of rheumatism and also due to a pending legal suit, "which if decided against me will bring utter ruin upon myself and family."

Peter Clarkson Ellmaker
103RD ENGINEER ARMORY COLLECTION, USAMHI.

Born: Aug. 11, 1813 Pequea, Lancaster Co., PA
Died: Oct. 12, 1890 Philadelphia, PA
Occupation: Dry goods merchant, grocer and notary public before war. Notary public, shoe and skate merchant, clerk and accountant after war.
Offices/Honors: Naval Officer of the Port of Philadelphia, 1848. US Marshal, Eastern District of PA, 1865–69.
Miscellaneous: Resided Philadelphia, PA
Buried: Mount Moriah Cemetery, Philadelphia, PA (Section 11, Lot 17)
References: Obituary, *Philadelphia Public Ledger*, Oct. 13, 1890. Pension File and Military Service File, National Archives. James W. Latta. *History of the 1st Regiment Infantry, National Guard of Pennsylvania (Gray Reserves).* Philadelphia and London, 1912. Harmon Y. Gordon. *History of the 1st Regiment Infantry of Pennsylvania.* Philadelphia, PA, 1961. Samuel P. Bates. *Martial Deeds of Pennsylvania.* Philadelphia, PA, 1875. Larry B. Maier. *Rough & Regular: A History of Philadelphia's 119th Regiment of Pennsylvania Volunteer Infantry, The Gray Reserves.* Shippensburg, PA, 1997.

JOHN BERNHARD EMBICH

Sergeant, Co. G, 5 PA Infantry, April 20, 1861. Honorably mustered out, July 24, 1861. 1 Lieutenant, Co. A, 93 PA Infantry, Oct. 21, 1861. Captain, Co. A, 93 PA Infantry, Aug. 26, 1862. Resigned Dec. 27, 1862, on account of physical disability. Captain, Co. E, 48 PA Militia, July 2, 1863. Colonel, 48 PA Militia, July 8, 1863. Honorably mustered out, Aug. 26, 1863.

Born: April 11, 1839 Lebanon, PA
Died: Dec. 23, 1912 Lebanon, PA
Occupation: Carpenter and builder
Offices/Honors: Associate Judge, Lebanon County Court, 1893–94
Miscellaneous: Resided Lebanon, Lebanon Co., PA
Buried: Mount Lebanon Cemetery, Lebanon, PA (Section N, Lot 118)
References: Obituary, *Lebanon Daily News*, Dec. 24, 1912. Pension File and Military Service File, National Archives. Penrose G. Mark. *Red: White: and Blue Badge Pennsylvania Veteran Volunteers. A History of the 93rd Regiment.* Harrisburg, PA, 1911.

Anthony H. Emley

From *Narrative History of the 109th Field Artillery Pennsylvania National Guard, 1775–1930.*

ANTHONY H. EMLEY

Colonel, 8 PA Infantry, April 23, 1861. Honorably mustered out, July 29, 1861.

Born: Feb. 22, 1813 NJ
Died: Aug. 16, 1868 Wilkes-Barre, PA
Occupation: Banker
Miscellaneous: Resided Wilkes-Barre, Luzerne Co., PA
Buried: Hollenback Cemetery, Wilkes-Barre, PA (Lot 1060)
References: Obituary, *Luzerne Union*, Aug. 19, 1868. *History of Luzerne, Lackawanna, and Wyoming Counties, PA.* New York City, NY, 1880. William H. Zierdt. *Narrative History of the 109th Field Artillery Pennsylvania National Guard, 1775–1930.* Wilkes-Barre, PA, 1932.

CHARLES ERNENWEIN

Lieutenant Colonel, 21 PA Infantry, April 29, 1861. Honorably mustered out, Aug. 8, 1861. *Colonel*, 156 PA Infantry, Sept. 18, 1862. Regiment did not complete organization and was consolidated with 157 PA Infantry.

Born: Germany
Died: Date and place of death unknown
Occupation: Eight years service as officer in Bavarian Army. Came to USA in 1850. Hatter.
Miscellaneous: Resided Philadelphia, PA
Buried: Burial place unknown
References: Letters Received, Volunteer Service Branch, Adjutant General's Office, File P808(VS)1862, National Archives.

JOHN HOLLIDAY FILLER

Captain, Co. G, 13 PA Infantry, April 25, 1861. Honorably mustered out, Aug. 6, 1861. Major, 55 PA Infantry, Sept. 16, 1861. Taken prisoner, Fort Wagner, SC, July 18, 1863. Confined at Camp Asylum, Columbia, SC. Paroled March 1, 1865. Lieutenant Colonel, 55 PA Infantry, Dec. 21, 1864. *Colonel*, 55 PA Infantry, March 25, 1865. Honorably mustered out, March 15, 1865.

Born: July 19, 1829 Bedford, PA
Died: Dec. 30, 1911 Warren, PA
Occupation: Regular Army (2 Lieutenant, 29 US Infantry; resigned April 21, 1868). Newspaper editor and lawyer.
Miscellaneous: Resided Bedford, Bedford Co., PA; Harrisburg, Dauphin Co., PA; and Philadelphia, PA
Buried: Oakland Cemetery, Warren, Warren Co., PA (Section O, Lot 122)
References: Obituary, *Philadelphia Record*, Dec. 31, 1911. Obituary, *Warren Evening Mirror*, Dec. 30, 1911. Pension File, National Archives. John W. Jordan, editor. *Genealogical and Personal History of the Allegheny Valley, PA.* New York City, NY, 1913. Letters Received, Commission Branch, Adjutant General's Office, File F39(CB)1868, National Archives. Letters Received, Volunteer Service Branch, Adjutant General's Office, File F181(VS)1862, National Archives.

JOHN BORLAND FINLAY

Organized and financed 103 PA Infantry. Although he had the sanction of the Secretary of War and also of Governor Curtin in recruiting troops, there is no official record that he was commissioned as colonel, but the title of colonel was assumed by him and no one ever questioned his right to use it. Not desiring to take troops into the field, he secured the services of Lt. Col. Theodore F. Lehmann (62 PA Infantry) to command the regiment. However, when Lehmann asserted his authority as colonel, this aroused the animosity of Finlay, and they became implacable, irreconcilable foes.

Born: Feb. 13, 1826 Moneyneagh, Ireland
Died: Sept. 18, 1897 New York City, NY (fatally injured in fall from cable car)
Education: Attended Royal College of Belfast, Ireland. Graduated University of Leipzig, Germany, 1846. Graduated Ohio State and Union Law College, Cleveland, OH, 1859.
Occupation: Reformed Presbyterian clergyman, 1850–56; lawyer; banker; and mining company executive
Miscellaneous: Resided Brooklyn, NY; Kittanning, Armstrong Co., PA; and New York City, NY
Buried: Kittanning Cemetery, Kittanning, PA (Section D, Lot 248)
References: Luther S. Dickey. *History of the 103rd Regiment Pennsylvania Veteran Volunteer Infantry.* Chicago, IL, 1910. Letters Received, Volunteer Service Branch, Adjutant General's Office, Files C228(VS)1862 and F61(VS)1862, National Archives. Obituary, *Kittanning Weekly Times,* Sept. 24, 1897. Obituary, *New York Times,* Sept. 19, 1897.

RICHARD MARIS FRAME

Colonel, 10 PA Militia, Sept. 16, 1862. Honorably discharged, Sept. 26, 1862.

Born: 1812? Delaware Co., PA
Died: June 16, 1875 West Chester, PA
Other Wars: Florida Indian War (Enlisted Jan. 25, 1835. Discharged as Sergeant, Co. H, 3 US Infantry, Jan. 25, 1841.)
Occupation: Blacksmith early in life. Railroad conductor and gas works superintendent later.
Miscellaneous: Resided West Chester, Chester Co., PA
Buried: Oaklands Cemetery, West Chester, PA

References: Obituary, *West Chester Daily Local News,* June 17, 1875. Enlistment Papers, Regular Army, National Archives. Douglas R. Harper. *"If Thee Must Fight": A Civil War History of Chester County, Pennsylvania.* West Chester, PA, 1990.

EMLEN FRANKLIN

Captain, Co. F, 1 PA Infantry, April 18, 1861. Honorably mustered out, July 26, 1861. Colonel, 122 PA Infantry, Aug. 14, 1862. Honorably mustered out, May 16, 1863. Colonel, 50 PA Militia, July 1, 1863. Discharged Aug. 15, 1863.

Born: April 7, 1827 Lancaster, PA
Died: June 19, 1891 Lancaster, PA
Education: Graduated Yale University, New Haven, CT, 1847
Occupation: Lawyer

Emlen Franklin
ROGER D. HUNT COLLECTION, USAMHI.
R. W. ADDIS, PHOTOGRAPHER, 308 PENNA. AVENUE,
WASHINGTON, DC.

Offices/Honors: PA House of Representatives, 1854. District Attorney, Lancaster Co., PA, 1859–62. Register of Wills, Lancaster Co., PA, 1863–66.

Miscellaneous: Resided Lancaster, Lancaster Co., PA

Buried: Woodward Hill Cemetery, Lancaster, PA

References: Pension File, National Archives. Obituary, *Lancaster Daily New Era*, June 19, 1891. George F. Sprenger. *Concise History of the Camp and Field Life of the 122nd Regiment Pennsylvania Volunteers.* Lancaster, PA, 1885. Franklin Ellis and Samuel Evans. *History of Lancaster County, PA.* Philadelphia, PA, 1883. Alexander Harris. *Biographical History of Lancaster County, PA.* Lancaster, PA, 1872.

WALTER SIMONDS FRANKLIN

1 Lieutenant, 12 US Infantry, May 14, 1861. 1 Lieutenant, RQM, 12 US Infantry, July 29, 1862. Captain, 12 US Infantry, Feb. 6, 1863. Commissary of Musters, 6 Army Corps, Army of the Potomac, Dec. 21, 1863–Aug. 5, 1864 and Dec. 7, 1864–Feb. 28, 1865. Commissary of Musters, 6 Army Corps, Army of the Shenandoah, Aug. 6–Dec. 6, 1864. *Colonel*, 87 PA Infantry, Jan. 31, 1865. Declined. Lieutenant Colonel, AIG, USV, assigned March 1, 1865–July 28, 1865 as AIG, 6 Army Corps, Army of the Potomac. Bvt. Colonel, USV, April 9, 1865, for gallant and meritorious services during the recent campaign terminating with the surrender of the insurgent army under General Robert E. Lee.

Born: March 1, 1836 York, PA

Died: Dec. 3, 1911 Baltimore, MD

Education: Graduated Lawrence Scientific School, Harvard University, Cambridge, MA, 1857

Occupation: Civil engineer before war. Regular Army (Captain, 21 US Infantry, discharged Sept. 30, 1870). Executive in the iron and steel industry and later railway president.

Offices/Honors: Member of the US Lighthouse Board, 1884–1910

Miscellaneous: Resided York, York Co., PA; Ashland, Baltimore Co., MD; and Baltimore, MD. Brother of Major Gen. William B. Franklin.

Buried: Prospect Hill Cemetery, York, PA (Section H, Lot 127)

References: Obituary, *Baltimore Sun*, Dec. 4, 1911. *Who Was Who in America, 1897–1942.* George R. Prowell. *History of York County, PA.* Chicago, IL, 1907. Letters Received, Commission Branch, Adjutant General's Office, File F456(CB)1864, National Archives. *The Union Army.* Maryland/Washington, DC, Edition. Madison, WI, 1908.

Walter Simonds Franklin
COURTESY OF EVERITT BOWLES.
CHARLES D. FREDRICKS & CO., "SPECIALITE,"
587 BROADWAY, NEW YORK.

JACOB GELLERT FRICK

Lieutenant Colonel, 96 PA Infantry, Sept. 23, 1861. Resigned July 29, 1862, since "I cannot consent to serve another day in the 96th PA Vols. under its present commander." Colonel, 129 PA Infantry, Aug. 15, 1862. Shell wound right thigh, Fredericksburg, VA, Dec. 13, 1862. Dismissed Jan. 25, 1863, for "positive and willful disobedience of orders and insubordinate conduct" and for "conduct subversive of good order and military discipline tending to mutiny," in refusing to obey an order to provide an estimate and requisition for frock coats for his regiment to enable them to appear on dress parades in the regulation frock coat. Disability resulting from dismissal removed, March 31, 1863, having been "sufficiently rebuked and admonished to prevent a recurrence of the offense." Colonel, 129 PA Infantry, April 10, 1863. Honorably mustered out, May 18, 1863. Colonel, 27 PA Emergency Troops, June 22, 1863. Honorably mustered out, July 31, 1863.

Born: Jan. 23, 1825 Northumberland, PA
Died: March 5, 1902 Pottsville, PA
Other Wars: Mexican War (2 Lieutenant, Co. K, 3 OH Infantry; and 2 Lieutenant, 11 US Infantry)
Occupation: Printer before war. Manufacturer of wire screens after war.
Offices/Honors: Medal of Honor, Fredericksburg, VA, Dec. 13, 1862, and Chancellorsville, VA, May 3, 1863. "At Fredericksburg seized the colors and led the command through a terrible fire of cannon and musketry. In a hand-to-hand fight at Chancellorsville, recaptured the colors of his regiment." Collector of Internal Revenue, 1871–81.
Miscellaneous: Resided Pottsville, Schuylkill Co., PA
Buried: Presbyterian Cemetery, Pottsville, PA
References: Obituary, *Pottsville Daily Republican*, March 6, 1902. Pension File, National Archives. Francis B. Wallace, compiler. *Memorial of the Patriotism of Schuylkill County in the American Slaveholder's Rebellion*. Pottsville, PA, 1865. St. Clair A. Mulholland. *Military Order Congress Medal of Honor Legion of the United States*. Philadelphia, PA, 1905. Samuel P. Bates. *Martial Deeds of Pennsylvania*. Philadelphia, PA, 1875. Letters Received, Volunteer Service Branch, Adjutant General's Office, Files M253(VS)1863 and P334(VS)1863, National Archives. William H. Armstrong. *Red-Tape and Pigeon-Hole Generals: Andrew A. Humphreys in the Army of the Potomac*. Commentary by Frederick B. Arner. Charlottesville, VA, 1999. Obituary, *Pottsville Miners' Journal*, March 6, 1902.

Jacob Gellert Frick
MASSACHUSETTS MOLLUS COLLECTION, USAMHI.

MAX FRIEDMAN

Colonel, 5 PA Cavalry, Aug. 3, 1861. Resigned March 9, 1862, due to physical disability caused by rheumatism.

Born: March 21, 1825 Muhlhausen, Bavaria, Germany
Died: Feb. 10, 1900 New York City, NY
Occupation: Merchant before war. Bank cashier and stock broker after war.
Miscellaneous: Resided Philadelphia, PA; and New York City, NY
Buried: Cypress Hills Cemetery, Brooklyn, NY
References: Simon Wolf. *The American Jew as Patriot, Soldier, and Citizen*. Philadelphia, PA, 1895. Obituary, *New York Times*, Feb. 12, 1900. Pension File and Military Service File, National Archives. Death certificate.

Max Friedman

WILLIAM FRISHMUTH

Colonel, 12 PA Cavalry, Nov. 7, 1861. Facing unproven charges brought by officers of his regiment that he collected false claims against the government, he resigned April 20, 1862.

Born: 1829? Saxe-Coburg-Gotha, Germany
Died: Aug. 1, 1893 Philadelphia, PA (committed suicide by pistol shot)
Occupation: Chemist and inventor

William Frishmuth (postwar)
FROM *A BIOGRAPHICAL ALBUM OF PROMINENT PENNSYLVANIANS.*

Miscellaneous: Resided Philadelphia, PA. Inventor of a patented aluminum process by which the metal was cheapened from $5 per pound to 18 cents per pound. Produced the aluminum capstone for the apex of the Washington Monument, Washington, DC.
Buried: North Cedar Hill Cemetery, Philadelphia, PA (Section R, Lot 404)
References: Pension File, National Archives. Obituary, *Philadelphia Public Ledger,* Aug. 2, 1893. *A Biographical Album of Prominent Pennsylvanians.* Third Series. Philadelphia, PA, 1890. Letters Received, Volunteer Service Branch, Adjutant General's Office, File R115(VS)1862, National Archives. Obituary, *New York Times,* Aug. 2, 1893. Larry B. Maier. *Leather & Steel: The 12th Pennsylvania Cavalry in the Civil War.* Shippensburg, PA, 2001.

PETER FRITZ

Captain, Co. B, 18 PA Infantry, April 24, 1861. Honorably mustered out, Aug. 7, 1861. Colonel, 99 PA Infantry, Feb. 25, 1862. Having received an adverse report from a Board of Examination, he resigned June 10, 1862.

Born: 1802 PA
Died: Aug. 9, 1878 Philadelphia, PA
Occupation: Marble worker and stone cutter
Offices/Honors: Member of the Board of Port Wardens. Prominent in the Masonic fraternity, becoming Grand Master of the Grand Lodge of Pennsylvania.
Miscellaneous: Resided Philadelphia, PA. Father of Bvt. Brig. Gen. Peter Fritz, Jr.
Buried: Laurel Hill Cemetery, Philadelphia, PA (Section 13, Lot 57)

Peter Fritz (prewar, as Major of the National Greys)
SOCIETY PORTRAIT COLLECTION,
THE HISTORICAL SOCIETY OF PENNSYLVANIA.

References: Obituary, *Philadelphia Public Ledger,* Aug. 10, 1878. Obituary, *Philadelphia Press,* Aug. 10, 1878. Letters Received, Volunteer Service Branch, Adjutant General's Office, File M686(VS)1862, National Archives. Military Service File, National Archives.

ANDREW J. FULTON

Corporal, Co. H, 16 PA Infantry, April 25, 1861. Honorably mustered out, July 30, 1861. Captain, Co. C, 87 PA Infantry, Sept. 14, 1861. Colonel, 166 PA Infantry, Nov. 25, 1862. Honorably mustered out, July 28, 1863.

Born: March 25, 1831 Hopewell Twp., York Co., PA
Died: Nov. 7, 1872 Stewartstown, PA (killed by accidental discharge of his gun while hunting)
Occupation: School teacher and civil engineer before war. Clerk in US Internal Revenue service after war.
Miscellaneous: Resided Stewartstown, York Co., PA
Buried: Presbyterian Cemetery, Stewartstown, PA
References: Obituary, *York Gazette,* Nov. 12, 1872. George R. Prowell. *History of the 87th Regiment Pennsylvania Volunteers.* York, PA, 1901. Letters Received, Volunteer Service Branch, Adjutant General's Office, File P1130(VS)1862, National Archives. Pension File and Military Service File, National Archives.

Andrew J. Fulton
FROM *HISTORY OF THE 87TH REGIMENT PENNSYLVANIA VOLUNTEERS.*

John H. Gallager
COLLECTION OF JOHN F. MCCORMACK, JR.

JOHN H. GALLAGER

Private, Co. I, 18 PA Infantry, April 24, 1861. Honorably mustered out, Aug. 6, 1861. Sergeant, Co. A, 106 PA Infantry, Aug. 17, 1861. 1 Lieutenant, Co. A, 106 PA Infantry, June 15, 1864. Captain, Co. K, 106 PA Infantry, Jan. 26, 1865. *Lieutenant Colonel*, 106 PA Infantry, May 27, 1865. *Colonel*, 106 PA Infantry, June 23, 1865. Honorably mustered out, June 30, 1865. 1 Lieutenant, Co. E, 7 US Veteran Volunteers, Oct. 24, 1865. Honorably mustered out, April 18, 1866.

Born: 1840? Philadelphia, PA
Died: Jan. 2, 1872 Philadelphia, PA
Occupation: Carpenter before war. Regular Army (Captain, 32 US Infantry, honorably mustered out Jan. 1, 1871).
Miscellaneous: Resided Philadelphia, PA
Buried: Sixth Street Union Cemetery, Philadelphia, PA. Probably removed to Philadelphia Memorial Park, Frazer, Chester Co., PA, when Sixth Street Union Cemetery was discontinued in 1970.

References: Pension File and Military Service File, National Archives. Constance Wynn Altshuler. *Cavalry Yellow & Infantry Blue.* Tucson, AZ, 1991. Letters Received, Commission Branch, Adjutant General's Office, File G61(CB)1866, National Archives. Joseph R. C. Ward. *History of the 106th Regiment Pennsylvania Volunteers.* Philadelphia, PA, 1906.

JAMES A. GALLIGHER

Captain, Co. A, 13 PA Cavalry, Dec. 28, 1861. Lieutenant Colonel, 13 PA Cavalry, April 28, 1862. Colonel, 13 PA Cavalry, July 1, 1862. Discharged for disability, Oct. 6, 1863, due to "a severe and protracted form of sciatica attended with partial paralysis of his left thigh and leg."

James A. Galligher
KEN TURNER COLLECTION.
ROOT GALLERY, FIFTH & CHESTNUT STREETS,
PHILADELPHIA, PA. C. COHILL, ARTIST.

Born: April 4, 1813 Philadelphia, PA

Died: March 19, 1891 New York City, NY

Occupation: Instructor of horsemanship and sword practice early in life. Later engaged in candle manufacturing.

Offices/Honors: Assistant Assessor of Internal Revenue, 1866–67

Miscellaneous: Resided Frankford, Philadelphia Co., PA; and New York City, NY

Buried: Calvary Cemetery, Long Island City, NY (Section 17, Range 2, Plot Z)

References: Samuel P. Bates. *Martial Deeds of Pennsylvania*. Philadelphia, PA, 1875. Pension File and Military Service File, National Archives. Letters Received, Volunteer Service Branch, Adjutant General's Office, File G670(VS)1863, National Archives. Harold Hand, Jr. *One Good Regiment: The 13th Pennsylvania Cavalry in the Civil War*. Victoria, B.C., 2000.

GEORGE SHELDON GALLUPE

1 Lieutenant, Co. C, 8 PA Reserves, April 17, 1861. Captain, Co. C, 8 PA Reserves, July 29, 1861. GSW left leg, Gaines' Mill, VA, June 27, 1862. GSW Glendale, VA, June 30, 1862. Acting AIG, 2 Brigade, PA Reserve Division, 22 Army Corps, Department of Washington, Feb.–April 1863. Acting AIG, 2 Brigade, PA Reserve Division, District of Alexandria, 22 Army Corps, Department of Washington, April 1863–Feb. 1864. Major, 8 PA Reserves, Nov. 2, 1863. Acting AIG, Staff of Brig. Gen. John P. Slough, Feb.–April, 1864. GSW face, Spotsylvania, VA, May 12, 1864. Honorably mustered out, May 24, 1864. Colonel, 5 PA Heavy Artillery, Sept. 10, 1864. Honorably mustered out, June 30, 1865.

Born: Aug. 4, 1832 Troy, NY

Died: April 5, 1900 Castle Shannon, Allegheny Co., PA

Occupation: Engaged in the oil business before war. Regular Army (Captain, 1 US Infantry, retired March 1, 1878).

Miscellaneous: Resided Castle Shannon, Allegheny Co., PA

Buried: Allegheny Cemetery, Pittsburgh, PA (Section 23, Lot 49, unmarked)

References: Obituary, *Pittsburgh Post*, April 6, 1900. Samuel P. Bates. *Martial Deeds of Pennsylvania*. Philadelphia, PA, 1875. Military Service File, National Archives. Letters Received, Commis-

George Sheldon Gallupe (postwar)
FROM *PITTSBURGH POST*, APRIL 6, 1900.

sion Branch, Adjutant General's Office, File G451(CB)1866, National Archives. Letters Received, Volunteer Service Branch, Adjutant General's Office, File M2219(VS)1864, National Archives.

ROBERT GALWAY, JR.

Captain, Co. D, 9 PA Reserves, May 3, 1861. GSW left leg, Dranesville, VA, Dec. 20, 1861. Discharged for disability, June 16, 1862, due to effects of his wound. Colonel, 15 PA Militia, Sept. 15, 1862. Discharged Sept. 28, 1862.

Born: 1837? Pittsburgh, PA

Died: Nov. 11, 1864 Pittsburgh, PA

Miscellaneous: Resided Pittsburgh, PA

Buried: Allegheny Cemetery, Pittsburgh, PA (Section 1, Lot 44)

References: Pension File and Military Service File, National Archives. Letters Received, Volunteer Service Branch, Adjutant General's Office, File G340(VS)1862, National Archives. Death notice, *Pittsburgh Gazette*, Nov. 12, 1864.

Augustus Abel Gibson
USAMHI.
Rehn & Hurn, No. 1319 Chestnut Street, Philadelphia, PA.

AUGUSTUS ABEL GIBSON

Captain, 2 US Artillery, July 9, 1853. Commanded Fort Delaware, DE, Feb. 7, 1861–July 31, 1862. Colonel, 2 PA Heavy Artillery, June 24, 1862. Major, 3 US Artillery, July 25, 1863. Commanded 1 Brigade, Defenses North of the Potomac, 22 Army Corps, Department of Washington, Feb. 2, 1863–March 26, 1864. Commanded 1 Brigade, Defenses South of the Potomac, 22 Army Corps, Department of Washington, March 10–May 16, 1864. Commanded 3 Brigade, 2 Division, 18 Army Corps, Army of the James, June 18–20, 1864. Having become involved in a bitter controversy with PA Governor Andrew G. Curtin over the issuance of commissions to newly-promoted officers and other matters, he was relieved of regimental command, July 22, 1864, and ordered to resume his position as major in the Regular Army. Commanded Fort Warren, Boston, MA, Sept. 8, 1864–Jan. 13, 1865.

Born: March 31, 1819 Brownfield, ME
Died: Feb. 11, 1893 Fryeburg, ME
Education: Graduated US Military Academy, West Point, NY, 1839
Other Wars: Mexican War (1 Lieutenant, 2 US Artillery)
Occupation: Regular Army (Lieutenant Colonel, 3 US Artillery, retired Dec. 15, 1870)
Miscellaneous: Resided Fryeburg, Oxford Co., ME
Buried: Mount Auburn Cemetery, Cambridge, MA (Palm Avenue, Lot 4197)
References: *Annual Reunion*, Association of the Graduates of the US Military Academy, 1893. Mehitable C. C. Wilson. *John Gibson of Cambridge, MA, and His Descendants.* Washington, DC, 1900. George W. Ward. *History of the 2nd Pennsylvania Veteran Heavy Artillery From 1861 to 1866.* Philadelphia, PA, 1904. George W. Cullum. *Biographical Register of the Officers and Graduates of the US Military Academy.* Third Edition. Boston and New York, 1891. Letters Received, Volunteer Service Branch, Adjutant General's Office, File G331(VS)1862, National Archives.

JAMES GILKYSON

Colonel, 17 PA Militia, Sept. 17, 1862. Honorably discharged, Sept. 27, 1862. Major, 31 PA Emergency Troops, July 17, 1863. Discharged Aug. 8, 1863.

Born: Feb. 15, 1815 Middletown Twp., Bucks Co., PA
Died: May 24, 1899 Richland Twp., Bucks Co., PA
Occupation: Lawyer
Offices/Honors: District Attorney, Bucks Co., PA, 1860–63 and 1873
Miscellaneous: Resided Doylestown, Bucks Co., PA. Brother of Colonel Stephen R. Gilkyson (40 NJ Infantry).
Buried: Doylestown Cemetery, Doylestown, PA
References: Obituary, *Doylestown Daily Intelligencer*, May 25, 1899. Richard Wynkoop. *Wynkoop Genealogy in the United States of America.* New York City, NY, 1904. J. H. Battle, editor. *History of Bucks County, PA.* Philadelphia, PA, 1887. William W. H. Davis. *History of the Doylestown Guards.* Doylestown, PA, 1887.

Samuel Irvin Givin (postwar)
FROM *MEN OF AMERICA: A BIOGRAPHICAL ALBUM OF THE CITY GOVERNMENT OF PHILADELPHIA.*

SAMUEL IRVIN GIVIN

Quartermaster Sergeant, Battery G, 3 PA Heavy Artillery, Sept. 26, 1862. Commissary Sergeant, 3 PA Heavy Artillery, Sept. 1, 1863. Captain, Co. K, 188 PA Infantry, April 13, 1864. Shell wound left shoulder, Cold Harbor, VA, June 3, 1864. GSW right ankle, Fort Harrison, VA, Sept. 29, 1864. Commanded Sharpshooters, 3 Division, 24 Army Corps, Nov. 10, 1864–June 1865. Lieutenant Colonel, 188 PA Infantry, May 31, 1865. Chief of Ambulances, Staff of Maj. Gen. John Gibbon, June 16–July 2, 1865. Commanded Sub-District of Danville, Department of Virginia, Sept.–Oct. 1865. *Colonel*, 188 PA Infantry, Nov. 26, 1865. Honorably mustered out, Dec. 14, 1865.

Born: April 18, 1833 County Antrim, Ireland
Died: April 17, 1904 Philadelphia, PA
Occupation: Carpenter and builder before war. Agent after war.
Offices/Honors: Philadelphia Chief of Police, 1879–84
Miscellaneous: Resided Philadelphia, PA
Buried: Graceland Memorial Cemetery, Yeadon, Delaware Co., PA. The site of Graceland Memorial Cemetery is now a city park, with only a few grave markers remaining.

References: *Men of America: A Biographical Album of the City Government of Philadelphia.* Philadelphia, PA, 1883. Obituary, *Philadelphia Public Ledger,* April 18, 1904. Pension File and Military Service File, National Archives. William H. Ward, editor. *Records of Members of the Grand Army of the Republic.* San Francisco, CA, 1886. William S. Settle. *History of the 3rd Pennsylvania Heavy Artillery and 188th Pennsylvania Volunteer Infantry.* Lewistown, PA, 1886.

CHARLES FREDERICK WILLIAM GLANZ

Major, 9 PA Infantry, April 24, 1861. Honorably mustered out, July 29, 1861. Colonel, 153 PA Infantry, Oct. 11, 1862. Taken prisoner, Chancellorsville, VA, May 3, 1863. Confined Libby Prison, Richmond, VA. Paroled May 23, 1863. Honorably mustered out, July 24, 1863.

Charles Frederick William Glanz
FROM *HISTORY OF THE 153RD REGIMENT PENNSYLVANIA VOLUNTEER INFANTRY.*

Born: 1823 Walkenreid, Brunswick, Germany
Died: July 24, 1880 Easton, PA
Education: Attended college at Blankenburg, Germany
Occupation: Brewer
Offices/Honors: US Consul, Stettin, Germany, 1857–58
Miscellaneous: Resided Easton, Northampton Co., PA
Buried: Easton Cemetery, Easton, PA (Section G, Lot 365)
References: Obituary, *Easton Daily Express*, July 24, 1880. Franklin Ellis. *History of Northampton County, PA.* Philadelphia, PA, 1877. Pension File, National Archives. William R. Kiefer. *History of the 153rd Regiment Pennsylvania Volunteer Infantry.* Easton, PA, 1909.

JOHN FRANCIS GLENN

Captain, Co. B, 23 PA Infantry, April 21, 1861. Honorably mustered out, July 31, 1861. Captain, Co. A, 23 PA Infantry, Aug. 8, 1861. GSW arm, Fair Oaks, VA, May 31, 1862. Major, 23 PA Infantry, July 20, 1862. Lieutenant Colonel, 23 PA Infantry, Dec. 13, 1862. Colonel, 23 PA Infantry, Jan. 19, 1864. Honorably mustered out, Sept. 8, 1864.

Born: Nov. 2, 1829 Philadelphia, PA
Died: Jan. 8, 1905 Philadelphia, PA

John Francis Glenn
FROM *HISTORY OF THE 23RD PENNSYLVANIA VOLUNTEER INFANTRY.*

Other Wars: Mexican War (Private, Co. D, 1 PA Infantry)
Occupation: Journalist before war. Manufacturer and gas contractor after war. Political boss of Philadelphia's 15th Ward for many years.
Miscellaneous: Resided Philadelphia, PA
Buried: Westminster Cemetery, Bala-Cynwyd, PA (Lakeview Section, Lot 18)
References: Obituary Circular, Whole No. 530, Pennsylvania MOLLUS. Obituary, *Philadelphia Public Ledger*, Jan. 9, 1905. Samuel P. Bates. *Martial Deeds of Pennsylvania.* Philadelphia, PA, 1875. Pension File, National Archives. William J. Wray. *History of the 23rd Pennsylvania Volunteer Infantry.* Philadelphia, PA, 1903.

TILGHMAN H. GOOD

Lieutenant Colonel, 1 PA Infantry, April 20, 1861. Honorably mustered out, July 27, 1861. Colonel, 47 PA Infantry, Aug. 5, 1861. Commanded District of Beaufort, SC, Department of the South, Aug. 22–Sept. 17, 1862 and Oct. 27–Nov. 1862. Commanded 1 Brigade, Expeditionary Forces, 10 Army Corps, Department of the South, Oct. 22–23, 1862. Commanded US Forces, Port Royal Island, SC, Department of the South, Nov.–Dec. 13, 1862 and Feb. 9–19, 1863. Commanded Post of Key West, FL, Department of the South, Dec. 19, 1862–Feb. 7, 1863. Commanded Fort Taylor, Key West, FL, Department of the South, Feb. 27, 1863–Feb. 1864. Honorably mustered out, Sept. 24, 1864.

Born: Oct. 6, 1830 South Whitehall Twp., Lehigh Co., PA
Died: July 18, 1887 Reading, PA
Occupation: Boot and shoe merchant, hotelkeeper, and bank teller before war. Engaged in real estate, insurance and banking activities after war, but resumed hotel management in 1879.
Offices/Honors: PA House of Representatives, 1859. Mayor of Allentown, PA, 1870–74.
Miscellaneous: Resided Allentown, Lehigh Co., PA; and Reading, Berks Co., PA
Buried: Linden Street Cemetery, Allentown, PA
References: Obituary, *Allentown Chronicle and News*, July 19, 1887. Samuel P. Bates. *Martial Deeds of Pennsylvania.* Philadelphia, PA, 1875. Alfred Mathews and Austin N. Hungerford. *History of the Counties of Lehigh and Carbon, in the Commonwealth of Pennsylvania.* Philadelphia, PA, 1884. Lewis G. Schmidt. *A*

Tilghman H. Good (postwar)
<small>From *History of the Counties of Lehigh and Carbon, in the Commonwealth of Pennsylvania.*</small>

Civil War History of the 47th Regiment of Pennsylvania Veteran Volunteers. Allentown, PA, 1986. Richard E. Matthews. *Lehigh County Pennsylvania in the Civil War.* Lehighton, PA, 1989. Military Service File, National Archives. *Proceedings and Papers Read Before the Lehigh County Historical Society.* Allentown, PA, 1922.

JOHN A. GORGAS

1 Sergeant, Co. C, 19 PA Infantry, April 18, 1861. Honorably mustered out, Aug. 9, 1861. 1 Lieutenant, Co. C, 90 PA Infantry, Dec. 2, 1861. Captain, Co. D, 90 PA Infantry, March 7, 1862. Discharged for disability, March 7, 1863, due to "articular rheumatism." Captain, Co. D, 52 PA Militia, July 9, 1863. Honorably mustered out, Sept. 1, 1863. Major, 196 PA Infantry, July 22, 1864. Honorably mustered out, Nov. 17, 1864. Colonel, 213 PA Infantry, March 4, 1865. Honorably mustered out, Nov. 18, 1865.

Born: March 18, 1828 Philadelphia, PA
Died: Jan. 2, 1899 Dayton, OH
Occupation: Blacksmith engaged in coachmaking before war. Employed US Mint, Philadelphia, PA, after war.

Miscellaneous: Resided Philadelphia, PA, to 1888; and Dayton, OH, after 1888
Buried: Dayton National Cemetery, Dayton, OH (Section L, Row 11, Grave 3)
References: Frank Conover, editor. *Centennial Portrait and Biographical Record of the City of Dayton and Montgomery County, OH.* Chicago, IL, 1897. Pension File and Military Service File, National Archives. Letters Received, Volunteer Service Branch, Adjutant General's Office, File G366(VS)1865, National Archives.

John A. Gorgas
<small>Massachusetts MOLLUS Collection, USAMHI.</small>

John M. Gosline
USAMHI.
R. W. ADDIS, PHOTOGRAPHER, MCCLEES GALLERY,
308 PENNA. AVENUE, WASHINGTON, DC.

JOHN M. GOSLINE

Captain, Co. A, 18 PA Infantry, April 24, 1861. Honorably mustered out, Aug. 7, 1861. Colonel, 95 PA Infantry, Oct. 12, 1861. GSW Gaines' Mill, VA, June 27, 1862.

Born: Feb. 7, 1826 Medford, NJ
Died: June 29, 1862 DOW Savage Station, VA
Occupation: Tailor
Miscellaneous: Resided Philadelphia, PA
Buried: Gettysburg National Cemetery, Gettysburg, PA (Section 2, Site 706)
References: Pension File, National Archives. Samuel P. Bates. *Martial Deeds of Pennsylvania.* Philadelphia, PA, 1875. G. Norton Galloway. *The 95th Pennsylvania Volunteers ("Gosline's Pennsylvania Zouaves") in the Sixth Corps: An Historical Paper.* Philadelphia, PA, 1884.

WILLIAM ALEXANDER GRAY

Captain, Co. F, 19 PA Infantry, May 18, 1861. Honorably mustered out, Aug. 29, 1861. Major, 109 PA Infantry, March 21, 1862. Contused GSW left side, Cedar Mountain, VA, Aug. 9, 1862. Honorably discharged, Sept. 30, 1862, to accept promotion. Appointed Colonel, 157 PA Infantry, Oct. 21, 1862. Regiment failed to complete organization. Colonel, 52 PA Militia, July 9, 1863. Honorably mustered out, Sept. 1, 1863.

Born: 1828? Philadelphia, PA
Died: June 6, 1869 Philadelphia, PA
Occupation: Jeweler
Miscellaneous: Resided Philadelphia, PA
Buried: Laurel Hill Cemetery, Philadelphia, PA (Section 3, Lot 278, unmarked)
References: Obituary, *Philadelphia Inquirer,* June 8, 1869. Pension File and Military Service File, National Archives. Letters Received, Volunteer Service Branch, Adjutant General's Office, Files G495(VS)1862 and P808(VS)1862, National Archives.

William Alexander Gray
ROGER D. HUNT COLLECTION, USAMHI.
TURNER'S GROUND FLOOR SKY-LIGHT PHOTOGRAPH ROOMS,
808 CHESTNUT STREET, PHILADELPHIA, PA.

WILLIAM H. GRAY

Colonel, 20 PA Infantry, April 30, 1861. Honorably mustered out, Aug. 3, 1861. Captain, Co. F, 192 PA Infantry, July 12, 1864. Provost Marshal, 2 Separate Brigade, 8 Army Corps, Fort McHenry, MD, Aug. 6–Sept. 23, 1864. Honorably mustered out, Nov. 11, 1864.

Born: March 12, 1824 Carlisle, PA
Died: Nov. 12, 1912 Lititz, PA
Other Wars: Mexican War (1 Lieutenant, 11 US Infantry)
Occupation: Clerk in the employ of the Pennsylvania Railroad Co.
Miscellaneous: Resided Philadelphia, PA; Erie, Erie Co., PA; and Lititz, Lancaster Co., PA
Buried: Mount Moriah Cemetery, Philadelphia, PA (Section 104, Lot 92, unmarked)
References: Pension File and Military Service File, National Archives. John C. Myers. *A Daily Journal of the 192nd Pennsylvania Volunteers.* Philadelphia, PA, 1864. Obituary, *Lancaster New Era*, Nov. 14, 1912.

JOHN GEORGE GREGG

Sergeant, Co. C, 15 OH Infantry, Aug. 30, 1861. 2 Lieutenant, Co. H, 15 OH Infantry, Jan. 9, 1862. 1 Lieutenant, Co. H, 15 OH Infantry, May 27, 1862. Resigned July 3, 1862, under pressure from Colonel Dickey, who described him as "utterly incompetent to perform the duties of his position." 1 Sergeant, Co. F, 3 PA Heavy Artillery, Sept. 16, 1862. 2 Lieutenant, Co. F, 3 PA Heavy Artillery, Nov. 18, 1863. Captain, Co. D, 188 PA Infantry, April 6, 1864. GSW right forearm, Cold Harbor, VA, June 1, 1864. Major, 188 PA Infantry, July 17, 1864. Lieutenant Colonel, 188 PA Infantry, March 28, 1865. *Colonel,* 188 PA Infantry, May 1, 1865. Resigned July 1, 1865, "to turn my attention to pressing private affairs which have been neglected these past four years."

Born: 1835? Maneylaggan, Ireland
Died: Oct. 31, 1880 Terre Haute, IN
Other Wars: Crimean War service. Regular army (6 US Infantry), 1856–59.
Occupation: Lawyer and school teacher
Miscellaneous: Resided Mansfield, Richland Co., OH; Neosho, Newton Co., MO; and Terre Haute, Vigo Co., IN, 1878–80
Buried: Woodlawn Cemetery, Terre Haute, IN (Division 38, Block 6B, Lot 12, unmarked)

References: Pension File and Military Service File, National Archives. Obituary, *Terre Haute Express*, Nov. 2, 1880. Applications for Civilian Appointments and Regular Army Commissions, Office of the Secretary of War, National Archives. Letters Received, Volunteer Service Branch, Adjutant General's Office, File G988(VS)1864, National Archives.

JOHN ARMSTRONG HAMM

Captain, Co. I, 74 PA Infantry, Aug. 20, 1861. Major, 74 PA Infantry, Sept. 30, 1861. Lieutenant Colonel, 74 PA Infantry, March 9, 1862. Colonel, 74 PA Infantry, Dec. 8, 1862. Honorably mustered out, March 2, 1863, his muster into service as colonel being revoked because no vacancy existed.

Born: Nov. 30, 1825 Alsatia
Died: Oct. 16, 1904 Montooth, PA
Occupation: Lumber merchant
Miscellaneous: Resided Montooth, Allegheny Co., PA; and Pittsburgh, PA
Buried: Allegheny Cemetery, Pittsburgh, PA (Section 33, Lot 164)
References: Obituary, *Pittsburgh Post*, Oct. 18, 1904. Pension File and Military Service File, National Archives. Letters Received, Volunteer Service Branch, Adjutant General's Office, File S298(VS)1863, National Archives. Obituary, *Pittsburgh Dispatch*, Oct. 17, 1904.

OLIVER P. HARDING

1 Lieutenant, Co. K, 89 NY Infantry, Oct. 31, 1861. Resigned March 4, 1863, on account of "continued ill health" from chronic diarrhea. Major, 203 PA Infantry, Oct. 7, 1864. Colonel, 203 PA Infantry, Jan. 16, 1865. Dismissed May 2, 1865, for "conduct unbecoming an officer and a gentleman" in embezzling bounty money and other funds belonging to enlisted men in his regiment and in exacting money from officers in return for the promise of promotion.

Born: 1834? Gibson, Susquehanna Co., PA
Died: Date and place of death unknown. No trace of him after the death of his son in New York City, March 31, 1869.
Occupation: Stone mason
Miscellaneous: Resided Binghamton, Broome Co., NY; and New York City, NY

Buried: Burial place unknown
References: Military Service File, National Archives. Letters Received, Volunteer Service Branch, Adjutant General's Office, File P2666(VS)1864, National Archives.

JOSIAH HARLAN

Colonel, Harlan's Light Cavalry, July 23, 1861. Colonel, 11 PA Cavalry, Nov. 13, 1861. Honorably discharged, Aug. 19, 1862, "as a means of promoting the harmony and efficiency of the regiment," upon the recommendation of Maj. Gen. John A. Dix, who called him "a source of dissension among the officers of the regiment."

Born: June 12, 1799 Newlin Twp., Chester Co., PA
Died: Oct. 21, 1871 San Francisco, CA
Occupation: Physician, and from 1823 to 1841 an adventurer in India and Afghanistan, commanding the military forces of various contending potentates
Miscellaneous: Resided Cochranville, Chester Co., PA; Philadelphia, PA; and San Francisco, CA

Josiah Harlan (prewar)
FROM *CENTRAL ASIA: PERSONAL NARRATIVE OF GENERAL JOSIAH HARLAN, 1823–1841.*

Buried: Masonic Cemetery, San Francisco, CA. Probably removed to Woodlawn Memorial Park, Colma, CA, when Masonic Cemetery was discontinued in 1932.
References: *Dictionary of American Biography.* Frank E. Ross. *Central Asia: Personal Narrative of General Josiah Harlan, 1823–1841.* London, England, 1939. *A Man of Enterprise: The Short Writings of Josiah Harlan.* Introduction, maps, chronology by Christopher J. Brunner. New York City, NY, 1987. Obituary, *West Chester Daily Local News,* Nov. 4, 1871. Alpheus H. Harlan. *History and Genealogy of the Harlan Family.* Baltimore, MD, 1912. Letters Received, Volunteer Service Branch, Adjutant General's Office, File M256(VS)1861, National Archives. Thomas P. Lowry. *Tarnished Eagles: The Courts-Martial of Fifty Union Colonels and Lieutenant Colonels.* Mechanicsburg, PA, 1997. *History of the 11th Pennsylvania Volunteer Cavalry.* Philadelphia, PA, 1902.

JOHN HARPER

Private, Co. G, 17 PA Infantry, April 18, 1861. Honorably mustered out, Aug. 2, 1861. 1 Sergeant, Co. G, 95 PA Infantry, Sept. 17, 1861. Sergeant Major, 95 PA Infantry, Nov. 6, 1861. 2 Lieutenant, Co. I, 95 PA Infantry, Dec. 14, 1861. 1 Lieutenant, Co. I, 95 PA Infantry, Nov. 21, 1862. Captain, Co. I, 95 PA Infantry, June 5, 1863. Major, 95 PA Infantry, Oct. 15, 1864. Lieutenant Colonel, 95 PA Infantry, Nov. 3, 1864. *Colonel,* 95 PA Infantry, April 3, 1865. Honorably mustered out, July 17, 1865. Bvt. Colonel, USV, April 6, 1865, for gallant and meritorious services before Petersburg and at the battle of Little Sailors Creek, VA.

Born: April 5, 1840 London, England
Died: Sept. 22, 1875 Roxborough, PA
Occupation: Bookkeeper
Miscellaneous: Resided Roxborough, Philadelphia Co., PA
Buried: West Laurel Hill Cemetery, Bala-Cynwyd, PA (Lansdowne Section, Lot 12, family marker)
References: Pension File and Military Service File, National Archives. Samuel P. Bates. *Martial Deeds of Pennsylvania.* Philadelphia, PA, 1875. G. Norton Galloway. *The 95th Pennsylvania Volunteers ("Gosline's Pennsylvania Zouaves") in the Sixth Corps: An Historical Paper.* Philadelphia, PA, 1884.

*John Harper (standing left, with officers of the 95th Pennsylvania Infantry,
left to right: Capt. Francis J. Randall, Capt. Samuel S. Ford, and Capt. Patrick Egan)*

FROM A PRIVATE COLLECTION.

ELISHA BOANERGES HARVEY

Colonel, 7 PA Reserves, June 26, 1861. Amid rumors of cowardly behavior at the battle of Gaines' Mill, VA, he resigned July 4, 1862, citing recurring rheumatism and the effects of injuries incurred during the Seven Days' battles before Richmond.

Born: Oct. 1, 1819 Huntington Twp., Luzerne Co., PA
Died: Aug. 20, 1872 Wilkes-Barre, PA
Education: Graduated Wesleyan University, Middletown, CT, 1845
Occupation: Lawyer
Offices/Honors: Register of Wills, Luzerne Co., PA, 1854–57
Miscellaneous: Resided Wilkes-Barre, Luzerne Co., PA
Buried: Hollenback Cemetery, Wilkes-Barre, PA (Lot 225)

Elisha Boanerges Harvey
D. Scott Hartzell Collection, USAMHI.

References: Oscar J. Harvey. *The Harvey Book.* Wilkes-Barre, PA, 1899. Samuel P. Bates. *Martial Deeds of Pennsylvania.* Philadelphia, PA, 1875. Oscar J. Harvey and Ernest G. Smith. *History of Wilkes-Barre, PA.* Wilkes-Barre, PA, 1929. Military Service File, National Archives. Josiah R. Sypher. *History of the Pennsylvania Reserve Corps.* Lancaster, PA, 1865. David G. Colwell. *The Bitter Fruits: The Civil War Comes to a Small Town in Pennsylvania.* Carlisle, PA, 1998. Obituary, *Scranton Weekly Republican,* Aug. 28, 1872.

JOHN R. HASLETT

Captain, Co. B, 66 PA Infantry, July 15, 1861. Captain, Co. B, 73 PA Infantry, March 1, 1862. "No longer desiring to serve in the 73rd Regt. P. V.," he resigned Dec. 28, 1862, "to enable me to take position in some regiment (if opportunity offers) that may wish my services." Captain, Co. A, 51 PA Militia, July 1, 1863. Honorably mustered out, Sept. 2, 1863. Colonel, 197 PA Infantry, July 22, 1864. Honorably mustered out, Nov. 11, 1864.

Born: Dec. 12, 1828 Philadelphia, PA
Died: Oct. 20, 1907 Hampton, VA
Occupation: Ship and house painter before war. Car driver after war.
Miscellaneous: Resided Philadelphia, PA; and New Rochelle, Westchester Co., NY, 1881–1901.
Buried: Mount Moriah Cemetery, Philadelphia, PA (Section 18, Lot 64, unmarked)
References: Pension File and Military Service File, National Archives. Death notice, *Philadelphia Public Ledger,* Oct. 23, 1907.

JOSEPH WILLIAMSON HAWLEY

Captain, Co. A, 124 PA Infantry, Aug. 8, 1862. Colonel, 124 PA Infantry, Aug. 18, 1862. GSW neck, Antietam, MD, Sept. 17, 1862. Honorably mustered out, May 17, 1863. Colonel, 29 PA Emergency Troops, June 23, 1863. Honorably mustered out, Aug. 1, 1863.

Born: July 14, 1836 Lionville, Chester Co., PA
Died: May 5, 1915 Media, PA
Education: Attended West Chester (PA) Academy
Occupation: School teacher and bank teller before war. Bank cashier and bank president after war.
Miscellaneous: Resided West Chester, Chester Co., PA; and Media, Delaware Co., PA
Buried: Media Cemetery, Media, PA

Joseph Williamson Hawley
ROGER D. HUNT COLLECTION, USAMHI.
F. GUTEKUNST, PHOTOGRAPHER, 704 & 706 ARCH STREET,
PHILADELPHIA, PA.

References: Samuel P. Bates. *Martial Deeds of Pennsylvania*. Philadelphia, PA, 1875. Obituary, *West Chester Daily Local News*, May 6, 1915. Robert M. Green, compiler. *History of the 124th Regiment Pennsylvania Volunteers*. Philadelphia, PA, 1907. Obituary Circular, Whole No. 823, Pennsylvania MOLLUS. Obituary, *Chester Times*, May 6, 1915.

GEORGE HAY

Captain, Co. K, 2 PA Infantry, April 20, 1861. Honorably mustered out, July 26, 1861. Colonel, 87 PA Infantry, Sept. 25, 1861. Commanded 2 Brigade, 2 Division, 8 Army Corps, Middle Department, Feb. 12, 1863–May 8, 1863. Discharged for disability, May 8, 1863, due to inguinal hernia caused by fall of his horse.

Born: Aug. 1, 1809 York, PA
Died: May 24, 1879 York, PA
Occupation: Cabinet maker and undertaker
Miscellaneous: Resided York, York Co., PA
Buried: Prospect Hill Cemetery, York, PA (Section E, Lot 284)

George Hay
NATIONAL ARCHIVES.
EVANS AND PRINCE, PHOTOGRAPHERS, YORK, PA.

References: George R. Prowell. *History of the 87th Regiment Pennsylvania Volunteers*. York, PA, 1901. Obituary, *York Daily*, May 26, 1879. Pension File, National Archives. John Gibson, editor. *History of York County, PA*. Chicago, IL, 1886.

GEORGE S. HAYS

Colonel, 8 PA Reserves, June 22, 1861. Resigned July 11, 1862, on account of "increasing ill health" due to injuries incurred in a fall from his horse at New Market Road, VA, June 30, 1862.

Born: Sept. 28, 1807 Allegheny Co., PA
Died: Feb. 24, 1884 Pittsburgh, PA
Occupation: Physician and stock raiser

George S. Hays
ROGER D. HUNT COLLECTION, USAMHI.

Offices/Honors: Prothonotary, Allegheny Co., PA, 1847–51
Miscellaneous: Resided Herriotsville, Allegheny Co., PA
Buried: Union Dale Cemetery, Pittsburgh, PA (Division 3, Section E, Range 12, Lot 51, unmarked)
References: Josiah R. Sypher. *History of the Pennsylvania Reserve Corps.* Lancaster, PA, 1865. Military Service File, National Archives. Obituary, *Pittsburgh Daily Post*, Feb. 26, 1884. Thomas P. Lowry. *Tarnished Eagles: The Courts-Martial of Fifty Union Colonels and Lieutenant Colonels.* Mechanicsburg, PA, 1997. Obituary, *Pittsburgh Evening Chronicle*, Feb. 25, 1884.

DENNIS HEENAN

Lieutenant Colonel, 24 PA Infantry, May 1, 1861. Honorably mustered out, Aug. 10, 1861. Colonel, 116 PA Infantry, Sept. 1, 1862. Shell wound right hand, Fredericksburg, VA, Dec. 13, 1862. Honorably discharged, Jan. 26, 1863, due to the consolidation of the regiment into a battalion of four companies.

Born: April 18, 1818 Barris O'Kane, County Tipperary, Ireland
Died: July 4, 1872 Philadelphia, PA (from injuries received when thrown from his carriage)
Occupation: Carpenter and builder before war. Liquor dealer, coal merchant, and public works contractor after war.
Miscellaneous: Resided Philadelphia, PA. Father-in-law of Bvt. Brig. Gen. St. Clair A. Mulholland.
Buried: Old Cathedral Cemetery, Philadelphia, PA (Section H, Range 6, Lots 63–64, unmarked)
References: John H. Campbell. *History of the Friendly Sons of St. Patrick and of the Hibernian Society for the Relief of Emigrants from Ireland.* Philadelphia, PA, 1892. Samuel P. Bates. *Martial Deeds of Pennsylvania.* Philadelphia, PA, 1875. Pension File and Military Service File, National Archives. St. Clair A. Mulholland. *The Story of the 116th Regiment Pennsylvania Volunteers in the War of the Rebellion.* Philadelphia, PA, 1903. Obituary, *Philadelphia Public Ledger*, July 6, 1872. Don Ernsberger. *Paddy Owen's Regulars: A History of the 69th Pennsylvania "Irish Volunteers."* N.p., 2004.

BAYNTON JAMES HICKMAN

Private, Co. F, 19 PA Infantry, May 18, 1861. 1 Lieutenant, Co. B, 49 PA Infantry, Aug. 20, 1861. Acting ADC, Staff of Brig. Gen. Winfield S. Hancock, Oct. 7, 1861–April 8, 1862. Captain, Co. B, 49 PA Infantry, April 8, 1862. Acting Ordnance Officer, 2 Division, 6 Army Corps, Army of the Potomac, Nov. 2, 1862–March 1864. Major, 49 PA Infantry, March 26, 1864. Lieutenant Colonel, 49 PA Infantry, May 11, 1864. Dismissed Aug. 9, 1864, for "misbehavior in presence of the enemy," having absented himself from and remained away from his regiment when it was engaged with the enemy at Scott's Farm, near Spotsylvania, VA, May 10, 1864. Sentence remitted and restored to command, in consideration of "the hitherto gallant and meritorious conduct of the accused and upon the recommendation of his division commander." *Colonel*, 49 PA Infantry, June 29, 1865. Resigned June 28, 1865, because "my business at home requires my attendance." Bvt. Colonel, USV, Dec. 5, 1864, for gallant and meritorious conduct throughout the present campaign before Richmond, VA, and in the Shenandoah Valley.

Baynton James Hickman
PAUL BRZOZOWSKI COLLECTION.
EDWARD P. HIPPLE, 820 ARCH STREET, PHILADELPHIA, PA.

Born: Feb. 1, 1841 East Bradford, Chester Co., PA
Died: Nov. 17, 1890 Martinsburg, WV
Occupation: Hosiery manufacturer
Miscellaneous: Resided West Chester, Chester Co., PA; and Philadelphia, PA
Buried: Birmingham-Lafayette Cemetery, near West Chester, PA
References: Robert S. Westbrook. *History of the 49th Pennsylvania Volunteers*. Altoona, PA, 1898. Obituary, *West Chester Daily Local News*, Nov. 18, 1890. Military Service File, National Archives. Obituary, *Philadelphia Public Ledger*, Nov. 19, 1890. Douglas R. Harper. *"If Thee Must Fight": A Civil War History of Chester County, Pennsylvania*. West Chester, PA, 1990.

JACOB C. HIGGINS

Captain, Brigade Quartermaster, 2 Brigade, 2 Division, Department of Pennsylvania, April 20, 1861. Honorably mustered out, July 25, 1861. Captain, Co. G, 1 PA Cavalry, Aug. 1, 1861. Lieutenant Colonel, 1 PA Cavalry, Sept. 27, 1861. Resigned Jan. 2, 1862, in anticipation of an adverse report from a Board of Examination. Colonel, 125 PA Infantry, Aug. 16, 1862. Honorably mustered out, May 18, 1863. Colonel, 22 PA Cavalry, March 5, 1864. Commanded 2 Brigade, 1 Cavalry Division, Army of West Virginia, July 22–30, 1864. Dismissed July 29, 1864, for "having, during the late battle near Winchester, by exaggerated statements and unsoldierly orders, created a panic among the teamsters, thereby causing a loss of stores and wagons." A Military Commission subsequently found that his dismissal was "founded on insufficient evidence," and his dismissal was revoked Oct. 25, 1864. Honorably mustered out, July 21, 1865.

Jacob Higgins
MASSACHUSETTS MOLLUS COLLECTION, USAMHI.

Born: March 7, 1826 Williamsburg, PA

Died: June 1, 1893 Johnstown, PA (accidental self-inflicted gunshot wound)

Other Wars: Mexican War (Private, Co. M, 2 PA Infantry)

Occupation: Carpenter and hotelkeeper

Miscellaneous: Resided Williamsburg, Blair Co., PA; Hollidaysburg, Blair Co., PA; and Johnstown, Cambria Co., PA

Buried: Grandview Cemetery, Johnstown, PA (Woodland Section, Division 3, Lot 93)

References: Milton V. Burgess. *Minute Men of Pennsylvania: With a Brief Biography of Their Leader in Blair, Bedford and Cambria Counties, Col. Jacob C. Higgins.* Martinsburg, PA, 1962. Pension File, National Archives. *History of the 125th Regiment Pennsylvania Volunteers.* Philadelphia, PA, 1906. Samuel C. Farrar. *The 22nd Pennsylvania Cavalry and the Ringgold Battalion, 1861–65.* Pittsburgh, PA, 1911. Letters Received, Volunteer Service Branch, Adjutant General's Office, Files H591(VS)1863 and D866(VS)1864, National Archives. Obituary, *Johnstown Weekly Tribune*, June 2 and June 9, 1893.

GOTTLIEB HOBURG

Sergeant, Co. I, 3 PA Infantry, April 20, 1861. Honorably mustered out, July 29, 1861. Sergeant, Co. K, 74 PA Infantry, Oct. 17, 1861. 2 Lieutenant, Co. G, 74 PA Infantry, Jan. 24, 1862. 1 Lieutenant, Adjutant, 74 PA Infantry, Feb. 14, 1862. 1 Lieutenant, Co. E, 74 PA Infantry, May 1, 1862. GSW right groin, Freeman's Ford, VA, Aug. 22, 1862. Discharged for disability, Oct. 31, 1862, on account of wounds. Captain, Co. I, 74 PA Infantry, May 2, 1863. Captain, Co. H, 74 PA Infantry, July 6, 1863. Colonel, 74 PA Infantry, April 1, 1865. Commanded Subdistrict of Clarksburg, WV, Department of West Virginia, May–June 1865. Honorably mustered out, Aug. 29, 1865.

Born: Nov. 21, 1827 Hanover, Germany

Died: July 18, 1870 New York City, NY

Occupation: Clerk and brewery worker

Miscellaneous: Resided Pittsburgh, PA; and Morrisania, Westchester Co., NY

Buried: Woodlawn Cemetery, New York City, NY (Section 25, Spruce Plot, Lot 1366)

References: Pension File and Military Service File, National Archives. Letters Received, Volunteer Service Branch, Adjutant General's Office, File H1085(VS)1862, National Archives.

Oliver Hopkinson

ROGER D. HUNT COLLECTION, USAMHI.
F. GUTEKUNST, PHOTOGRAPHER, 704 & 706 ARCH STREET, PHILADELPHIA, PA.

OLIVER HOPKINSON

Lieutenant Colonel, 1 DE Infantry, Oct. 15, 1861. GSW knee, Antietam, MD, Sept. 17, 1862. Resigned Dec. 14, 1862, due to disability from scorbutic disease. Colonel, 51 PA Militia, July 10, 1863. Honorably mustered out, Sept. 2, 1863.

Born: July 24, 1812 Philadelphia, PA

Died: March 10, 1905 Philadelphia, PA

Education: Graduated University of Pennsylvania, Philadelphia, PA, 1832

Occupation: Lawyer

Miscellaneous: Resided Philadelphia, PA. Grandson of Francis Hopkinson, Signer of the Declaration of Independence.

Buried: Laurel Hill Cemetery, Philadelphia, PA (Section 9, Lot 125)

References: John W. Jordan, editor. *Colonial Families of Philadelphia.* New York and Chicago, 1911. Military Service File, National Archives. Obituary, *Philadelphia Public Ledger,* March 11, 1905. Moses King. *Philadelphia and Notable Philadelphians.* New York City, NY, 1902.

MELCHIOR HAY HORN

Major, 5 PA Militia, Sept. 11, 1862. Discharged Sept. 27, 1862. Colonel, 38 PA Militia, July 3, 1863. Honorably mustered out, Aug. 7, 1863.

Born: April 9, 1822 Easton, PA
Died: Feb. 28, 1890 Catasauqua, PA
Occupation: Merchant, civil engineer, canal weighmaster, and bank cashier
Miscellaneous: Resided Easton, Northampton Co., PA; and Catasauqua, Lehigh Co., PA, after 1857. Brother-in-law of Col. Samuel Yohe.
Buried: Fairview Cemetery, West Catasauqua, PA
References: Frank B. Copp. *Biographical Sketches of Some of Easton's Prominent Citizens.* Easton, PA, 1879. James F. Lambert and Henry J. Reinhard. *A History of Catasauqua in Lehigh County, PA.* Allentown, PA, 1914. Charles R. Roberts. *History of Lehigh County, PA.* Allentown, PA, 1914. Obituary, *Catasauqua Valley Record,* March 6, 1890.

HENRY SHIPPEN HUIDEKOPER

Captain, Co. K, 150 PA Infantry, Aug. 30, 1862. Lieutenant Colonel, 150 PA Infantry, Sept. 4, 1862. GSW right arm (amputated), Gettysburg, PA, July 1, 1863. *Colonel,* 150 PA Infantry, Feb. 23, 1864. Resigned March 5, 1864, on account of physical disability from the debilitating effects of the amputation of his arm.

Born: July 17, 1839 Meadville, PA
Died: Nov. 9, 1918 Philadelphia, PA
Education: Graduated Harvard University, Cambridge, MA, 1862
Occupation: Manufacturer of woollen goods
Offices/Honors: Medal of Honor, Gettysburg, PA, July 1, 1863. "While engaged in repelling an attack of the enemy, received a severe wound of the right arm, but instead of retiring remained at the front in command of his regiment." Major Gen., Pennsylvania National Guard, 1870–81. Postmaster, Philadelphia, PA, 1880–85.

Melchior Hay Horn
FROM *A HISTORY OF CATASAUQUA IN LEHIGH COUNTY, PA.*

Henry Shippen Huidekoper
ALEX. CHAMBERLAIN COLLECTION, USAMHI.
R. W. ADDIS, PHOTOGRAPHER, 308 PENNA. AVENUE, WASHINGTON, DC.

Miscellaneous: Resided Meadville, Crawford Co., PA; and Philadelphia, PA

Buried: Greendale Cemetery, Meadville, PA (Section 2, Lots 5–6)

References: Samuel P. Bates. *Martial Deeds of Pennsylvania*. Philadelphia, PA, 1875. Obituary, *Philadelphia Public Ledger*, Nov. 10, 1918. Thomas Chamberlin. *History of the 150th Regiment Pennsylvania Volunteers*. Philadelphia, PA, 1905. *Class of 'Sixty-Two, Harvard University, Fiftieth Anniversary*. Cambridge, MA, 1912. St. Clair A. Mulholland. *Military Order Congress Medal of Honor Legion of the United States*. Philadelphia, PA, 1905. Pension File and Military Service File, National Archives. Letters Received, Volunteer Service Branch, Adjutant General's Office, File W2005(VS)1863, National Archives. *Companions of the Military Order of the Loyal Legion of the United States*. New York City, NY, 1901.

Thomas Marcus Hulings
COURTESY OF PERRY M. FROHNE.
F. GUTEKUNST, PHOTOGRAPHER, 704 & 706 ARCH STREET, PHILADELPHIA, PA.

THOMAS MARCUS HULINGS

1 Lieutenant, Co. E, 25 PA Infantry, April 18, 1861. Captain, Co. E, 25 PA Infantry, May 28, 1861. Honorably mustered out, July 29, 1861. Major, 49 PA Infantry, July 31, 1861. Captain, 12 US Infantry, Feb. 19, 1862. Lieutenant Colonel, 49 PA Infantry, Oct. 16, 1862. Colonel, 49 PA Infantry, March 26, 1864. GSW head, Spotsylvania, VA, May 10, 1864.

Born: Feb. 7, 1835 Lewistown, PA
Died: May 10, 1864 KIA Spotsylvania, VA
Occupation: Lawyer
Miscellaneous: Resided Lewistown, Mifflin Co., PA. Son-in-law of Brig. Gen. Lorenzo Thomas.
Buried: Spotsylvania, VA (Body never recovered). Cenotaph in Green Mount Cemetery, Baltimore, MD (Area VV, Lots 91–94).
References: F. Ellis and Austin N. Hungerford, editors. *History of the Susquehanna and Juniata Valleys in Pennsylvania*. Philadelphia, PA, 1886. Pension File and Military Service File, National Archives. Samuel P. Bates. *Martial Deeds of Pennsylvania*. Philadelphia, PA, 1875. Robert S. Westbrook. *History of the 49th Pennsylvania Volunteers*. Altoona, PA, 1898. Obituary, *Lewistown Gazette*, June 1, 1864. Obituary, *Philadelphia Inquirer*, May 19, 1864.

CHARLES H. HUNTER

Colonel, 42 PA Militia, July 6, 1863. Honorably mustered out, Aug. 12, 1863.

Born: Sept. 29, 1817 Rockland Twp., Berks Co., PA
Died: June 3, 1870 Reading, PA
Education: Graduated Princeton (NJ) University, 1837. Graduated University of Pennsylvania Medical School, 1841.
Occupation: Physician
Offices/Honors: Prothonotary, Berks Co., PA, 1851–54
Miscellaneous: Resided Reading, Berks Co., PA
Buried: Charles Evans Cemetery, Reading, PA (Section M, Lots 25–30)
References: Obituary, *Reading Daily Eagle*, June 4, 1870.

John Irvin
CHARLES FAUST COLLECTION, USAMHI.

JOHN IRVIN

Captain, Co. B, 149 PA Infantry, Aug. 26, 1862. Major, 149 PA Infantry, March 26, 1863. Shell wound head, Gettysburg, PA, July 1, 1863. Lieutenant Colonel, 149 PA Infantry, April 5, 1864. Colonel, 149 PA Infantry, Jan. 28, 1865. Honorably mustered out, Aug. 4, 1865.

Born: March 8, 1836 Curwensville, PA
Died: Feb. 22, 1897 Curwensville, PA
Occupation: Engaged in mercantile, milling and lumbering enterprises
Miscellaneous: Resided Curwensville, Clearfield Co., PA
Buried: Oak Hill Cemetery, Curwensville, PA
References: Obituary, *Clearfield Republican*, Feb. 24, 1897. John W. Nesbit. *General History of Company D, 149th Pennsylvania Volunteers*. Oakdale, PA, 1908. Richard E. Matthews. *The 149th Pennsylvania Volunteer Infantry Unit in the Civil War*. Jefferson, NC, 1994. Lewis C. Aldrich, editor. *History of Clearfield County, PA*. Syracuse, NY, 1887. Letters Received, Volunteer Service Branch, Adjutant General's Office, File I444(VS)1865, National Archives.

JOSEPH JACK

Colonel, 168 PA Infantry, Dec. 1, 1862. Honorably mustered out, July 25, 1863.

Born: Feb. 9, 1808 Pleasant Unity, Westmoreland Co., PA
Died: April 18, 1893 Decatur, IL
Occupation: Farmer and grocer
Miscellaneous: Resided Pleasant Unity, Westmoreland Co., PA, to 1869; and Decatur, Macon Co., IL, after 1869
Buried: Greenwood Cemetery, Decatur, IL
References: Pension File, National Archives. Obituary, *Decatur Daily Republican*, April 19, 1893. Samuel P. Bates. *Martial Deeds of Pennsylvania*. Philadelphia, PA, 1875.

THOMAS CHALKLEY JAMES

Captain, 1 Troop, Philadelphia City Cavalry, May 13, 1861. Honorably mustered out, Aug. 17, 1861. Lieutenant Colonel, 9 PA Cavalry, Nov. 10, 1861. *Colonel*, 9 PA Cavalry, Oct. 14, 1862.

Thomas Chalkley James
ROGER D. HUNT COLLECTION, USAMHI.

Born: Jan. 8, 1813 Philadelphia, PA
Died: Jan. 13, 1863 Philadelphia, PA
Occupation: Commission merchant
Miscellaneous: Resided Philadelphia, PA
Buried: Laurel Hill Cemetery, Philadelphia, PA (Section 10, Lot 19)
References: Joseph L. Wilson, editor. *Book of the First Troop Philadelphia City Cavalry, 1774–1914.* Philadelphia, PA, 1915. Robert C. Moon. *The Morris Family of Philadelphia.* Philadelphia, PA, 1898. Obituary, *Philadelphia Public Ledger,* Jan. 15, 1863.

Phaon Jarrett
KEN TURNER COLLECTION.
N. PARKER, WEST CHESTER, PA.

PHAON JARRETT

Colonel, 11 PA Infantry, April 26, 1861. Honorably mustered out, Aug. 1, 1861.

Born: Feb. 9, 1809 Lower Nazareth, Northampton Co., PA
Died: Sept. 16, 1876 Lock Haven, PA
Education: Attended US Military Academy, West Point, NY (Class of 1832)
Occupation: Civil engineer and surveyor
Miscellaneous: Resided Allentown, Lehigh Co., PA; and Lock Haven, Clinton Co., PA
Buried: Linden Street Cemetery, Allentown, PA
References: John B. Linn. *History of Centre and Clinton Counties, PA.* Philadelphia, PA, 1883. William H. Locke. *The Story of the Regiment.* Philadelphia, PA, 1868. Cindy Stouffer and Shirley Cubbison. *A Colonel, a Flag, and a Dog.* Gettysburg, PA, 1998. Obituary, *Clinton Democrat,* Sept. 21, 1876.

WILLIAM WESLEY JENNINGS

1 Lieutenant, Co. F, 25 PA Infantry, May 2, 1861. Honorably mustered out, July 26, 1861. Captain, Co. F, 127 PA Infantry, Aug. 6, 1862. Colonel, 127 PA Infantry, Aug. 16, 1862. Shell wound foot, Fredericksburg, VA, Dec. 13, 1862. Honorably mustered out, May 29, 1863. Colonel, 26 PA Emergency Troops, June 22, 1863. Honorably mustered out, July 30, 1863.

Born: July 22, 1838 Harrisburg, PA
Died: Feb. 28, 1894 Harrisburg, PA
Occupation: Iron manufacturer and banker
Offices/Honors: Sheriff of Dauphin Co., PA, 1863–66 and 1876–79
Miscellaneous: Resided Harrisburg, Dauphin Co., PA
Buried: Harrisburg Cemetery, Harrisburg, PA (Section I, Lot 42)
References: Luther R. Kelker. *History of Dauphin County, PA.* New York and Chicago, 1907. *Commemorative Biographical Encyclopedia of Dauphin County, PA.* Chambersburg, PA, 1896. Obituary, *Harrisburg Patriot,* March 1, 1894. Pension File, National Archives. William H. Egle. *Pennsylvania Genealogies.* Harrisburg, PA, 1896. Obituary Circular, Whole No. 270, Pennsylvania MOLLUS. *History of the 127th Regiment Pennsylvania Volunteers.* Lebanon, Pa, 1902. William H. Egle. *History of the Counties of Dauphin and Lebanon in the Commonwealth of Pennsylvania.* Philadelphia, PA, 1883.

William Wesley Jennings

Charles Francis Johnson

CHARLES FRANCIS JOHNSON

Lieutenant Colonel, 81 PA Infantry, Sept. 16, 1861. Colonel, 81 PA Infantry, June 1, 1862. GSW both thighs and groin, Glendale, VA, June 30, 1862. Resigned Nov. 24, 1862, on account of physical disability from "sympathetic inflammation of the spermatic cord," caused by his wounds. Major, VRC, June 5, 1863. Lieutenant Colonel, 16 VRC, Sept. 29, 1863. Colonel, 18 VRC, Dec. 7, 1863. Commanded 2 Provisional Brigade, Garrison of Washington, DC, Aug. 1865.

Born: Sept. 22, 1827 Philadelphia, PA
Died: July 28, 1867 Bowling Green, KY (chronic diarrhea and cystitis)
Occupation: Clerk and engraver
Miscellaneous: Resided Philadelphia, PA; and Camden, NJ
Buried: Fairview Cemetery, Bowling Green, KY

References: Pension File and Military Service File, National Archives. Death notice, *Philadelphia Public Ledger*, Aug. 3, 1867. Charles F. Johnson Papers, USAMHI. Fred Pelka, editor. *The Civil War Letters of Colonel Charles F. Johnson, Invalid Corps.* Amherst and Boston, 2004. Letters Received, Volunteer Service Branch, Adjutant General's Office, File J356(VS)1865, National Archives.

JAMES JOHNSON

1 Lieutenant, Co. N, 71 PA Infantry, July 1, 1861. Captain, Co. N, 71 PA Infantry, Jan. 23, 1862. GSW right leg, White Oak Swamp, VA, June 30, 1862. Captain, Co. G, 71 PA Infantry, July 27, 1862. Resigned Sept. 3, 1862. Colonel, 13 PA Militia, Sept. 17, 1862. Honorably discharged, Sept. 26, 1862. Colonel, 178 PA Infantry, Dec. 2, 1862. Honorably mustered out, July 27, 1863. Major, 14 VRC, Dec. 14, 1863. Superintendent, Freedmen's Bureau, Fredericksburg, VA, Nov. 30, 1865–Dec. 31, 1867. Honorably mustered out, Jan. 1, 1868.

Born: Feb. 22, 1820 Pittsgrove (now Elmer), Salem Co., NJ

Died: May 11, 1915 Bala-Cynwyd, PA

Occupation: Farmer before war. Clerk in the New York City Post Office after war.

Miscellaneous: Resided near Deerfield, Cumberland Co., NJ, to 1857; Philadelphia, PA, 1857–69; Brooklyn, NY, 1869–99; and Bala-Cynwyd, Montgomery Co., PA

Buried: Lawnview Cemetery, Rockledge, PA (Broad Lawn, Range 32, Grave 61)

References: Pension File and Military Service File, National Archives. Obituary, *Philadelphia Public Ledger*, May 13, 1915. Letters Received, Volunteer Service Branch, Adjutant General's Office, File J3(VS)1866, National Archives.

JOHN D. COCKERELL JOHNSON

Major, 110 PA Infantry, Oct. 7, 1861. Resigned June 16, 1862, "on the plea of physical disability," due to "congestion of the liver of a chronic nature." *Colonel,* 146 PA Infantry, July 1862. Regiment did not complete organization.

Born: Jan. 21, 1827 Christiana, DE

Died: July 31, 1894 Philadelphia, PA

Occupation: Stock broker

Offices/Honors: Secretary and Treasurer, Philadelphia Stock Exchange, 1871–94

Miscellaneous: Resided Philadelphia, PA

Buried: Woodlands Cemetery, Philadelphia, PA (Section H, Lot 282)

References: Letters Received, Volunteer Service Branch, Adjutant General's Office, File J278(VS)1862, National Archives. Obituary Circular, Whole No. 282, Pennsylvania MOLLUS. Pension File and Military Service File, National Archives. Obituary, *Philadelphia Public Ledger*, Aug. 2, 1894. Commissions File, Records of the Department of Military and Veterans' Affairs, Pennsylvania State Archives.

JOHN WILLIAMS JOHNSTON

Colonel, 14 PA Infantry, April 30, 1861. Honorably mustered out, Aug. 7, 1861. Lieutenant Colonel, 93 PA Infantry, Sept. 14, 1861. Resigned July 10, 1862.

Born: May 22, 1820 Kingston, PA

Died: Dec. 17, 1902 Kingston, PA

John Williams Johnston
MASSACHUSETTS MOLLUS COLLECTION, USAMHI.

Other Wars: Mexican War (Captain, Co. E, 2 PA Volunteers)

Occupation: Railroad construction engineer and farmer

Miscellaneous: Resided Kingston, Unity Twp., Westmoreland Co., PA

Buried: St. Clair Cemetery, Greensburg, PA (Section U, Lot 58)

References: George D. Albert, editor. *History of the County of Westmoreland*. Philadelphia, PA, 1882. Obituary, *Greensburg Daily Tribune*, Dec. 18, 1902. Penrose G. Mark. *Red: White: and Blue Badge Pennsylvania Veteran Volunteers. A History of the 93rd Regiment*. Harrisburg, PA, 1911. Military Service File, National Archives.

EDWARD S. JONES

Captain, Co. C, 3 PA Cavalry, Aug. 1, 1861. Lieutenant Colonel, 3 PA Cavalry, Nov. 20, 1862. *Colonel*, 3 PA Cavalry, Aug. 16, 1864. Honorably mustered out, Aug. 24, 1864.

Born: Aug. 14, 1818 Philadelphia, PA
Died: Nov. 25, 1886 Nashville, TN
Occupation: Publisher before war. Paper bag manufacturer and US steamboat inspector after war.
Offices/Honors: Commander of Department of Tennessee and Georgia, GAR
Miscellaneous: Resided Philadelphia, PA; and Nashville, TN
Buried: Nashville National Cemetery, Nashville, TN (Section MM, Grave 16520)
References: Obituary, *Nashville Daily American*, Nov. 26, 1886. Pension File, National Archives. Letters Received, Volunteer Service Branch, Adjutant General's Office, File J603(VS)1863, National Archives. *History of the 3rd Pennsylvania Cavalry in the American Civil War.* Philadelphia, PA, 1905.

Edward S. Jones
FROM *HISTORY OF THE 3RD PENNSYLVANIA CAVALRY IN THE AMERICAN CIVIL WAR.*

GEORGE W. JONES

Sergeant, Co. F, 22 PA Infantry, April 23, 1861. Honorably mustered out, Aug. 7, 1861. 1 Sergeant, Co. G, Phelps' Regiment MO Infantry, Dec. 1, 1861. Honorably mustered out, May 12, 1862. Captain, Co. B, 150 PA Infantry, Aug. 25, 1862. Dismissed March 12, 1863, for presenting a "false and fraudulent" claim for subsistence. Dismissal revoked, April 3, 1863, upon evidence of the validity of the claim. Major, 150 PA Infantry, March 18, 1864. Lieutenant Colonel, 150 PA Infantry, May 16, 1865. *Colonel*, 150 PA Infantry, June 15, 1865. Honorably mustered out, June 23, 1865.

Born: Nov. 4, 1833 Germantown, PA
Died: Nov. 26, 1913 Germantown, PA
Occupation: Carpenter and builder. Janitor in later life.
Miscellaneous: Resided Philadelphia, PA
Buried: Holy Sepulchre Cemetery, Philadelphia, PA (Section G, Range 4, Lot 13)

George W. Jones
ALEX. CHAMBERLAIN COLLECTION, USAMHI.

References: Obituary, *Philadelphia Public Ledger,* Nov. 27, 1913. Pension File, National Archives. Letters Received, Volunteer Service Branch, Adjutant General's Office, File J63(VS)1863, National Archives. Thomas Chamberlin. *History of the 150th Regiment Pennsylvania Volunteers.* Philadelphia, PA, 1905.

JOHN RICHTER JONES

Colonel, 58 PA Infantry, Feb. 13, 1862. GSW heart, Batchelder's Creek, NC, May 23, 1863

Born: Oct. 2, 1803 Salem, NJ
Died: May 23, 1863 KIA Batchelder's Creek, NC
Education: Graduated University of Pennsylvania, Philadelphia, PA, 1821
Occupation: Lawyer, judge, and agriculturist

Offices/Honors: Judge, Court of Common Pleas, Philadelphia, PA, 1836–47
Miscellaneous: Resided Roxborough, Philadelphia Co., PA; and Eaglesmere, Sullivan Co., PA. Uncle of Bvt. Brig. Gen. Cecil Clay.
Buried: Leverington Cemetery, Roxborough, Philadelphia Co., PA
References: J. Richter Jones Papers, Lewis Leigh Collection, USAMHI. *The Volunteers' Roll of Honor.* Philadelphia, PA, 1864. William Cathcart. *The Baptist Encyclopedia.* Philadelphia, PA, 1881. Samuel P. Bates. *Martial Deeds of Pennsylvania.* Philadelphia, PA, 1875. *University of Pennsylvania: Biographical Catalogue of the Matriculates of the College.* Philadelphia, PA, 1894. *Appletons' Cyclopedia of American Biography.* Military Service File, National Archives.

John Richter Jones
KEN TURNER COLLECTION.

Owen Jones
COURTESY OF THE AUTHOR.
PUBLISHED BY E. ANTHONY, 501 BROADWAY, NEW YORK,
FROM PHOTOGRAPHIC NEGATIVE IN
BRADY'S NATIONAL PORTRAIT GALLERY.

OWEN JONES

Major, 1 PA Cavalry, Aug. 16, 1861. Lieutenant Colonel, 1 PA Cavalry, Jan. 3, 1862. Colonel, 1 PA Cavalry, May 5, 1862. Commanded 1 Brigade, Bayard's Cavalry Division, Army of the Potomac, Oct. 1862. Resigned Jan. 29, 1863.

Born: Dec. 29, 1819 near Ardmore, Montgomery Co., PA

Died: Dec. 25, 1878 near Ardmore, PA

Education: Attended University of Pennsylvania, Philadelphia, PA (Class of 1840)

Occupation: Although educated for a law career, he preferred to engage in agricultural pursuits

Offices/Honors: US House of Representatives, 1857–59

Miscellaneous: Resided near Ardmore, Montgomery Co., PA

Buried: Laurel Hill Cemetery, Philadelphia, PA (Section G, Lot 262)

References: Theodore W. Bean. *History of Montgomery County, PA.* Philadelphia, PA, 1884. William P. Lloyd. *History of the 1st Regiment Pennsylvania Reserve Cavalry.* Philadelphia, PA, 1864. *Biographical Directory of the American Congress.* Military Service File, National Archives. Obituary, *Philadelphia Public Ledger,* Dec. 27, 1878.

TOBIAS B. KAUFMAN

Corporal, Co. I, 1 PA Reserves, June 10, 1861. 2 Lieutenant, Co. I, 1 PA Reserves, July 26, 1861. Captain, Co. I, 1 PA Reserves, Nov. 14, 1861. GSW right forearm, Antietam, MD, Sept. 17, 1862. Major, 1 PA Reserves, March 1, 1863. Honorably mustered out, June 13, 1864. Colonel, 209 PA Infantry, Sept. 16, 1864. Taken prisoner, Bermuda Hundred, VA, Nov. 17, 1864. Confined Libby Prison, Richmond, VA; and Danville, VA. Paroled Feb. 22, 1865. Honorably mustered out, May 31, 1865.

Born: Aug. 19, 1837 Boiling Springs, PA

Died: Oct. 21, 1912 Belmond, IA

Occupation: School teacher before war. Grain merchant and farmer after war.

Miscellaneous: Resided Boiling Springs, Cumberland Co., PA, to 1873; Belmond, Wright Co., IA, 1873–1909; and Tulsa, Tulsa Co., OK, 1909–12

Buried: Belmond Cemetery, Belmond, IA

Tobias B. Kaufman
DOUG KAUFFMANN COLLECTION, USAMHI.

References: Obituary, *Tulsa Daily World,* Oct. 23, 1912. Obituary, *Iowa Valley Press,* Oct. 24, 1912. *Biographical Record and Portrait Album of Hamilton and Wright Counties, IA.* Chicago, IL, 1889. Pension File and Military Service File, National Archives. Letters Received, Volunteer Service Branch, Adjutant General's Office, File K188(VS)1865, National Archives.

JOSIAH HOLCOMB KELLOGG

1 Lieutenant, 1 US Dragoons, May 13, 1861. 1 Lieutenant, 1 US Cavalry, Aug. 3, 1861. 1 Lieutenant, Adjutant, 1 US Cavalry, Jan. 13, 1862. Captain, 1 US Cavalry, May 20, 1862. Colonel, 17 PA Cavalry, Nov. 19, 1862. Commanded 2 Brigade, 1 Division, Cavalry Corps, Army of the Potomac, June 6–9, 1863 and Jan. 10–25, 1864. Honorably discharged from volunteer service, Dec. 17, 1864, on account of physical disability due to variocele. Retired from regular service, Feb. 6, 1865.

Josiah Holcomb Kellogg
FREDERICK H. MESERVE. HISTORICAL PORTRAITS.
COURTESY OF NEW YORK STATE LIBRARY.

Born: Oct. 1, 1836 Erie, PA
Died: June 19, 1919 Chicago, IL
Education: Attended Hobart College, Geneva, NY. Graduated US Military Academy, West Point, NY, 1860.
Occupation: College professor, civil engineer, insurance actuary and publisher of an insurance journal
Miscellaneous: Resided Chicago, IL
Buried: Rosehill Cemetery, Chicago, IL (Rosehill Mausoleum, Niche A-205)
References: Timothy Hopkins. *The Kelloggs in the Old World and the New.* San Francisco, CA, 1903. Letters Received, Volunteer Service Branch, Adjutant General's Office, File K18(VS)1863, National Archives. Henry P. Moyer. *History of the 17th Regiment Pennsylvania Volunteer Cavalry.* Lebanon, PA, 1911. *Annual Report,* Association of the Graduates of the US Military Academy, 1920. Obituary, *Chicago Daily Tribune,* June 21, 1919.

THEOPHILUS G. KEPHART

Corporal, Co. I, 25 PA Infantry, April 20, 1861. Honorably mustered out, July 26, 1861. 1 Lieutenant, Co. B, 104 PA Infantry, Sept. 15, 1861. GSW right foot, Fair Oaks, VA, May 31, 1862. Captain, Co. B, 104 PA Infantry, Sept. 16, 1862. Shell wound left side, Morris Island, SC, Oct. 1, 1863. GSW right hand, Johns' Island, SC, July 9, 1864. Major, 104 PA Infantry, Dec. 17, 1864. Lieutenant Colonel, 104 PA Infantry, Feb. 24, 1865. Colonel, 104 PA Infantry, May 2, 1865. Honorably mustered out, Aug. 25, 1865.

Born: April 19, 1835 New Britain, Bucks Co., PA
Died: April 20, 1912 Chicago, IL
Occupation: Farmer before war. American Express Co. employee after war.
Miscellaneous: Resided New Britain, Bucks Co., PA, to 1866; Tuscola, Douglas Co., IL, 1866–69; and Chicago, IL, 1869–1912
Buried: Oakwoods Cemetery, Chicago, IL (Section D, Division 4, Lot 72)
References: Samuel P. Bates. *Martial Deeds of Pennsylvania.* Philadelphia, PA, 1875. Pension File and Military Service File, National Archives. William W. H. Davis. *History of the 104th Pennsylvania Regiment.* Philadelphia, PA, 1866. Obituary, *Bucks County Intelligencer,* April 25, 1912. Letters Received, Volunteer Service Branch, Adjutant General's Office, File K165(VS)1866, National Archives.

JAMES K. KERR

Major, 4 PA Cavalry, Oct. 18, 1861. Lieutenant Colonel, 4 PA Cavalry, March 12, 1862. Colonel, 4 PA Cavalry, Sept. 18, 1862. Commanded Cavalry Brigade, Center Grand Division, Army of the Potomac, Jan.–Feb. 1863. Commanded 2 Brigade, 2 Division, Cavalry Corps, Army of the Potomac, March 1863. Resigned May 17, 1863, on account of "a failure of health" from chronic diarrhea and a "sub-acute form of rheumatism."

Born: 1824 Titusville, Crawford Co., PA
Died: Feb. 25, 1876 Pittsburgh, PA
Occupation: Lawyer. Law partner of Bvt. Brig. Gen. Alfred B. McCalmont.
Miscellaneous: Resided Franklin, Venango Co., PA; and Pittsburgh, PA
Buried: Allegheny Cemetery, Pittsburgh, PA (Section 20, Lot 50)

References: Military Service File, National Archives. *A Brief History of the 4th Pennsylvania Veteran Cavalry.* Pittsburgh, PA, 1891. *Proceedings of the Celebration of the First Centennial of the Organization of the County of Venango, PA.* N.p., 1905. Herbert C. Bell, editor. *History of Venango County, PA; Its Past and Present.* Chicago, IL, 1890. Obituary, *Pittsburgh Daily Post*, Feb. 26 and 28, 1876. Obituary, *Pittsburgh Evening Chronicle*, Feb. 25, 1876.

MICHAEL KERWIN

1 Sergeant, Co. H, 24 PA Infantry, May 1, 1861. Honorably mustered out, Aug. 10, 1861. Captain, Co. B, 13 PA Cavalry, March 27, 1862. Major, 13 PA Cavalry, Oct. 20, 1862. Colonel, 13 PA Cavalry, April 22, 1864. Commanded 2 Brigade, 2 Division, Cavalry Corps, Army of the Potomac, Aug. 2–6, 1864, Aug. 16–27, 1864, Oct. 11–Nov. 10, 1864, and Feb. 9–17, 1865. Commanded 3 Brigade, 3 Division, Cavalry Corps, Military Division of the Mississippi, April 1865. Honorably mustered out, July 14, 1865.

Michael Kerwin
COURTESY OF THE AUTHOR.

Born: Aug. 15, 1837 County Wexford, Ireland

Died: June 20, 1912 New York City, NY

Occupation: Coal merchant, railroad contractor, postal clerk, newspaper editor and US pension agent

Offices/Honors: Collector of Internal Revenue. New York City Police Commissioner.

Miscellaneous: Resided Philadelphia, PA, to 1870; and New York City, NY, after 1870. Married widow of Colonel Denis F. Burke (88 NY Infantry).

Buried: Arlington National Cemetery, Arlington, VA (Section 3, Lot 2169)

References: Pension File and Military Service File, National Archives. Obituary, *New York Times*, June 21, 1912. Samuel P. Bates. *Martial Deeds of Pennsylvania.* Philadelphia, PA, 1875. William H. Powell, editor. *Officers of the Army and Navy (Volunteer) Who Served in the Civil War.* Philadelphia, PA, 1893. Thomas W. Smith. *The Story of a Cavalry Regiment, "Scott's 900," 11th New York Cavalry, From the St. Lawrence River to the Gulf of Mexico.* Chicago, IL, 1897. Harold Hand, Jr. *One Good Regiment: The 13th Pennsylvania Cavalry in the Civil War.* Victoria, B. C., 2000.

JOSEPH McCULLOUGH KINKEAD

1 Lieutenant, Adjutant, 13 PA Infantry, April 25, 1861. Honorably mustered out, Aug. 6, 1861. Lieutenant Colonel, 102 PA Infantry, Aug. 6, 1861. Colonel, 102 PA Infantry, Jan. 15, 1863. Facing charges of cowardice preferred by "a clique of line officers of the regiment," he resigned May 27, 1863, "believing that it will be for the best interest of the service to have the regiment placed under command of some officer thoroughly conversant with the business, but entirely unacquainted with its line officers or their antecedents." Brig. Gen. Frank Wheaton endorsed his resignation, "He has not the energy and force requisite for the command of a regiment."

Born: May 7, 1825 Pittsburgh, PA

Died: April 18, 1892 Turtle Creek, Allegheny Co., PA

Education: Attended Western University (now University of Pittsburgh), Pittsburgh, PA

Other Wars: Mexican War (Corporal, Co. K, 1 PA Infantry)

Occupation: Printer and railroad station agent

Miscellaneous: Resided Pittsburgh, PA; and Turtle Creek, Allegheny Co., PA

Buried: Allegheny Cemetery, Pittsburgh, PA (Section 17, Lot 120)

References: Thomas Cushing, editor. *History of Allegheny County, PA.* Chicago, IL, 1889. Death notice, *Pittsburgh Dispatch*, April 20, 1892. John H. Niebaum. *History of the Pittsburgh Washington Infantry, 102nd (Old 13th) Regiment Pennsylvania Veteran Volunteers and Its Forebears.* Pittsburgh, PA, 1931. Military Service File, National Archives.

James Thompson Kirk
CHARLES MANUEL COLLECTION, USAMHI.

Joseph McCullough Kinkead
RONN PALM COLLECTION.

JAMES THOMPSON KIRK

Lieutenant Colonel, 10 PA Reserves, June 29, 1861. Colonel, 10 PA Reserves, May 13, 1862. GSW right hip, 2nd Bull Run, VA, Aug. 30, 1862. Resigned Oct. 18, 1862, due to "dyspepsia and chronic diarrhea resulting from the fatigue and exhaustion suffered during the Seven Days' fighting before Richmond."

Born: Sept. 21, 1825 Canonsburg, PA
Died: Dec. 7, 1886 Washington, PA
Education: Attended Jefferson College, Canonsburg, PA
Occupation: Merchant tailor before war. Hotelkeeper for several years after war and then established a gentleman's furnishing and notion business.

Miscellaneous: Resided Washington, Washington Co., PA

Buried: Washington Cemetery, Washington, PA

References: *Commemorative Biographical Record of Washington County, PA.* Chicago, IL, 1893. Obituary, *Washington Daily Reporter*, Dec. 8, 1886. Samuel P. Bates. *Martial Deeds of Pennsylvania.* Philadelphia, PA, 1875. Josiah R. Sypher. *History of the Pennsylvania Reserve Corps.* Lancaster, PA, 1865. Pension File and Military Service File, National Archives. Letters Received, Volunteer Service Branch, Adjutant General's Office, File K168(VS)1866, National Archives.

WILLIAM SPEER KIRKWOOD

Captain, Co. B, 63 PA Infantry, Aug. 26, 1861. Major, 63 PA Infantry, June 20, 1862. GSW right leg, Groveton, VA, Aug. 29, 1862. Lieutenant Colonel, 63 PA Infantry, Nov. 6, 1862. *Colonel*, 63 PA Infantry, April 18, 1863. GSW leg and breast, Chancellorsville, VA, May 3, 1863.

William Speer Kirkwood
FROM *UNDER THE RED PATCH: STORY OF THE 63RD REGIMENT PENNSYLVANIA VOLUNTEERS.*

Born: July 4, 1835 Fairview, Allegheny Co., PA

Died: June 25, 1863 DOW Alexandria, VA

Occupation: Farmer and ferryman

Miscellaneous: Resided Pittsburgh, PA

Buried: Allegheny Cemetery, Pittsburgh, PA (Section 22, Lot 57)

References: Gilbert A. Hays. *Under the Red Patch: Story of the 63rd Regiment Pennsylvania Volunteers.* Pittsburgh, PA, 1908. Samuel P. Bates. *Martial Deeds of Pennsylvania.* Philadelphia, PA, 1875. Military Service File, National Archives.

CHARLES KLECKNER

Private, Co. K, 6 PA Infantry, April 22, 1861. Honorably mustered out, July 26, 1861. 2 Lieutenant, Co. D, 48 PA Infantry, Aug. 30, 1861. 1 Lieutenant, Co. D, 48 PA Infantry, Nov. 30, 1861. Colonel, 172 PA Infantry, Nov. 19, 1862. Commanded 3 Brigade, 1 Division, 4 Army Corps, Department of Virginia, June 17–July 8, 1863. Honorably mustered out, Aug. 1, 1863. Major, 184 PA Infantry, May 13, 1864. Shell wound left leg and GSW both hips, Reams' Station, VA, Aug. 25, 1864. Lieutenant Colonel, 184 PA Infantry, Oct. 13, 1864. Honorably mustered out, July 14, 1865.

Born: Dec. 10, 1831 New Berlin, PA

Died: July 1, 1911 Shamokin, PA

Occupation: Merchant before war. Hotelkeeper and boarding stable keeper after war.

Offices/Honors: PA House of Representatives, 1868–69

Miscellaneous: Resided New Berlin, Union Co., PA; Philadelphia, PA; and Shamokin, Northumberland Co., PA

Buried: New Berlin Cemetery, New Berlin, PA

References: Pension File, National Archives. Obituary, *Mifflinburg Telegraph*, July 7, 1911. Samuel P. Bates. *Martial Deeds of Pennsylvania.* Philadelphia, PA, 1875. Letters Received, Volunteer Service Branch, Adjutant General's Office, File M3637(VS)1864, National Archives.

Charles Kleckner (seated left) with officers of the 184th Pennsylvania,
including, from left to right, Col. John Hubler Stover, Maj. George L. Ritman, and Surgeon William B. Brinton
RONN PALM COLLECTION.
D. C. BURNITE & CO., 110 MARKET STREET, HARRISBURG, PA.

ROBERT KLOTZ

Volunteer ADC, Staff of Major General Robert Patterson, April–July 1861. Colonel, 19 PA Militia, Sept. 15, 1862. Honorably discharged, Sept. 27, 1862.

Born: Oct. 27, 1819 Mahoning Twp., Carbon Co., PA
Died: May 1, 1895 Mauch Chunk, PA
Other Wars: Mexican War (1 Lieutenant, Adjutant, 2 PA Infantry)

Occupation: Merchant and hotel operator
Offices/Honors: PA House of Representatives, 1849–50. Treasurer, Carbon Co., PA, 1859–61. US House of Representatives, 1879–83.
Miscellaneous: Resided Mauch Chunk (now Jim Thorpe), Carbon Co., PA; except for the years 1854–57, spent in Kansas, where he founded the town of Pawnee and served as a member of the Topeka Constitutional Convention
Buried: Mauch Chunk Cemetery, Jim Thorpe, PA

Robert Klotz (postwar)
LIBRARY OF CONGRESS.

References: *Portrait and Biographical Record of Lehigh, Northampton, and Carbon Counties, PA.* Chicago, IL, 1894. *National Cyclopedia of American Biography. Biographical Directory of the American Congress.* Obituary, *Mauch Chunk Democrat,* May 4, 1895. Charles R. Roberts. *History of Lehigh County, PA.* Allentown, PA, 1914. Alfred Mathews and Austin N. Hungerford. *History of the Counties of Lehigh and Carbon, in the Commonwealth of Pennsylvania.* Philadelphia, PA, 1884. Pension File, National Archives.

NAPOLEON BONAPARTE KNEASS

Colonel, 7 PA Militia, Sept. 12, 1862. Honorably discharged, Sept. 26, 1862.

Born: April 17, 1818 Philadelphia, PA
Died: March 16, 1888 Philadelphia, PA
Education: Attended US Military Academy, West Point, NY (Class of 1836)
Occupation: Manufacturer and importer of saddlery and saddlery hardware

Napoleon Bonaparte Kneass
103RD ENGINEER ARMORY COLLECTION, USAMHI.
J. CREMER & CO., 18 SOUTH 8TH STREET, PHILADELPHIA, PA.

Miscellaneous: Resided New Orleans, LA; and Philadelphia, PA. Great-great grandson of John Hart, Signer of the Declaration of Independence.
Buried: Woodlands Cemetery, Philadelphia, PA (Section I, Lots 194–197, family vault)
References: Anna J. Magee. "Memorials of the Kneass Family of Philadelphia," *Publications of the Genealogical Society of Pennsylvania,* Vol. 7, No. 2 (March 1919). James W. Latta. *History of the 1st Regiment Infantry, National Guard of Pennsylvania (Gray Reserves).* Philadelphia and London, 1912. Harmon Y. Gordon. *History of the 1st Regiment Infantry of Pennsylvania.* Philadelphia, PA, 1961. Frederick W. Pyne. *Descendants of the Signers of the Declaration of Independence.* Camden, ME, 1998. Obituary, *Philadelphia Inquirer,* March 19, 1888.

CHARLES AUGUST KNODERER

Captain of Engineers, Staff of Brig. Gen. Franz Sigel, Sept. 1861. Colonel, 11 PA Militia, Sept. 12, 1862. Honorably discharged, Sept. 25, 1862. Colonel, 167 PA Infantry, Nov. 6, 1862. Shell wound left hip, Deserted House, near Suffolk, VA, Jan. 30, 1863.

Born: 1823? Emmendingen, Baden, Germany
Died: Feb. 15, 1863 DOW Suffolk, VA
Education: Attended Carlsruhe (Germany) Polytechnic School
Other Wars: Participated in the German Revolution of 1848–49
Occupation: Civil engineer with Schuylkill Navigation Company
Miscellaneous: Resided Reading, Berks Co., PA
Buried: Charles Evans Cemetery, Reading, PA (Section L, Lot 36)

Charles August Knoderer
FROM *MARTIAL DEEDS OF PENNSYLVANIA*.

References: Samuel P. Bates. *Martial Deeds of Pennsylvania*. Philadelphia, PA, 1875. Joseph G. Rosengarten. *The German Soldier in the Wars of the United States*. Second edition, revised and enlarged. Philadelphia, PA, 1890. Pension File and Military Service File, National Archives. Obituary, *Reading Daily Times*, Feb. 17, 1863.

JOHN A. KOLTES

Colonel, 73 PA Infantry, Aug. 2, 1861. Commanded 2 Brigade, Blenker's Division, Mountain Department, June 1862. Commanded 1 Brigade, 2 Division, 1 Army Corps, Army of Virginia, June 26–Aug. 30, 1862. Shell wound head, 2nd Bull Run, VA, Aug. 30, 1862.

Born: 1823 (or 1825) (or 1827) Baldringen (or Treves), Germany
Died: Aug. 30, 1862 KIA 2nd Bull Run, VA
Other Wars: Mexican War (Sergeant, Co. E, 1 PA Infantry)
Occupation: Employee of US Mint, Philadelphia, PA
Miscellaneous: Resided Philadelphia, PA
Buried: Glenwood Cemetery, Philadelphia, PA. Probably removed to Glenwood Memorial Gardens, Broomall, PA, when Glenwood Cemetery was discontinued in 1938.
References: Barbara Endres. *The Koltes Family Genealogy*. N.p., 1981. William J. Tenney. *The Military and Naval History of the Rebellion in the United States*. New York City, NY, 1865. *Appletons' Cyclopedia of American Biography*. Wilhelm Kaufmann. *The Germans in the American Civil War*. Translated by Steven Rowan and edited by Don Heinrich Tolzmann with Werner D. Mueller and Robert E. Ward. Carlisle, PA, 1999. Joseph G. Rosengarten. *The German Soldier in the Wars of the United States*. Second edition, revised and enlarged. Philadelphia, PA, 1890. Pension File and Military Service File, National Archives. Obituary, *Philadelphia Public Ledger*, Sept. 4, 1862.

FRANCIS A. LANCASTER

Major, 115 PA Infantry, June 26, 1862. GSW left arm, Bristoe Station, VA, Aug. 27, 1862. Colonel, 115 PA Infantry, Dec. 2, 1862. GSW head, Chancellorsville, VA, May 3, 1863.

John A. Koltes
Courtesy of Jacqueline T. Eubanks.

Francis A. Lancaster
Mike Waskul Collection.
M. P. Simons, Photographer, 1320 Chestnut Street,
Philadelphia, PA.

Born: Jan. 23, 1839 Philadelphia, PA

Died: May 3, 1863 KIA Chancellorsville, VA

Occupation: Associated with his brothers in the grain business

Miscellaneous: Resided Philadelphia, PA

Buried: Old Cathedral Cemetery, Philadelphia, PA (Section E, Range 3, Lots 61–64)

References: Samuel P. Bates. *Martial Deeds of Pennsylvania.* Philadelphia, PA, 1875. Death report, *Philadelphia Public Ledger,* May 7, 1863. Military Service File, National Archives.

JOHN JACOB LAWRENCE

Captain, Co. F, 125 PA Infantry, Aug. 15, 1862. Major, 125 PA Infantry, Aug. 16, 1862. GSW Chancellorsville, VA, May 3, 1863. Honorably mustered out, May 18, 1863. Colonel, 46 PA Militia, July 8, 1863. Honorably mustered out, Aug. 19, 1863.

Born: March 7, 1827 near Washington, PA

Died: March 27, 1893 Pittsburgh, PA

Occupation: Railroad superintendent. Pursued manufacturing and coal mining interests after 1875.

Miscellaneous: Resided Huntingdon, Huntingdon Co., PA; and Pittsburgh, PA

Buried: Harrisburg Cemetery, Harrisburg, PA (Section M, Lot 189)

References: Obituary Circular, Whole No. 272, Pennsylvania MOLLUS. Pension File and Military Service File, National Archives. Obituary, *Harrisburg Patriot,* March 30, 1893. *History of the 125th Regiment Pennsylvania Volunteers.* Philadelphia, PA, 1906. William H. Egle. *Pennsylvania Genealogies.* Harrisburg, PA, 1896. Obituary, *Pittsburgh Dispatch,* March 29, 1893.

John Jacob Lawrence
RONN PALM COLLECTION.

Henry Allen Laycock
FROM *WILKES-BARRE RECORD*, AUG. 6, 1897

HENRY ALLEN LAYCOCK

1 Lieutenant, Co. I, 56 PA Infantry, Nov. 17, 1861. Captain, Co. B, 56 PA Infantry, Nov. 13, 1862. Acting AQM, 2 Brigade, 1 Division, 1 Army Corps, Army of the Potomac, Jan. 1863–Feb. 1864. Provost Marshal, 3 Division, 5 Army Corps, Army of the Potomac, Nov. 1864–Jan. 1865. Major, 56 PA Infantry, Dec. 26, 1864. Lieutenant Colonel, 56 PA Infantry, March 16, 1865. *Colonel,* 56 PA Infantry, June 12, 1865. GSW elbow, White Oak Road, VA, March 31, 1865. Bvt. Colonel, USV, April 1, 1865, for gallant and meritorious services at the battle of Five Forks, VA. Honorably mustered out, July 1, 1865.

Born: Nov. 11, 1833 Warren Co., NJ
Died: Aug. 5, 1897 Wyoming, PA
Occupation: Iron moulder and hotel clerk before war. Hotelkeeper after war.
Miscellaneous: Resided Pittston, Luzerne Co., PA; Wilkes-Barre, Luzerne Co., PA; and Wyoming, Luzerne Co., PA
Buried: Forty Fort Cemetery, Forty Fort, Luzerne Co., PA
References: Obituary, *Wilkes-Barre Record,* Aug. 6, 1897. Obituary Circular, Whole No. 348, Pennsylvania MOLLUS. Henry C. Bradsby, editor. *History of Luzerne County, PA.* Chicago, IL, 1893. Military Service File, National Archives. Letters Received, Volunteer Service Branch, Adjutant General's Office, File G589(VS)1864, National Archives.

DANIEL LEASURE

Captain, Co. H, 12 PA Infantry, April 25, 1861. Honorably mustered out, Aug. 5, 1861. Colonel, 100 PA Infantry, Aug. 31, 1861. GSW left leg, 2nd Bull Run, VA, Aug. 29, 1862. Commanded 2 Brigade, 1 Division, 9 Army Corps, Army of the Potomac, July 22–Aug. 3, 1862 and April–May 10, 1864. Commanded 3 Brigade, 1 Division, 9 Army Corps, Army of the Potomac, Oct. 22–26, 1862; Nov. 2, 1862–Jan. 27, 1863; and Feb. 7–March 18, 1863. Commanded 1 Division, 9 Army Corps, Army of the Potomac, Oct. 26–Nov. 2, 1862 and May 10–12, 1864. Commanded 3 Brigade, 1 Division, 9 Army Corps, Army of the Ohio, March 19–June 14, 1863 and Sept. 22–Nov. 5, 1863. Commanded 3 Brigade, 1 Division, 9 Army Corps, Army of the Tennessee, June 14–Aug. 18, 1863. Honorably mustered out, Aug. 30, 1864.

Born: March 18, 1819 near Madison, Westmoreland Co., PA

Died: Oct. 4, 1886 St. Paul, MN

Education: Graduated Jefferson Medical College, Philadelphia, PA, 1846

Occupation: Physician

Miscellaneous: Resided New Castle, Lawrence Co., PA; Pittsburgh, PA; and St. Paul, MN

Buried: Greenwood Cemetery, New Castle, PA (Section 1, Lot 193)

References: Paul E. Steiner. *Physician-Generals in the Civil War.* Springfield, IL, 1966. Obituary, *St. Paul Pioneer Press*, Oct. 5, 1886. Pension File, National Archives. Samuel P. Bates. *Martial Deeds of Pennsylvania.* Philadelphia, PA, 1875. William G. Gavin. *Campaigning with the Roundheads: The History of the 100th Pennsylvania Veteran Volunteer Infantry Regiment in the American Civil War.* Dayton, OH, 1989. Letters Received, Volunteer Service Branch, Adjutant General's Office, File W211(VS)1863, National Archives.

Daniel Leasure
ROGER D. HUNT COLLECTION, USAMHI.
A. W. PHIPPS, PHOTOGRAPHER, NEW CASTLE, PA.

AMBROSE A. LECHLER

2 Lieutenant, Co. G, 4 PA Reserves, May 29, 1861. Resigned July 22, 1862, due to "dyspepsia, diarrhea, liver complaint, and an exceedingly debilitated constitution, which is daily growing worse." Colonel, 176 PA Infantry, Nov. 28, 1862. Dismissed Sept. 17, 1863, for "receiving compensation from the sutler of the regiment for his appointment; appropriating to his own use rations drawn for the enlisted men of the regiment; and taking from the mail and destroying newspapers addressed to the officers and men." Due to "the contradictory character of the testimony in the case," his dismissal was revoked, April 28, 1864, and he was honorably mustered out to date, Sept. 17, 1863. Lieutenant Colonel, 199 PA Infantry, Sept. 21, 1864. Resigned Oct. 22, 1864, having been "promised the colonelcy," and never intending "to serve with less rank than that previously held by myself."

Born: 1832? PA

Died: Oct. 17, 1890 New York City, NY

Occupation: Bookseller before war. Agent and watchman after war.

Miscellaneous: Resided Philadelphia, PA; San Francisco, CA; and New York City, NY

Buried: Cypress Hills National Cemetery, Brooklyn, NY (Section 2, Grave 4954)

References: Pension File and Military Service File, National Archives. Letters Received, Volunteer Service Branch, Adjutant General's Office, Files P1265(VS)1862 and L514(VS)1863, National Archives.

THEODORE FREDERICK LEHMANN

Lieutenant Colonel, 62 PA Infantry, July 1, 1861. Colonel, 103 PA Infantry, Oct. 30, 1861. Commanded 4 Division, 18 Army Corps, Department of North Carolina, March 14–April 14, 1863. Commanded 1 Brigade, 4 Division, 18 Army Corps, May–Aug. 1863. Commanded District of the Albemarle, Department of North Carolina, May 3–Aug. 1, 1863. Taken prisoner, Plymouth, NC, April 20, 1864. Confined Charleston, SC. Paroled Aug. 3, 1864. Commanded Sub-district of the Albemarle, District of North Carolina, Department of Virginia and North Carolina, Dec. 1864. Commanded Post of Roanoke Island, District of North Carolina, Department of North Carolina, Jan.–Feb. 1865. Commanded Post of Roanoke Island, District of Beaufort, Department of North Carolina, March–June 1865. Honorably mustered out, June 25, 1865.

Theodore Frederick Lehmann
RONN PALM COLLECTION.
SAMUEL MASURY, 289 WASHINGTON STREET, BOSTON, MA.

Born: March 1, 1812 Eystrup, Hanover, Germany

Died: Dec. 6, 1894 Washington, DC

Occupation: School teacher before war. Civil engineer after war. Although talented as an artist, a musician, a chemist, a civil engineer, a linguist, and an inventor, he lacked the business ability to convert those talents into profit.

Offices/Honors: President, Western Pennsylvania Military Academy

Miscellaneous: Resided Frankfort, Franklin Co., KY; Henderson, Henderson Co., KY; Pittsburgh, PA; and Washington, DC

Buried: Congressional Cemetery, Washington, DC (Range 77, Site 335)

References: Luther S. Dickey. *History of the 103rd Regiment Pennsylvania Veteran Volunteer Infantry.* Chicago, IL, 1910. Samuel P. Bates. *Martial Deeds of Pennsylvania.* Philadelphia, PA, 1875. Pension File and Military Service File, National Archives. Letters Received, Volunteer Service Branch, Adjutant General's Office, File F61(VS)1862, National Archives.

ASHER S. LEIDY

1 Lieutenant, Adjutant, 22 PA Infantry, April 23, 1861. Honorably mustered out, Aug. 7, 1861. Major, 99 PA Infantry, Aug. 19, 1861. Lieutenant Colonel, 99 PA Infantry, Feb. 1, 1862. Colonel, 99 PA Infantry, June 11, 1862. GSW left thigh, Fredericksburg, VA, Dec. 13, 1862. Discharged for disability, Oct. 7, 1863, due to rheumatism and chronic diarrhea. Restored to command, Nov. 11, 1863. Dismissed April 9, 1864, for "absence without leave." Dismissal revoked, Oct. 22, 1866, and he was honorably discharged to date, April 9, 1864.

Asher S. Leidy
WILLIAM B. STYPLE COLLECTION, USAMHI.
O. H. WILLARD, 1628 MARKET STREET, PHILADELPHIA, PA.

Born: July 30, 1830 Philadelphia, PA
Died: July 6, 1878 Philadelphia, PA
Education: Attended Philadelphia (PA) College of Pharmacy. Attended University of Pennsylvania Medical School, Philadelphia, PA.
Occupation: Druggist and chemist. Also briefly a hotel proprietor and a pension claim agent.
Miscellaneous: Resided Philadelphia, PA
Buried: Machpelah Cemetery, Philadelphia, PA. Probably removed to Graceland Memorial Cemetery, Yeadon, Delaware Co., PA, when Machpelah Cemetery was discontinued in 1895. The site of Graceland Memorial Cemetery is now a city park, with only a few grave markers remaining.
References: Pension File and Military Service File, National Archives. Obituary, *Philadelphia Public Ledger,* July 8, 1878. Samuel P. Bates. *Martial Deeds of Pennsylvania.* Philadelphia, PA, 1875. Letters Received, Volunteer Service Branch, Adjutant General's Office, File G409(VS)1864, National Archives.

CHARLES LESPES

Captain, Co. I, 1 DE Infantry, Sept. 2, 1861. Resigned July 21, 1862, "my presence being required in my country." Authorized as Colonel, 1 PA Chasseurs, June 16, 1863. Only five companies were raised (as 3 Independent Battalion, PA Infantry, under Lt. Col. T. Ellwood Zell). Authority as colonel revoked, Aug. 30, 1863. 1 Sergeant, Co. C, 3 NJ Cavalry, Jan. 22, 1864. Deserted June 7, 1864.

Born: 1817? France
Died: Date and place of death unknown
Occupation: Seventeen years as an officer in the French army
Miscellaneous: Resided New York City, NY; and Philadelphia, PA
Buried: Burial place unknown
References: Letters Received, Volunteer Service Branch, Adjutant General's Office, Files L640(VS)1862 and L254(VS)1863, National Archives. Military Service File, National Archives.

WILLIAM HENRY LESSIG

Captain, Co. C, 96 PA Infantry, Sept. 23, 1861. Major, 96 PA Infantry, Sept. 15, 1862. Lieutenant Colonel, 96 PA Infantry, Dec. 23, 1862. *Colonel,* 96 PA Infantry, March 13, 1863. Honorably mustered out, Oct. 21, 1864.

William Henry Lessig
KEN TURNER COLLECTION.
BRADY'S NATIONAL PHOTOGRAPHIC PORTRAIT GALLERIES,
BROADWAY AND TENTH STREETS, NEW YORK.

Born: Oct. 30, 1831 Lebanon, PA
Died: July 18, 1910 Monte Vista, CO
Occupation: Mining engineer before war. Hotelkeeper, real estate developer and capitalist after war. Described in a newspaper obituary as a "soldier, politician, bon vivant and once wealthy man of affairs."
Offices/Honors: Surveyor General, Colorado Territory, 1867–74
Miscellaneous: Resided Pottsville, Schuylkill Co., PA, to 1867; Denver, CO, 1867–1900; and Chicago, IL. According to a newspaper obituary, "No more picturesque figure ever moved across the stage of Colorado and Denver events."
Buried: Charles Baber Cemetery, Pottsville, PA (Section G, Lot 4)
References: Obituary, *Rocky Mountain News,* July 19, 1910. Obituary, *Pottsville Republican,* July 22, 1910. Francis B. Wallace, compiler. *Memorial of the Patriotism of Schuylkill County in the American Slaveholder's Rebellion.* Pottsville, PA, 1865. Samuel P. Bates. *Martial Deeds of Pennsylvania.* Philadelphia, PA, 1875. Pension File, National Archives. John H. Monnett and Michael McCarthy. *Colorado Profiles: Men and Women Who Shaped the Centennial State.* Evergreen, CO, 1987.

Robert Litzinger
RONN PALM COLLECTION.
P. L. PERKINS, 205 & 207 BALTIMORE STREET,
SECOND FLOOR, BALTIMORE, MD.

ROBERT LITZINGER

Captain, Co. A, 11 PA Reserves, April 23, 1861. Major, 11 PA Reserves, Oct. 29, 1861. Resigned April 1, 1862, on account of illness caused by "an abscess, formed upon my liver." Colonel, 4 PA Militia, Sept. 15, 1862. Honorably discharged, Sept. 25, 1862. Captain, Co. A, Independent Battalion, PA Militia, June 23, 1863. Lieutenant Colonel, Independent Battalion, PA Militia, July 26, 1863. Honorably discharged, Aug. 8, 1863. Captain, Co. C, 209 PA Infantry, Sept. 15, 1864. Honorably discharged, June 4, 1865.

Born: Nov. 28, 1830 Ebensburg, PA
Died: April 28, 1898 Johnstown, PA
Other Wars: Mexican War (Fifer, Co. D, 2 PA Volunteers)
Occupation: Printer and lumber merchant. Later held a position in the shipping department of the Cambria Iron Co.
Miscellaneous: Resided Belsano, Cambria Co., PA; Ebensburg, Cambria Co., PA; and Johnstown, Cambria Co., PA, after 1873
Buried: Grandview Cemetery, Johnstown, PA (Central Section, Division 4, Lot 173)
References: Obituary, *Johnstown Weekly Democrat*, April 29, 1898. Joseph Gibbs. *Three Years in the Bloody Eleventh: The Campaigns of a Pennsylvania Reserves Regiment.* University Park, PA, 2002. Military Service File, National Archives. Letters Received, Volunteer Service Branch, Adjutant General's Office, File L101(VS)1865, National Archives.

HENRY CLAY LONGNECKER

Colonel, 9 PA Infantry, April 24, 1861. Commanded 4 Brigade, 1 Division, Department of Pennsylvania, June 1861. Honorably mustered out, July 29, 1861. Colonel, 5 PA Militia, Sept. 11, 1862. Honorably discharged, Sept. 27, 1862.

Born: April 17, 1820 Allen Twp., Cumberland Co., PA
Died: Sept. 16, 1871 Allentown, PA
Education: Attended Norwich (VT) University. Attended Lafayette College, Easton, PA.
Other Wars: Mexican War (1 Lieutenant, Adjutant, US Voltigeurs)
Occupation: Lawyer and judge
Offices/Honors: US House of Representatives, 1859–61
Miscellaneous: Resided Allentown, Lehigh Co., PA
Buried: Fairview Cemetery, Allentown, PA
References: *Biographical Directory of the American Congress.* Pension File, National Archives. William A. Ellis, editor. *History of Norwich University, 1819–1911.* Montpelier, VT, 1911.

RUSSELL FARNUM LORD, JR.

Colonel, 24 PA Militia, Sept. 20, 1862. Honorably discharged, Sept. 22, 1862.

Born: Oct. 1, 1837 Honesdale, PA
Died: July 12, 1899 New York City, NY

Henry Clay Longnecker
Ken Turner Collection.

Russell Farnum Lord, Jr. (postwar)
Courtesy of the Minisink Valley Historical Society,
Port Jervis, NY.
W. L. Bates, Tabor Block, Denver, CO.

Education: Attended Sheffield Scientific School, Yale University, New Haven, CT

Occupation: Civil and mining engineer. Assistant Engineer of the Delaware & Hudson Canal.

Offices/Honors: Government Engineer of the Republic of Salvador, 1885–91

Miscellaneous: Resided Honesdale, Wayne Co., PA; San Joaquin River Valley, CA; Retalhuleu, Guatemala; and New York City, NY. His half-sister, Mary Dimmick, was the second wife of President Benjamin Harrison.

Buried: Laurel Grove Cemetery, Port Jervis, NY (Section B, Lot 66, unmarked)

References: Obituary, *Wayne County Herald*, July 20, 1899. Obituary, *Port Jervis Union*, July 13, 1899. Obituary, *New York Times*, July 15, 1899. Peter Osborne. *Russel Farnum Lord: His Life, His Times, His Letters* (Unpublished Manuscript, Minisink Valley Historical Society, Port Jervis, NY).

ROMAIN LUJEANE

Colonel, 99 PA Infantry, July 22, 1861. Resigned Nov. 7, 1861. 1 Lieutenant, Adjutant, 58 OH Infantry, Dec. 18, 1861. Resigned Feb. 7, 1862.

Born: 1830? Italy

Died: Prior to 1890. Place of death unknown.

Occupation: Professor of German, Philadelphia Central High School, 1859–60

Miscellaneous: Resided Philadelphia, PA

Buried: Burial place unknown

References: Military Service File, National Archives. *General Catalogue of the Central High School of Philadelphia from 1838 to 1890.* Philadelphia, PA, 1890.

RALPH LASHELLS MACLAY

Captain, Co. H, 49 PA Infantry, Aug. 15, 1861. Resigned July 16, 1862. Colonel, 18 PA Militia, Sept. 12, 1862. Honorably discharged, Sept. 27, 1862. Lieutenant Colonel, 36 PA Militia, July 4, 1863. Honorably discharged, August 11, 1863.

Born: March 1, 1836 PA
Died: June 11, 1866 Milroy, PA
Occupation: School teacher
Miscellaneous: Resided Milroy, Mifflin Co., PA
Buried: Presbyterian Cemetery, Milroy, PA
References: Obituary, *Lewistown Gazette,* June 13, 1866. Robert S. Westbrook. *History of the 49th Pennsylvania Volunteers.* Altoona, PA, 1898. William H. Egle. *Pennsylvania Genealogies.* Harrisburg, PA, 1896. Military Service File, National Archives. A. Monroe Aurand, Jr. *The Genealogy of Samuel Maclay, 1741–1811.* Harrisburg, PA, 1938.

ALBERT LEWIS MAGILTON

Lieutenant Colonel, 2 PA Reserves, June 21, 1861. Colonel, 4 PA Reserves, Oct. 4, 1861. GSW Charles City Cross Roads, VA, June 30, 1862. Commanded 2 Brigade, 3 Division, 5 Army Corps, Army of the Potomac, June 30–Aug. 26, 1862. Commanded 2 Brigade, 3 Division, 1 Army Corps, Army of the Potomac, Sept. 12–Dec. 23, 1862. Resigned Dec. 23, 1862.

Albert Lewis Magilton

Born: July 8, 1826 New Castle Co., DE
Died: Dec. 28, 1875 Philadelphia, PA
Education: Attended Philadelphia (PA) Central High School. Graduated US Military Academy, West Point, NY, 1846.
Other Wars: Mexican War (2 Lieutenant, 4 US Artillery)
Occupation: Deputy Collector of US Internal Revenue, 1864–75
Offices/Honors: Professor of Infantry Tactics, Philadelphia Free Military School (for applicants for the command of colored troops), 1864
Miscellaneous: Resided Philadelphia, PA
Buried: West Laurel Hill Cemetery, Bala-Cynwyd, PA (Washington Section, Lot 38)
References: Obituary, *Philadelphia Public Ledger,* Dec. 30, 1875. Samuel P. Bates. *Martial Deeds of Pennsylvania.* Philadelphia, PA, 1875. Obituary, *New York Times,* Dec. 30, 1875. George W. Cullum. *Biographical Register of the Officers and Graduates of the US Military Academy.* Third Edition. Boston and New York, 1891. *Annual Reunion,* Association of the Graduates of the US Military Academy, 1876. Josiah R. Sypher. *History of the Pennsylvania Reserve Corps.* Lancaster, PA, 1865. Military Service File, National Archives. *Second Brigade of the Pennsylvania Reserves at Antietam.* Harrisburg, PA, 1908.

FRANCIS MAHLER

Lieutenant Colonel, 75 PA Infantry, Aug. 9, 1861. Colonel, 75 PA Infantry, July 30, 1862. GSW buttocks, 2nd Bull Run, VA, Aug. 30, 1862. GSW leg, Gettysburg, PA, July 1, 1863.

Born: Aug. 1, 1826 Baden, Germany
Died: July 4, 1863 DOW Gettysburg, PA
Other Wars: Participated in the German Revolution of 1848–49. Captured and sentenced to be shot, he escaped and came to the United States.
Occupation: Cordwainer
Miscellaneous: Resided Philadelphia, PA
Buried: Mount Peace Cemetery, Philadelphia, PA (Section B, Lot 263)
References: Pension File and Military Service File, National Archives. Samuel P. Bates. *Martial Deeds of Pennsylvania.* Philadelphia, PA, 1875. Wilhelm Kaufmann. *The Germans in the American Civil War.* Translated by Steven Rowan and edited by Don Heinrich Tolzmann with Werner D. Mueller and

Francis Mahler

Robert E. Ward. Carlisle, PA, 1999. Herrmann Nachtigall. *History of the 75th Regiment Pennsylvania Volunteers.* Translated by Heinz D. Schwinge and Karl E. Sundstrom. North Riverside, IL, 1987. Obituary, *Philadelphia Public Ledger,* July 8, 1863.

LEVI MAISH

Captain, Co. K, 130 PA Infantry, Aug. 8, 1862. Lieutenant Colonel, 130 PA Infantry, Aug. 17, 1862. GSW right shoulder and lung, Antietam, MD, Sept. 17, 1862. Colonel, 130 PA Infantry, Dec. 14, 1862. GSW right hip, Chancellorsville, VA, May 3, 1863. Honorably mustered out, May 21, 1863.

Born: Nov. 22, 1837 Conewago Twp., York Co., PA
Died: Feb. 26, 1899 Washington, DC
Education: Attended University of Pennsylvania, Philadelphia, PA
Occupation: Lawyer
Offices/Honors: PA House of Representatives, 1867–68. US House of Representatives, 1875–79, 1887–91.
Miscellaneous: Resided York, York Co., PA; and Washington, DC
Buried: Arlington National Cemetery, Arlington, VA (Section 2, Lot 3742)
References: Pension File, National Archives. *Biographical Directory of the American Congress.* Samuel P. Bates. *Martial Deeds of Pennsylvania.* Philadelphia, PA, 1875. George R. Prowell. *History of York County, PA.* Chicago, IL, 1907. George H. Washburn. *A Complete Military History and Record of the 108th Regiment New York Volunteers.* Rochester, NY, 1894. Obituary, *York Gazette,* Feb. 27, 1899. Obituary, *Washington Evening Star,* Feb. 27, 1899.

Levi Maish

William Benson Mann (1856)
SOCIETY PORTRAIT COLLECTION,
THE HISTORICAL SOCIETY OF PENNSYLVANIA.

WILLIAM BENSON MANN

Colonel, 2 PA Reserves, June 21, 1861. Resigned Oct. 30, 1861, "in order to discharge the duties of the office of District Attorney" of Philadelphia. Captain, Independent Co., PA Emergency Troops, June 17, 1863. Honorably mustered out, July 24, 1863.

Born: Oct. 27, 1816 Mount Holly, Burlington Co., NJ
Died: Oct. 17, 1896 Philadelphia, PA
Occupation: Lawyer and judge
Offices/Honors: US District Attorney for Philadelphia, 1856–1868. Prothonotary of the Common Pleas Court of Philadelphia, 1876–96.
Miscellaneous: Resided Philadelphia, PA
Buried: Lawnview Cemetery, Rockledge, PA (Broad Lawn, Range 26, Grave 26)
References: *Men of America: A Biographical Album of the City Government of Philadelphia.* Philadelphia, PA, 1883. *Encyclopedia of Contemporary Biography of Pennsylvania.* New York City, NY, 1890. Charles Morris, editor. *Makers of Philadelphia.* Philadelphia,

PA, 1894. Obituary, *Philadelphia Public Ledger,* Oct. 19, 1896. *A Biographical Album of Prominent Pennsylvanians.* Second Series. Philadelphia, PA, 1889. Josiah R. Sypher. *History of the Pennsylvania Reserve Corps.* Lancaster, PA, 1865. Pension File and Military Service File, National Archives. Moses King. *Philadelphia and Notable Philadelphians.* New York City, NY, 1902.

ROBERT G. MARCH

Colonel, 4 PA Reserves, May 9, 1861. Resigned Oct. 1, 1861, due to physical debility from "gastric rheumatic fever." Captain, Co. B, 20 PA Emergency Troops, June 17, 1863. GSW left leg, Wrightsville, PA, June 28, 1863. Honorably discharged, Aug. 10, 1863.

Born: Oct. 5, 1819 Philadelphia, PA
Died: Feb. 1, 1875 Philadelphia, PA
Occupation: Morocco finisher. Later held a position in the US Internal Revenue service.
Miscellaneous: Resided Philadelphia, PA
Died: Laurel Hill Cemetery, Philadelphia, PA (Section O, Lot 213)
References: Josiah R. Sypher. *History of the Pennsylvania Reserve Corps.* Lancaster, PA, 1865. Pension File and Military Service File, National Archives. Death notice, *Philadelphia Inquirer,* Feb. 4, 1875.

JOHN MILLER MARK

Captain, Co. D, 93 PA Infantry, Oct. 3, 1861. GSW right forearm, Fair Oaks, VA, May 31, 1862. Major, 93 PA Infantry, June 1, 1862. Colonel, 93 PA Infantry, Nov. 27, 1862. Resigned March 12, 1863, in response to an adverse report from a Board of Examination, which found him "without capacity or efficiency and utterly unqualified for his position." Brig. Gen. Frank Wheaton endorsed his resignation, "Respectfully forwarded with the request that this honest farmer who is utterly inefficient and incompetent as a soldier may be honorably discharged."

Born: March 15, 1822 near Jonestown, Lebanon Co., PA
Died: Dec. 21, 1905 Lebanon, PA
Occupation: Hotelkeeper and tavern keeper before war. Hotelkeeper and detective after war.
Offices/Honors: Register, Lebanon Co., PA, 1854–57. Storekeeper and gauger in US Internal Revenue service after war.

Miscellaneous: Resided Lebanon, Lebanon Co., PA

Buried: Mount Lebanon Cemetery, Lebanon, PA (Section M, Lot 97)

References: *Biographical Annals of Lebanon County, PA.* Chicago, IL, 1904. Pension File and Military Service File, National Archives. Obituary, *Lebanon Daily News*, Dec. 22, 1905. Penrose G. Mark. *Red: White: and Blue Badge Pennsylvania Veteran Volunteers. A History of the 93rd Regiment.* Harrisburg, PA, 1911. Letters Received, Volunteer Service Branch, Adjutant General's Office, File M465(VS)1863, National Archives. William H. Egle. *History of the Counties of Dauphin and Lebanon in the Commonwealth of Pennsylvania.* Philadelphia, PA, 1883.

John Miller Mark (postwar)
FROM *RED: WHITE: AND BLUE BADGE PENNSYLVANIA VETERAN VOLUNTEERS. A HISTORY OF THE 93RD REGIMENT.*

William Maxwell (postwar)
FROM *HISTORY OF THE 57TH REGIMENT, PENNSYLVANIA VETERAN VOLUNTEER INFANTRY.*

WILLIAM MAXWELL

Colonel, 57 PA Infantry, Aug. 24, 1861. Resigned Feb. 27, 1862, "owing to difficulties which have arisen in the regiment, owing in part to the inefficiency of officers, and that from my efforts at discipline acquired a faction against me in the regiment."

Born: Feb. 28, 1809 Gettysburg, PA

Died: Dec. 13, 1890 Greenville, PA

Education: Attended US Military Academy, West Point, NY (Class of 1830)

Occupation: Lawyer and judge

Miscellaneous: Resided Mercer, Mercer Co., PA; and Greenville, Mercer Co., PA

Buried: Shenango Valley Cemetery, Greenville, PA

References: Obituary, *Greenville Advance-Argus*, Dec. 18, 1890. *History of the 57th Regiment, Pennsylvania Veteran Volunteer Infantry.* Meadville, PA, 1904. Military Service File, National Archives. *History of Mercer County, PA; Its Past and Present.* Chicago, IL, 1888.

EDWARD RODMAN MAYER

Colonel, 41 PA Militia, July 5, 1863. Honorably mustered out, Aug. 4, 1863.

Born: July 18, 1823 Philadelphia, PA
Died: Aug. 16, 1891 Wilkes-Barre, PA
Education: Graduated University of Pennsylvania, Philadelphia, PA, 1841. M.D., University of Pennsylvania Medical School, 1844.
Occupation: Physician
Miscellaneous: Resided Wilkes-Barre, Luzerne Co., PA
Buried: Hollenback Cemetery, Wilkes-Barre, PA (Lot 618)
References: Obituary, *Wilkes-Barre Record*, Aug. 17, 1891. *University of Pennsylvania: Biographical Catalogue of the Matriculates of the College*. Philadelphia, PA, 1894.

JOHN SWAYZE McCALMONT

Colonel, 10 PA Reserves, June 29, 1861. Commanded 3 Brigade, McCall's Division, Army of the Potomac, Oct.–Nov. 1861. Resigned May 9, 1862, "on account of ill health and physical inability to withstand the continued exposures of field service."

Born: April 25, 1822 Franklin, PA
Died: Dec. 2, 1906 Washington, DC
Education: Attended Allegheny College, Meadville, PA. Graduated US Military Academy, West Point, NY, 1842.
Occupation: Lawyer and judge
Offices/Honors: PA House of Representatives, 1849–50 (Speaker, 1850). President Judge, 18th Judicial District, 1853–61. US Commissioner of Customs, 1885–89.
Miscellaneous: Resided Franklin, Venango Co., PA; Clarion, Clarion Co., PA; and Washington, DC. Brother of Bvt. Brig. Gen. Alfred B. McCalmont.
Buried: Franklin Cemetery, Franklin, PA
References: Charles F. Ritter and Jon L. Wakelyn. *American Legislative Leaders, 1850–1910*. Westport, CT, 1989. *Annual Reunion*, Association of the Graduates of the US Military Academy, 1908. Josiah R. Sypher. *History of the Pennsylvania Reserve Corps*. Lancaster, PA, 1865. Samuel P. Bates. *Martial Deeds of Pennsylvania*. Philadelphia, PA, 1875. Military Service File, National Archives. Herbert C. Bell, editor. *History of Venango County, PA; Its Past and Present*. Chicago, IL, 1890. *The Union Army*. Maryland/Washington, DC, Edition. Madison, WI, 1908.

John Swayze McCalmont
RONN PALM COLLECTION.

WILLIAM McCANDLESS

Major, 2 PA Reserves, Aug. 1, 1861. Lieutenant Colonel, 2 PA Reserves, Oct. 24, 1861. Colonel, 2 PA Reserves, Nov. 1, 1861. GSW groin, 2nd Bull Run, VA, Aug. 30, 1862. Commanded 1 Brigade, 3 Division, 1 Army Corps, Army of the Potomac, Dec. 13, 1862–Feb. 17, 1863. Commanded 1 Brigade, Pennsylvania Reserves Division, Department of Washington, Feb. 17–March 29, 1863 and May 29–June 26, 1863. Commanded 1 Brigade, 3 Division, 5 Army Corps, Army of the Potomac, June 28–Aug. 28, 1863, Nov. 1, 1863–Feb. 20, 1864, and May 1–8, 1864. Commanded 3 Division, 5 Army Corps, Army of the Potomac, Aug. 28–Nov. 1, 1863 and Feb. 20–May 1, 1864. GSW left forearm, Spotsylvania, VA, May 8, 1864. Honorably mustered out, June 16, 1864. Appointed Brigadier General, USV, July 21, 1864, but declined.

William McCandless
COURTESY OF GIL BARRETT.
WENDEROTH & TAYLOR, 912, 914, & 916 CHESTNUT STREET,
PHILADELPHIA, PA.

Born: Sept. 29, 1834 Philadelphia, PA

Died: June 17, 1884 Philadelphia, PA

Occupation: Machinist and civil engineer early in life. Later became a lawyer.

Offices/Honors: PA Senate, 1867–69. PA Secretary of Internal Affairs, 1876–79.

Miscellaneous: Resided Philadelphia, PA

Buried: Mount Moriah Cemetery, Philadelphia, PA (Section 107, Lot 88)

References: Josiah R. Sypher. *History of the Pennsylvania Reserve Corps.* Lancaster, PA, 1865. Samuel P. Bates. *Martial Deeds of Pennsylvania.* Philadelphia, PA, 1875. Obituary, *Philadelphia Public Ledger,* June 18, 1884. John H. Campbell. *History of the Friendly Sons of St. Patrick and of the Hibernian Society for the Relief of Emigrants from Ireland.* Philadelphia, PA, 1892. Military Service File, National Archives. *The Union Army.* Maryland/Washington, DC, Edition. Madison, WI, 1908.

JAMES MAYLAND McCARTER

Chaplain, 14 PA Infantry, April 30, 1861. Honorably mustered out, Aug. 7, 1861. Colonel, 93 PA Infantry, Oct. 28, 1861. Shell wound (contused) left side, Fair Oaks, VA, May 31, 1862. Dismissed Nov. 27, 1862, for "drunkenness on duty." Disability resulting from dismissal removed, April 13, 1863, since it is "at least probable that his condition was the result of an incautious use of opiates" in the treatment of his wound. Colonel, 93 PA Infantry, April 13, 1863. Discharged Aug. 21, 1863, upon the recommendation of a Board of Examination, which found him guilty of "appearing at a General Court Martial of which he was President in a state of intoxication." His discharge was revoked in orders dated Nov. 1, 1882, and his resignation tendered Aug. 7, 1863, in anticipation of the adverse recommendation of the Board of Examination, was accepted to date Aug. 19, 1863.

James Mayland McCarter
MASSACHUSETTS MOLLUS COLLECTION, USAMHI.

Born: 1822 New York City, NY
Died: June 18, 1900 Preston, MD
Education: Attended Norristown (PA) Academy
Occupation: Methodist clergyman, farmer and author
Miscellaneous: Resided Smyrna, Kent Co., DE; Lancaster, Lancaster Co., PA; Philadelphia, PA; West Chester, Chester Co., PA; Reading, Berks Co., PA; Lebanon, Lebanon Co., PA; and Preston, Caroline Co., MD
Buried: Bethesda Methodist Churchyard, Preston, MD
References: *The Biographical Cyclopedia of Representative Men of Maryland and District of Columbia.* Baltimore, MD, 1879. *Portrait and Biographical Record of the Eastern Shore of Maryland.* New York and Chicago, 1898. Pension File, National Archives. Penrose G. Mark. *Red: White: and Blue Badge Pennsylvania Veteran Volunteers. A History of the 93rd Regiment.* Harrisburg, PA, 1911. Letters Received, Volunteer Service Branch, Adjutant General's Office, Files M1266(VS)1862 and M1598(VS)1863, National Archives. Richard E. Matthews. *Colonel McCarter, The Fighting Parson. Bassler and His Jackson Guards.* Lebanon, PA, 1987.

William Moore McClure
KEN TURNER COLLECTION.
R. W. ADDIS, PHOTOGRAPHER, 308 PENNA. AVENUE,
WASHINGTON, DC.

WILLIAM MOORE McCLURE

Captain, Co. H, 11 PA Infantry, April 26, 1861. Honorably mustered out, July 31, 1861. Captain, Co. F, 2 PA Heavy Artillery, Jan. 4, 1862. *Colonel*, 4 PA Heavy Artillery, April 30, 1864. Colonel, 2 PA Heavy Artillery, Sept. 30, 1864. Commanded 3 Brigade, 2 Division, 18 Army Corps, Army of the James, Nov. 5–26, 1864. Commanded Provisional Brigade, Defenses of Bermuda Hundred, Army of the James, Dec. 3, 1864–March 7, 1865. Resigned March 7, 1865, in order to "fulfill private obligations which I am in honor bound to respect."

Born: March 5, 1831 Glenmoore, Chester Co., PA
Died: Oct. 2, 1893 Lancaster, PA
Occupation: Marble works proprietor
Offices/Honors: KS Territorial House of Representatives, 1857–59
Miscellaneous: Resided Leavenworth, Leavenworth Co., KS; Columbia, Lancaster Co., PA; Danville, Montour Co., PA; and Lancaster, Lancaster Co., PA
Buried: Fairview Cemetery, Glenmoore, PA
References: George W. Martin, editor. *Transactions of the Kansas State Historical Society, 1907–08.* Topeka, KS, 1908. Obituary, *Lancaster New Era,* Oct. 2, 1893. George W. Ward. *History of the 2nd Pennsylvania Veteran Heavy Artillery.* Philadelphia, PA, 1904. Samuel P. Bates. *Martial Deeds of Pennsylvania.* Philadelphia, PA, 1875. Pension File, National Archives. Letters Received, Volunteer Service Branch, Adjutant General's Office, File W2410(VS)1864, National Archives.

ROBERT BRICE McCOMB

Colonel, 14 PA Militia, Sept. 16, 1862. Honorably discharged, Sept. 28, 1862. Colonel, 55 PA Militia, July 3, 1863. Honorably mustered out, Aug. 26, 1863.

Born: Aug. 15, 1820 Indian Run, Mercer Co., PA
Died: Sept. 22, 1907 Sandy Lake, PA
Occupation: Lawyer, after early career as cabinetmaker
Offices/Honors: PA House of Representatives, 1854–56
Miscellaneous: Resided New Castle, Lawrence Co., PA. Brother of CSA General William McComb.
Buried: Graceland Cemetery, New Castle, PA
References: Aaron L. Hazen, editor. *Twentieth Century History of New Castle and Lawrence County, PA.* Chicago, IL, 1908. Obituary, *New Castle News,* Sept. 23, 1907. *Book of Biographies: Lawrence County, PA.* Buffalo, NY, 1897. Samuel W. Durant. *History of Lawrence County, PA.* Philadelphia, PA, 1877.

Robert Brice McComb (postwar)

HENRY McCORMICK

Captain, Co. F, 25 PA Infantry, May 2, 1861. Honorably mustered out, July 26, 1861. Colonel, 1 PA Militia, Sept. 11, 1862. Honorably discharged, Sept. 25, 1862.

Born: March 10, 1831 Harrisburg, PA
Died: July 14, 1900 Rosegarten, Cumberland Co., PA
Education: Attended Partridge's Collegiate and Commercial Institute, New Haven, CT. Graduated Yale University, New Haven, CT, 1852.
Occupation: Iron manufacturer
Miscellaneous: Resided Harrisburg, Dauphin Co., PA
Buried: Harrisburg Cemetery, Harrisburg, PA (Section L, Lot 106)
References: Luther R. Kelker. *History of Dauphin County, PA.* New York and Chicago, 1907. *Commemorative Biographical Encyclopedia of Dauphin County, PA.* Chambersburg, PA, 1896. Obituary, *Harrisburg Patriot,* July 14, 1900. Leander J. McCormick. *Family Record and Biography.* Chicago, IL, 1896. William H. Egle. *Pennsylvania Genealogies.* Harrisburg, PA, 1896. *Obituary Record of Grad-*

Henry McCormick
USAMHI.

uates of Yale College Deceased during the Academical Year Ending in June, 1901. William W. H. Davis. *History of the Doylestown Guards.* Doylestown, PA, 1887. William H. Egle. *History of the Counties of Dauphin and Lebanon in the Commonwealth of Pennsylvania.* Philadelphia, PA, 1883.

JOHN FULTON McCULLOUGH

Private, Co. F, 1 PA Cavalry, Aug. 16, 1861. Honorably discharged, Jan. 16, 1862. Captain, Co. A, 140 PA Infantry, Sept. 4, 1862. GSW Gettysburg, PA, July 2, 1863. *Colonel,* 183 PA Infantry, May 28, 1864. GSW leg, Totopotomy Creek, VA, May 31, 1864.

Born: May 12, 1841 near Jefferson, PA
Died: May 31, 1864 KIA Totopotomy Creek, VA
Education: Attended Waynesburg (PA) College. Attended Jefferson College, Canonsburg, PA.
Occupation: Student

John Fulton McCullough
MEADE ALBUM, CIVIL WAR LIBRARY & MUSEUM,
PHILADELPHIA, PA.

Miscellaneous: Resided Jefferson, Greene Co., PA
Buried: Presbyterian Churchyard, Jefferson, PA
References: Robert L. Stewart. *History of the 140th Regiment Pennsylvania Volunteers.* Philadelphia, PA, 1912.

ROBERT P. McDOWELL

Colonel, 5 PA Infantry, April 21, 1861. Honorably mustered out, July 24, 1861.

Born: May 12, 1826 Pittsburgh, PA
Died: Aug. 12, 1864 Washington, DC
Occupation: Clerk
Offices/Honors: PA House of Representatives, 1859
Miscellaneous: Resided Pittsburgh, PA
Buried: Allegheny Cemetery, Pittsburgh, PA (Section 8 1/2, Lot 1)
References: Thomas P. Lowry. *Tarnished Eagles: The Courts-Martial of Fifty Union Colonels and Lieutenant Colonels.* Mechanicsburg, PA, 1997. Obituary, *Pittsburgh Daily Post*, Aug. 15, 1864. Obituary, *Pittsburgh Evening Chronicle*, Aug. 13, 1864.

HENRY BENJAMIN McKEAN

1 Lieutenant, Adjutant, 6 PA Reserves, June 22, 1861. Lieutenant Colonel, 6 PA Reserves, April 1, 1862. Resigned Nov. 25, 1862, due to physical disability from chronic diarrhea. Colonel, 35 PA Militia, July 4, 1863. Honorably mustered out, Aug. 7, 1863.

Born: Sept. 13, 1831 Troy, PA
Died: March 22, 1903 Washington, DC
Occupation: Lawyer. Held a position in the US Pension Bureau in later life.
Miscellaneous: Resided Towanda, Bradford Co., PA; and Washington, DC
Buried: Arlington National Cemetery, Arlington, VA (Section 3, Lot 1359)
References: Pension File and Military Service File, National Archives. Obituary, *Washington Evening Star*, March 24, 1903. Obituary Circular, Whole No. 343, District of Columbia MOLLUS. Samuel P. Bates. *Martial Deeds of Pennsylvania.* Philadelphia, PA, 1875. Obituary, *Bradford Argus*, March 26, 1903.

Henry Benjamin McKean (postwar)
CIVIL WAR LIBRARY & MUSEUM, PHILADELPHIA, PA.

HENRY BOYD McKEEN

1 Lieutenant, Adjutant, 81 PA Infantry, Oct. 27, 1861. Major, 81 PA Infantry, June 1, 1862. GSW Malvern Hill, VA, July 1, 1862. Lieutenant Colonel, 81 PA Infantry, July 2, 1862. Colonel, 81 PA Infantry, Nov. 24, 1862. GSW side and foot, Fredericksburg, VA, Dec. 13, 1862. Shell wound Chancellorsville, VA, May 3, 1863. Commanded 1 Brigade, 1 Division, 2 Army Corps, Army of the Potomac, July 2–4, 1863 and Dec. 25, 1863–March 14, 1864. Commanded 1 Brigade, 2 Division, 2 Army Corps, Army of the Potomac, May 12–June 3, 1864. GSW Cold Harbor, VA, June 3, 1864.

Born: Sept. 18, 1835 Philadelphia, PA
Died: June 3, 1864 KIA Cold Harbor, VA
Education: Graduated Princeton (NJ) University, 1853
Occupation: Lumber merchant
Miscellaneous: Resided Philadelphia, PA
Buried: Woodlands Cemetery, Philadelphia, PA (Section D, Lot 2)
References: *Semi-Centennial Register of the Members of the Phi Kappa Sigma Fraternity, 1850–1900.* Philadelphia, PA, 1900. Samuel P. Bates. *Martial Deeds of Pennsylvania.* Philadelphia, PA, 1875. Military Service File, National Archives. Edmund J. Raus, Jr. *A Generation on the March: The Union Army at Gettysburg.* Gettysburg, PA, 1996. Joseph T. Duryea. *An Oration Commemorative of the Restoration of the Union, with a Tribute to the Alumni and Under-Graduates of the College of New Jersey, Who Fell in the National Struggle.* Philadelphia, PA, 1866.

AMOR ARCHER McKNIGHT

Captain, Co. I, 8 PA Infantry, April 24, 1861. Honorably mustered out, July 29, 1861. Colonel, 105 PA Infantry, Aug. 28, 1861. GSW side, Fair Oaks, VA, May 31, 1862. Resigned July 29, 1862, "fifteen months of unremitting service, in various positions" having "so shattered what was previously a weak constitution." Colonel, 105 PA Infantry, Sept. 20, 1862. GSW head, Chancellorsville, VA, May 3, 1863.

Born: April 19, 1832 Blairsville, PA
Died: May 3, 1863 KIA Chancellorsville, VA

Henry Boyd McKeen

Amor Archer McKnight

Education: Attended Brookville (PA) Academy
Occupation: Lawyer, after early career as printer
Miscellaneous: Resided Brookville, Jefferson Co., PA
Buried: Chancellorsville, VA (Body never recovered)
References: William J. McKnight. *Jefferson County, PA: Her Pioneers and People.* Chicago, IL, 1917. Samuel P. Bates. *Martial Deeds of Pennsylvania.* Philadelphia, PA, 1875. Letters Received, Volunteer Service Branch, Adjutant General's Office, File M454(VS)1863, National Archives. Kate M. Scott. *History of the 105th Regiment of Pennsylvania Volunteers.* Philadelphia, PA, 1877.

JOHN WHITE McLANE

Colonel, Erie Regiment, PA Infantry, April 27, 1861. Honorably mustered out, July 20, 1861. Colonel, 83 PA Infantry, July 24, 1861. Shell wound head and GSW right breast, Gaines' Mill, VA, June 27, 1862.

Born: Aug. 24, 1820 Wilmington, DE
Died: June 27, 1862 KIA Gaines' Mill, VA
Other Wars: Mexican War (Captain, 1 IN Volunteers)

John White McLane
RONN PALM COLLECTION.

Occupation: Farmer, miller and fire insurance agent
Offices/Honors: Sheriff of Erie Co., PA, 1858–61
Miscellaneous: Resided Fort Wayne, Allen Co., IN; and Erie, Erie Co., PA
Buried: Erie Cemetery, Erie, PA (Section L, Lot 2)
References: Samuel P. Bates. *Martial Deeds of Pennsylvania.* Philadelphia, PA, 1875. Michael Schellhammer. *The 83rd Pennsylvania Volunteers in the Civil War.* Jefferson, NC, 2003. Amos M. Judson. *History of the 83rd Regiment Pennsylvania Volunteers.* Erie, PA, 1865. Obituary, *Erie Weekly Gazette,* July 10, 1862.

GEORGE POTTS McLEAN

Major, 22 PA Infantry, April 23, 1861. Honorably mustered out, Aug. 5, 1861. Colonel, 88 PA Infantry, Aug. 9, 1861. Acting Military Governor, Alexandria, VA, Dec. 1861. Resigned Dec. 1, 1862, due to physical disability from rheumatism and chronic diarrhea. Colonel, 59 PA Militia, June 27, 1863. Honorably mustered out, Sept. 9, 1863. Colonel, 183 PA Infantry, March 8, 1864. Resigned May 3, 1864, "on account of having received an order to appear before the Board of Examination."

George Potts McLean
BONNIE YUHAS COLLECTION, USAMHI.

Hugh Watson McNeil

Born: July 13, 1817 Philadelphia, PA
Died: Oct. 23, 1900 Philadelphia, PA
Occupation: Merchant engaged in the manufacture of picture frames and mirrors before war. Served as US Government Storekeeper at the Philadelphia Custom House for about 18 years after the war.
Miscellaneous: Resided Philadelphia, PA
Buried: Mount Moriah Cemetery, Philadelphia, PA (Section 51, Lot 69)
References: Samuel P. Bates. *Martial Deeds of Pennsylvania.* Philadelphia, PA, 1875. Pension File and Military Service File, National Archives. Obituary, *Philadelphia Public Ledger,* Oct. 24, 1900. Letters Received, Volunteer Service Branch, Adjutant General's Office, File M145(VS)1861, National Archives. John D. Vautier. *History of the 88th Pennsylvania Volunteers in the War for the Union.* Philadelphia, PA, 1894.

HUGH WATSON McNEIL

1 Lieutenant, Co. D, 13 PA Reserves, May 29, 1861. Captain, Co. D, 13 PA Reserves, June 12, 1861. Colonel, 13 PA Reserves, Jan. 22, 1862. GSW lungs, Antietam, MD, Sept. 16, 1862.

Born: Jan. 10, 1830 Owasco, Cayuga Co., NY
Died: Sept. 16, 1862 KIA Antietam, MD
Education: Attended Yale University, New Haven, CT. Graduated Delaware College, Newark, DE.
Occupation: Held positions in the US Coast Survey and the US Treasury Department for several years, after which he was a lawyer in New York City and a bank cashier in Warren, PA

Hugh Watson McNeil

Miscellaneous: Resided Auburn, Cayuga Co., NY; Washington, DC; New York City, NY; and Warren, Warren Co., PA

Buried: Fort Hill Cemetery, Auburn, NY (Laurel Hill Section, Lots 1–6)

References: O. R. Howard Thomson and William H. Rauch. *History of the "Bucktails," Kane Rifle Regiment of the Pennsylvania Reserve Corps.* Philadelphia, PA, 1906. Josiah R. Sypher. *History of the Pennsylvania Reserve Corps.* Lancaster, PA, 1865. Samuel P. Bates. *Martial Deeds of Pennsylvania.* Philadelphia, PA, 1875. Hugh W. McNeil Collection, Pennsylvania State Archives.

WILLIAM WILLIAMSON McNULTY

Captain, Co. I, 1 PA Cavalry, Aug. 13, 1861. Colonel, 6 PA Cavalry, Sept. 6, 1861. Honorably discharged, Oct. 12, 1861, the regiment having failed to complete its organization.

Born: April 6, 1808 West Middletown, Washington Co., PA

Died: May 11, 1879 Boonville, MO

Occupation: Hotelkeeper

Miscellaneous: Resided Hopewell Twp. and Buffalo Twp., Washington Co., PA; and Boonville, Cooper Co., MO

Buried: Grove Presbyterian Churchyard, West Middletown, PA

References: Military Service File, National Archives. Boyd Crumrine, editor. *History of Washington County, PA.* Philadelphia, PA, 1882. William P. Lloyd. *History of the 1st Regiment Pennsylvania Reserve Cavalry.* Philadelphia, PA, 1864. Obituary, *Washington (PA) Daily Evening Reporter,* May 13, 1879.

DAVID WHITE MEGRAW

Sergeant, Co. D, 123 PA Infantry, Aug. 8, 1862. GSW left thigh, Fredericksburg, VA, Dec. 13, 1862. Honorably mustered out, May 13, 1863. 2 Lieutenant, Capt. Tyler's Park Battery, PA Volunteers, July 20, 1863. Honorably mustered out, Jan. 28, 1864. Captain, Co. H, 116 PA Infantry, March 2, 1864. Major, 116 PA Infantry, Jan. 17, 1865. Lieutenant Colonel, 116 PA Infantry, Jan. 18, 1865. GSW left thigh, White Oak Road, VA, March 31, 1865. *Colonel,* 116 PA Infantry, June 4, 1865. Honorably mustered out, July 14, 1865.

Born: June 12, 1839 County Down, Ireland

Died: April 2, 1888 Chicago, IL

Occupation: Carpenter and later police captain

Miscellaneous: Resided Pittsburgh, PA; Lake Geneva, Walworth Co., WI; and Chicago, IL

Buried: Union Dale Cemetery, Pittsburgh, PA (Division 1, Section 7, Range 6 1/2, Grave 739)

References: Pension File and Military Service File, National Archives. Samuel P. Bates. *Martial Deeds of Pennsylvania.* Philadelphia, PA, 1875. Obituary, *Pittsburgh Press,* April 3, 1888. St. Clair A. Mulholland. *The Story of the 116th Regiment Pennsylvania Volunteers in the War of the Rebellion.* Philadelphia, PA, 1903. Obituary, *Pittsburgh Dispatch,* April 3, 1888.

ADOLPH MEHLER

Major, 21 PA Infantry, April 29, 1861. Honorably mustered out, Aug. 9, 1861. Lieutenant Colonel, 98 PA Infantry, Aug. 31, 1861. Colonel, 98 PA Infantry, Nov. 26, 1862. Dismissed March 12, 1863, for "certifying to a false and fraudulent account." Dismissal revoked, June 18, 1863, upon evidence that the account was valid. Honorably discharged to date, March 12, 1863.

Born: 1824? Prussia

Died: Oct. 26, 1871 Philadelphia, PA

Other Wars: Prussian cavalry officer in Schleswig-Holstein war of 1848–49

Occupation: Hotelkeeper

Miscellaneous: Resided Philadelphia, PA; and Atlantic City, Atlantic Co., NJ

Buried: Mount Moriah Cemetery, Philadelphia, PA (Section 104, Lot 18)

References: Pension File, National Archives. Letters Received, Volunteer Service Branch, Adjutant General's Office, File J332(VS)1863, National Archives. Death notice, *Philadelphia Public Ledger,* Oct. 27, 1871.

GABRIEL MIDDLETON

Private, 1 Troop, Philadelphia City Cavalry, May 13, 1861. Honorably mustered out, Aug. 17, 1861. Captain, Co. E, 2 PA Cavalry, Sept. 16, 1861. Lieutenant Colonel, 20 PA Cavalry (3 years), Feb. 23, 1864. Colonel, 20 PA Cavalry (3 years), March 1, 1865. Honorably mustered out, June 20, 1865, upon consolidation of regiment with 2 PA Cavalry.

Gabriel Middleton

Born: 1836? Philadelphia, PA
Died: Feb. 24, 1886 Orlando, FL
Occupation: Cotton broker
Miscellaneous: Resided Philadelphia, PA
Buried: Laurel Hill Cemetery, Philadelphia, PA (Section 7, Lots 338–340)
References: Obituary, *Philadelphia Public Ledger*, Feb. 27, 1886. Joseph L. Wilson, editor. *Book of the First Troop Philadelphia City Cavalry, 1774–1914*. Philadelphia, PA, 1915. Military Service File, National Archives. Commissions File, Records of the Department of Military and Veterans' Affairs, Pennsylvania State Archives.

James Miller (81 PA)

JAMES MILLER

Colonel, 81 PA Infantry, Aug. 8, 1861. GSW heart, Fair Oaks, VA, June 1, 1862.

Born: April 21, 1823 County Antrim, Ireland
Died: June 1, 1862 KIA Fair Oaks, VA
Other Wars: Mexican War (Captain, Co. K, 2 PA Infantry)
Occupation: Jeweler and coal merchant
Miscellaneous: Resided Mauch Chunk (now Jim Thorpe), Carbon Co., PA; South Easton, Northampton Co., PA; and New York City, NY
Buried: Easton Cemetery, Easton, PA (Section E, Lot 175)

References: Franklin Ellis. *History of Northampton County, PA.* Philadelphia, PA, 1877. Pension File, National Archives. Obituary, *New York Daily Tribune,* June 5, 1862. Samuel P. Bates. *Martial Deeds of Pennsylvania.* Philadelphia, PA, 1875.

JAMES MILLER

Sergeant, Co. K, 105 PA Infantry, Sept. 25, 1861. 2 Lieutenant, Co. K, 105 PA Infantry, March 20, 1863. 1 Lieutenant, Co. K, 105 PA Infantry, May 25, 1863. GSW left knee, Auburn, VA, Oct. 13, 1863. Captain, Co. K, 105 PA Infantry, Nov. 10, 1863. GSW left arm, Wilderness, VA, May 5, 1864. Major, 105 PA Infantry, Oct. 28, 1864. Colonel, 105 PA Infantry, April 25, 1865. Honorably mustered out, July 11, 1865.

Born: April 15, 1835 Jefferson Co., PA
Died: July 1, 1896 Grampian Hills, PA (from injuries received in a carriage accident)
Occupation: Farmer and lumberman
Miscellaneous: Resided Grampian Hills, Clearfield Co., PA

James Miller (105 PA)
USAMHI.

Buried: Friends Cemetery, Grampian Hills, PA
References: Pension File, National Archives. Samuel P. Bates. *Martial Deeds of Pennsylvania.* Philadelphia, PA, 1875. Kate M. Scott. *History of the 105th Regiment of Pennsylvania Volunteers.* Philadelphia, PA, 1877.

FRANCIS PATTERSON MINIER

Colonel, 3 PA Infantry, April 20, 1861. Honorably mustered out, July 29, 1861. Captain, 12 US Infantry, May 14, 1861. Appointment expired, Aug. 6, 1861. Captain, Co. A, 21 MI Infantry, Aug. 12, 1862. Resigned April 6, 1863, due to "general debility and great prostration of nervous energy."

Born: Sept. 19, 1820 Bloomsburg, PA
Died: Oct. 3, 1873 Palo, MI
Other Wars: Mexican War (Corporal, General Recruiting Service, USA)
Occupation: Regular Army (Sergeant, General Recruiting Service), 1847–54. Farmer after war.
Miscellaneous: Resided Hollidaysburg, Blair Co., PA; Syracuse, NY; and Ronald Center, Ionia Co., MI
Buried: Palo Van Vleck Cemetery, Palo, Ionia Co., MI (Lot 156)
References: Pension File, National Archives. H. H. Hardesty. *Presidents, Soldiers, Statesmen.* Ionia County, MI, Edition. New York, Toledo and Chicago, 1896. Letters Received, Volunteer Service Branch, Adjutant General's Office, File I650(VS)1862, National Archives. Enlistment Papers, Regular Army, National Archives.

WILLIAM N. MONIES

Captain, Co. B, 136 PA Infantry, Aug. 16, 1862. Honorably mustered out, May 29, 1863. Colonel, 30 PA Emergency Troops, June 25, 1863. Honorably mustered out, July 27, 1863.

Born: May 10, 1827 New Dailly, Ayrshire, Scotland
Died: Jan. 10, 1881 Scranton, PA
Occupation: Engaged in the milling business and later in the wholesale bakery business
Offices/Honors: Mayor of Scranton, PA, 1869–72. Treasurer of Lackawanna Co., PA, 1878–80.
Miscellaneous: Resided Scranton, Lackawanna Co., PA
Buried: Dunmore Cemetery, Scranton, PA (Block 10, Lot 94)

William N. Monies (postwar)
FROM *HISTORY OF LUZERNE, LACKAWANNA, AND WYOMING COUNTIES, PA.*

References: Frederick L. Hitchcock. *History of Scranton and Its People.* New York City, NY, 1914. *History of Luzerne, Lackawanna, and Wyoming Counties, PA.* New York City, NY, 1880. Obituary, *Scranton Republican,* Jan. 11, 1881.

JOHN WILLIAM MOORE

Captain, Co. G, 66 PA Infantry, July 9, 1861. Captain, Co. K, 99 PA Infantry, March 3, 1862. Major, 99 PA Infantry, Feb. 20, 1863. GSW Gettysburg, PA, July 2, 1863. Accidental bayonet wound foot, near Culpeper, VA, Sept. 25, 1863. Lieutenant Colonel, 99 PA Infantry, April 10, 1864. Colonel, 203 PA Infantry, Sept. 10, 1864. GSW abdomen, Fort Fisher, NC, Jan. 15, 1865.

Born: 1836 Philadelphia, PA
Died: Jan. 15, 1865 KIA Fort Fisher, NC
Miscellaneous: Resided Philadelphia, PA
Buried: Mount Moriah Cemetery, Philadelphia, PA (Section 36, Lot 68)
References: Pension File and Military Service File, National Archives. Samuel P. Bates. *Martial Deeds of Pennsylvania.* Philadelphia, PA, 1875. Funeral account, *Philadelphia Public Ledger,* Feb. 1, 1865.

John William Moore
KEN TURNER COLLECTION.
C. EVANS, PHOTOGRAPHER, NO. 1520 MARKET STREET, PHILADELPHIA, PA.

WILLIAM MOORE

1 Lieutenant, Adjutant, 73 PA Infantry, Aug. 3, 1861. Captain, Co. D, 73 PA Infantry, May 1, 1862. Lieutenant Colonel, 73 PA Infantry, Aug. 30, 1862. Colonel, 73 PA Infantry, Jan. 28, 1863. GSW left chest, the ball passing through left lung and injuring the spine, Chancellorsville, VA, May 2, 1863. Resigned Feb. 8, 1864, "on account of continued disability" from his wound "after an absence of more than sixty days."

Born: July 2, 1831 Germany
Died: March 26, 1910 Philadelphia, PA
Occupation: Engaged in furnishing business and later in the grocery business
Miscellaneous: Resided Philadelphia, PA
Buried: Mount Peace Cemetery, Philadelphia, PA (Section D, Lot 152)
References: Pension File and Military Service File, National Archives. Obituary, *Philadelphia Press,* March 27, 1910. Letters Received, Volunteer Service Branch, Adjutant General's Office, File M209(VS)1864, National Archives.

Algernon Sidney Mountain Morgan
RONN PALM COLLECTION.

ALGERNON SIDNEY MOUNTAIN MORGAN

2 Lieutenant, Co. K, 12 PA Infantry, April 25, 1861. Honorably mustered out, July 31, 1861. Lieutenant Colonel, 63 PA Infantry, Aug. 1, 1861. GSW both hips, Fair Oaks, VA, May 31, 1862. Colonel, 63 PA Infantry, Sept. 29, 1862. Discharged for disability, April 18, 1863, due to effects of his wound, "which has kept him from his command since May 31, 1862." Appointed Military Storekeeper, Ordnance Department, USA, Dec. 5, 1863.

Born: May 9, 1831 Morganza, Washington Co., PA
Died: March 10, 1914 Pittsburgh, PA
Education: Graduated Western University (now University of Pittsburgh), Pittsburgh, PA, 1849
Occupation: Civil engineer and coke manufacturer before war. Regular Army (Captain, Military Storekeeper, retired June 6, 1894) and bank president after war.
Miscellaneous: Resided Pittsburgh, PA
Buried: Allegheny Cemetery, Pittsburgh, PA (Section 11, Lot 50)
References: Gilbert A. Hays. *Under the Red Patch: Story of the 63rd Regiment Pennsylvania Volunteers.* Pittsburgh, PA, 1908. Obituary, *Pittsburgh Dispatch*, March 12, 1914. Pension File, National Archives. Samuel P. Bates. *Martial Deeds of Pennsylvania.* Philadelphia, PA, 1875. *Companions of the Military Order of the Loyal Legion of the United States.* New York City, NY, 1901.

David Boyd Morris
FROM *HISTORY OF THE 101ST PENNSYLVANIA VETERAN VOLUNTEER INFANTRY.*

DAVID BOYD MORRIS

Captain, Co. A, 13 PA Infantry, April 25, 1861. Honorably mustered out, Aug. 6, 1861. Lieutenant Colonel, 101 PA Infantry, Dec. 7, 1861. GSW left leg, Fair Oaks, VA, May 31, 1862. Colonel, 101 PA Infantry, July 21, 1862. Honorably mustered out, Jan. 24, 1865.

Born: Dec. 17, 1825 Elizabeth, NJ
Died: Feb. 27, 1908 Pittsburgh, PA
Occupation: Stucco worker before war. Stucco and cement contractor after war.
Miscellaneous: Resided Pittsburgh, PA
Buried: Homewood Cemetery, Pittsburgh, PA (Section 19, Lot 488)
References: Pension File, National Archives. John A. Reed. *History of the 101st Pennsylvania Veteran Volunteer Infantry*. Chicago, IL, 1910. Samuel P. Bates. *Martial Deeds of Pennsylvania*. Philadelphia, PA, 1875. Obituary, *Pittsburgh Dispatch*, Feb. 28, 1908. John H. Niebaum. *History of the Pittsburgh Washington Infantry 102nd (Old 13th) Regiment Pennsylvania Veteran Volunteers and its Forebears*. Pittsburgh, PA, 1931.

ALBERT P. MOULTON

1 Lieutenant, Co. F, 3 PA Reserves, June 11, 1861. Captain, Co. F, 3 PA Reserves, Sept. 5, 1863. Captain, Co. M, 54 PA Infantry, July 4, 1864. Lieutenant Colonel, 54 PA Infantry, March 20, 1865. *Colonel*, 54 PA Infantry, April 3, 1865. Taken prisoner, High Bridge, VA, April 6, 1865. Paroled April 9, 1865. Honorably discharged, May 30, 1865, his services being no longer required.

Born: 1823?
Died: Date and place of death unknown
Occupation: Manufacturer (1861). Hatter (1870–71).
Miscellaneous: Resided Reading, Berks Co., PA (1861–65); and New York City, NY (1870–71)
Buried: Burial place unknown
References: Military Service File, National Archives. Evan M. Woodward. *History of the 3rd Pennsylvania Reserve*. Trenton, NJ, 1883. William Swinton. *History of the 7th Regiment, National Guard, State of New York, During the War of the Rebellion*. New York City, NY, 1886. Letters Received, Volunteer Service Branch, Adjutant General's Office, Files M1521(VS)1865 and M1993(VS)1865, National Archives.

George Adolph Muhleck
LIBRARY OF CONGRESS.
BRADY'S NATIONAL PHOTOGRAPHIC PORTRAIT GALLERIES, 352 PENNSYLVANIA AVE., WASHINGTON, DC.

GEORGE ADOLPH MUHLECK

Captain, Co. F, 21 PA Infantry, April 29, 1861. Lieutenant Colonel, 73 PA Infantry, Aug. 3, 1861. Colonel, 73 PA Infantry, Aug. 30, 1862. Commanded 1 Brigade, 2 Division, 1 Army Corps, Army of Virginia, Aug. 30–Sept. 12, 1862. Commanded 1 Brigade, 2 Division, 11 Army Corps, Army of the Potomac, Sept. 12–Oct. 27, 1862 and Nov. 27–Dec. 1862. Resigned Jan. 27, 1863, on account of "divorce from my wife, care of three little children, and distracted state of mind which renders me unfit for a faithful discharge of my duties." Later served in US Sanitary Commission.

Born: 1829? Wurtemberg, Germany
Died: Jan. 8, 1869 Egg Harbor City, NJ
Miscellaneous: Resided Philadelphia, PA; and Egg Harbor City, Atlantic Co., NJ

Buried: Burial place unknown
References: Pension File and Military Service File, National Archives.

ALEXANDER MURPHY

Captain, Co. F, 17 PA Infantry, April 25, 1861. Honorably mustered out, Aug. 3, 1861. Colonel, 21 PA Militia, Sept. 15, 1862. Honorably discharged, Sept. 26, 1862. Colonel, 49 PA Militia, July 14, 1863. Honorably mustered out, Sept. 3, 1863.

Born: 1822? Philadelphia, PA
Died: Nov. 22, 1865 Philadelphia, PA
Occupation: Custom House broker
Miscellaneous: Resided Philadelphia, PA
Buried: Woodlands Cemetery, Philadelphia, PA (Section F, Lot 89, unmarked)
References: Pension File, National Archives. Obituary, *Philadelphia Public Ledger*, Nov. 23, 1865.

WILLIAM GRAY MURRAY

Colonel, 84 PA Infantry, Aug. 30, 1861. GSW head, Kernstown, VA, March 23, 1862.

Born: July 25, 1825 County Longford, Ireland
Died: March 23, 1862 KIA Kernstown, VA
Other Wars: Mexican War (2 Lieutenant, 11 US Infantry)
Occupation: Merchant
Offices/Honors: Postmaster, Hollidaysburg, PA, 1853–61
Miscellaneous: Resided Hollidaysburg, Blair Co., PA
Buried: St. Marys Cemetery, Hollidaysburg, PA
References: Samuel P. Bates. *Martial Deeds of Pennsylvania*. Philadelphia, PA, 1875. Military Service File, National Archives. Gary L. Ecelbarger. *"We Are In For It!" The First Battle of Kernstown, March 23, 1862*. Shippensburg, PA, 1997. Obituary, *Altoona Tribune*, April 17, 1862.

Alexander Murphy
103RD ENGINEER ARMORY COLLECTION, USAMHI.

William Gray Murray
BLAIR COUNTY HISTORICAL SOCIETY, ALTOONA, PA.

Daniel Nagle
ROGER D. HUNT COLLECTION, USAMHI.
A. M. ALLEN, PHOTOGRAPHER, CORNER CENTRE & MARKET STREET,
POTTSVILLE, PA.

DANIEL NAGLE

Captain, Co. D, 6 PA Infantry, April 22, 1861. Honorably mustered out, July 27, 1861. Captain, Co. D, 48 PA Infantry, Aug. 20, 1861. Major, 48 PA Infantry, Nov. 30, 1861. Resigned July 21, 1862. Lieutenant Colonel, 19 PA Militia, Sept. 15, 1862. Honorably discharged, Sept. 27, 1862. Colonel, 173 PA Infantry, Nov. 17, 1862. Honorably mustered out, Aug. 17, 1863.

Born: April 1, 1828 Womelsdorf, PA
Died: Jan. 11, 1918 Pottsville, PA
Other Wars: Mexican War (Drummer, Co. B, 1 PA Infantry)
Occupation: Engaged in painting and paper hanging business
Miscellaneous: Resided Pottsville, Schuylkill Co., PA. Brother of Brig. Gen. James Nagle.

Buried: Presbyterian Cemetery, Pottsville, PA
References: Henry W. Ruoff, editor. *Biographical and Portrait Cyclopedia of Schuylkill County, PA.* Philadelphia, PA, 1893. Obituary, *Pottsville Republican,* Jan. 12, 1918. *Schuylkill County, PA. Genealogy-Family History-Biography.* Chicago, IL, 1916. Francis B. Wallace, compiler. *Memorial of the Patriotism of Schuylkill County in the American Slaveholder's Rebellion.* Pottsville, PA, 1865. Joseph Gould. *The Story of the Forty-Eighth.* Philadelphia, PA, 1908. Military Service File, National Archives.

HARMANUS NEFF

Captain, Co. C, 19 PA Infantry, May 18, 1861. Honorably mustered out, Aug. 29, 1861. Colonel, 196 PA Infantry, July 9, 1864. Honorably mustered out, Nov. 22, 1864.

Harmanus Neff
COURTESY OF THE AUTHOR.
GIHON & RIXON, PHOTOGRAPHIC ARTISTS, 1024 CHESTNUT STREET,
PHILADELPHIA, PA.

Born: March 27, 1831 Philadelphia, PA
Died: March 9, 1877 Philadelphia, PA
Occupation: Printer
Miscellaneous: Resided Philadelphia, PA
Buried: Laurel Hill Cemetery, Philadelphia, PA (Section U, Lot 559)
References: Pension File, National Archives. Obituary, *Philadelphia Public Ledger*, March 10, 1877.

JOHN NEWKUMET

Lieutenant Colonel, 2 Regiment, Philadelphia City Home Guard, Aug. 19, 1861. Colonel, 9 PA Militia, Sept. 12, 1862. Honorably discharged, Sept. 27, 1862. Colonel, 31 PA Emergency Troops, June 30, 1863. Honorably mustered out, Aug. 8, 1863.

Born: Nov. 1, 1827 Eich, Hesse-Darmstadt, Germany
Died: May 8, 1869 Philadelphia, PA
Occupation: Architect and fire brick manufacturer
Miscellaneous: Resided Philadelphia, PA
Buried: Glenwood Memorial Gardens, Broomall, PA (Section R, Lot 235, unmarked)

John Newkumet
MASSACHUSETTS MOLLUS COLLECTION, USAMHI.

References: Death notice, *Philadelphia Public Ledger*, May 11, 1869. *Biographical Encyclopedia of Pennsylvania of the Nineteenth Century*. Philadelphia, PA, 1874. Obituary, *Philadelphia Sunday Dispatch*, May 16, 1869. Commissions File, Records of the Department of Military and Veterans' Affairs, Pennsylvania State Archives.

JOHN NYCE

2 Lieutenant, Co. F, 4 PA Reserves, June 8, 1861. 1 Lieutenant, Adjutant, 4 PA Reserves, July 17, 1861. Major, 4 PA Reserves, June 1, 1862. Saber wound right arm and shell wound left knee, Charles City Crossroads, VA, June 30, 1862. GSW left arm, Malvern Hill, VA, July 1, 1862. GSW right breast and right hand, Antietam, MD, Sept. 17, 1862. Colonel, 174 PA Infantry, Nov. 19, 1862. Honorably mustered out, Aug. 7, 1863.

Born: July 22, 1831 Sandyston Twp., Sussex Co., NJ
Died: April 13, 1880 Milford, PA
Occupation: Lawyer
Miscellaneous: Resided Stroudsburg, Monroe Co., PA; and Milford, Pike Co., PA, after 1864
Buried: Milford Cemetery, Milford, PA
References: Pension File and Military Service File, National Archives. Alfred Mathews. *History of Wayne, Pike and Monroe Counties, PA*. Philadelphia, PA, 1886. Obituary, *Port Jervis Evening Gazette*, April 13, 1880. Obituary, *Port Jervis Daily Union*, April 14, 1880. Obituary, *New York Times*, April 14, 1880. Letters Received, Volunteer Service Branch, Adjutant General's Office, File P1065(VS)1862, National Archives.

EDWARD O'BRIEN

Captain, Co. F, 12 PA Infantry, April 25, 1861. Honorably mustered out, Aug. 5, 1861. Captain, Co. D, 134 PA Infantry, Aug. 14, 1862. Lieutenant Colonel, 134 PA Infantry, Aug. 20, 1862. Colonel, 134 PA Infantry, Dec. 8, 1862. Honorably mustered out, May 26, 1863.

Born: Oct. 10, 1823 Pittsburgh, PA
Died: July 9, 1877 Dixmont, Allegheny Co., PA
Other Wars: Mexican War (Corporal, Co. I, 2 PA Infantry)
Occupation: Iron moulder
Miscellaneous: Resided Pittsburgh, PA; and New Castle, Lawrence Co., PA

Edward O'Brien

Dennis O'Kane

Buried: St. Mary's Cemetery, New Castle, PA
References: Samuel P. Bates. *Martial Deeds of Pennsylvania*. Philadelphia, PA, 1875. Samuel W. Durant. *History of Lawrence County, PA*. Philadelphia, PA, 1877. Obituary, *New Castle Courant*, July 13, 1877. Obituary, *Lawrence Guardian*, July 14, 1877.

DENNIS O'KANE

Major, 24 PA Infantry, May 1, 1861. Honorably mustered out, Aug. 10, 1861. Lieutenant Colonel, 69 PA Infantry, Aug. 19, 1861. Colonel, 69 PA Infantry, Dec. 1, 1862. GSW abdomen, Gettysburg, PA, July 3, 1863.

Born: 1818 County Derry, Ireland
Died: July 4, 1863 DOW Gettysburg, PA
Occupation: Tavern keeper
Miscellaneous: Resided Philadelphia, PA
Buried: Old Cathedral Cemetery, Philadelphia, PA (Section U, Range 3, Lot 27)

References: Samuel P. Bates. *Martial Deeds of Pennsylvania*. Philadelphia, PA, 1875. Anthony W. McDermott. *A Brief History of the 69th Regiment Pennsylvania Veteran Volunteers*. Philadelphia, PA, 1889. Edmund J. Raus, Jr. *A Generation on the March: The Union Army at Gettysburg*. Gettysburg, PA, 1996. Pension File and Military Service File, National Archives. Don Ernsberger. *Paddy Owen's Regulars: A History of the 69th Pennsylvania "Irish Volunteers."* N.p., 2004.

RICHARD ADOLPHUS OAKFORD

Colonel, 15 PA Infantry, April 27, 1861. Honorably mustered out, Aug. 8, 1861. Colonel, 132 PA Infantry, Aug. 22, 1862. GSW left shoulder, Antietam, MD, Sept. 17, 1862.

Born: Dec. 8, 1820 Philadelphia, PA
Died: Sept. 17, 1862 KIA Antietam, MD

Richard Adolphus Oakford

FROM WAR FROM THE INSIDE: THE STORY OF THE 132ND REGIMENT
PENNSYLVANIA VOLUNTEER INFANTRY IN THE WAR FOR THE
SUPPRESSION OF THE REBELLION.

Education: Attended Lafayette College, Easton, PA
Occupation: Civil engineer, farmer, and justice of the
  peace
Miscellaneous: Resided Scranton, Lackawanna Co., PA
Buried: Hollenback Cemetery, Wilkes-Barre, PA (Lot
  524)
References: Samuel P. Bates. *Martial Deeds of Pennsylvania*. Philadelphia, PA, 1875. *Portrait and Biographical Record of Wyoming and Lackawanna Counties, PA.* New York and Chicago, 1897. Pension File, National Archives. Frederick L. Hitchcock. *War from the Inside: The Story of the 132nd Regiment Pennsylvania Volunteer Infantry in the War for the Suppression of the Rebellion.* Philadelphia, PA, 1904. Benjamin H. Throop. *A Half Century in Scranton.* Scranton, PA, 1895. Charles E. Slocum. *A Short History of the Slocums, Slocumbs, and Slocombs of America.* Syracuse, NY, 1882.

ROBERT LEVAN ORR

1 Lieutenant, Co. I, 17 PA Infantry, April 25, 1861. Honorably mustered out, Aug. 2, 1861. Captain, Co. O, 23 PA Infantry, Sept. 4, 1861. Captain, Co. H, 61 PA Infantry, March 1, 1862. Acting AAG, Staff of Brig. Gen. John J. Abercrombie, May 12–June 30, 1864. Acting AAG, Staff of Brig. Gen. George W. Getty, June 30–July 26, 1864. Acting ACM, Staff of Brig. Gen. George W. Getty, July 26–Nov. 1864. Major, 61 PA Infantry, Dec. 1, 1864. Dismissed Jan. 7, 1865, for "whilst in the city of Philadelphia, absent from his command, and not in the execution of his office, violating the mustering regulations, by mustering into an advanced grade, an officer physically unfit for duty with his regiment, thereby creating a vacancy in the grade of Major, into which he caused and permitted himself to be mustered." Dismissal revoked, Feb. 8, 1865. GSW Petersburg, VA, April 2, 1865. Lieutenant Colonel, 61 PA Infantry, April 3, 1865. Colonel, 61 PA Infantry, April 27, 1865. Honorably mustered out, June 28, 1865. Bvt. Colonel, USV, April 2, 1865, for gallant and meritorious services in the assault before Petersburg, VA.

Robert Levan Orr
RONN PALM COLLECTION.
W. L. GERMON'S ATELIER, NO. 702 CHESTNUT STREET,
PHILADELPHIA, PA.

Born: March 28, 1836 Philadelphia, PA

Died: Nov. 14, 1894 Philadelphia, PA

Education: Attended Philadelphia (PA) Central High School

Occupation: Salesman before war. Auditor and dry goods merchant after war.

Offices/Honors: Mercantile Appraiser, Philadelphia, PA, 1877–81. Medal of Honor, Petersburg, VA, April 2, 1865. "Carried the colors at the head of the column in the assault after two color bearers had been shot down."

Miscellaneous: Resided Philadelphia, PA

Buried: Lawnview Cemetery, Rockledge, PA (Susquehanna Lawn, Range 68, Grave 40)

References: Obituary, *Philadelphia Public Ledger*, Nov. 15, 1894. Pension File and Military Service File, National Archives. Obituary Circular, Whole No. 291, Pennsylvania MOLLUS. William H. Powell, editor. *Officers of the Army and Navy (Volunteer) Who Served in the Civil War*. Philadelphia, PA, 1893. Samuel P. Bates. *Martial Deeds of Pennsylvania*. Philadelphia, PA, 1875. Abraham T. Brewer. *History 61st Regiment Pennsylvania Volunteers, 1861–65*. Pittsburgh, PA, 1911. Letters Received, Volunteer Service Branch, Adjutant General's Office, File O1748(VS)1864, National Archives. *Companions of the Military Order of the Loyal Legion of the United States*. New York City, NY, 1901.

John Emory Parsons
FROM *HISTORY OF THE 1ST BATTALION PENNSYLVANIA SIX MONTHS VOLUNTEERS AND 187TH REGIMENT PENNSYLVANIA VOLUNTEER INFANTRY.*

JOHN EMORY PARSONS

1 Lieutenant, Adjutant, 149 PA Infantry, Aug. 30, 1862. Acting AAG, 2 Brigade, 3 Division, 1 Army Corps, Army of the Potomac, April–Dec. 1863. GSW Gettysburg, PA, July 1, 1863. Taken prisoner, Gettysburg, PA, July 1, 1863. Paroled July 4, 1863. Acting AAG, 1 Brigade, 3 Division, 1 Army Corps, Dec. 1863–March 1864. Acting AAG, 3 Brigade, 4 Division, 5 Army Corps, Army of the Potomac, March–June 1864. Captain, AAG, USV, June 30, 1864. Assigned as AAG, 1 Brigade, 1 Division, 5 Army Corps, July 27, 1864. Resigned Jan. 30, 1865. Lieutenant Colonel, 187 PA Infantry, Jan. 31, 1865. Colonel, 187 PA Infantry, May 1, 1865. Honorably mustered out, Aug. 3, 1865.

Born: Dec. 23, 1837 Duncan's Island, near Harrisburg, PA

Died: July 18, 1914 Toledo, OH (crushed in elevator accident)

Occupation: Civil engineer before war. Engaged in life insurance, real estate, and banking enterprises after war.

Offices/Honors: PA House of Representatives, 1870–71

Miscellaneous: Resided Halifax, Dauphin Co., PA, to 1872; Harrisburg, Dauphin Co., PA, 1872–75; and Toledo, Lucas Co., OH, after 1875

Buried: Woodlawn Cemetery, Toledo, OH (Section 3, Lot 15)

References: Obituary, *Toledo Blade*, July 20, 1914. James M. Gibbs. *History of the 1st Battalion Pennsylvania Six Months Volunteers and 187th Regiment Pennsylvania Volunteer Infantry*. Harrisburg, PA, 1905. Samuel P. Bates. *Martial Deeds of Pennsylvania*. Philadelphia, PA, 1875. Pension File and Military Service File, National Archives.

JAMES PATCHELL

Sergeant, Co. D, 13 PA Infantry, April 25, 1861. Honorably mustered out, Aug. 6, 1861. 1 Lieutenant, Co. D, 102 PA Infantry, Aug. 16, 1861. Captain, Co. D, 102 PA Infantry, July 7, 1862. Major, 102 PA Infantry, Sept. 18, 1864. GSW right leg, Cedar Creek, VA, Oct. 19, 1864. Lieutenant Colonel, 102 PA Infantry, Oct. 20, 1864. GSW right hand, Petersburg, VA, April 2, 1865. Colonel, 102 PA Infantry, April 18, 1865. Honorably mustered out, June 28, 1865. Bvt. Colonel, USV, Sept. 19, 1864, for gallantry at the battle of Winchester, VA.

Born: July 6, 1832 Londonderry, Ireland
Died: Feb. 28, 1920 Union City, IN

Occupation: Iron moulder before war. Foundry and machine shop operator and railroad car inspector after war.
Miscellaneous: Resided Pittsburgh, PA; and Union City, Randolph Co., IN, after 1867
Buried: Union City Cemetery, Union City, IN
References: Pension File and Military Service File, National Archives. Obituary, *Union City Evening Times*, Feb. 28, 1920. John H. Niebaum. *History of the Pittsburgh Washington Infantry 102nd (Old 13th) Regiment Pennsylvania Veteran Volunteers and its Forebears.* Pittsburgh, PA, 1931. *A Portrait and Biographical Record of Delaware and Randolph Counties, IN.* Chicago, IL, 1894.

James Patchell with officers of the 102nd Pennsylvania Infantry.
Seated, left to right: Patchell, Capt. Luman S. Clark (of 62nd New York), Col. John W. Patterson, and Lt. Col. William McIlwaine. Standing, left to right: Capt. James D. Duncan, Capt. William D. Jones, Capt. James H. Coleman, and Capt. W. Stewart Day.

JOHN PATRICK

Lieutenant Colonel, 66 PA Infantry, Aug. 19, 1861. Colonel, 66 PA Infantry, Jan. 20, 1862. Resigned Feb. 6, 1862.

Born: 1806 PA
Died: Nov. 8, 1873 Omaha, NE
Occupation: Physician, college professor, and newspaper editor
Miscellaneous: Resided Uniontown, Fayette Co., PA; Philadelphia, PA; and Omaha, Douglas Co., NE
Buried: Oak Grove Cemetery, Uniontown, PA (Section B, Lot 15, family marker)
References: Military Service File, National Archives. *Baptismal, Marriage, Burial Roster of Trinity Cathedral Episcopal Church, Omaha, NE.* N.p., 1944. Obituary, *Uniontown American Standard*, Nov. 13, 1873. Funeral account, *Omaha Daily Herald*, Nov. 11, 1873.

JOHN WILLIAMS PATTERSON

Captain, Co. B, 13 PA Infantry, April 25, 1861. Honorably mustered out, Aug. 6, 1861. Captain, Co. E, 102 PA Infantry, Aug. 16, 1861. GSW left breast, Fair Oaks, VA, May 31, 1862. Major, 102 PA Infantry, July 3, 1862. Lieutenant Colonel, 102 PA Infantry, Jan. 16, 1863. Taken prisoner, Salem Heights, VA, May 4, 1863. Confined Libby Prison, Richmond, VA. Paroled May 23, 1863. Colonel, 102 PA Infantry, May 27, 1863. GSW head, Wilderness, VA, May 5, 1864.

Born: May 4, 1835 Pittsburgh, PA
Died: May 5, 1864 KIA Wilderness, VA
Occupation: Civil engineer
Miscellaneous: Resided Pittsburgh, PA
Buried: Southside Cemetery, Pittsburgh, PA (Section 31, Plot 200)
References: Research Files of William A. Phillis. "Civil War Letters of Colonel John W. Patterson and Almira Wendt Patterson," *Michigan Genealogical Records*, Series 2, Volume 12. N.p., 1990. Military Service File, National Archives. John H. Niebaum. *History of the Pittsburgh Washington Infantry 102nd (Old 13th) Regiment Pennsylvania Veteran Volunteers and its Forebears.* Pittsburgh, PA, 1931. John N. Boucher. *A Century and a Half of Pittsburgh and Her People.* New York City, NY, 1908.

John Williams Patterson
WILLIAM A. PHILLIS COLLECTION.
T. H. MCBRIDE, ARTIST, NO. 64 FOURTH ST., PITTSBURGH, PA.

LEWIS B. PIERCE

Lieutenant Colonel, 12 PA Cavalry, Nov. 7, 1861. Colonel, 12 PA Cavalry, April 21, 1862. Commanded Post of Manassas, VA, May–Aug. 1862. Acting AIG, Staff of Major Gen. Robert H. Milroy, April–June 1863. Commanded Post of Martinsburg, WV, Sept.–Nov. 1863. Dismissed Aug. 7, 1864, for "utter worthlessness and inefficiency as an officer." Restored to command, Oct. 15, 1864, upon the recommendation of a Military Commission, which found that his dismissal was "founded on insufficient evidence." Mustered out Dec. 15, 1864, "for incompetency, upon the recommendation of the Commanding General, Middle Military Division."

Born: Sept. 2, 1831 LeRaysville, Bradford Co., PA
Died: Oct. 30, 1876 Baltimore, MD
Education: M.D., Geneva (NY) Medical College, 1870

Lewis B. Pierce
RONN PALM COLLECTION.
F. GUTEKUNST, PHOTOGRAPHER, 704 & 706 ARCH STREET,
PHILADELPHIA, PA.

Occupation: Merchant and farmer before war. Received medical education but did not practice. General agent of the Phoenix Mutual Life Insurance Co. after war.

Offices/Honors: Auditor of Public Accounts, Bradford Co., PA, 1858–61

Miscellaneous: Resided LeRaysville, Bradford Co., PA, before war; and Baltimore, MD, after war

Buried: LeRaysville Borough Cemetery, LeRaysville, PA

References: H. C. Bradsby. *History of Bradford County, PA.* Chicago, IL, 1891. Obituary, *Baltimore Sun*, Oct. 31, 1876. Military Service File, National Archives. Eugene F. Cordell. *The Medical Annals of Maryland.* Baltimore, MD, 1903. Larry B. Maier. *Leather & Steel: The 12th Pennsylvania Cavalry in the Civil War.* Shippensburg, PA, 2001. Letters Received, Volunteer Service Branch, Adjutant General's Office, File W1814(VS)1864, National Archives.

JAMES REED PORTER

Captain, Co. B, 11 PA Reserves, June 10, 1861. Lieutenant Colonel, 11 PA Reserves, July 1, 1861. Resigned Oct. 22, 1861, due to physical disability from rheumatism. Colonel, 135 PA Infantry, Aug. 19, 1862. Commanded 1 Brigade, 3 Division, 1 Army Corps, Army of the Potomac, Feb. 17–March 28, 1863. Honorably mustered out, May 24, 1863. Colonel, 57 PA Militia, July 8, 1863. Honorably mustered out, Aug. 17, 1863.

Born: 1825? Westmoreland Co., PA
Died: March 9, 1895 Dayton, OH
Occupation: Saltworks superintendent and merchant before war. Short term as Deputy Internal Revenue Collector after war.
Offices/Honors: Prothonotary, Indiana Co., PA, 1857–61
Miscellaneous: Resided Saltsburg, Indiana Co., PA; Indiana, Indiana Co., PA; Harrisburg, Dauphin Co., PA; Pittsburgh, PA; Dayton, OH; and Piqua, Miami Co., OH

Buried: Forest Hill Cemetery, Piqua, OH (Section 7, Lot 13)

James Reed Porter
COURTESY OF OLAF.
R. W. ADDIS, PHOTOGRAPHER, 308 PENNA. AVENUE,
WASHINGTON, DC.

References: Clarence D. Stephenson. *Indiana County 175th Anniversary History.* Indiana, PA, 1983. Pension File and Military Service File, National Archives. Joseph Gibbs. *Three Years in the Bloody Eleventh: The Campaigns of a Pennsylvania Reserves Regiment.* University Park, PA, 2002. Letters Received, Volunteer Service Branch, Adjutant General's Office, File S1408(VS)1863, National Archives. Manuscript biography, Samuel Penniman Bates Papers, Pennsylvania State Archives.

JOHN MITCHELL POWER

Lieutenant Colonel, 3 PA Infantry, April 20, 1861. Honorably mustered out, July 29, 1861. Colonel, 76 PA Infantry, Aug. 10, 1861. Resigned Aug. 7, 1862, "on account of ill health" due to "anemia and functional disease of the heart."

Born: Aug. 1829 Venango Co., PA
Died: Sept. 10, 1897 Old Orchard, St. Louis Co., MO
Occupation: Charcoal furnace operator, oil operator, and ironworks bookkeeper
Miscellaneous: Resided Johnstown, Cambria Co., PA, before war; New Castle, Lawrence Co., PA, to 1884; and Old Orchard, St. Louis Co., MO, after 1884
Buried: Greenwood Cemetery, New Castle, PA (Section G, Lot 78, unmarked)
References: Pension File and Military Service File, National Archives. Death Notice, *St. Louis Globe-Democrat,* Sept. 12, 1897. Obituary, *New Castle News,* Sept. 11, 1897.

MATTHEW STANLEY QUAY

1 Lieutenant, Co. F, 10 PA Reserves, April 25, 1861. Appointed Assistant Commissary General of PA, July 5, 1861. Colonel, 134 PA Infantry, Aug. 23, 1862. Resigned Dec. 7, 1862, "on account of continued ill health" due to typho-malarial fever. Volunteer ADC, Staff of Brig. Gen. Erastus B. Tyler, Dec. 13, 1862. Military Secretary to PA Governor Andrew G. Curtin, 1863–65.

Born: Sept. 30, 1833 Dillsburg, PA
Died: May 28, 1904 Beaver, PA
Education: Graduated Jefferson College, Canonsburg, PA, 1850
Occupation: Lawyer
Offices/Honors: PA House of Representatives, 1865–67. Secretary of the (PA) Commonwealth, 1873–78, 1879–82. PA Treasurer, 1885–87. US Senate, 1887–1904. Medal of Honor, Fredericksburg, VA,

Matthew Stanley Quay
FROM *UNDER THE MALTESE CROSS: ANTIETAM TO APPOMATTOX: CAMPAIGNS 155TH PENNSYLVANIA REGIMENT.*

Dec. 13, 1862. "Although out of service, he voluntarily resumed duty on the eve of the battle and took a conspicuous part in the charge on the heights."
Miscellaneous: Resided Beaver, Beaver Co., PA; and Washington, DC
Buried: Beaver Cemetery, Beaver, PA
References: *Dictionary of American Biography.* James A. Kehl. *Boss Rule in the Gilded Age.* Pittsburgh, PA, 1981. Joseph H. Bausman. *History of Beaver County, PA.* New York City, NY, 1904. John W. Oliver. "Matthew Stanley Quay," *The Western Pennsylvania Historical Magazine,* Vol. 17, No. 1 (March 1934). *History of Beaver County, PA.* Philadelphia and Chicago, 1888. St. Clair A. Mulholland. *Military Order Congress Medal of Honor Legion of the United States.* Philadelphia, PA, 1905. Samuel P. Bates. *Martial Deeds of Pennsylvania.* Philadelphia, PA, 1875. *Biographical Directory of the American Congress.* Letters Received, Volunteer Service Branch, Adjutant General's Office, File Q91(VS)1863, National Archives. Military Service File, National Archives. *Under the Maltese Cross: Antietam to Appomattox: Campaigns 155th Pennsylvania Regiment.* Pittsburgh, PA, 1910. *Companions of the Military Order of the Loyal Legion of the United States.* New York City, NY, 1901.

Lewis Waln Ralston
LEACH'S PHILADELPHIA PORTRAITS,
THE HISTORICAL SOCIETY OF PENNSYLVANIA.

LEWIS WALN RALSTON

1 Lieutenant, Co. F, 109 PA Infantry, Feb. 12, 1862. GSW abdomen, Cedar Mountain, VA, Aug. 9, 1862. Captain, Co. A, 109 PA Infantry, Oct. 14, 1862. Lieutenant Colonel, 109 PA Infantry, Oct. 25, 1862. *Colonel,* 109 PA Infantry, May 4, 1863. Volunteer ADC, Staff of Colonel George A. Cobham, Jr., commanding 2 Brigade, 2 Division, 12 Army Corps, Army of the Cumberland, Nov. 1863. Commanded 2 Brigade, 2 Division, 12 Army Corps, Dec. 27, 1863–Jan. 24, 1864. Dismissed April 12, 1864, for "absence without leave from the General Rendezvous for Veteran Volunteers at Chester Hospital from the 11th of March to the 24th of March, 1864." Dismissal revoked, July 8, 1864, and he was honorably discharged to date April 12, 1864.

Born: Aug. 26, 1832 Philadelphia, PA
Died: Feb. 7, 1873 Philadelphia, PA
Education: Attended University of Pennsylvania, Philadelphia, PA (Class of 1851)
Occupation: Iron broker
Miscellaneous: Resided Philadelphia, PA

Buried: Churchyard of St. James the Less, Philadelphia, PA (Lot 61)
References: *University of Pennsylvania: Biographical Catalogue of the Matriculates of the College.* Philadelphia, PA, 1894. Death Notice, *Philadelphia Evening Bulletin,* Feb. 8, 1873. J. Robert T. Craine, compiler. *The Ancestry and Posterity of Matthew Clarkson (1664–1702).* N.p., 1971. Military Service File, National Archives. Letters Received, Volunteer Service Branch, Adjutant General's Office, File G387(VS)1864, National Archives.

WILLIAM RICKARDS, JR.

Captain, Co. I, 29 PA Infantry, June 6, 1861. Shell wound right shoulder, Winchester, VA, May 25, 1862. Taken prisoner, Winchester, VA, May 25, 1862. Confined Libby Prison, Richmond, VA, and Salisbury (NC) Prison. Paroled Aug. 17, 1862. Lieutenant Colonel, 29 PA Infantry, Oct. 4, 1862. Colonel, 29 PA Infantry, April 24, 1863. Commanded 3 Brigade, 2 Division, 20 Army Corps, Army of the Cumberland, May 15–16, 1864. GSW left breast, Pine Knob, GA, June 15, 1864. Dismissed July 8, 1864, for "making application to be mustered out, by reason of expiration of term of service, after having availed himself of the veteran furlough granted his regiment, his command at the time being in front of the enemy." Dismissal revoked, July 28, 1864. Honorably discharged, Nov. 2, 1864, on account of physical disability from wounds received in action.

Born: Nov. 18, 1824 Philadelphia, PA
Died: May 25, 1900 Franklin, PA
Occupation: Jewelry manufacturer before the war. After the war engaged in the oil business until 1873, when he became a dentist.
Miscellaneous: Resided Philadelphia, PA, to 1865; and Franklin, Venango Co., PA, after 1865
Buried: Franklin Cemetery, Franklin, PA
References: Pension File and Military Service File, National Archives. H. H. Hardesty. *Presidents, Soldiers, Statesmen.* Western Pennsylvania Edition. New York, Toledo and Chicago, 1896. John W. Jordan, editor. *Genealogical and Personal History of the Allegheny Valley, PA.* New York City, NY, 1913. Herbert C. Bell, editor. *History of Venango County, PA; Its Past and Present.* Chicago, IL, 1890. Samuel P. Bates. *Martial Deeds of Pennsylvania.* Philadelphia, PA, 1875. Letters Received, Volunteer Service Branch, Adjutant General's Office, File K525(VS)1864, National Archives.

ROBERT BRUCE RICKETTS

1 Lieutenant, Battery F, 1 PA Light Artillery, July 8, 1861. Captain, Battery F, 1 PA Light Artillery, March 16, 1863. Major, 1 PA Light Artillery, June 28, 1864. *Colonel*, 1 PA Light Artillery, March 15, 1865. Honorably discharged, July 3, 1865. Bvt. Colonel, USV, March 13, 1865, for gallant and meritorious services during the recent rebellion.

Born: April 29, 1839 Orangeville, PA
Died: Nov. 13, 1918 near Ganoga Lake, Sullivan Co., PA
Education: Attended Wyoming Seminary, Kingston, PA
Occupation: Lumber manufacturer and land speculator
Miscellaneous: Resided Wilkes-Barre, Luzerne Co., PA. Brother of Colonel William W. Ricketts.
Buried: Family Cemetery, North Mountain, Ricketts Glen State Park, PA
References: Horace E. Hayden, Alfred Hand & John W. Jordan, editors. *Genealogical and Family History of the Wyoming and Lackawanna Valleys, PA.* New York and Chicago, 1906. Lephia French Oncley. *Our Ricketts Cousins.* Ann Arbor, MI, 1987. Richard A. Sauers and Peter Tomasak. *Ricketts' Battery: A History of Battery F, 1st PA Light Artillery.* Wilkes-Barre, PA, 2001. Letters Received, Volunteer Service Branch, Adjutant General's Office, File R551(VS)1862, National Archives. William H. Powell, editor. *Officers of the Army and Navy (Volunteer) Who Served in the Civil War.* Philadelphia, PA, 1893. Josiah R. Sypher. *History of the Pennsylvania Reserve Corps.* Lancaster, PA, 1865. Oscar J. Harvey and Ernest G. Smith. *A History of Wilkes-Barre, Luzerne County, PA.* Wilkes-Barre, PA, 1929. *Companions of the Military Order of the Loyal Legion of the United States.* New York City, NY, 1901.

Robert Bruce Ricketts
USAMHI.
J. E. McCLEES, ARTIST, 910 CHESTNUT STREET, PHILADELPHIA, PA.

WILLIAM WALLACE RICKETTS

Colonel, 6 PA Reserves, June 22, 1861. Discharged for disability, Feb. 27, 1862, due to "a severe and long continued attack of typhoid fever."

Born: Jan. 22, 1837 Rohrsburg, Columbia Co., PA
Died: Aug. 10, 1862 Orangeville, PA
Education: Attended US Military Academy, West Point, NY (Class of 1860). Graduated Philadelphia (PA) Medical College, 1860.
Occupation: Physician
Miscellaneous: Resided Orangeville, Columbia Co., PA. Brother of Colonel Robert B. Ricketts.
Buried: Laurel Hill Cemetery, Orangeville, PA
References: Josiah R. Sypher. *History of the Pennsylvania Reserve Corps.* Lancaster, PA, 1865. Lephia French Oncley. *Our Ricketts Cousins.* Ann Arbor, MI, 1987. Pension File and Military Service File, National Archives.

OLIVER HAZZARD RIPPEY

Lieutenant Colonel, 7 PA Infantry, April 23, 1861. Honorably mustered out, July 23, 1861. Colonel, 61 PA Infantry, July 24, 1861. GSW Fair Oaks, VA, May 31, 1862.

Born: Aug. 19, 1825 Pittsburgh, PA
Died: May 31, 1862 KIA Fair Oaks, VA
Education: Attended Western University (now University of Pittsburgh), Pittsburgh, PA. Attended Allegheny College, Meadville, PA.
Other Wars: Mexican War (Private, Co. K, 1 PA Infantry)
Occupation: Lawyer
Miscellaneous: Resided Pittsburgh, PA
Buried: Allegheny Cemetery, Pittsburgh, PA (Section 12, Lot 22)

Oliver Hazzard Rippey

From Under the Maltese Cross: Antietam to Appomattox: Campaigns 155th Pennsylvania Regiment.

References: Samuel P. Bates. *Martial Deeds of Pennsylvania*. Philadelphia, PA, 1875. Obituary, *New York Daily Tribune*, June 5, 1862. A. T. Brewer. *History 61st Regiment Pennsylvania Volunteers, 1861–65*. Pittsburgh, PA, 1911. Military Service File, National Archives.

RICHARD BIDDLE ROBERTS

Captain, Co. I, 12 PA Infantry, April 15, 1861. Lieutenant Colonel, ADC, Staff of PA Governor Andrew G. Curtin, April 25, 1861. Colonel, 1 PA Reserves, June 9, 1861. Provost Marshal, Washington, DC, March 1862. Commanded 1 Brigade, 3 Division, 5 Army Corps, Army of the Potomac, June 30–July 5, 1862. Nominated as Brig. Gen., USV, July 15, 1862, but the US Senate adjourned without acting on the nomination. Commanded 1 Brigade, 3 Division, 1 Army Corps, Army of the Potomac, Sept. 17–29, 1862. Resigned Nov. 1, 1862, "having been tendered a position in Pennsylvania under the military organization of that state by his Excellency Governor Curtin which he desires me to accept at once and which I do not feel myself at liberty to decline." Continuing on Governor Curtin's staff with the rank of colonel until April 10, 1866, he served as State Military Agent in Washington, DC, from April 27, 1863 to Dec. 31, 1863 and later had charge of the issuance of commissions to Pennsylvania officers.

Born: Aug. 25, 1825 Pittsburgh, PA
Died: April 19, 1886 Chicago, IL
Occupation: Lawyer
Offices/Honors: US District Attorney, Western District of Pennsylvania, 1857–61
Miscellaneous: Resided Pittsburgh, PA; and Chicago, IL, after 1869
Buried: Allegheny Cemetery, Pittsburgh, PA (Section 1, Lot 60)

Richard Biddle Roberts

References: Josiah R. Sypher. *History of the Pennsylvania Reserve Corps*. Lancaster, PA, 1865. Samuel P. Bates. *Martial Deeds of Pennsylvania*. Philadelphia, PA, 1875. Pension File and Military Service File, National Archives. Obituary, *Chicago Daily Tribune*, April 20, 1886. Obituary, *Philadelphia Times*, April 21, 1886. *Annual Report of the Adjutant General of Pennsylvania for the Year 1866*. Harrisburg, PA, 1867.

RICHARD PETIT ROBERTS

Captain, Co. F, 140 PA Infantry, Aug. 21, 1862. Colonel, 140 PA Infantry, Sept. 8, 1862. Commanded 3 Brigade, 1 Division, 2 Army Corps, Army of the Potomac, Jan. 24–Feb. 12, 1863. GSW heart, Gettysburg, PA, July 2, 1863.

Born: June 5, 1820 near Frankfort Springs, Beaver Co., PA
Died: July 2, 1863 KIA Gettysburg, PA
Occupation: Lawyer
Miscellaneous: Resided Beaver, Beaver Co., PA
Buried: Beaver Cemetery, Beaver, PA

Richard Petit Roberts

References: Samuel P. Bates. *Martial Deeds of Pennsylvania*. Philadelphia, PA, 1875. *History of Beaver County, PA*. Philadelphia and Chicago, 1888. Joseph H. Bausman. *History of Beaver County, PA*. New York City, NY, 1904. Robert L. Stewart. *History of the 140th Regiment Pennsylvania Volunteers*. Philadelphia, PA, 1912.

CHAUNCEY P. ROGERS

2 Lieutenant, Co. C, Erie Regiment, PA Infantry, April 21, 1861. Honorably discharged, July 25, 1861. 1 Lieutenant, Co. D, 83 PA Infantry, Aug. 26, 1861. GSW right shoulder, right knee and right foot, Malvern Hill, VA, July 1, 1862. Acting ADC, 3 Brigade, 1 Division, 5 Army Corps, Army of the Potomac, Oct.–Dec. 1863. Captain, Co. D, 83 PA Infantry, March 28, 1864. Lieutenant Colonel, 83 PA Infantry, Nov. 10, 1864. Colonel, 83 PA Infantry, March 7, 1865. Honorably mustered out, June 28, 1865.

Born: Oct. 28, 1838 Springfield, Erie Co., PA
Died: Feb. 20, 1920 Corry, PA

Chauncey P. Rogers

Richard Biddle Roberts with members of Governor Curtin's military staff, left to right: Roberts, Col. Francis Jordan, Col. John A. Wright, Commissary General William W. Irwin, Governor Andrew G. Curtin, Col. Samuel B. Thomas, Quartermaster General James L. Reynolds, Inspector General Lemuel Todd, Adjutant General Alexander L. Russell, and Surgeon General Joseph A. Phillips).

Occupation: Bookkeeper and surveyor before war. Civil engineer after war.

Offices/Honors: PA House of Representatives, 1872. Prothonotary, Erie Co., PA, 1873–76.

Miscellaneous: Resided Edinboro, Erie Co., PA; Corry, Erie Co., PA; Titusville, Crawford Co., PA; Memphis, TN; Richmond, VA; and Mechanicsburg, Cumberland Co., PA

Buried: Pine Grove Cemetery, Corry, PA

References: *History of Erie County, PA.* Chicago, IL, 1884. Obituary, *Erie Dispatch*, Feb. 22, 1920. Michael Schellhammer. *The 83rd Pennsylvania Volunteers in the Civil War.* Jefferson, NC, 2003. Amos M. Judson. *History of the 83rd Regiment Pennsylvania Volunteers.* Erie, PA, 1865. Pension File and Military Service File, National Archives.

ISAAC ROGERS

1 Lieutenant, Co. B, 110 PA Infantry, Sept. 7, 1861. Captain, Co. B, 110 PA Infantry, Dec. 1, 1862. Chief of Pioneers, 2 Brigade, 3 Division, 3 Army Corps, Army of the Potomac, Dec. 1862. Major, 110 PA Infantry, Dec. 21, 1862. Lieutenant Colonel, 110 PA Infantry, Oct. 10, 1863. *Colonel*, 110 PA Infantry, April 23, 1864. GSW right thigh (amputated), Spotsylvania, VA, May 12, 1864.

Isaac Rogers
ROGER D. HUNT COLLECTION, USAMHI.

Born: Nov. 5, 1834 Cromwell Twp., Huntingdon Co., PA

Died: May 23, 1864 DOW Fredericksburg, VA

Occupation: Farmer

Miscellaneous: Resided Orbisonia, Huntingdon Co., PA. Although the spelling "Rodgers" is on his gravestone and his father used the same spelling, the colonel used the spelling "Rogers."

Buried: Orbisonia Cemetery, Orbisonia, PA

References: Samuel P. Bates. *Martial Deeds of Pennsylvania.* Philadelphia, PA, 1875. Pension File and Military Service File, National Archives. *A Civil War Remembrance at the Grave of Colonel Isaac Rogers.* N.p., 1988. Obituary, *Huntingdon Globe*, June 8, 1864.

HENRY ROYER

1 Lieutenant, Co. H, 96 PA Infantry, Sept. 23, 1861. Captain, Co. H, 96 PA Infantry, March 1, 1862. Resigned Jan. 11, 1863. Colonel, 53 PA Militia, July 13, 1863. Honorably mustered out, Aug. 20, 1863.

Born: July 9, 1837 Trappe, PA

Died: Feb. 13, 1903 Denver, CO

Education: Graduated Yale University, New Haven, CT, 1858

Henry Royer (postwar)
CIVIL WAR LIBRARY & MUSEUM, PHILADELPHIA, PA.

Occupation: Lawyer before war. Dry goods merchant after war.

Miscellaneous: Resided Pottsville, Schuylkill Co., PA; and Denver, CO, after 1893

Buried: Charles Baber Cemetery, Pottsville, PA (Section Y, Lot 3)

References: Obituary Circular, Whole No. 549, Pennsylvania MOLLUS. Aldice G. Warren, editor. *Catalogue of the Delta Kappa Epsilon Fraternity.* New York City, NY, 1910. William P. Bacon. *Fourth Biographical Record of the Class of Fifty-Eight, Yale University.* New Britain, CT, 1897. Obituary, *Pottsville Miners' Journal*, Feb. 17, 1903. Obituary, *Pottsville Daily Republican*, Feb. 16, 1903. Pension File and Military Service File, National Archives. Obituary, *Rocky Mountain News*, Feb. 15, 1903.

RICHARD HENRY RUSH

Colonel, 6 PA Cavalry, July 27, 1861. Commanded 3 Brigade, Pleasanton's Cavalry Division, Army of the Potomac, Sept.–Nov. 1862. Detailed as Assistant to the Provost Marshal General, in charge of the organization of the Veteran Reserve Corps, May 10, 1863. Resigned Sept. 29, 1863, to accept appointment in Veteran Reserve Corps. Colonel, 1 VRC, Oct. 1, 1863. Commanded Rock Island (IL) Prison, Nov.–Dec. 1863.

Richard Henry Rush
KEN TURNER COLLECTION.
F. GUTEKUNST, PHOTOGRAPHER, 704 & 706 ARCH STREET, PHILADELPHIA, PA.

Richard Henry Rush
RONN PALM COLLECTION.
BROADBENT & CO., 814 CHESTNUT STREET, PHILADELPHIA, PA.

Commanded 1 Brigade, Veteran Reserve Corps, District of Washington, 22 Army Corps, Department of Washington, March 23–May 21, 1864. Resigned July 1, 1864.

Born: Jan. 14, 1825 London, England

Died: Oct. 17, 1893 Philadelphia, PA

Education: Graduated US Military Academy, West Point, NY, 1846

Other Wars: Mexican War (1 Lieutenant, 2 US Artillery)

Occupation: Regular Army (1 Lieutenant, 2 US Artillery, resigned July 1, 1854). Gentleman of leisure.

Miscellaneous: Resided Philadelphia, PA. Descended from two Signers of the Declaration of Independence, being the grandson of Benjamin Rush, who married the daughter of Richard Stockton.

Buried: Laurel Hill Cemetery, Philadelphia, PA (Section P, Lots 37/40)

References: *Annual Reunion*, Association of the Graduates of the US Military Academy, 1894. Frederick W. Pyne. *Descendants of the Signers of the Declaration of Independence*. Camden, ME, 1998. Letters Received, Volunteer Service Branch, Adjutant General's Office, File P615(VS)1863, National Archives. Samuel L. Gracey. *Annals of the 6th Pennsylvania Cavalry*. Philadelphia, PA, 1868. George W. Cullum. *Biographical Register of the Officers and Graduates of the US Military Academy*. Third Edition. Boston and New York, 1891. Military Service File, National Archives. Obituary, *Philadelphia Public Ledger*, Oct. 18, 1893.

William Wilkins Sanders

WILLIAM WILKINS SANDERS

1 Lieutenant, 6 US Infantry, May 9, 1861. 1 Lieutenant, Adjutant, 6 US Infantry, Dec. 1, 1861. Captain, 6 US Infantry, June 27, 1862. GSW Chancellorsville, VA, May 1, 1863. Acting ADC and Commissary of Musters, Staff of Major Gen. George G. Meade, July 1863–March 1865. Chief Commissary of Musters, Army of the Potomac, Feb. 17, 1865. Colonel, 2 PA Cavalry, March 26, 1865. Colonel, 1 PA Provisional Cavalry, June 17, 1865. Honorably mustered out, July 13, 1865. Lieutenant Colonel, 1 US Veteran Volunteer Infantry, Aug. 4, 1865. Honorably mustered out of volunteer service, March 1, 1866. Bvt. Colonel, USA, April 9, 1865, for gallant and meritorious services in the campaign terminating with the surrender of the insurgent army under General Robert E. Lee.

Born: Oct. 8, 1839 Pittsburgh, PA

Died: Jan. 26, 1883 Fort Snelling, MN

Occupation: Regular Army (Major, 8 US Infantry, died Jan. 26, 1883)

Miscellaneous: Resided Pittsburgh, PA; and Philadelphia, PA

Buried: Woodlands Cemetery, Philadelphia, PA (Section L, Lots 187–189)

References: Letters Received, Appointment, Commission and Personal Branch, Adjutant General's Office, File 2307(ACP)1876, National Archives. Anna V. Parker. *The Sanders Family of Grass Hills*. Madison, IN, 1966. Guy V. Henry. *Military Record of Civilian Appointments in the United States Army*. New York City, NY, 1869. Letters Received, Volunteer Service Branch, Adjutant General's Office, File S949(VS)1865, National Archives.

EDWIN SCHALL

Major, 4 PA Infantry, April 20, 1861. Honorably mustered out, July 26, 1861. Major, 51 PA Infantry, July 27, 1861. Lieutenant Colonel, 51 PA Infantry, Sept. 17, 1862. Commanded 2 Brigade, 2 Division, 9 Army Corps, Army of the Ohio, Aug. 22–Dec. 12, 1863. *Colonel*, 51 PA Infantry, May 13, 1864. GSW neck, Cold Harbor, VA, June 3, 1864.

Born: Feb. 15, 1835 Marlborough Twp., Montgomery Co., PA

Died: June 3, 1864 KIA Cold Harbor, VA

Education: Attended Norwich (VT) University. Graduated Ohio State Law College, Cleveland, OH.

Occupation: Lawyer and newspaper editor

Edwin Schall

Miscellaneous: Resided Norristown, Montgomery Co., PA

Buried: Montgomery Cemetery, Norristown, PA (Section B, Lots 218–221)

References: Samuel P. Bates. *Martial Deeds of Pennsylvania.* Philadelphia, PA, 1875. M. Auge. *Lives of the Eminent Dead of Montgomery County, PA.* Norristown, PA, 1879. Obituary, *Army and Navy Journal,* June 25, 1864. Thomas H. Parker. *History of the 51st Regiment of Pennsylvania Volunteers and Veteran Volunteers.* Philadelphia, PA, 1869.

JOHN W. SCHALL

1 Lieutenant, Co. K, 2 PA Infantry, April 20, 1861. Honorably mustered out, July 26, 1861. Captain, Co. K, 87 PA Infantry, Aug. 24, 1861. Lieutenant Colonel, 87 PA Infantry, Sept. 14, 1861. Colonel, 87 PA Infantry, May 9, 1863. Commanded 3 Brigade, 3 Division, 3 Army Corps, Army of the Potomac, Aug. 28–Sept. 17, 1863. Commanded 1 Brigade, 3 Division, 6 Army Corps, Army of the Potomac, May 13–14, 1864 and June 2–3, 1864. GSW right arm, Cold Harbor, VA, June 3, 1864. Honorably mustered out, Oct. 13, 1864.

Born: June 22, 1834 Dale, Berks Co., PA
Died: April 16, 1920 Norristown, PA
Education: Attended Norwich (VT) University (Class of 1855)

Other Wars: Spanish American War (Colonel, 6 PA Infantry)
Occupation: Civil engineer and dry goods merchant before war. Iron manufacturer and Philadelphia Custom House inspector after war.
Offices/Honors: Recorder of Deeds, Montgomery Co., PA, 1875–82. Postmaster, Norristown, PA, 1890–94. Served 37 years as officer in Pennsylvania National Guard, retiring as Major Gen., Sept. 1, 1907.
Miscellaneous: Resided York, York Co., PA; and Norristown, Montgomery Co., PA
Buried: Montgomery Cemetery, Norristown, PA
References: Pension File, National Archives. George R. Prowell. *History of the 87th Regiment, Pennsylvania Volunteers.* York, PA, 1901. William A. Ellis, editor. *History of Norwich University, 1819–1911.* Montpelier, VT, 1911. Henry W. Ruoff, editor. *Biographical and Portrait Cyclopedia of Montgomery County, PA.* Philadelphia, PA, 1895. Ellwood Roberts, editor. *Biographical Annals of Montgomery County, PA.* New York and Chicago, 1904. Obituary, *Philadelphia Public Ledger,* April 17, 1920. Moses King. *Philadelphia and Notable Philadelphians.* New York City, NY, 1902. William P. Clarke. *Official History of the Militia and the National Guard of the State of Pennsylvania.* N.p., 1909.

John W. Schall

MATTHEW SCHLAUDECKER

Major, Erie Regiment, PA Infantry, April 27, 1861. Honorably discharged, July 16, 1861. Lieutenant Colonel, 111 PA Infantry, Sept. 2, 1861. Colonel, 111 PA Infantry, Jan. 24, 1862. Commanded 2 Brigade, 2 Division, 2 Army Corps, Army of Virginia, Aug. 12–30, 1862. Resigned Nov. 6, 1862, "on account of disability" due to intermittent fever.

Born: July 10, 1829 Rulzheim, Bavaria
Died: Sept. 20, 1907 San Francisco, CA (committed suicide by cutting his throat with a razor)
Occupation: Merchant
Offices/Honors: Major Gen., PA Militia, before war
Miscellaneous: Resided Erie, Erie Co., PA; and San Francisco, CA
Buried: San Francisco National Cemetery, San Francisco, CA (Section OS, Plot 63, Grave 1)

Matthew Schlaudecker
RONN PALM COLLECTION.
P. L. PERKINS, 99 BALTIMORE STREET,
OPPOSITE HOLLIDAY STREET, BALTIMORE, MD.

References: Obituary Circular, Whole No. 871, California MOLLUS. John R. Boyle. *Soldiers True: The Story of the 111th Regiment Pennsylvania Veteran Volunteers.* New York and Cincinnati, 1903. Military Service File, National Archives. Obituary, *San Francisco Chronicle*, Sept. 21, 1907.

JAMES MARTINUS SCHOONMAKER

Quartermaster Sergeant, Co. G, 1 MD Cavalry, Aug. 25, 1861. Sergeant Major, 1 MD Cavalry, June 1, 1862. 2 Lieutenant, Co. A, 1 MD Cavalry, July 19, 1862. Resigned Aug. 4, 1862. Colonel, 14 PA Cavalry, Nov. 24, 1862. Commanded 2 Brigade, 4 Division, Army of West Virginia, Dec. 1863–April 1864. Commanded 2 Brigade, 2 Cavalry Division, Army of West Virginia, April 26–May 1864. Commanded 1 Brigade, 2 Cavalry Division, Army of West Virginia, June 6–9, 1864 and July–Oct. 1864. Honorably discharged, July 31, 1865, upon consolidation of the regiment into a battalion of six companies.

James Martinus Schoonmaker
RONN PALM COLLECTION.
C. D. FREDRICKS & CO., 587 BROADWAY, NEW YORK.

Born: June 30, 1842 Pittsburgh, PA
Died: Oct. 11, 1927 Pittsburgh, PA
Education: Attended Western University (now University of Pittsburgh), Pittsburgh, PA
Occupation: Railroad executive, banker, coal operator and coke manufacturer
Offices/Honors: Medal of Honor, Winchester, VA, Sept. 19, 1864. "At a critical period, gallantly led a cavalry charge against the left of the enemy's line of battle, drove the enemy out of his works, and captured many prisoners."
Miscellaneous: Resided Pittsburgh, PA
Buried: Homewood Cemetery, Pittsburgh, PA (Section 14, Lot 83)
References: Franklin Ellis, editor. *History of Fayette County, PA.* Philadelphia, PA, 1882. Obituary, *Pittsburgh Press,* Oct. 12, 1927. Harrington Emerson. *Col. J. M. Schoonmaker and the Pittsburgh & Lake Erie Railroad.* New York City, NY, 1913. William D. Slease. *The 14th Pennsylvania Cavalry in the Civil War.* Pittsburgh, PA, 1915. St. Clair A. Mulholland. *Military Order Congress Medal of Honor Legion of the United States.* Philadelphia, PA, 1905. Military Service File, National Archives.

Philip Jacob Schopp
PHMC COLLECTION, USAMHI.

PHILIP JACOB SCHOPP

Captain, Co. D, 75 PA Infantry, Aug. 27, 1861. Captain, Acting AAG, Staff of Brig. Gen. Henry Bohlen, Feb. 10–May 15, 1862. Captain, AAG, USV, May 16, 1862. AAG, Staff of Brig. Gen. Henry Bohlen, May 16–Aug. 22, 1862. Resigned Sept. 13, 1862, to accept appointment as colonel. Colonel, 75 PA Infantry, Sept. 14, 1862. Lt. Col. Francis Mahler, being senior in rank and holding a colonel's commission of the same date as Schopp, protested his appointment. In support of Mahler's protest, Maj. Gen. Franz Sigel refused to allow Schopp to take command of the regiment, and he was honorably discharged, Nov. 7, 1862.

Born: Aug. 16, 1827 Orb, Bavaria
Died: Feb. 8, 1893 Greenville, OH
Occupation: Civil engineer
Miscellaneous: Resided Reading, Berks Co., PA; and Greenville, Darke Co., OH
Buried: Greenville Cemetery, Greenville, OH
References: Pension File and Military Service File, National Archives. Letters Received, Volunteer Service Branch, Adjutant General's Office, File S1357(VS)1862, National Archives. Obituary, *Greenville Democrat,* Feb. 15, 1893.

JOHN SMYTHE SCHULTZE

1 Lieutenant, RQM, 93 PA Infantry, Oct. 28, 1861. Acting Quartermaster, Staff of Brig. Gen. John J. Peck, May–June 1862. Acting Quartermaster and Acting ADC, Staff of Major Gen. Darius N. Couch, Nov. 1862–April 1863. GSW Fredericksburg, VA, Dec. 13, 1862. Captain, ADC, USV, April 25, 1863. ADC, Staff of Maj. Gen. Darius N. Couch, April–June 1863. Major, AAG, USV, June 23, 1863. AAG, Staff of Maj. Gen. Darius N. Couch, commanding Department of the Susquehanna, June 25, 1863–Dec. 1864. *Colonel,* 187 PA Infantry, April 1, 1864. Declined. AAG, Staff of George Cadwalader, commanding Department of Pennsylvania, Dec. 1864–June 1865. AAG, District of Pennsylvania, Middle Military Department, July–Nov. 1865. Honorably mustered out, Nov. 22, 1865. Bvt. Colonel, USV, March 13, 1865, for faithful and meritorious services.

Born: Sept. 1, 1836 Centre Co., PA
Died: April 8, 1912 Boonton, NJ
Education: Attended Dickinson Seminary, Williamsport, PA
Occupation: Iron works superintendent and lumberman before war. Business agent and trust manager after war.

Offices/Honors: NJ Assembly, 1873. NJ Senate, 1875–77.

Miscellaneous: Resided Lock Haven, Clinton Co., PA; Toms River, Ocean Co., NJ; and Boonton, Morris Co., NJ

Buried: Riverside Cemetery, Toms River, NJ

References: Obituary, *New Jersey Courier,* April 11, 1912. Obituary, *Newark Evening News,* April 9, 1912. *Biographical Encyclopedia of New Jersey of the Nineteenth Century.* Philadelphia, PA, 1877. Letters Received, Commission Branch, Adjutant General's Office, File S1938(CB)1865, National Archives. Military Service File, National Archives. James M. Gibbs. *History of the 1st Battalion Pennsylvania Six Months Volunteers and 187th Regiment Pennsylvania Volunteer Infantry.* Harrisburg, PA, 1905. Letters Received, Volunteer Service Branch, Adjutant General's Office, File E320(VS)1864, National Archives.

William Sergeant
KEN TURNER COLLECTION.
D. C. BURNITE & CO., 110 MARKET STREET, HARRISBURG, PA.

WILLIAM SERGEANT

Captain, 12 US Infantry, May 14, 1861. Colonel, 210 PA Infantry, Sept. 24, 1864. Commanded 3 Brigade, 2 Division, 5 Army Corps, Army of the Potomac, Nov. 1–17, 1864 and Dec. 22, 1864–Feb. 2, 1865. GSW thigh, Gravelly Run, VA, March 31, 1865.

Born: Aug. 29, 1829 Philadelphia, PA

Died: April 11, 1865 DOW James River, VA (en route from City Point, VA, to Fort Monroe, VA)

Education: Graduated Princeton (NJ) University, 1847

Occupation: Lawyer

Offices/Honors: PA House of Representatives, 1853

Miscellaneous: Resided Philadelphia, PA. Brother-in-law of Major Gen. George G. Meade. Brother-in-law of CSA Brig. Gen. Henry A. Wise.

Buried: Laurel Hill Cemetery, Philadelphia, PA (Section L, Lot 1)

References: Henry B. Munn and Alfred Martien, compilers. *Class of 1847. The Centennial Class of the College of New Jersey.* Philadelphia, PA, 1907. *Commemorative Biographical Encyclopedia of Dauphin County, PA.* Chambersburg, PA, 1896. William J. Tenney. *The Military and Naval History of the Rebellion in the United States.* New York City, NY, 1865. William H. Egle. *Pennsylvania Genealogies.* Harrisburg, PA, 1896. Obituary, *Philadelphia Public Ledger,* April 17, 1865. Joseph T. Duryea. *An Oration Commemorative of the Restoration of the Union, with a Tribute to the Alumni and Under-Graduates of the College of New Jersey, Who Fell in the National Struggle.* Philadelphia, PA, 1866. Jennings C. Wise. *Col. John Wise of England and Virginia (1617–1695): His Ancestors and Descendants.* Richmond, VA, 1918.

JAMES SHEAFER

1 Lieutenant, Co. A, 101 PA Infantry, Nov. 28, 1861. Captain, Co. A, 101 PA Infantry, July 21, 1862. Commanded Roanoke Island, NC, July 18–Oct. 1863. Taken prisoner, Plymouth, NC, April 20, 1864. Confined Columbia, SC. Paroled March 1, 1865. Colonel, 101 PA Infantry, May 31, 1865. Honorably mustered out, June 25, 1865.

Born: Nov. 8, 1834 Carlisle, PA

Died: June 22, 1908 Pittsburgh, PA

Occupation: Hatter before war. Jeweler after war.

Miscellaneous: Resided Pittsburgh, PA

James Sheafer
ROGER D. HUNT COLLECTION, USAMHI.
KEET & GEMMILL, CORNER THIRD AND MARKET STREETS,
HARRISBURG, PA.

Buried: Homewood Cemetery, Pittsburgh, PA (Section 7, Lot 60)

References: Pension File and Military Service File, National Archives. John A. Reed. *History of the 101st Regiment Pennsylvania Veteran Volunteer Infantry.* Chicago, IL, 1910. Obituary, *Pittsburgh Dispatch*, June 23, 1908. Letters Received, Volunteer Service Branch, Adjutant General's Office, File S793(VS)1865, National Archives.

PETER SIDES

Captain, Co. A, 57 PA Infantry, Sept. 4, 1861. Lieutenant Colonel, 57 PA Infantry, Sept. 15, 1862. Colonel, 57 PA Infantry, March 12, 1863. GSW left hand, Gettysburg, PA, July 2, 1863. GSW left forearm, Wilderness, VA, May 5, 1864. Discharged for disability, Nov. 28, 1864, due to wounds received in action.

Born: 1820 Philadelphia, PA
Died: Oct. 23, 1878 Philadelphia, PA
Occupation: Merchant
Miscellaneous: Resided Philadelphia, PA
Buried: Lawnview Cemetery, Rockledge, PA (Susquehanna Lawn, Range 57, Grave 39, unmarked)

Peter Sides
COURTESY OF DAVID L. RICHARDS.

References: Pension File and Military Service File, National Archives. Obituary, *Philadelphia Public Ledger*, Oct. 25, 1878. *History of the 57th Regiment, Pennsylvania Veteran Volunteer Infantry.* Meadville, PA, 1904. Edmund J. Raus, Jr. *A Generation on the March: The Union Army at Gettysburg.* Gettysburg, PA, 1996.

SENECA GALUSHA SIMMONS

Colonel, 5 PA Reserves, June 21, 1861. Major, 4 US Infantry, Sept. 9, 1861. Commanded 1 Brigade, 3 Division, 5 Army Corps, Army of the Potomac, June 27–30, 1862. GSW liver and lung, Glendale, VA, June 30, 1862. Taken prisoner, Glendale, VA, June 30, 1862.

Born: Dec. 27, 1808 Windsor, VT
Died: July 1, 1862 DOW Glendale, VA
Education: Graduated Norwich Military Academy, Middletown, CT, 1829. Graduated US Military Academy, West Point, NY, 1834.

Seneca Galusha Simmons
MASSACHUSETTS MOLLUS COLLECTION, USAMHI.
R. W. ADDIS, PHOTOGRAPHER, 308 PENNA. AVENUE, WASHINGTON, DC.

Other Wars: Mexican War (Captain, 7 US Infantry)

Occupation: Regular Army (Major, 4 US Infantry)

Miscellaneous: Resided Pottsville, Schuylkill Co., Pa; and Harrisburg, Dauphin Co., PA

Buried: Probably Richmond National Cemetery, Richmond, VA (removed as an unknown soldier from Oakwood Cemetery, Richmond, VA)

References: *Commemorative Biographical Encyclopedia of Dauphin County, PA.* Chambersburg, PA, 1896. William A. Ellis, editor. *History of Norwich University, 1819–1911.* Montpelier, VT, 1911. *Field and Post-Room*, Vol. 1, No. 2 (Feb. 1886). Josiah R. Sypher. *History of the Pennsylvania Reserve Corps.* Lancaster, PA, 1865. Samuel P. Bates. *Martial Deeds of Pennsylvania.* Philadelphia, PA, 1875. William H. Egle. *History of the Counties of Dauphin and Lebanon in the Commonwealth of Pennsylvania.* Philadelphia, PA, 1883.

William Sinclair
MASSACHUSETTS MOLLUS COLLECTION, USAMHI.

WILLIAM SINCLAIR

1 Lieutenant, 3 US Artillery, April 30, 1861. Colonel, 6 PA Reserves, April 1, 1862. Commanded 1 Brigade, 3 Division, 5 Army Corps, Army of the Potomac, July 5–Aug. 26, 1862. GSW thigh, 2nd Bull Run, VA, Aug. 30, 1862. Commanded 1 Brigade, 3 Division, 1 Army Corps, Army of the Potomac, Nov. 14–Dec. 13, 1862. GSW left foot, Fredericksburg, VA, Dec. 13, 1862. Commanded 1 Brigade, Pennsylvania Reserves Division, 22 Army Corps, Department of Washington, March 29–May 29, 1863. Resigned volunteer commission, June 6, 1863, because "I can get the command of a battery and I wish to serve with the artillery." Acting AIG, 13 Army Corps, Army of the Gulf, July 27–Oct. 12, 1863. Assigned to duty as Lieutenant Colonel, AIG, USV, Oct. 12, 1863–July 3, 1865. AIG, 13 Army Corps, Army of the Gulf, Oct. 12, 1863–June 26, 1864. Captain, 3 US Artillery, Dec. 11, 1865.

Born: Feb. 15, 1835 Woodsfield, OH

Died: Oct. 3, 1905 Washington, DC

Education: Graduated US Military Academy, West Point, NY, 1857

Occupation: Regular Army (Brig. Gen., retired Feb. 13, 1899)

Miscellaneous: Resided Washington, DC

Buried: Arlington National Cemetery, Arlington, VA (Section 1, Lot 156-B)

References: Pension File and Military Service File, National Archives. *Annual Reunion*, Association of the Graduates of the US Military Academy, 1907. Josiah R. Sypher. *History of the Pennsylvania Reserve Corps.* Lancaster, PA, 1865. George W. Cullum. *Biographical Register of the Officers and Graduates of the US Military Academy.* Third Edition. Boston and New York, 1891. Obituary, *Washington Evening Star,* Oct. 4, 1905.

WILLIAM BARTON SIPES

Captain, Co. I, 2 PA Infantry, April 20, 1861. Honorably mustered out, July 26, 1861. Lieutenant Colonel, 7 PA Cavalry, Oct. 31, 1861. Colonel, 7 PA Cavalry, June 25, 1863. Commanded 1 Brigade, 2 Division, Cavalry Corps, Army of the Cumberland, Dec. 1863–Jan. 24, 1864. Commanded Post of Columbia, TN, June–Nov. 1864. Resigned Nov. 30, 1864, due to physical disability from "chronic dyspepsia, nervous debility induced by malarial disease, and irritability of the heart manifested on increased exertion."

Born: 1831 PA

Died: Sept. 4, 1905 Phenix, RI

Occupation: Newspaper editor, lawyer and journalist

Miscellaneous: Resided Pottsville, Schuylkill Co., PA; Harrisburg, Dauphin Co., PA; Philadelphia, PA; and Bath Beach, Kings Co., NY

Buried: Green-Wood Cemetery, Brooklyn, NY (Section 205, Lot 29071)

References: Pension File and Military Service File, National Archives. William B. Sipes. *The 7th Pennsylvania Veteran Volunteer Cavalry, Its Record, Reminiscences and Roster.* Pottsville, PA, 1906. Obituary, *Brooklyn Daily Eagle,* Sept. 6, 1905. Letters Received, Volunteer Service Branch, Adjutant General's Office, File P257(VS)1864, National Archives.

William Barton Sipes
MANUSCRIPT GROUP 218, PENNSYLVANIA STATE ARCHIVES.

WILLIAM GRAHAM SIRWELL

Captain, Co. B, 9 PA Infantry, April 22, 1861. Honorably mustered out, July 24, 1861. Colonel, 78 PA Infantry, Aug. 26, 1861. Commanded 3 Brigade, 2 Division, 14 Army Corps, Army of the Cumberland, June 9–Oct. 10, 1863. Commanded 3 Brigade, 1 Division, 14 Army Corps, Oct. 10–Nov. 17, 1863. Discharged for disability, Nov. 17, 1863, due to chronic otitis, rendering him partially deaf and unfit for field service. Colonel, 78 PA Infantry, March 9, 1864. Honorably mustered out, Nov. 4, 1864.

Born: Aug. 10, 1820 Pittsburgh, PA

Died: Sept. 9, 1885 Kittanning, PA

Occupation: Watch maker and jeweler

William Graham Sirwell
RONN PALM COLLECTION.

William Francis Small
USAMHI.
J. E. MCCLEES, ARTIST, 910 CHESTNUT STREET, PHILADELPHIA, PA.

Miscellaneous: Resided Kittanning, Armstrong Co., PA
Buried: St. Marys Cemetery, Kittanning, PA
References: *Armstrong County: Her People, Past and Present*. Chicago, IL, 1914. Pension File, National Archives. Obituary, *Kittanning Weekly Times*, Sept. 11, 1885. Letters Received, Volunteer Service Branch, Adjutant General's Office, File F175(VS)1862, National Archives. Joseph T. Gibson, editor. *History of the 78th Pennsylvania Volunteer Infantry*. Pittsburgh, PA, 1905. Samuel P. Bates. *Martial Deeds of Pennsylvania*. Philadelphia, PA, 1875. Ron Gancas. *The Gallant Seventy-eighth, Colonel William Sirwell and the Pennsylvania Seventy-eighth*. Plum Boro, PA, 1997.

WILLIAM FRANCIS SMALL

Brig. Gen., PA State Militia. Commanded Washington Brigade, April 1861. Colonel, 26 PA Infantry, May 5, 1861. GSW right leg, Williamsburg, VA, May 5, 1862. On July 9, 1862, he was notified that Special Orders No. 82, Adjutant General's Office, dated April 15, 1862, had discharged him to take effect April 10, 1862, for "having refused to appear before an examining board when duly summoned." This discharge was revoked by Special Orders No. 475, Adjutant General's Office, dated Sept. 25, 1866, and he was honorably discharged to date June 30, 1862, upon tender of resignation. Colonel, 60 PA Militia, June 19, 1863. Honorably mustered out, Sept. 8, 1863.

Born: Sept. 16, 1819 Montgomery Co., PA
Died: June 13, 1877 Philadelphia, PA
Other Wars: Mexican War (Captain, Co. C, 1 PA Infantry)
Occupation: Lawyer
Offices/Honors: PA Senate, 1847–49
Miscellaneous: Resided Philadelphia, PA
Buried: Laurel Hill Cemetery, Philadelphia, PA (Section X, Lots 439–441)
References: Pension File, National Archives. Samuel P. Bates. *Martial Deeds of Pennsylvania*. Philadelphia, PA, 1875. Thomas P. Lowry. *Tarnished Eagles: The Courts-Martial of Fifty Union Colonels and Lieutenant Colonels*. Mechanicsburg, PA, 1997. Letters Received, Volunteer Service Branch, Adjutant General's Office, Files H178(VS)1862 and S546(VS)1862, National Archives. Obituary, *Philadelphia Public Ledger*, June 14, 1877. Frank H. Taylor. *Philadelphia in the Civil War, 1861–65*. Philadelphia, PA, 1913.

CHARLES ROSS SMITH

1 Lieutenant, Co. A, 17 PA Infantry, April 25, 1861. Honorably mustered out, Aug. 2, 1861. Captain, Co. A, 6 PA Cavalry, Aug. 27, 1861. Major, 6 PA Cavalry, Oct. 1, 1861. Lieutenant Colonel, 6 PA Cavalry, March 29, 1862. Provost Marshal, Staff of Major Gen. George Stoneman, Feb. 15–June 13, 1863. Chief Ordnance Officer, Staff of Major Gen. Alfred Pleasanton, June 13–July 29, 1863. Chief of Staff and Ordnance Officer, Staff of Major Gen. Alfred Pleasanton, July 29, 1863–April 25, 1864. *Colonel*, 6 PA Cavalry, Sept. 30, 1863. Provost Marshal, Staff of Major Gen. Philip H. Sheridan, April 25–Sept. 18, 1864. Honorably mustered out, Sept. 19, 1864. Bvt. Colonel, USV, March 13, 1865, for gallant and meritorious services at the battles of Todd's Tavern, Yellow Tavern, and Hawes' Shop.

Born: May 18, 1829 Philadelphia, PA
Died: Nov. 9, 1897 Philadelphia, PA
Occupation: Chemist and druggist before war. Engaged in the chemical business and later in the grain business after war.

Offices/Honors: Secretary of the Philadelphia Commercial Exchange, 1885–97
Miscellaneous: Resided Philadelphia, PA
Buried: Woodlands Cemetery, Philadelphia, PA (Section N, Lot 267)
References: Obituary, *Philadelphia Public Ledger*, Nov. 10, 1897. Samuel L. Gracey. *Annals of the 6th Pennsylvania Cavalry*. Philadelphia, PA, 1868. Military Service File, National Archives.

CHARLES SOMERS SMITH

Captain, Co. A, 7 PA Militia, Sept. 12, 1862. Honorably discharged, Sept. 26, 1862. Colonel, 32 PA Militia, June 26, 1863. Honorably mustered out, Aug. 1, 1863.

Born: April 9, 1798 PA
Died: Aug. 21, 1884 Jenkintown, Montgomery Co., PA
Occupation: Superintendent of the Stephen Girard Estate

Charles Ross Smith
MEADE ALBUM, CIVIL WAR LIBRARY & MUSEUM, PHILADELPHIA, PA.

Charles Somers Smith
FROM *HISTORY OF THE 1ST REGIMENT INFANTRY, NATIONAL GUARD OF PENNSYLVANIA (GRAY RESERVES)*.

Miscellaneous: Resided Philadelphia, PA

Buried: Laurel Hill Cemetery, Philadelphia, PA (Section 7, Lot 198)

References: Obituary, *Philadelphia Public Ledger*, Aug. 23, 1884. James W. Latta. *History of the 1st Regiment Infantry, National Guard of Pennsylvania (Gray Reserves)*. Philadelphia and London, 1912. Harmon Y. Gordon. *History of the 1st Regiment Infantry of Pennsylvania*. Philadelphia, PA, 1961.

GEORGE FAIRLAMB SMITH

1 Lieutenant, RQM, 2 PA Infantry, April 20, 1861. Honorably mustered out, July 26, 1861. Captain, Co. B, 49 PA Infantry, Aug. 2, 1861. Major, 61 PA Infantry, March 14, 1862. GSW Fair Oaks, VA, May 31, 1862. Taken prisoner, Fair Oaks, VA, May 31, 1862. Confined Libby Prison, Richmond, VA; and Salisbury (NC) Prison. Lieutenant Colonel, 61 PA Infantry, June 1, 1862. Paroled Aug. 17, 1862. Discharged for disability, April 23, 1863, due to "diarrhea and derangement of the liver accompanied with typhoid symptoms." Colonel, 61 PA Infantry, May 4, 1863. GSW right thigh, Spotsylvania, VA, May 12, 1864. Honorably mustered out, Sept. 7, 1864. Colonel, 61 PA Infantry, Sept. 29, 1864. Resigned April 26, 1865, "on account of the close of the war and . . . my business at home demands my immediate attention."

Born: Feb. 28, 1840 West Chester, PA

Died: Oct. 18, 1877 West Chester, PA

Education: Graduated Yale University, New Haven, CT, 1858

Occupation: Lawyer

Offices/Honors: PA House of Representatives, 1875–76

Miscellaneous: Resided West Chester, Chester Co., PA

Buried: Oaklands Cemetery, West Chester, PA (Section G, Lot 72)

References: J. Smith Futhey and Gilbert Cope. *History of Chester County, PA*. Philadelphia, PA, 1881. Obituary, *West Chester Daily Local News*, Oct. 19, 1877. Pension File, National Archives. William P. Bacon. *Fourth Biographical Record of the Class of Fifty-Eight, Yale University*. New Britain, CT, 1897. Abraham T. Brewer. *History 61st Regiment Pennsylvania Volunteers, 1861–65*. Pittsburgh, PA, 1911. Samuel P. Bates. *Martial Deeds of Pennsylvania*. Philadelphia, PA, 1875. Letters Received, Volunteer Service Branch, Adjutant General's Office, File S592(VS)1863, National Archives.

George Fairlamb Smith
RONN PALM COLLECTION.
H. MANGERS, 1200 CHESTNUT STREET, PHILADELPHIA, PA.

LEWIS W. SMITH

Captain, Co. A, 9 PA Reserves, June 26, 1861. Resigned June 17, 1862, due to physical disability from "a very weak back, the result of fistula." Colonel, 169 PA Infantry, Nov. 28, 1862. Honorably mustered out, July 27, 1863.

Born: Oct. 4, 1812 Hesse Darmstadt, Germany

Died: May 17, 1886 Oak Park, Cook Co., IL

Other Wars: Mexican War (Captain, Co. L, 2 PA Infantry)

Occupation: Railroad conductor. Bookkeeper in later life.

Miscellaneous: Resided Loysburg, Bedford Co., PA; Pittsburgh, PA; and Oak Park, Cook Co., IL

Buried: Rosehill Cemetery, Chicago, IL (Section 3, Lot 85)

References: Pension File and Military Service File, National Archives. Death notice, *Chicago Daily Tribune*, May 20, 1886.

RICHARD PENN SMITH

1 Lieutenant, Co. F, 71 PA Infantry, May 28, 1861. 1 Lieutenant, Adjutant, 71 PA Infantry, Feb. 15, 1862. Captain, Co. A, 71 PA Infantry, July 4, 1862. GSW left ankle, Antietam, MD, Sept. 17, 1862. Major, 71 PA Infantry, Nov. 1, 1862. Colonel, 71 PA Infantry, Feb. 1, 1863. Commanded 1 Brigade, 2 Division, 2 Army Corps, Army of the Potomac, Sept. 28–Oct. 6, 1863. Commanded 2 Brigade, 2 Division, 2 Army Corps, Jan. 8–March 18, 1864. Honorably mustered out, July 2, 1864.

Born: May 9, 1837 Philadelphia, PA
Died: Nov. 27, 1887 West New Brighton, NY
Occupation: Merchant before war. Wholesale coal merchant and manufacturer after war.
Miscellaneous: Resided Philadelphia, PA; and West New Brighton, Staten Island, NY

Richard Penn Smith
USAMHI.
E. P. Hipple, 820 Arch Street, Philadelphia, PA.

Buried: Moravian Cemetery, New Dorp, Staten Island, NY (Section A, Lot 58)
References: Charles Morris, editor. *Makers of Philadelphia.* Philadelphia, PA, 1894. Obituary circular, Whole No. 276, New York MOLLUS. Richard M. Bayles, editor. *History of Richmond County, Staten Island, NY.* New York City, NY, 1887. *A Biographical Album of Prominent Pennsylvanians.* Third Series. Philadelphia, PA, 1890. Gary G. Lash. *"Duty Well Done," The History of Edward Baker's California Regiment.* Baltimore, MD, 2001. Pension File and Military Service File, National Archives.

FRANKLIN BAILY SPEAKMAN

Captain, Co. G, 133 PA Infantry, Aug. 16, 1862. Colonel, 133 PA Infantry, Aug. 21, 1862. Honorably mustered out, May 26, 1863.

Born: Jan. 9, 1833 Londonderry Twp., Chester Co., PA
Died: Sept. 9, 1900 Coatesville, PA
Occupation: Hotel proprietor

Franklin Baily Speakman
Ronn Palm Collection.
Amey & Lemer, Wyeth's Hall, Harrisburg, PA.

Miscellaneous: Resided New Bloomfield, Perry Co., PA; and Coatesville, Chester Co., PA

Buried: Fairview Cemetery, Coatesville, PA

References: Obituary, *Coatesville Weekly Times*, Sept. 15, 1900. Obituary, *West Chester Daily Local News*, Sept. 10, 1900. Obituary Circular, Whole No. 558, Pennsylvania MOLLUS. Emma Speakman Webster, compiler. *The Speakman Family in America*. Philadelphia, PA, 1930. Samuel P. Bates. *Martial Deeds of Pennsylvania*. Philadelphia, PA, 1875. Military Service File, National Archives.

GEORGE C. SPEAR

Major, 23 PA Infantry, April 21, 1861. Honorably mustered out, July 31, 1861. Major, 23 PA Infantry, Aug. 2, 1861. Lieutenant Colonel, 61 PA Infantry, March 1, 1862. GSW neck, Fair Oaks, VA, May 31, 1862. Taken prisoner, Fair Oaks, VA, May 31, 1862. Confined Richmond, VA. Paroled July 17, 1862. Colonel, 61 PA Infantry, June 1, 1862. Commanded Light Division, 6 Army Corps, Army of the Potomac, April 28–May 3, 1863. GSW through body, Fredericksburg, VA, May 3, 1863.

George C. Spear
Ronn Palm Collection.
W. L. Germon's Atelier, No. 702 Chestnut Street, Philadelphia, PA.

Born: 1822? PA

Died: May 3, 1863 KIA Fredericksburg, VA

Occupation: Clerk in city gas office

Miscellaneous: Resided Philadelphia, PA

Buried: Mount Moriah Cemetery, Philadelphia, PA (Section 36, Lot 19)

References: Samuel P. Bates. *Martial Deeds of Pennsylvania*. Philadelphia, PA, 1875. Pension File and Military Service File, National Archives. Obituary/funeral, *Philadelphia Public Ledger*, May 14, 1863. A. T. Brewer. *History 61st Regiment Pennsylvania Volunteers, 1861–65*. Pittsburgh, PA, 1911.

HENRY J. STAINROOK

Captain, Co. C, 22 PA Infantry, April 23, 1861. Honorably mustered out, Aug. 7, 1861. Colonel, 109 PA Infantry, Nov. 8, 1861. Shell wound abdomen, Cedar Mountain, VA, Aug. 9, 1862. Commanded 2 Brigade, 2 Division, 12 Army Corps, Army of the Potomac, Sept. 15–17, 1862 and Dec. 22, 1862–Jan. 3, 1863. GSW Chancellorsville, VA, May 3, 1863.

Henry J. Stainrook
Roger D. Hunt Collection, USAMHI.
J. Cremer & Co., Artists, No. 18 South Eighth Street, Philadelphia, PA.

Born: 1826? PA

Died: May 3, 1863 KIA Chancellorsville, VA

Other Wars: Mexican War (Private, Co. G, 1 PA Infantry)

Occupation: Wood grainer

Miscellaneous: Resided Philadelphia, PA

Buried: Lawnview Cemetery, Rockledge, PA (Norris Lawn, Range 54, Grave 14, unmarked)

References: Samuel P. Bates. *Martial Deeds of Pennsylvania*. Philadelphia, PA, 1875. Obituary, *Philadelphia Public Ledger*, May 11, 1863. Pension File and Military Service File, National Archives.

JOHN FRANCIS STAUNTON

Colonel, 67 PA Infantry, July 24, 1861. Commanded Post of Annapolis, 8 Army Corps, Middle Department, Sept. 1862–Jan. 1863. Commanded 3 Brigade, 2 Division, 8 Army Corps, Middle Department, Feb.–March 1863. Commanded 2 Brigade, 3 Division, 6 Army Corps, Army of the Potomac, July 6–Aug. 6, 1864. Commanded 2 Brigade, 3 Division, 6 Army Corps, Army of the Shenandoah, Aug. 6–10, 1864. Dismissed Sept. 1, 1864, for "disobedience of orders and neglect of duty, to the prejudice of good order and military discipline," for failing to "use all possible dispatch in forwarding" his brigade from Baltimore in time to take part in the battle of Monocacy, July 9, 1864. Disability resulting from dismissal removed, Jan. 31, 1865.

Born: March 20, 1821 Newark, NJ

Died: Feb. 8, 1875 Philadelphia, PA

Other Wars: Mexican War (Private, Co. F, 1 PA Infantry)

Occupation: Clerk and Assistant Assessor of Internal Revenue.

Miscellaneous: Resided Philadelphia, PA

Buried: Odd Fellows Cemetery, Philadelphia, PA (Section V, Lot 454). Cemetery records indicate that he was removed from the cemetery before Odd Fellows Cemetery was discontinued in 1951. Although cemetery records seem to indicate that he was removed to West Laurel Hill Cemetery, Bala-Cynwyd, PA, the records of West Laurel Hill Cemetery fail to show his burial there.

References: Obituary, *Philadelphia Public Ledger*, Feb. 11, 1875. Letters Received, Volunteer Service Branch, Adjutant General's Office, File H1905(VS)1863, National Archives. Military Service File, National Archives.

Franklin Bell Stewart
ROGER D. HUNT COLLECTION, USAMHI.
D. C. BURNITE & CO., 110 MARKET STREET, HARRISBURG, PA.

FRANKLIN BELL STEWART

Musician, Co. D, 3 PA Infantry, April 20, 1861. Honorably mustered out, July 29, 1861. Principal Musician, 110 PA Infantry, Sept. 16, 1862. 1 Sergeant, Co. H, 110 PA Infantry, May 1, 1863. 2 Lieutenant, Co. H, 110 PA Infantry, May 30, 1863. GSW right shoulder, Gettysburg, PA, July 2, 1863. 1 Lieutenant, Co. H, 110 PA Infantry, May 13, 1864. Captain, Co. H, 110 PA Infantry, Dec. 3, 1864. Acting AIG, 2 Brigade, 3 Division, 2 Army Corps, Army of the Potomac, March 10–June 2, 1865. Major, 110 PA Infantry, March 28, 1865. Lieutenant Colonel, 110 PA Infantry, June 9, 1865. *Colonel*, 110 PA Infantry, June 19, 1865. Honorably mustered out, June 28, 1865.

Born: 1837 Huntingdon Co., PA

Died: Aug. 30, 1904 Lima, OH

Occupation: Artist before war. Held a responsible position in the US Pension Bureau after war.

Offices/Honors: Postmaster, Altoona, PA, 1869–77

Miscellaneous: Resided Altoona, Blair Co., PA; and Washington, DC

Buried: Fairview Cemetery, Altoona, PA

References: Pension File and Military Service File, National Archives. Obituary, *Altoona Morning Times*, Aug. 31, 1904. Death notice, *Washington Evening Star*, Aug. 31, 1904. Letters Received, Volunteer Service Branch, Adjutant General's Office, File S1217(VS)1864, National Archives.

WILLIAM WELLS STOTT

Corporal, Co. E, 9 PA Infantry, April 22, 1861. Honorably mustered out, July 24, 1861. Captain, Co. K, 124 PA Infantry, Aug. 14, 1862. Honorably mustered out, May 17, 1863. Colonel, 43 PA Militia, July 6, 1863. Discharged Aug. 13, 1863.

Born: 1841 Stottsville, Chester Co., PA
Died: Oct. 14, 1891 Tucson, AZ
Occupation: School teacher before war. After the war engaged for a number of years in mining operations in the West. Returning to West Chester, he engaged in the coal business and several manufacturing ventures. A few months before his death he took an appointment in the US Interior Department as Chinese and Indian Inspector in Arizona.

William Wells Stott
ROBERT W. ECK COLLECTION, USAMHI.

Offices/Honors: Clerk of Courts, Chester Co., PA, 1874–77
Miscellaneous: Resided West Chester, Chester Co., PA; Kansas City, MO; and Tucson, Pima Co., AZ
Buried: Arlington National Cemetery, Arlington, VA (Section 3, Lot 1955)
References: Pension File and Military Service File, National Archives. Obituary, *West Chester Daily Local News*, Oct. 15, 1891. Obituary, *Coatesville Weekly Times*, Oct. 17, 1891. Obituary, *Tucson Daily Citizen*, Oct. 14, 1891. Robert M. Green, compiler. *History of the 124th Regiment Pennsylvania Volunteers in the War of the Rebellion*. Philadelphia, PA, 1907.

JOHN HUBLER STOVER

Captain, Co. B, 10 PA Infantry, April 24, 1861. Honorably mustered out, July 31, 1861. Major, 106 PA Infantry, Nov. 5, 1861. Colonel, 184 PA Infantry, April 4, 1864. Described by mustering officer Major Richard I. Dodge as "unprincipled, drunken, and worthless, and unfit to be in the Army of the United States," he was nevertheless mustered as colonel, Dec. 30, 1864, upon direct orders from President Lincoln, who observed, "I do not believe the charges against him." Honorably mustered out, July 14, 1865.

Born: April 24, 1833 Aaronsburg, PA
Died: Oct. 27, 1889 Aurora Springs, MO
Occupation: Lawyer and newspaper editor before war. Lawyer and real estate agent after war.
Offices/Honors: District Attorney, Centre Co., PA, 1860–62. District Attorney, Morgan Co., MO, 1866–68. US House of Representatives, 1868–69.
Miscellaneous: Resided Bellefonte, Centre Co., PA; Versailles, Morgan Co., MO; and Aurora Springs, Miller Co., MO
Buried: City Cemetery, Versailles, MO
References: *Biographical Directory of the American Congress.* Joseph R. C. Ward. *History of the 106th Regiment Pennsylvania Volunteers.* Philadelphia, PA, 1906. Pension File and Military Service File, National Archives. Letters Received, Volunteer Service Branch, Adjutant General's Office, File P947(VS)1864, National Archives. Thomas W. Herringshaw, editor. *Herringshaw's National Library of American Biography.* Chicago, IL, 1909–14.

John Hubler Stover
USAMHI.
F. Gutekunst, Photographer, 704 & 706 Arch Street,
Philadelphia, PA.

DEWITT CLINTON STRAWBRIDGE

Sergeant, Co. B, 19 OH Infantry, April 27, 1861. 1
Sergeant, Co. B, 19 OH Infantry, June 8, 1861. Honorably mustered out, Aug. 29, 1861. Captain, Co. B, 76
PA Infantry, Sept. 24, 1861. Colonel, 76 PA Infantry,
Aug. 9, 1862. Commanded Post of Hilton Head, SC,
Aug.–Oct. 1863. Resigned Nov. 20, 1863, "on account
of physical disability" due to "inguinal hernia of rather
large size." 1 Lieutenant, Adjutant, 17 KS Infantry, July
8, 1864. Honorably mustered out, Nov. 16, 1864.

Born: Aug. 5, 1837 Millerstown, PA
Died: Oct. 8, 1886 Kansas City, MO
Occupation: Merchant, banker, and real estate agent
Miscellaneous: Resided Sharon, Mercer Co., PA; Leav-
 enworth, Leavenworth Co., KS; Brookfield, Linn
 Co., MO, 1870–81; and Kansas City, MO, 1881–86
Buried: Oakwood Cemetery, Sharon, PA (Section A,
 Lot 38)

DeWitt Clinton Strawbridge (postwar)
From *Martial Deeds of Pennsylvania.*

References: Samuel P. Bates. *Martial Deeds of Pennsyl-
vania.* Philadelphia, PA, 1875. Obituary, *Sharon
Herald,* Oct. 15, 1886. Pension File and Military
Service File, National Archives. Letters Received,
Volunteer Service Branch, Adjutant General's
Office, File S1181(VS)1863, National Archives.
Death Notice, *Kansas City Times,* Oct. 9, 1886.

SAMUEL DALE STRAWBRIDGE

1 Lieutenant, Co. F, 2 PA Heavy Artillery, Jan. 8, 1862.
Captain, Co. I, 2 PA Heavy Artillery, Dec. 13, 1862.
Major, 4 PA Heavy Artillery, April 30, 1864. Acting
AIG, Provisional Brigade, Army of the James, Dec. 4,
1864–Jan. 10, 1865. Honorably mustered out, Jan. 10,
1865. Colonel, 2 PA Heavy Artillery, April 4, 1865.
Commanded Sub-District of the Blackwater, Department of Virginia, July 1865–Jan. 1866. Honorably mustered out, Jan. 29, 1866.

Born: Aug. 31, 1825 Liberty Twp., Montour Co., PA
Died: Jan. 16, 1902 Hampton, VA
Occupation: Superintendent of the night watch at Kirk-
 bride, West Philadelphia, after war
Miscellaneous: Resided Danville, Montour Co., PA;
 Philadelphia, PA

Samuel Dale Strawbridge
USAMHI.

Buried: Hampton National Cemetery, Hampton, VA (Phoebus Addition, Section C, Grave 8243)
References: Samuel P. Bates. *Martial Deeds of Pennsylvania.* Philadelphia, PA, 1875. Pension File and Military Service File, National Archives. Mary Stiles Guild. *Genealogy Strobridge, Morrison or Morison, Strawbridge.* Lowell, MA, 1891. George W. Ward. *History of the 2nd Pennsylvania Veteran Heavy Artillery.* Philadelphia, PA, 1904. Obituary, *Philadelphia Inquirer,* Jan. 18, 1902.

CHARLES LEWIS KALBFUS SUMWALT

Colonel, 138 PA Infantry, Aug. 30, 1862. Dismissed March 30, 1863, for "drunkenness whilst on duty" and "conduct prejudicial to good order and military discipline." Private, Co. K, 1 Potomac Home Brigade MD Cavalry, March 28, 1864. Sergeant, Co. K, 1 Potomac Home Brigade MD Cavalry, Sept. 1, 1864. Sergeant Major, 1 Potomac Home Brigade MD Cavalry, Jan. 6, 1865. Honorably mustered out, June 28, 1865.

Born: 1826? Baltimore, MD
Died: Aug. 29, 1875 Baltimore, MD
Occupation: Methodist clergyman before war. Plasterer after war.

Miscellaneous: Resided Gettysburg, Adams Co., PA; and Baltimore, MD
Buried: Mount Olivet Cemetery, Baltimore, MD (Section A, Lot 108, unmarked)
References: Pension File and Military Service File, National Archives. Thomas P. Lowry. *Tarnished Eagles: The Courts-Martial of Fifty Union Colonels and Lieutenant Colonels.* Mechanicsburg, PA, 1997. Letters Received, Volunteer Service Branch, Adjutant General's Office, File S790(VS)1863, National Archives. Osceola Lewis. *History of the 138th Regiment Pennsylvania Volunteer Infantry.* Norristown, PA, 1866. J. Howard Wert, "Old Time Notes of Adams County," *Gettysburg Star & Sentinel,* March 6, 1907.

THOMAS WORTHINGTON SWENEY

1 Lieutenant, RQM, 99 PA Infantry, July 26, 1861. Colonel, 99 PA Infantry, Nov. 7, 1861. Resigned Jan. 24, 1862, due to "physical inability."

Born: May 22, 1812 West Chester, PA
Died: April 7, 1872 Philadelphia, PA
Occupation: Member of the real estate firm of Morris L. Hallowell & Co.
Offices/Honors: US Assessor of Internal Revenue, 1863–66
Miscellaneous: Resided Philadelphia, PA
Buried: Laurel Hill Cemetery, Philadelphia, PA (Section 7, Lots 1–2)
References: William P. Hallowell. *Record of a Branch of the Hallowell Family.* Philadelphia, PA, 1893. Obituary, *Philadelphia Public Ledger,* April 9, 1872. Military Service File, National Archives. Obituary, *Philadelphia Evening Bulletin,* April 9, 1872.

JOHN HENRY TAGGART

Colonel, 12 PA Reserves, July 25, 1861. Resigned July 8, 1862, "believing that I can be of much service to my country in Pennsylvania, in the present crisis, and considerations of a domestic and business character imperatively demanding my presence there." Reinstated as Colonel, 12 PA Reserves, Aug. 19, 1862, despite the fact that Lt. Col. Martin D. Hardin had been promoted to fill the position. Commanded 3 Brigade, 3 Division, 3 Army Corps, Army of Virginia, Sept. 2–9, 1862. Mustered out, Sept. 23, 1862, as a supernumerary officer. Chief Preceptor, Free Military School for Applicants for the Command of Colored Troops, 1864–65.

John Henry Taggart

Born: Jan. 22, 1821 Georgetown, Kent Co., MD
Died: June 4, 1892 Grubb's Landing, DE
Occupation: Newspaper editor and publisher
Miscellaneous: Resided Philadelphia, PA
Buried: West Laurel Hill Cemetery, Bala-Cynwyd, PA (Summit Section, Lot 131)
References: *National Cyclopedia of American Biography.* Martin D. Hardin. *History of the 12th Regiment Pennsylvania Reserve Volunteer Corps.* New York City, NY, 1890. Samuel P. Bates. *Martial Deeds of Pennsylvania.* Philadelphia, PA, 1875. Obituary, *Philadelphia Public Ledger,* June 6, 1892. Thomas P. Lowry. *Tarnished Eagles: The Courts-Martial of Fifty Union Colonels and Lieutenant Colonels.* Mechanicsburg, PA, 1997. Military Service File, National Archives. Letters Received, Volunteer Service Branch, Adjutant General's Office, File R574(VS)1862, National Archives. *A Biographical Album of Prominent Pennsylvanians.* First Series. Philadelphia, PA, 1888. James H. Stine. *History of the Army of the Potomac.* Philadelphia, PA, 1892.

THOMAS FOREST BETTON TAPPER

Captain, Co. G, 4 PA Reserves, May 29, 1861. Sabre wound right forearm and bayonet wound left leg, Charles City Cross Roads, VA, June 30, 1862. Lieutenant Colonel, 4 PA Reserves, Dec. 24, 1862. *Colonel,* 4 PA Reserves, May 10, 1864. Honorably mustered out, June 17, 1864.

Born: Aug. 31, 1823 Germantown, PA
Died: Feb. 2, 1885 Philadelphia, PA
Occupation: Machinist, engineer, and dry goods merchant. Chief Engineer of the Philadelphia Post Office for eighteen years after war.
Miscellaneous: Resided Philadelphia, PA
Buried: Laurel Hill Cemetery, Philadelphia, PA (Section 16, Lot 233)

Thomas Forest Betton Tapper

References: Samuel P. Bates. *Martial Deeds of Pennsylvania.* Philadelphia, PA, 1875. Obituary, *Philadelphia Public Ledger,* Feb. 3, 1885. Josiah R. Sypher. *History of the Pennsylvania Reserve Corps.* Lancaster, PA, 1865. Pension File and Military Service File, National Archives. Robert E. Hoagland. "Identifying John Tapper, a German Immigrant Laborer in Early Nineteenth-Century Philadelphia, through the Records of His Children," *National Genealogical Society Quarterly,* Vol. 92, No. 3 (Sept. 2004).

CHARLES FREDERICK TAYLOR

Captain, Co. H, 13 PA Reserves, July 22, 1861. Taken prisoner, Harrisonburg, VA, June 6, 1862. Exchanged and returned to regiment, Nov. 22, 1862. Colonel, 13 PA Reserves, Sept. 17, 1862. GSW shoulder Fredericksburg, VA, Dec. 13, 1862. GSW heart, Gettysburg, PA, July 2, 1863.

Charles Frederick Taylor
Courtesy of Alan J. Sessarego.
R. W. Addis, Photographer, McClees' Gallery,
308 Penna. Avenue, Washington, DC.

Born: Feb. 6, 1840 West Chester, PA
Died: July 2, 1863 KIA Gettysburg, PA
Education: Attended University of Michigan, Ann Arbor, MI
Occupation: Farmer
Miscellaneous: Resided Kennett Square, Chester Co., PA. Brother of noted author Bayard Taylor. Brother of Colonel William W. Taylor.
Buried: Longwood Cemetery, Kennett Square, PA (Section B, Lot 43)
References: Samuel P. Bates. *Martial Deeds of Pennsylvania.* Philadelphia, PA, 1875. J. Smith Futhey and Gilbert Cope. *History of Chester County, PA.* Philadelphia, PA, 1881. Charles F. Hobson and Arnold Shankman. "Colonel of the Bucktails: Civil War Letters of Charles Frederick Taylor," *Pennsylvania Magazine of History and Biography,* Vol. 97, No. 3 (July 1973). O. R. Howard Thomson and William H. Rauch. *History of the "Bucktails," Kane Rifle Regiment of the Pennsylvania Reserve Corps.* Philadelphia, PA, 1906. Alfred R. Justice. *Descendants of Robert Taylor.* Philadelphia, PA, 1925. Military Service File, National Archives. Douglas R. Harper. *"If Thee Must Fight": A Civil War History of Chester County, Pennsylvania.* West Chester, PA, 1990.

WILLIAM W. TAYLOR

Lieutenant Colonel, 8 PA Militia, Sept. 12, 1862. Honorably discharged Sept. 25, 1862. Colonel, 33 PA Emergency Troops, June 26, 1863. Honorably mustered out, Aug. 4, 1863.

Born: Oct. 22, 1829 Kennett Square, PA
Died: Nov. 26, 1896 Philadelphia, PA
Occupation: Civil engineer, engaged before the war in railroad construction and after the war in building water works
Miscellaneous: Resided West Chester, Chester Co., PA; and Philadelphia, PA. Brother of Colonel Charles F. Taylor. Brother of noted author Bayard Taylor.
Buried: Longwood Cemetery, Kennett Square, PA
References: Obituary, *West Chester Daily Local News,* Nov. 27, 1896. Obituary, *Oxford Press,* Dec. 3, 1896. D. Herbert Way. *Descendants of Robert and Hannah Hickman Way.* Woodstown, NJ, 1975. Death Certificate.

James Tearney
COURTESY OF GIL BARRETT.
GILL'S CITY GALLERY, NO. 20 EAST KING STREET, LANCASTER, PA.

JAMES TEARNEY

Private, Co. F, 1 PA Infantry, April 20, 1861. Honorably mustered out, July 27, 1861. Sergeant, Co. B, 87 PA Infantry, Sept. 14, 1861. 1 Sergeant, Co. B, 87 PA Infantry, May 26, 1863. Taken prisoner, Winchester, VA, June 15, 1863. Confined Richmond, VA. Paroled July 8, 1863. 1 Lieutenant, Co. B, 87 PA Infantry, July 28, 1864. GSW right thigh, Winchester, VA, Sept. 19, 1864. Captain, Co. A, 87 PA Infantry, Oct. 29, 1864. Colonel, 87 PA Infantry, May 10, 1865. Honorably mustered out, June 29, 1865.

Born: Oct. 9, 1836 Lancaster, PA
Died: Feb. 9, 1900 Roaring Spring, Blair Co., PA
Occupation: Tinsmith
Miscellaneous: Resided Millersville, Lancaster Co., PA; and Hollidaysburg, Blair Co., PA
Buried: Lutheran Cemetery, Hollidaysburg, PA

References: Samuel P. Bates. *Martial Deeds of Pennsylvania*. Philadelphia, PA, 1875. Pension File and Military Service File, National Archives. Obituary, *Hollidaysburg Democratic Standard*, Feb. 14, 1900. George R. Prowell. *History of the 87th Regiment Pennsylvania Volunteers*. York, PA, 1901.

WILLIAM H. TELFORD

Captain, Co. G, 50 PA Infantry, Aug. 8, 1861. GSW right leg, Spotsylvania, VA, May 12, 1864. Taken prisoner, Spotsylvania, VA, May 12, 1864. Confined at Danville, VA; Lynchburg, VA; Macon, GA; Charleston, SC; and Columbia, SC. Escaped Jan. 12, 1865. Lieutenant Colonel, 50 PA Infantry, Feb. 8, 1865. Colonel, 50 PA Infantry, May 1, 1865. Commanded 2 Brigade, 1 Division, 9 Army Corps, Army of the Potomac, June 11–July 1, 1865. Although his name was included on the muster-out roll of the Field and Staff of the 50 PA Infantry, July 30, 1865, he was subsequently dishonorably dismissed, Aug. 31, 1865, for "defrauding the Government of the United States," due to his involvement in the buying and selling of horses known to have been the property of the United States.

William H. Telford
FROM *HISTORY OF THE 50TH REGIMENT PENNSYLVANIA VETERAN VOLUNTEERS.*

William H. Telford
Massachusetts MOLLUS Collection, USAMHI.

Born: 1840 Ireland

Died: April 12, 1909 Susquehanna, PA

Occupation: Marble cutter before war. Engaged in the furniture and undertaking business and operated a livery stable after war.

Miscellaneous: Resided Susquehanna, Susquehanna Co., PA; and Towanda, Bradford Co., PA

Buried: Grand Street Cemetery, Susquehanna, PA

References: Rhamanthus M. Stocker. *Centennial History of Susquehanna County, PA.* Philadelphia, PA, 1887. Obituary, *Montrose Independent Republican*, April 16, 1909. C. F. Heverly. *Our Boys in Blue.* Towanda, PA, 1898. Pension File and Military Service File, National Archives. Lewis Crater. *History of the 50th Regiment Pennsylvania Veteran Volunteers.* Reading, PA, 1884. Letters Received, Volunteer Service Branch, Adjutant General's Office, File T107(VS)1865, National Archives.

HAMPTON SIDNEY THOMAS

Corporal, Co. E, 9 PA Infantry, April 22, 1861. Honorably mustered out, July 29, 1861. 2 Lieutenant, Co. G, 1 PA Cavalry, Aug. 28, 1861. 1 Lieutenant, Co. G, 1 PA Cavalry, Sept. 27, 1861. Captain, Co. M, 1 PA Cavalry, May 1, 1862. Acting AIG, 2 Brigade, 3 Division, Cavalry Corps, Army of the Potomac, April–June 1863. Acting AIG, 1 Brigade, 2 Division, Cavalry Corps, June 1863–Oct. 1864. Major, 1 PA Cavalry, Nov. 11, 1864. *Colonel*, 1 PA Cavalry, Jan. 4, 1865. Shell wound right leg (amputated), Amelia Springs, VA, April 5, 1865. Major, 2 PA Provisional Cavalry, June 17, 1865. Honorably discharged, Aug. 17, 1865, "on account of services being no longer required and physical disability from wounds." Bvt. Colonel, USV, April 5, 1865, for great gallantry near Jetersville, VA, in assisting to capture a rebel battery.

Born: Nov. 3, 1837 Quakertown, PA

Died: May 21, 1899 Philadelphia, PA

Occupation: Coal and wood business until 1874, after which he served in a succession of municipal appointive offices, including Collector of Delinquent Taxes, 1890–95, and Police Magistrate

Offices/Honors: Register of Wills, Chester Co., PA, 1866–69. Medal of Honor, Amelia Springs, VA, April 5, 1865. "Conspicuous gallantry in the capture of a field battery and a number of battle flags and in the destruction of the enemy's wagon train. Major Thomas lost a leg in this action."

Hampton Sidney Thomas
KEN TURNER COLLECTION.
HENSZEY, N0. 812 ARCH STREET, PHILADELPHIA, PA.

Miscellaneous: Resided Oxford, Chester Co., PA; West Chester, Chester Co., PA; and Philadelphia, PA

Buried: Lawnview Cemetery, Rockledge, PA (Broad Lawn, Range 20, Grave 26)

References: Obituary, *Philadelphia Public Ledger*, May 22, 1899. Obituary, *West Chester Morning Republican*, May 22, 1899. William H. Powell, editor. *Officers of the Army and Navy (Volunteer) Who Served in the Civil War.* Philadelphia, PA, 1893. St. Clair A. Mulholland. *Military Order Congress Medal of Honor Legion of the United States.* Philadelphia, PA, 1905. William P. Lloyd. *History of the 1st Regiment Pennsylvania Reserve Cavalry.* Philadelphia, PA, 1864. Pension File and Military Service File, National Archives. Letters Received, Volunteer Service Branch, Adjutant General's Office, File B2131(VS)1865, National Archives.

WILLIAM BROOKE THOMAS

Colonel, 20 PA Militia, Sept. 18, 1862. Discharged Sept. 28, 1862. Colonel, 20 PA Emergency Troops, June 17, 1863. Honorably mustered out, Aug. 10, 1863. Colonel, 192 PA Infantry, July 15, 1864. Honorably mustered out, Nov. 11, 1864.

Born: May 25, 1811 Haverford, PA
Died: Dec. 12, 1887 Philadelphia, PA
Occupation: Miller and flour manufacturer
Offices/Honors: Collector of Customs, Port of Philadel-
phia, 1861–64
Miscellaneous: Resided Philadelphia, PA
Buried: Laurel Hill Cemetery, Philadelphia, PA (Sec-
tion 10, Lot 146)
References: Stephen N. Winslow. *Biographies of Successful
Philadelphia Merchants.* Philadelphia, PA, 1864. John
W. Jordan, editor. *Colonial Families of Philadelphia.*
Philadelphia, PA, 1911. Anna M. Holstein. *Swedish
Holsteins in America.* Norristown, PA, 1892. Pension
File, National Archives. John C. Myers. *A Daily
Journal of the 192nd Regiment Pennsylvania Volunteers.*
Philadelphia, PA, 1864. Obituary, *Philadelphia Pub-
lic Ledger,* Dec. 13, 1887. Letters Received, Volun-
teer Service Branch, Adjutant General's Office, File
H2171(VS)1864, National Archives.

William Brooke Thomas
COURTESY OF THE AUTHOR.
MORGAN & BRUSSTAR, 1109 SPRING GARDEN STREET,
PHILADELPHIA, PA.

ANDREW HART TIPPIN

Major, 20 PA Infantry, April 26, 1861. Honorably mustered out, Aug. 6, 1861. Colonel, 68 PA Infantry, June
26, 1862. Commanded 1 Brigade, 1 Division, 3 Army
Corps, Army of the Potomac, May–June 1863 and July
2–3, 1863. Taken prisoner, Auburn, VA, Oct. 14, 1863.
Confined Libby Prison, Richmond, VA. Paroled March
14, 1864. Returned to regiment, June 19, 1864. Honorably mustered out, June 9, 1865.

Born: Dec. 25, 1823 Plymouth, Montgomery Co., PA
Died: Feb. 6, 1870 Philadelphia, PA
Other Wars: Mexican War (1 Lieutenant, 11 US Infantry)
Occupation: Clerk
Offices/Honors: Deputy US Marshal of the Eastern
District of PA
Miscellaneous: Resided Pottstown, Montgomery Co.,
PA; and Philadelphia, PA
Buried: Pottstown Cemetery, Pottstown, PA
References: Samuel P. Bates. *Martial Deeds of Pennsylva-
nia.* Philadelphia, PA, 1875. Letters Received, Vol-
unteer Service Branch, Adjutant General's Office,
File C1466(VS)1863, National Archives. Pension
File and Military Service File, National Archives.
Obituary, *Philadelphia Public Ledger,* Feb. 7, 1870.

GUSTAVUS WASHINGTON TOWN

1 Lieutenant, Co. A, 18 PA Infantry, April 24, 1861.
Honorably mustered out, Aug. 7, 1861. Lieutenant
Colonel, 95 PA Infantry, Sept. 17, 1861. Colonel, 95 PA
Infantry, June 28, 1862. Commanded 3 Brigade, 1 Divi-
sion, 6 Army Corps, Army of the Potomac, Oct.–Dec.
10, 1862 and Feb. 23–March 15, 1863. GSW heart,
Salem Heights, VA, May 3, 1863.

Born: Aug. 28, 1839 Philadelphia, PA
Died: May 3, 1863 KIA Salem Heights, VA
Education: Attended Philadelphia (PA) Central High
School
Occupation: Printer
Miscellaneous: Resided Philadelphia, PA. Brother of
Colonel Thomas J. Town.
Buried: West Laurel Hill Cemetery, Bala-Cynwyd, PA
(River Section, Lot 273)
References: Samuel P. Bates. *Martial Deeds of Pennsyl-
vania.* Philadelphia, PA, 1875. Pension File and
Military Service File, National Archives. G. Nor-
ton Galloway. *The 95th Pennsylvania Volunteers
("Gosline's Pennsylvania Zouaves") in the Sixth Corps:
An Historical Paper.* Philadelphia, PA, 1884.

Gustavus Washington Town
ROGER D. HUNT COLLECTION, USAMHI.
F. GUTEKUNST, PHOTOGRAPHER, 704 & 706 ARCH STREET,
PHILADELPHIA, PA.

Thomas Jefferson Town
USAMHI.
R. W. ADDIS, PHOTOGRAPHER, McCLEES GALLERY,
308 PENNA. AVENUE, WASHINGTON, DC.

References: Samuel P. Bates. *Martial Deeds of Pennsylvania.* Philadelphia, PA, 1875. Pension File and Military Service File, National Archives. John H. Campbell. *History of the Friendly Sons of St. Patrick and of the Hibernian Society for the Relief of Emigrants from Ireland.* Philadelphia, PA, 1892. G. Norton Galloway. *The 95th Pennsylvania Volunteers ("Gosline's Pennsylvania Zouaves") in the Sixth Corps: An Historical Paper.* Philadelphia, PA, 1884. Obituary, *Philadelphia Public Ledger,* April 16, 1916.

THOMAS JEFFERSON TOWN

2 Lieutenant, Co. A, 18 PA Infantry, April 24, 1861. Honorably mustered out, Aug. 6, 1861. Captain, Co. A, 95 PA Infantry, Sept. 4, 1861. Major, 95 PA Infantry, Nov. 14, 1862. Colonel, 95 PA Infantry, May 3, 1863. GSW left hip, Salem Heights, VA, May 3, 1863. Resigned Aug. 5, 1863, "having been wounded . . . and being still disabled . . . with no early prospect of recovery."

Born: Oct. 9, 1841 Philadelphia, PA
Died: April 15, 1916 Philadelphia, PA
Occupation: Printer, stationer and later US Internal Revenue clerk
Miscellaneous: Resided Philadelphia, PA. Brother of Colonel Gustavus W. Town
Buried: Mount Peace Cemetery, Philadelphia, PA (Section R, Lot 117)

JAMES HARVEY TRIMBLE

Captain, Co. C, 4 PA Cavalry, Sept. 16, 1861. Major, 4 PA Cavalry, Nov. 1, 1861. Resigned Aug. 6, 1862, being "disabled and unfit for military duty in the mounted service" due to "a severe form of internal hemorrhoids." Captain, Co. E, 1 Battalion, PA Cavalry, July 24, 1863. Honorably mustered out, Dec. 28, 1863. Colonel, 211 PA Infantry, Sept. 16, 1864. Resigned March 18, 1865, due to "neuralgia in the head and neck, which added to my advanced age, incapacitates me from performing the duties of my office." In recommending the acceptance of his resignation, his brigade commander, Joseph A. Mathews, described him as "hopelessly inefficient as a commanding officer, although a gentleman of many good qualities and many friends."

James Harvey Trimble
SOLDIERS AND SAILORS NATIONAL MILITARY MUSEUM
AND MEMORIAL, PITTSBURGH, PA.

Born: March 21, 1814 New Alexander, Westmoreland
Co., PA
Died: May 10, 1897 McKeesport, PA
Occupation: Tanner before war. Provision dealer and
clerk after war.
Miscellaneous: Resided near Latrobe, Westmoreland
Co., PA, until 1877; and McKeesport, Allegheny
Co., PA, 1877–97
Buried: McKeesport and Versailles Cemetery, Mc-
Keesport, PA (Section D, Lot A)
References: Pension File and Military Service File,
National Archives. Obituary, *McKeesport Daily
News*, May 11, 1897. Letters Received, Volunteer
Service Branch, Adjutant General's Office, File
K314(VS)1862, National Archives.

JOHN TROUT

Colonel, 37 PA Militia, July 4, 1863. Honorably mustered out, Aug. 4, 1863.

Born: 1822 Bedford Co., PA
Died: June 18, 1876 Williamsport, PA
Other Wars: Mexican War (Artificer, Battery G, 1 US
Artillery)

Occupation: Gunsmith
Miscellaneous: Resided Williamsport, Lycoming Co.,
PA
Buried: Williamsport Cemetery, Williamsport, PA
References: Obituary, *Williamsport Daily Gazette and
Bulletin*, June 19, 1876. Obituary, *Williamsport Sun
and Democrat*, June 21, 1876. Register of Enlist-
ments in the US Army, National Archives.

ADOLPH VON HARTUNG

Captain, Co. A, 74 PA Infantry, July 23, 1861. Major, 74
PA Infantry, Oct. 17, 1862. Lieutenant Colonel, 74 PA
Infantry, Jan. 15, 1863. Colonel, 74 PA Infantry, April 4,
1863. GSW left leg, Gettysburg, PA, July 1, 1863. Honorably discharged July 11, 1864, on account of physical
disability from wounds received in action.

Adolph Von Hartung
USAMHI.
EDWARD LUPUS, NO. 23 BALTIMORE STREET, BALTIMORE, MD.

Born: June 24, 1833 Kuestrin, Prussia

Died: April 10, 1902 Baltimore, MD

Occupation: Prussian army officer and merchant before war. After war held a position in the money order department of the Baltimore Post Office. Pension attorney and insurance agent in later life.

Miscellaneous: Resided Baltimore, MD

Buried: Loudon Park Cemetery, Baltimore, MD (Section W, Lot 174)

References: Pension File and Military Service File, National Archives. Obituary, *Baltimore Sun*, April 11, 1902. Obituary, *Baltimore American*, April 11, 1902. Edmund J. Raus, Jr. *A Generation on the March: The Union Army at Gettysburg.* Gettysburg, PA, 1996. Letters Received, Volunteer Service Branch, Adjutant General's Office, File H66(VS)1864, National Archives.

John Wainwright

SPECIAL COLLECTIONS RESEARCH CENTER, SYRACUSE UNIVERSITY LIBRARY, SYRACUSE, NY.

JOHN WAINWRIGHT

Private, Co. G, 2 PA Infantry, April 20, 1861. Honorably mustered out, July 26, 1861. 1 Sergeant, Co. F, 97 PA Infantry, Sept. 23, 1861. 2 Lieutenant, Co. F, 97 PA Infantry, Jan. 10, 1862. GSW right thigh, James Island, SC, June 12, 1862. 1 Lieutenant, Co. F, 97 PA Infantry, March 9, 1863. Captain, Co. F, 97 PA Infantry, Nov. 1, 1864. Shell wound right shoulder, Fort Fisher, NC, Jan. 15, 1865. Lieutenant Colonel, 97 PA Infantry, Jan. 15, 1865. Colonel, 97 PA Infantry, June 1, 1865. Honorably mustered out, Aug. 28, 1865.

Born: July 13, 1839 Syracuse, NY

Died: April 15, 1915 Wilmington, DE

Occupation: Coach painter before war. Dry goods merchant and pension attorney after war.

Offices/Honors: Medal of Honor, Fort Fisher, NC, Jan. 15, 1865. "Gallant and meritorious conduct, where, as first lieutenant, he commanded the regiment."

Miscellaneous: Resided West Chester, Chester Co., PA; and Wilmington, New Castle Co., DE

Buried: Arlington National Cemetery, Arlington, VA (Section 2, Lot 1061)

John Wainwright

FROM *COMPANIONS OF THE MILITARY ORDER OF THE LOYAL LEGION OF THE UNITED STATES.*

References: Pension File and Military Service File, National Archives. J. Smith Futhey and Gilbert Cope. *History of Chester County, PA*. Philadelphia, PA, 1881. Obituary, *Wilmington Every Evening*, April 15, 1915. William H. Powell, editor. *Officers of the Army and Navy (Volunteer) Who Served in the Civil War*. Philadelphia, PA, 1893. Isaiah Price. *History of the 97th Regiment Pennsylvania Volunteer Infantry during the War of the Rebellion*. Philadelphia, PA, 1875. St. Clair A. Mulholland. *Military Order Congress Medal of Honor Legion of the United States*. Philadelphia, PA, 1905. Joseph B. Mitchell. *The Badge of Gallantry*. New York City, NY, 1968. *Companions of the Military Order of the Loyal Legion of the United States*. Second Edition. New York City, NY, 1901. Letters Received, Volunteer Service Branch, Adjutant General's Office, File W1280(VS)1865, National Archives.

AMOR WILLIAM WAKEFIELD

1 Sergeant, Co. I, 7 PA Infantry, April 22, 1861. Honorably mustered out, July 27, 1861. 1 Lieutenant, Co. E, 49 PA Infantry, Aug. 6, 1861. Captain, Co. E, 49 PA Infantry, Aug. 5, 1862. Major, 49 PA Infantry, May 11, 1864. Shell wound right shoulder and back, Cold Harbor, VA, June 1, 1864. Taken prisoner, Winchester, VA, Sept. 19, 1864. Confined Richmond, VA; Salisbury, NC; and Danville, VA. Paroled Feb. 22, 1865. Lieutenant Colonel, 49 PA Infantry, June 29, 1865. *Colonel*, 49 PA Infantry, July 14, 1865. Honorably mustered out, July 15, 1865.

Born: Aug. 30, 1829 Mifflin Co., PA
Died: Dec. 17, 1891 Culver, KS
Occupation: Farmer and district court clerk
Miscellaneous: Resided McVeytown, Mifflin Co., PA, to 1877; Culver and Minneapolis, Ottawa Co., KS, after 1877
Buried: Highland Cemetery, Minneapolis, KS (Block 10, Lot 25)
References: Samuel P. Bates. *Martial Deeds of Pennsylvania*. Philadelphia, PA, 1875. Pension File, National Archives. Robert S. Westbrook. *History of the 49th Pennsylvania Volunteers*. Altoona, PA, 1898. Letters Received, Volunteer Service Branch, Adjutant General's Office, File W221(VS)1863, National Archives.

Amor William Wakefield
RONN PALM COLLECTION.
D. C. BURNITE & CO., 110 MARKET STREET, HARRISBURG, PA.

WILLIAM CLARK WARD

Sergeant, Co. A, 17 PA Infantry, April 25, 1861. Honorably mustered out, Aug. 2, 1861. 1 Lieutenant, Adjutant, 115 PA Infantry, Nov. 21, 1861. Lieutenant Colonel, 115 PA Infantry, Jan. 16, 1863. Resigned April 13, 1863, since his business, being "the only support my aged parents have, is now needing my personal attention to prevent my parents from coming to absolute want." *Colonel*, 115 PA Infantry, June 19, 1864. Did not join regiment since its low strength did not permit the muster of a colonel.

Born: Oct. 27, 1837 Philadelphia, PA
Died: Nov. 27, 1896 Philadelphia, PA
Occupation: Clerk in clothing house before war. Railroad freight agent after war.
Offices/Honors: Prominently identified with the Artillery Corps of Washington Grays, serving as its captain, 1866–74
Miscellaneous: Resided Philadelphia, PA
Buried: Laurel Hill Cemetery, Philadelphia, PA (Section 16, Lot 84)
References: Obituary Circular, Whole No. 327, Pennsylvania MOLLUS. Obituary, *Philadelphia Inquirer*, Nov. 29, 1896. Pension File and Military Service File, National Archives.

HORATIO NELSON WARREN

Captain, Co. A, 142 PA Infantry, Aug. 23, 1862. Major, 142 PA Infantry, Jan. 6, 1863. Acting AIG, 1 Brigade, 3 Division, 1 Army Corps, Army of the Potomac, July–Oct. 1863. Lieutenant Colonel, 142 PA Infantry, Sept. 10, 1864. GSW right side, White Oak Road, VA, March 31, 1865. *Colonel*, 142 PA Infantry, June 3, 1865. Honorably mustered out, May 29, 1865.

Born: Dec. 26, 1838 Clarence, Erie Co., NY
Died: Aug. 22, 1916 Buffalo, NY
Occupation: Mercantile clerk and bookkeeper before war. Merchant, US pension agent, and life insurance agent after war.

Horatio Nelson Warren

FROM *THE DECLARATION OF INDEPENDENCE AND WAR HISTORY: BULL RUN TO THE APPOMATTOX.*

Miscellaneous: Resided West Middlesex, Mercer Co., PA, to 1876; Philadelphia, PA, 1876–79; and Buffalo, NY, after 1879
Buried: Forest Lawn Cemetery, Buffalo, NY (Section 14, Lot 202)
References: William R. Cutter. *Genealogical and Family History of Western New York.* New York City, NY, 1912. Obituary, *Buffalo Morning Express*, Aug. 23, 1916. Pension File and Military Service File, National Archives. Horatio N. Warren. *The Declaration of Independence and War History: Bull Run to the Appomattox.* Buffalo, NY, 1894. Samuel P. Bates. *Martial Deeds of Pennsylvania.* Philadelphia, PA, 1875. Letters Received, Volunteer Service Branch, Adjutant General's Office, File S2620(VS)1864, National Archives.

JAMES FREDERICK WEAVER

2 Lieutenant, Co. B, 148 PA Infantry, Aug. 5, 1862. Captain, Co. B, 148 PA Infantry, Sept. 1, 1862. Shell wound head, Po River, VA, May 9, 1864. Major, 148 PA Infantry, Feb. 1, 1865. Lieutenant Colonel, 148 PA Infantry, May 6, 1865. *Colonel*, 148 PA Infantry, June 1, 1865. Honorably mustered out, June 1, 1865.

Born: Nov. 6, 1830 Spring Twp., Centre Co., PA
Died: Aug. 13, 1904 Milesburg, PA
Occupation: Newspaper editor and merchant
Offices/Honors: County Treasurer, Centre Co., PA, 1872–74. PA House of Representatives, 1877–78.
Miscellaneous: Resided Bellefonte, Centre Co., PA; and Milesburg, Centre Co., PA
Buried: Union Cemetery, Bellefonte, PA
References: Samuel P. Bates. *Martial Deeds of Pennsylvania.* Philadelphia, PA, 1875. Pension File and Military Service File, National Archives. Obituary, *Bellefonte Democratic Watchman*, Aug. 19, 1904. *Commemorative Biographical Record of Central Pennsylvania, Including the Counties of Centre, Clinton, Union and Snyder.* Chicago, IL, 1898. Letters Received, Volunteer Service Branch, Adjutant General's Office, File W1462(VS)1863, National Archives. Joseph W. Muffly, editor. *The Story of Our Regiment: A History of the 148th Pennsylvania Volunteers.* Des Moines, IA, 1904.

James Frederick Weaver
ROGER D. HUNT COLLECTION, USAMHI.

Richard White
HARRISBURG CIVIL WAR ROUND TABLE COLLECTION, USAMHI.

Born: Feb. 5, 1826 Indiana, PA
Died: April 14, 1865 near Indiana, PA
Education: Attended Yale University, New Haven, CT
Occupation: Early in life engaged in tanning and lumber business and was also involved in several iron furnaces. Later edited and published several newspapers.
Miscellaneous: Resided Indiana, Indiana Co., PA; and Ebensburg, Cambria Co., PA. Brother of Bvt. Brig. Gen. Harry White.
Buried: St. Bernard's Cemetery, Indiana, PA
References: Clarence D. Stephenson. *Indiana County 175th Anniversary History*. Indiana, PA, 1983. *Indiana County Heritage*, Vol. 2, No. 1 (Fall 1967). Pension File and Military Service File, National Archives. W. Wayne Smith. *The Price of Patriotism: Indiana County, Pennsylvania, and the Civil War*. Shippensburg, PA, 1998. Letters Received, Volunteer Service Branch, Adjutant General's Office, Files P1726(VS)1864 and W1933(VS)1864, National Archives. Obituary, *Indiana Democrat*, April 20, 1865.

RICHARD WHITE

Major, 10 PA Infantry, April 24, 1861. Honorably mustered out, July 31, 1861. Colonel, 55 PA Infantry, Aug. 2, 1861. Commanded 1 Brigade, 3 Division, 10 Army Corps, Army of the James, April 28–May 16, 1864. Taken prisoner, Drewry's Bluff, VA, May 16, 1864. Confined Libby Prison, Richmond, VA; Macon, GA; and Charleston, SC. Paroled Aug. 3, 1864. In Dec. 1864 he was tried on charges of conspiring to defraud the men of his regiment of their bounty moneys, but the charges were not sustained. Honorably mustered out, March 24, 1865.

JAMES PYLE WICKERSHAM

Colonel, 47 PA Militia, July 9, 1863. Honorably mustered out, Aug. 14, 1863

James Pyle Wickersham
SARTAIN ENGRAVINGS, THE HISTORICAL SOCIETY
OF PENNSYLVANIA.

Born: March 5, 1825 Newlin Twp., Chester Co., PA
Died: March 25, 1891 Lancaster, PA
Education: Attended Unionville (PA) Academy
Occupation: School principal and educator
Offices/Honors: PA Superintendent of Public Instruction, 1866–81. US Minister to Denmark, 1882.
Miscellaneous: Resided Lancaster, Lancaster Co., PA. Brother of Colonel Morris D. Wickersham (Quartermaster, USV)
Buried: Lancaster Cemetery, Lancaster, PA
References: *Dictionary of American Biography.* Obituary, *Lancaster Daily New Era*, March 25, 1891. *National Cyclopedia of American Biography.* Obituary, *Pennsylvania School Journal*, Vol. 39 (April 1891). Obituary, *West Chester Daily Local News*, March 26, 1891. Paul K. Adams. "Lancaster's Educational Reformer: James P. Wickersham, The Early Years," *Journal of the Lancaster County Historical Society*, Vol. 97, No. 4 (Winter 1995).

SAMUEL MORRIS WICKERSHAM

Colonel, 22 PA Militia, Sept. 16, 1862. Honorably discharged, Oct. 1, 1862. Lieutenant Colonel, 169 PA Infantry, Dec. 2, 1862. Honorably mustered out, July 27, 1863.

Born: 1819 Philadelphia, PA
Died: March 15, 1894 Pittsburgh, PA
Occupation: Proprietor of a lumber mill and wire works. Iron broker in later life.
Miscellaneous: Resided Pittsburgh, PA
Buried: Allegheny Cemetery, Pittsburgh, PA (Section 21, Lot 34)
References: Obituary, *Pittsburgh Press*, March 16, 1894. Pension File and Military Service File, National Archives. Obituary, *Pittsburgh Dispatch*, March 16, 1894.

GEORGE BERRYHILL WIESTLING

Colonel, 23 PA Militia, Sept. 21, 1862. Honorably discharged, Oct. 1, 1862. Colonel, 177 PA Infantry, Nov. 28, 1862. Honorably mustered out, Aug. 7, 1863.

George Berryhill Wiestling
ROBERT MCALLISTER PAPERS, SPECIAL COLLECTIONS AND
UNIVERSITY ARCHIVES, RUTGERS UNIVERSITY LIBRARIES.
CHARLES D. FREDRICKS & CO., "SPECIALITE,"
587 BROADWAY, NEW YORK.

Born: Jan. 28, 1835 Harrisburg, PA
Died: June 17, 1891 Mont Alto, Franklin Co., PA
Occupation: Civil engineer and railroad contractor (business partner of Bvt. Brig. Gen. Robert McAllister) before war. Railroad superintendent and iron works manager after war.
Miscellaneous: Resided Harrisburg, Dauphin Co., PA; and Mont Alto, Franklin Co., PA
Buried: Harrisburg Cemetery, Harrisburg, PA (Section D, Lot 58)
References: *Biographical Directory of the Railway Officials of America.* Chicago, IL, 1887. Obituary, *Harrisburg Patriot*, June 18, 1891. William H. Egle. *Pennsylvania Genealogies.* Harrisburg, PA, 1896. James I. Robertson, Jr., editor. *The Civil War Letters of General Robert McAllister.* New Brunswick, NJ, 1965. Military Service File, National Archives. Obituary, *Chambersburg Valley Spirit*, June 17, 1891.

VINCENT MEIGS WILCOX

Lieutenant Colonel, 132 PA Infantry, Aug. 26, 1862. Colonel, 132 PA Infantry, Sept. 18, 1862. Resigned Jan. 21, 1863, on account of physical disability due to "persistent chronic diarrhea."

Born: Oct. 17, 1828 Madison, CT
Died: May 9, 1896 New York City, NY
Occupation: School teacher and dry goods merchant before war. President of E. & H.T. Anthony & Co., manufacturers and importers of photography supplies, after war.
Miscellaneous: Resided Madison, New Haven Co., CT; Scranton, Lackawanna Co., PA; and New York City, NY
Buried: West Cemetery, Madison, CT
References: Pension File and Military Service File, National Archives. Henry P. Phelps. *Personal Records, Department of New York, GAR.* N.p., 1896. William H. Powell, editor. *Officers of the Army and Navy (Volunteer) Who Served in the Civil War.* Philadelphia, PA, 1893. Frederick L. Hitchcock. *War from the Inside: The Story of the 132nd Regiment Pennsylvania Volunteer Infantry in the War for the Suppression of the Rebellion.* Philadelphia, PA, 1904. Obituary Circular, Whole No. 519, New York MOLLUS. Samuel P. Bates. *Martial Deeds of Pennsylvania.* Philadelphia, PA, 1875. Obituary, *New York Times*, May 12, 1896. Charles Morris, editor. *Makers of New York.* Philadelphia, PA, 1895.

Vincent Meigs Wilcox
MASSACHUSETTS MOLLUS COLLECTION, USAMHI.

JOSEPH WILLCOX

Colonel, 16 PA Militia, Sept. 17, 1862. Honorably discharged, Sept. 27, 1862.

Born: Aug. 11, 1829 Concord, PA
Died: Sept. 30, 1918 Philadelphia, PA
Occupation: Paper manufacturer. Retired at age of 38 to devote his time to scientific and literary pursuits, primarily involving geology and mineralogy.
Miscellaneous: Resided Ivy Mills, Delaware Co., PA; and Bridgewater, Delaware Co., PA
Buried: St. Thomas the Apostle Catholic Churchyard, Chester Heights, Delaware Co., PA
References: Martha S. Albertson. *A Willcox Family History, 1689–1977.* N.p., 1977. Obituary, *West Chester Daily Local News*, Oct. 2, 1918. John W. Jordan, editor. *Colonial Families of Philadelphia.* New York and Chicago, 1911.

Joseph Willcox (postwar)
LEACH'S PHILADELPHIA PORTRAITS,
THE HISTORICAL SOCIETY OF PENNSYLVANIA.

EDWARD CHARLES WILLIAMS

Brig. Gen., PA Volunteers, April 19, 1861. Honorably mustered out, July 20, 1861. Colonel, 9 PA Cavalry, Oct. 20, 1861. Resigned Oct. 9, 1862, due to "a question of rank."

Born: Feb. 10, 1820 Philadelphia, PA

Died: Feb. 16, 1900 Chapman, Snyder Co., PA

Other Wars: Mexican War (Captain, Co. G, 2 PA Infantry)

Occupation: Bookbinder and stationer before war. Merchant and postmaster after war.

Offices/Honors: Sheriff of Dauphin Co., PA, 1850–54. Brig. Gen., PA State Militia, 1854–61. Postmaster, Chapman, PA, 1875–1900.

Miscellaneous: Resided Harrisburg, Dauphin Co., PA; and Chapman, Snyder Co., PA, after 1871

Buried: St. Johns Evangelical United Brethren Churchyard, Chapman, PA

References: Dewey S. Herrold. "Brigadier General Edward Charles Williams," *The Snyder County Historical Society Bulletin*, Vol. 2, No. 4 (1942). *Commemorative Biographical Encyclopedia of Dauphin County, PA.* Chambersburg, PA, 1896. Pension File and Military Service File, National Archives. F. Ellis and A. N. Hungerford. *History of That Part of the Susquehanna and Juniata Valleys Embraced in the Counties of Mifflin, Juniata, Perry, Union and Snyder.* Philadelphia, PA, 1886. John W. Rowell. *Yankee Cavalrymen: Through the Civil War With the 9th Pennsylvania Cavalry.* Knoxville, TN, 1971. William H. Egle. *History of the Counties of Dauphin and Lebanon in the Commonwealth of Pennsylvania.* Philadelphia, PA, 1883.

Edward Charles Williams
RANDY HACKENBURG COLLECTION.

Joseph Hemphill Wilson (second from left) with officers of the 101st Pennsylvania, from left to right, Maj. Joseph S. Hoard, Lt. Col. David B. Morris, and Adjutant Robert F. Cooper

FROM *HISTORY OF THE 101ST REGIMENT PENNSYLVANIA VETERAN VOLUNTEER INFANTRY.*

JOSEPH HEMPHILL WILSON

Colonel, 101 PA Infantry, Oct. 4, 1861

Born: May 16, 1820 Franklin Twp., Beaver Co., PA
Died: May 30, 1862 Roper Church, VA (typhoid fever)
Education: Graduated Jefferson College, Canonsburg, PA, 1848
Occupation: Lawyer
Offices/Honors: District Attorney, Beaver Co., PA, 1853–56. PA House of Representatives, 1859–61.
Miscellaneous: Resided Beaver, Beaver Co., PA
Buried: Zelienople Cemetery, Zelienople, PA
References: Samuel P. Bates. *Martial Deeds of Pennsylvania.* Philadelphia, PA, 1875. John A. Reed. *History of the 101st Regiment Pennsylvania Veteran Volunteer Infantry.* Chicago, IL, 1910. William H. Egle. *Pennsylvania Genealogies.* Harrisburg, PA, 1896. Military Service File, National Archives.

WILLIAM WILSON

1 Lieutenant, Co. B, 81 PA Infantry, Aug. 10, 1861. Captain, Co. E, 81 PA Infantry, Dec. 9, 1861. GSW left hand, Malvern Hill, VA, July 1, 1862. Shell wound left side of head, Fredericksburg, VA, Dec. 13, 1862. Major, 81 PA Infantry, July 24, 1863. Lieutenant Colonel, 81 PA Infantry, March 15, 1864. GSW left knee, Spotsylvania, VA, May 13, 1864. Commanded Consolidated Brigade, 1 Division, 2 Army Corps, Army of the Potomac, Aug. 29–Sept. 12, 1864. Commanded 1 Brigade, 1 Division, 2 Army Corps, Oct. 6–Nov. 3, 1864 and June 20–28, 1865. Colonel, 81 PA Infantry, Oct. 30, 1864. Muster as colonel cancelled, Dec. 8, 1864, since "he neither had a sufficient number of companies nor men to muster a colonel." Honorably mustered out, June 29, 1865. Bvt. Colonel, USV, March 13, 1865, for gallant and meritorious conduct during the war.

Born: 1835? County Tyrone, Ireland
Died: Sept. 18, 1894 Camden, NJ
Occupation: Carriage painter. Inspector in Philadelphia Custom House, 1865–71.
Miscellaneous: Resided Camden, Camden Co., NJ
Buried: Evergreen Cemetery, Camden, NJ
References: Pension File and Military Service File, National Archives. Obituary, *Camden Daily Telegram,* Sept. 18, 1894. Letters Received, Volunteer Service Branch, Adjutant General's Office, Files S3079(VS)1864 and W2703(VS)1864, National Archives.

FRANCIS WISTER

Captain, 12 US Infantry, Aug. 5, 1861. Acting ADC, Staff of Major Gen. Andrew A. Humphreys, Nov. 1864–April 1865. Colonel, 215 PA Infantry, April 21, 1865. Commanded Provisional Brigade, 9 Army Corps, Army of the Potomac, May 1865. Honorably mustered out, July 31, 1865. Resigned regular army commission, April 5, 1866.

Born: June 2, 1841 Germantown, PA
Died: Nov. 22, 1905 Philadelphia, PA
Education: Graduated University of Pennsylvania, Philadelphia, PA, 1860
Occupation: Coal and iron merchant
Miscellaneous: Resided Philadelphia, PA. Brother of Bvt. Brig. Gen. Langhorne Wister.
Buried: Holy Cross Cemetery, Yeadon, Delaware Co., PA (Section 9, Range 10, Lot 6)

Francis Wister
MEADE ALBUM, CIVIL WAR LIBRARY & MUSEUM, PHILADELPHIA, PA. F. GUTEKUNST, NO. 704 & 706 ARCH STREET, PHILADELPHIA, PA.

References: Obituary Circular, Whole No. 550, Pennsylvania MOLLUS. Pension File and Military Service File, National Archives. Charles Morris, editor. *Makers of Philadelphia.* Philadelphia, PA, 1894. John M. Bullard. *The Rotches.* New Bedford, MA, 1947. Obituary, *Philadelphia Public Ledger,* Nov. 23, 1905. William H. Powell and Edward Shippen, editors. *Officers of the Army and Navy (Regular) Who Served in the Civil War.* Philadelphia, PA, 1892. Letters Received, Volunteer Service Branch, Adjutant General's Office, File P1437(VS)1865, National Archives.

Edward Lawrence Witman
KEN TURNER COLLECTION.
J. C. ELROD'S GALLERY, 409 MAIN STREET, LOUISVILLE, KY.

EDWARD LAWRENCE WITMAN

Private, Co. F, 25 PA Infantry, May 2, 1861. Honorably mustered out, July 26, 1861. 1 Lieutenant, Co. D, 46 PA Infantry, Sept. 2, 1861. Acting ADC, 1 Brigade, 1 Division, 5 Army Corps, Army of the Potomac, March 20–April 4, 1862. Acting ADC, 1 Brigade, 1 Division, Department of the Shenandoah, April 4–June 26, 1862. Acting ADC, 1 Brigade, 1 Division, 2 Army Corps, Army of Virginia, June 26–Sept. 12, 1862. Acting ADC, 1 Brigade, 1 Division, 12 Army Corps, Army of the Potomac, Sept. 12–Oct. 1862. Captain, Co. D, 46 PA Infantry, Sept. 14, 1862. Acting AAG, 1 Brigade, 1 Division, 12 Army Corps, Army of the Potomac, Aug. 17–Sept. 25, 1863. Acting AAG, 1 Brigade, 1 Division, 12 Army Corps, Army of the Cumberland, Sept. 25, 1863–Feb. 1, 1864. Acting AAG, 1 Brigade, 1 Division, 20 Army Corps, Army of the Cumberland, April 14–June 30, 1864. GSW right leg, Resaca, GA, May 15, 1864. Lieutenant Colonel, 210 PA Infantry, Sept. 27, 1864. *Colonel,* 210 PA Infantry, April 12, 1865. Honorably mustered out, May 30, 1865.

Born: Oct. 19, 1838 Harrisburg, PA
Died: April 24, 1912 Harrisburg, PA
Occupation: Druggist and later civil engineer engaged in railroad construction
Miscellaneous: Resided Harrisburg, Dauphin Co., PA; and San Francisco, CA
Buried: Harrisburg Cemetery, Harrisburg, PA (Section H-2, Lot 106)
References: Pension File and Military Service File, National Archives. Obituary, *Harrisburg Patriot,* April 25, 1912. William H. Egle. *Pennsylvania Genealogies.* Harrisburg, PA, 1896. Letters Received, Volunteer Service Branch, Adjutant General's Office, File P2687(VS)1864, National Archives.

ENOS WOODWARD

Captain, Co. L, 71 PA Infantry, July 1, 1861. Captain, Co. B, 71 PA Infantry, July 23, 1862. Resigned Sept. 19, 1862, because "fifteen months of constant, arduous and much exposed service with my regiment has so injured my health that I am no longer fitted for the duties which my position and rank involve." Colonel, 44 PA Militia, July 6, 1863. Honorably mustered out, Aug. 27, 1863.

Born: June 1, 1833 Steubenville, OH
Died: Dec. 17, 1898 New Holland, PA

Occupation: Wholesale grocer before war. Commercial broker and newspaper correspondent after war.

Miscellaneous: Resided Philadelphia, PA; Pittsburgh, PA; and Wernersville, Berks Co., PA

Buried: Woodlands Cemetery, Philadelphia, PA (Section I, Lots 682–685)

References: Obituary, *Philadelphia Public Ledger*, Dec. 19, 1898. Pension File and Military Service File, National Archives. Norma S. Woodward. *Descendants of Richard Woodward, New England, 1589–1982.* Baltimore, MD, 1982. Obituary, *Pittsburgh Dispatch*, Dec. 18, 1898. Obituary, *Lancaster New Era*, Dec. 20, 1898.

RICHARD HOBSON WOOLWORTH

Major, 3 PA Reserves, June 21, 1861. Lieutenant Colonel, 4 PA Reserves, June 1, 1862. GSW Charles City Cross Roads, VA, June 30, 1862. Taken prisoner, Charles City Cross Roads, VA, July 1, 1862. Confined Richmond, VA. Paroled July 17, 1862. GSW left groin, Fredericksburg, VA, Dec. 13, 1862. Colonel, 4 PA Reserves, Dec. 24, 1862. Shell wound left groin, Cloyd's Mountain, VA, May 9, 1864.

Richard Hobson Woolworth

KEN TURNER COLLECTION.

SLAGLE, 288 PENNA. AVENUE, CORNER 11TH STREET, WASHINGTON, DC.

Born: Nov. 1824 Mantuaville (now part of Philadelphia), PA

Died: May 9, 1864 KIA Cloyd's Mountain, VA

Occupation: Stock broker

Miscellaneous: Resided Philadelphia, PA

Buried: Lawnview Cemetery, Rockledge, PA (Glenwood Lawn, Range 26, Grave 30, unmarked)

References: Josiah R. Sypher. *History of the Pennsylvania Reserve Corps.* Lancaster, PA, 1865. Pension File and Military Service File, National Archives. Samuel P. Bates. *Martial Deeds of Pennsylvania.* Philadelphia, PA, 1875.

John Louden Wright

USAMHI.

R. W. ADDIS, PHOTOGRAPHER, McCLEES' GALLERY, 308 PENNA. AVENUE, WASHINGTON, DC.

JOHN LOUDEN WRIGHT

1 Lieutenant, Co. K, 5 PA Reserves, June 21, 1861. Colonel, 2 PA Militia, Sept. 13, 1862, while detailed on recruiting service at Camp Curtin, Harrisburg, PA. Honorably discharged as colonel Sept. 25, 1862. Acting ADC, 3 Brigade, 3 Division, 1 Army Corps, Army of the Potomac, Jan. 10–Feb. 1863. Acting ADC, 3 Brigade, PA Reserve Division, 22 Army Corps, Department of Washington, Feb.–June 1863. 1 Lieutenant, Adjutant, 5 PA Reserves, May 28, 1863. Acting AAG, 3 Brigade, 3 Division, 5 Army Corps, Army of the Potomac, June 1863–May 31, 1864. Captain, Co. F, 5 PA Reserves, May 7, 1864. Honorably mustered out, June 11, 1864.

Born: Oct. 1, 1838 Columbia, PA
Died: Feb. 16, 1916 Columbia, PA
Occupation: Farmer and machinist
Offices/Honors: Postmaster, Columbia, PA, 1890–94
Miscellaneous: Resided Columbia, Lancaster Co., PA
Buried: Mount Bethel Cemetery, Columbia, PA
References: Pension File and Military Service File, National Archives. *Portrait and Biographical Record of Lancaster County, PA.* Chicago, IL, 1894. Obituary, *Lancaster New Era*, Feb. 17, 1916.

GEORGE CAMPBELL WYNKOOP

Brig. Gen., PA Volunteers, April 20, 1861. Commanded 2 Brigade, 2 Division, Department of Pennsylvania, June–July 25, 1861. Honorably mustered out, Aug. 1, 1861. Colonel, 7 PA Cavalry, Aug. 21, 1861. Discharged for disability, June 25, 1863, due to "neuralgic rheumatism affecting both of his arms and shoulders."

Born: Feb. 27, 1806 Brookeville, Montgomery Co., MD
Died: Sept. 29, 1882 Pottsville, PA
Occupation: Coal agent
Offices/Honors: Sheriff of Schuylkill Co., PA, 1867–70
Miscellaneous: Resided Pottsville, Schuylkill Co., PA. Uncle of Colonel John E. Wynkoop.
Buried: Presbyterian Cemetery, Pottsville, PA
References: Richard Wynkoop. *Wynkoop Genealogy in the United States of America.* New York City, NY, 1904. Pension File and Military Service File, National Archives. Obituary, *Pottsville Miners' Journal*, Sept. 30, 1882. Francis B. Wallace, compiler. *Memorial of the Patriotism of Schuylkill County in the American Slaveholder's Rebellion.* Pottsville, PA, 1865. Letters Received, Volunteer Service Branch,

George Campbell Wynkoop
MASSACHUSETTS MOLLUS COLLECTION, USAMHI.

Adjutant General's Office, File S1086(VS)1863, National Archives. William B. Sipes. *The 7th Pennsylvania Veteran Volunteer Cavalry, Its Record, Reminiscences and Roster.* Pottsville, PA, 1906.

JOHN ESTILL WYNKOOP

Major, 6 PA Infantry, April 22, 1861. Honorably mustered out, July 27, 1861. Major, 7 PA Cavalry, Oct. 25, 1861. Colonel, 20 PA Cavalry (6 months), July 7, 1863. Honorably mustered out, Jan. 7, 1864. Colonel, 20 PA Cavalry (3 years), Feb. 16, 1864. Commanded 2 Brigade, 1 Cavalry Division, Army of West Virginia, April–July 1864, Aug. 29–Sept. 15, 1864, and Oct. 14–20, 1864. Dismissed July 28, 1864, for "drunkenness and conduct unbecoming an officer and a gentleman." President Lincoln disapproved his dismissal, Aug. 13, 1864, with the endorsement, "Induced to believe the

John Estill Wynkoop
FROM *THE 7TH PENNSYLVANIA VETERAN VOLUNTEER CAVALRY,
ITS RECORD, REMINISCENCES AND ROSTER.*

intoxication of Col. Wynkoop was a single instance, contrary to the whole habit of his life." Commanded 1 Cavalry Division, Army of West Virginia, Sept.–Oct. 1864. In forwarding Wynkoop's application for extension of leave of absence, Jan. 3, 1865, Brig. Gen. Alfred T. A. Torbert took issue with his statements, mentioned another instance of Wynkoop being "disgustingly drunk," and recommended that he be at once ordered back to his regiment or mustered out of the service. Upon Maj. Gen. Philip Sheridan's added recommendation that he "be mustered out of service for the benefit of the service," and in view of his former conduct, he was dismissed Jan. 18, 1865.

Born: May 9, 1825 Newtown, Bucks Co., PA
Died: Jan. 17, 1901 Philadelphia, PA
Occupation: Engaged in the coal and timber business and in the operation of iron furnaces. Later engaged in contracting and paving business.
Miscellaneous: Resided Pottsville, Schuylkill Co., PA; and Philadelphia, PA. Nephew of Colonel George C. Wynkoop.
Buried: Charles Baber Cemetery, Pottsville, PA (Section L, Lot 1)
References: Richard Wynkoop. *Wynkoop Genealogy in the United States of America.* New York City, NY, 1904. Obituary, *Pottsville Republican,* Jan. 18, 1901. Obituary, *Philadelphia Public Ledger,* Jan. 19, 1901. Francis B. Wallace, compiler. *Memorial of the Patriotism of Schuylkill County in the American Slaveholder's Rebellion.* Pottsville, PA, 1865. William B. Sipes. *The 7th Pennsylvania Veteran Volunteer Cavalry, Its Record, Reminiscences and Roster.* Pottsville, PA, 1906. Pension File and Military Service File, National Archives. Letters Received, Volunteer Service Branch, Adjutant General's Office, File P2264(VS)1864, National Archives.

SAMUEL YOHE

Colonel, 1 PA Infantry, April 20, 1861. Honorably mustered out, July 27, 1861. Provost Marshal, 11 District of Pennsylvania, May 1863–April, 1865.

Born: April 15, 1805 Easton, PA
Died: July 5, 1880 Philadelphia, PA
Occupation: Dry goods merchant and miller before war. Banker and broker after war.
Offices/Honors: Prothonotary, Northampton Co., PA, 1836–39. Treasurer, Northampton Co., PA, 1848–50.
Miscellaneous: Resided Easton, Northampton Co., PA; and Philadelphia, PA, after 1867. Brother-in-law of Colonel Melchior H. Horn.
Buried: Easton Cemetery, Easton, PA (Section N, Lot 161)
References: Frank B. Copp. *Biographical Sketches of Some of Easton's Prominent Citizens.* Easton, PA, 1879. Obituary, *Easton Daily Express,* July 6, 1880. Pension File, National Archives. Obituary, *Philadelphia Public Ledger,* July 8, 1880.

Samuel Yohe (postwar)
FROM *BIOGRAPHICAL SKETCHES OF SOME OF
EASTON'S PROMINENT CITIZENS.*

WILLIAM HENRY YOUNG

Colonel, KY Light Cavalry (later 3 PA Cavalry), July 10, 1861. Having been improperly mustered as colonel before the regiment was complete and facing unsubstantiated charges of having a "very pernicious influence among the men of the regiment" and conspiring to defraud the government of a "very considerable amount of property in horses, equipments and rations," he was superseded as colonel, Oct. 12, 1861, by William W. Averell. When he protested Averell's muster as colonel, he was immediately arrested by Brig. Gen. George Stoneman, and after several weeks of close confinement at Old Capitol Prison with no charges preferred against him, he was ordered to leave Washington, DC. Unable to obtain redress of his grievances, he resigned April 14, 1862, to date from Oct. 31, 1861.

Born: 1819? NY
Died: Date and place of death unknown
Occupation: Lawyer and editor
Miscellaneous: Resided Louisville, KY; Philadelphia, PA; Washington, DC; and Buffalo, NY
Buried: Burial place unknown

References: Pension File and Military Service File, National Archives. Letters Received, Volunteer Service Branch, Adjutant General's Office, Files Y1(VS)1861 and Y1(VS)1862, National Archives. William Brooke Rawle. *History of the 3rd Pennsylvania Cavalry in the American Civil War.* Philadelphia, PA, 1905.

THOMAS A. ZIEGLE

Captain, Co. A, 16 PA Infantry, April 20, 1861. Colonel, 16 PA Infantry, May 3, 1861. Honorably mustered out, Aug. 1, 1861. Colonel, 107 PA Infantry, March 6, 1862.

Thomas A. Ziegle
COURTESY OF THE AUTHOR.

Born: Sept. 8, 1824 York, PA
Died: July 15, 1862 near Warrenton, VA (congestion of the brain)
Education: Attended Gettysburg (PA) College
Other Wars: Mexican War (1 Sergeant, Co. C, 1 PA Infantry)
Occupation: Lawyer
Miscellaneous: Resided York, York Co., PA
Buried: Prospect Hill Cemetery, York, PA (Section D, Lot 208)
References: Samuel P. Bates. *Martial Deeds of Pennsylvania*. Philadelphia, PA, 1875. John Gibson, editor. *History of York County, PA*. Chicago, IL, 1886. Franklin B. Hough. *History of Duryee's Brigade*. Albany, NY, 1864. Pension File and Military Service File, National Archives. Obituary, *York Democratic Press*, July 25, 1862.

HENRY I. ZINN

1 Lieutenant, Co. H, 7 PA Reserves, May 8, 1861. Captain, Co. H, 7 PA Reserves, June 28, 1861. Resigned Nov. 30, 1861, "feeling it due myself to sever my connection with the regiment." Captain, Co. F, 130 PA Infantry, Aug. 9, 1862. Colonel, 130 PA Infantry, Aug. 17, 1862. GSW head, Fredericksburg, VA, Dec. 13, 1862.

Born: Dec. 11, 1834 Dover Twp., York Co., PA
Died: Dec. 13, 1862 KIA Fredericksburg, VA
Education: Attended Cumberland Valley Institute, Mechanicsburg, PA
Occupation: School teacher
Miscellaneous: Resided Allen, Cumberland Co., PA
Buried: Mount Zion Cemetery, near Allen, PA

Henry I. Zinn
FROM *CUMBERLAND COUNTY PENNSYLVANIA IN THE CIVIL WAR.*

References: Samuel P. Bates. *Martial Deeds of Pennsylvania*. Philadelphia, PA, 1875. John D. Hemminger. *Cumberland County Pennsylvania in the Civil War*. Carlisle, PA, 1926. Pension File and Military Service File, National Archives. Obituary, *Cumberland Valley Journal*, Dec. 18, 1862.

NEW JERSEY

1st Cavalry

William Halsted	Sept. 1, 1861	Discharged Feb. 18, 1862
Percy Wyndham	Feb. 19, 1862	Discharged July 5, 1864
John W. Kester	July 6, 1864	Mustered out Sept. 25, 1864
Hugh H. Janeway	Oct. 11, 1864	KIA April 5, 1865
Myron H. Beaumont	May 4, 1865	Mustered out July 24, 1865

2nd Cavalry

Joseph Karge	June 23, 1863	Mustered out Nov. 1, 1865, **Bvt. Brig. Gen.**

3rd Cavalry

Andrew J. Morrison	Nov. 4, 1863	Resigned Aug. 29, 1864
Alexander C. M. Pennington	Sept. 8, 1864	Mustered out Aug. 1, 1865, **Bvt. Brig. Gen.**
William P. Robeson, Jr.	Aug. 4, 1865	Not mustered, **Bvt. Brig. Gen.**

1st Militia

Adolphus J. Johnson	April 30, 1861	Mustered out July 31, 1861

1st Infantry

William R. Montgomery	May 21, 1861	Promoted **Brig. Gen., USV**, Aug. 29, 1861
Alfred T. A. Torbert	Sept. 1, 1861	Promoted **Brig. Gen., USV**, Nov. 29, 1862
Mark W. Collet	Nov. 29, 1862	KIA May 3, 1863
William Henry, Jr.	March 11, 1864	Mustered out June 23, 1864

2nd Militia

Henry M. Baker	May 1, 1861	Mustered out July 31, 1861

2nd Infantry

George W. McLean	May 22, 1861	Resigned Dec. 31, 1861
Isaac M. Tucker	Jan. 20, 1862	KIA June 27, 1862
Samuel L. Buck	July 2, 1862	Mustered out June 21, 1864
William H. Penrose	June 22, 1865	Promoted **Brig. Gen., USV**, July 1, 1865
James W. McNeely	July 10, 1865	Mustered out July 11, 1865

3rd Militia

William Napton	April 27, 1861	Mustered out July 31, 1861

3rd Infantry

George W. Taylor	May 23, 1861	Promoted **Brig. Gen., USV**, May 9, 1862
Henry W. Brown	May 15, 1862	Mustered out June 23, 1864

4th Militia

Matthew Miller, Jr.	April 27, 1861	Mustered out July 31, 1861

4th Infantry

James H. Simpson	Aug. 12, 1861	Resigned Aug. 24, 1862, **Bvt. Brig. Gen.**
William B. Hatch	Aug. 26, 1862	DOW Dec. 18, 1862
William Birney	Jan. 8, 1863	Promoted **Brig. Gen., USV**, May 22, 1863
James N. Duffy	Sept. 29, 1863	Not mustered
David Vickers	March 21, 1865	Mustered out May 18, 1865, **Bvt. Brig. Gen.**
Edward L. Campbell	May 29, 1865	Mustered out July 9, 1865, **Bvt. Brig. Gen.**

5th Infantry

Samuel H. Starr	Aug. 28, 1861	Resigned Oct. 20, 1862
William J. Sewell	Oct. 21, 1862	Resigned July 2, 1864, **Bvt. Brig. Gen.**
Ashbel W. Angel	July 2, 1864	Mustered out Sept. 7, 1864

6th Infantry

James T. Hatfield	Sept. 2, 1861	Resigned April 27, 1862
Gershom Mott	May 7, 1862	Promoted **Brig. Gen., USV**, Sept. 7, 1862
George C. Burling	Sept. 10, 1862	Resigned March 4, 1864, **Bvt. Brig. Gen.**
Stephen R. Gilkyson	June 1, 1864	Mustered out Sept. 7, 1864

7th Infantry

Joseph W. Revere	Aug. 31, 1861	Promoted **Brig. Gen., USV**, Oct. 25, 1862
Louis R. Francine	Dec. 9, 1862	DOW July 16, 1863, **Bvt. Brig. Gen.**
Francis Price, Jr.	July 23, 1863	Mustered out July 17, 1865, **Bvt. Brig. Gen.**

8th Infantry

Adolphus J. Johnson	Sept. 14, 1861	Resigned March 19, 1863
John Ramsey	April 1, 1863	Mustered out July 17, 1865, **Bvt. Brig. Gen.**

9th Infantry

Joseph W. Allen	Sept. 23, 1861	Died Jan. 15, 1862
Charles A. Heckman	Feb. 10, 1862	Promoted **Brig. Gen., USV**, Nov. 29, 1862
Abram Zabriskie	Jan. 8, 1863	DOW May 24, 1864
James Stewart, Jr.	June 15, 1864	Mustered out July 12, 1865, **Bvt. Brig. Gen.**

10th Infantry

William Bryan	Dec. 26, 1861	Discharged March 6, 1862
William R. Murphy	Jan. 19, 1862	Resigned March 12, 1863
Henry O. Ryerson	March 26, 1863	DOW May 12, 1864
Enos Fourat	March 31, 1865	Declined
Henry A. Perrine	June 30, 1865	Not mustered

11th Infantry

Robert McAllister	June 30, 1862	Mustered out June 6, 1865, **Bvt. Brig. Gen.**

12th Infantry

Robert C. Johnson	July 9, 1862	Discharged Feb. 27, 1863
J. Howard Willets	Feb. 27, 1863	Discharged Dec. 19, 1864
John Willian, Jr.	Feb. 23, 1865	Mustered out July 15, 1865, **Bvt. Brig. Gen.**

13th Infantry

Ezra A. Carman	July 8, 1862	Mustered out June 8, 1865, **Bvt. Brig. Gen.**

14th Infantry

William S. Truex	July 7, 1862	Mustered out June 18, 1865, **Bvt. Brig. Gen.**

15th Infantry

Samuel Fowler	July 10, 1862	Resigned March 6, 1863
Alexander C. M. Pennington	March 28, 1863	Declined, **Bvt. Brig. Gen.**
William H. Penrose	April 10, 1863	To 2nd NJ Infantry, June 22, 1865, **Brig. Gen., USV**

16th Infantry
See 1st Cavalry

17th Infantry
See 1st Militia

18th Infantry
See 2nd Militia

19th Infantry
See 3rd Militia

20th Infantry
See 4th Militia

21st Infantry

Gilliam Van Houten	Sept. 6, 1862	DOW May 6, 1863

22nd Infantry

Cornelius Fornet	Sept. 9, 1862	Commission revoked
Abraham G. Demarest	Jan. 26, 1863	Mustered out June 25, 1863

23rd Infantry

John S. Cox	Sept. 11, 1862	Resigned Nov. 9, 1862
Henry O. Ryerson	Nov. 12, 1862	To 10th NJ Infantry, March 26, 1863
E. Burd Grubb	April 9, 1863	Mustered out June 27, 1863, **Bvt. Brig. Gen.**

24th Infantry

William B. Robertson	Sept. 16, 1862	Mustered out June 29, 1863

25th Infantry

Andrew Derrom	Sept. 24, 1862	Mustered out June 20, 1863

26th Infantry

Andrew J. Morrison	Sept. 16, 1862	Dismissed June 11, 1863

27th Infantry

George W. Mindil	Oct. 3, 1862	Mustered out July 2, 1863, **Bvt. Brig. Gen.**

28th Infantry
    Moses N. Wisewell   Sept. 15, 1862   Mustered out July 6, 1863, **Bvt. Brig. Gen.**

29th Infantry
    Edwin F. Applegate   Sept. 12, 1862   Resigned Jan. 16, 1863
    William R. Taylor   Jan. 27, 1863   Mustered out June 30, 1863

30th Infantry
    Alexander E. Donaldson   Sept. 11, 1862   Resigned March 1, 1863
    John J. Cladek   March 4, 1863   Mustered out June 27, 1863

31st Infantry
    Alexander P. Berthoud   Sept. 11, 1862   Mustered out June 24, 1863

32nd Infantry
    See 2nd Cavalry

33rd Infantry
    George W. Mindil   July 10, 1863   Mustered out July 17, 1865, **Bvt. Brig. Gen.**

34th Infantry
    William Hudson Lawrence   Sept. 16, 1863   Resigned Aug. 3, 1865, **Bvt. Brig. Gen.**
    Timothy C. Moore   Nov. 8, 1865   Mustered out April 30, 1866, **Bvt. Brig. Gen.**

35th Infantry
    John J. Cladek   Aug. 15, 1863   Dismissed Aug. 12, 1865

36th Infantry
    See 3rd Cavalry

37th Infantry
    E. Burd Grubb   June 23, 1864   Mustered out Oct. 1, 1864, **Bvt. Brig. Gen.**

38th Infantry
    William J. Sewell   Aug. 31, 1864   Mustered out June 30, 1865, **Bvt. Brig. Gen.**

39th Infantry
    Abram C. Wildrick   Sept. 23, 1864   Mustered out June 17, 1865, **Bvt. Brig. Gen.**

40th Infantry
    Stephen R. Gilkyson   March 7, 1865   Mustered out July 13, 1865

JOSEPH WARNER ALLEN

Colonel, 9 NJ Infantry, Sept. 23, 1861

Born: July 22, 1811 near Bristol, PA
Died: Jan. 15, 1862 Hatteras Inlet, NC (drowned)
Occupation: Civil engineer engaged in railroad and public works construction
Offices/Honors: NJ Senate, 1853–58
Miscellaneous: Resided Bordentown, Burlington Co., NJ
Buried: Christ Episcopal Churchyard, Bordentown, NJ
References: J. Madison Drake. *The History of the 9th New Jersey Veteran Vols.* Elizabeth, NJ, 1889. John Y. Foster. *New Jersey and the Rebellion.* Newark, NJ, 1868. Samuel F. Bigelow and George J. Hagar, editors. *Biographical Cyclopedia of New Jersey.* New York City, NY, 1908. Civil War Officer Memorials, Department of Defense, New Jersey Archives.

Joseph Warner Allen
US MILITARY ACADEMY LIBRARY.

ASHBEL WELCH ANGEL

Captain, Co. E, 3 NJ Militia, April 25, 1861. Honorably mustered out, July 31, 1861. Captain, Co. A, 5 NJ Infantry, Aug. 14, 1861. GSW right thigh and right groin, Fair Oaks, VA, June 1, 1862. Captain, Co. I, 5 NJ Infantry, Aug. 11, 1862. Major, 5 NJ Infantry, Oct. 21, 1862. GSW right side, Chancellorsville, VA, May 3, 1863. Acting Topographical Engineer, Staff of Major Gen. Winfield S. Hancock, April 5–Aug. 27, 1864. *Colonel*, 5 NJ Infantry, July 2, 1864. Honorably mustered out, Sept. 7, 1864. Lieutenant Colonel, 38 NJ Infantry, Oct. 3, 1864. Honorably mustered out, June 30, 1865.

Born: Dec. 15, 1839 Lambertville, NJ
Died: July 5, 1884 Panama City, Panama
Occupation: Merchant and railroad contractor. Later engaged in superintending marine excavations in the harbor at Panama.
Offices/Honors: Postmaster, Lambertville, NJ, 1869–75
Miscellaneous: Resided Lambertville, Hunterdon Co., NJ

Ashbel Welch Angel
NEW JERSEY STATE ARCHIVES.
GOOD & STOKES, PHOTOGRAPHERS,
No. 27 EAST STATE & 36 GREENE STREETS, TRENTON, NJ.

Buried: Unknown location in Panama. Cenotaph, Mount Hope Presbyterian Cemetery, Lambertville, NJ (Row G, Lot 119).

References: Pension File and Military Service File, National Archives. Obituary, *Lambertville Record*, July 9, 1884. Obituary, *Trenton Daily True American*, July 8, 1884. Obituary, *Hunterdon County Democrat*, July 15, 1884.

EDWIN FORREST APPLEGATE

Colonel, 29 NJ Infantry, Sept. 12, 1862. Resigned Jan. 16, 1863, "on account of ill health."

Born: June 3, 1831 New York City, NY
Died: Jan. 23, 1885 Freehold, NJ
Occupation: Newspaper editor
Offices/Honors: Auditor, Monmouth Co., NJ, 1873–74. Postmaster, Freehold, NJ, 1874–83.
Miscellaneous: Resided Red Bank, Monmouth Co., NJ; and Freehold, Monmouth Co., NJ
Buried: Maplewood Cemetery, Freehold, NJ

Edwin Forrest Applegate (postwar)
FROM *HISTORY OF MONMOUTH COUNTY, NJ, 1664–1920*.

References: *History of Monmouth County, NJ, 1664–1920*. New York and Chicago, 1922. Obituary, *Monmouth Democrat*, Jan. 29, 1885. Military Service File, National Archives. Civil War Officer Memorials, Department of Defense, New Jersey Archives.

HENRY MICHAEL BAKER

Colonel, 2 NJ Militia, May 1, 1861. Honorably mustered out, July 31, 1861. Colonel, 88 NY Infantry, Sept. 28, 1861. Dismissed Sept. 22, 1862 for "absence from his command without authority" and for "cowardice in the face of the enemy" at Fair Oaks, VA, June 28, 1862. Dismissal revoked July 1, 1871, and he was honorably discharged, upon tender of resignation, to date Sept. 30, 1862.

Born: 1820? Dublin, Ireland
Died: Nov. 8, 1872 Jersey City, NJ
Occupation: Proprietor of a clothing store

Henry Michael Baker
COLLECTION OF THE NEW-YORK HISTORICAL SOCIETY.
BAILEY, PHOTOGRAPHER, MONTICELLO AVE., JERSEY CITY, NJ.

Miscellaneous: Resided Jersey City, Hudson Co., NJ

Buried: St. Peters Catholic Cemetery, Jersey City, NJ (South Division, Lot 88)

References: Pension File, National Archives. Obituary, *Jersey City Times*, Nov. 8, 9 and 11, 1872. Letters Received, Volunteer Service Branch, Adjutant General's Office, Files B1834(VS)1862 and M1226(VS)1862, National Archives. David P. Conyngham. *The Irish Brigade and Its Campaigns.* Boston, MA, 1869.

MYRON HOLLEY BEAUMONT

1 Lieutenant, RQM, 3 NJ Militia, April 30, 1861. Honorably mustered out, July 31, 1861. Major, 1 NJ Cavalry, Aug. 16, 1861. Lieutenant Colonel, 1 NJ Cavalry, Nov. 1, 1864. GSW left leg, Hatcher's Run, VA, Feb. 6, 1865. Colonel, 1 NJ Cavalry, May 4, 1865. Honorably mustered out, July 24, 1865.

Born: 1837 Wayne Co., NY

Died: Feb. 5, 1878 Ukiah, CA (committed suicide by taking morphine)

Occupation: Private, US Mounted Rifles, 1856–57. Printer and newspaper editor. Pension broker and saloon keeper in later life.

Miscellaneous: Resided Rahway, Union Co., NJ; New York City, NY; Coos Bay, Coos Co., OR; San Francisco, CA; and Ukiah, Mendocino Co., CA. Deserted his family in the early 1870s, fled to Oregon with his brother-in-law's wife, engaged in various criminal pursuits, and committed suicide while using the alias Thomas B. Edwards.

Buried: Ukiah City Cemetery, Ukiah, CA (unmarked)

References: Pension File and Military Service File, National Archives. Joseph G. Bilby. "Col. Myron Beaumont, 1st NJ Cavalry," *Military Images*, Vol. 11, No. 1 (July–Aug. 1989). Letters Received, Volunteer Service Branch, Adjutant General's Office, File P1436(VS)1863, National Archives. Edmund J. Raus, Jr. *A Generation on the March: The Union Army at Gettysburg.* Gettysburg, PA, 1996. Earl Schenck Miers, editor. *Ride to War: The History of the 1st New Jersey Cavalry*, by Henry R. Pyne. New Brunswick, NJ, 1961. Edward G. Longacre. *Jersey Cavaliers: A History of the 1st New Jersey Volunteer Cavalry, 1861–65.* Hightstown, NJ, 1992. Civil War Officer Memorials, Department of Defense, New Jersey Archives.

Myron Holley Beaumont

ALEXANDER PETER BERTHOUD

Colonel, 31 NJ Infantry, Sept. 11, 1862. Commanded 3 Brigade, 1 Division, 1 Army Corps, Army of the Potomac, March 29–April 20, 1863. Honorably mustered out, June 24, 1863.

Born: 1824 Switzerland

Died: June 19, 1894 Newton, NJ

Education: Graduated Union College, Schenectady, NY, 1844

Occupation: Civil engineer and railroad superintendent

Offices/Honors: One of the founders of the Chi Psi Fraternity

Miscellaneous: Resided Washington, Warren Co., NJ, to 1866; Morristown, Morris Co., NJ, 1866–69; New York City, NY, 1869–72, 1880–90; Dover, Morris Co., NJ, 1872–76; Newark, NJ, 1876–80; and Newton, Sussex Co., NJ, 1890–94

Buried: Fort Plain Cemetery, Fort Plain, NY

References: Pension File, National Archives. Obituary, *Sussex Register*, June 20, 1894. H. Seger Slifer, editor. *Catalogue of Chi Psi Fraternity, 1841–1932.* Ann Arbor, MI, 1929.

Alexander Peter Berthoud
MASSACHUSETTS MOLLUS COLLECTION, USAMHI.

HENRY WILLIS BROWN

Captain, Co. A, 3 NJ Infantry, May 22, 1861. Lieutenant Colonel, 3 NJ Infantry, May 27, 1861. Colonel, 3 NJ Infantry, May 15, 1862. Commanded 1 Brigade, 1 Division, 6 Army Corps, Army of the Potomac, Dec. 24, 1862–Feb. 8, 1863, April 10–May 3, 1863, and March 25–May 9, 1864. GSW left hip, Salem Heights, VA, May 3, 1863. Provost Marshal, Warrenton, VA, Aug. 1863. GSW left thigh, Spotsylvania, VA, May 12, 1864. Honorably mustered out, June 23, 1864.

Henry Willis Brown
NEW JERSEY STATE ARCHIVES.
G. W. FREEMAN, PHOTOGRAPHER, CHARLESTOWN, MA.

Born: July 5, 1816 Boston, MA
Died: Oct. 25, 1892 Deer Island, Boston Harbor, MA
Occupation: Corporal, Co. E, 4 US Artillery, 1839–44. Soap and candle manufacturer before war. China merchant, US Customs clerk, and night watchman after war.
Miscellaneous: Resided Philadelphia, PA; Chelsea, Suffolk Co., MA; and Beverly, Essex Co., MA. Born Henry Willis Barnes, he changed his name to Brown in 1839, when he enlisted in the US Army and deserted his family. Without the benefit of a divorce, he subsequently married and raised children with two other women.
Buried: Beverly Central Cemetery, Beverly, MA (Section 4, Lot 16)

References: Pension File and Military Service File, National Archives. Joseph G. Bilby. "An Officer and a Gentleman . . . Sort Of," *Military Images*, Vol. 13, No. 4 (Jan.–Feb. 1992). Samuel Toombs. *New Jersey Troops in the Gettysburg Campaign*. Orange, NJ, 1888. Edmund J. Raus, Jr. *A Generation on the March: The Union Army at Gettysburg*. Gettysburg, PA, 1996. Letters Received, Volunteer Service Branch, Adjutant General's Office, File M3930(VS)1864, National Archives.

WILLIAM BRYAN

Colonel, 10 NJ Infantry, Dec. 26, 1861. Discharged March 6, 1862 upon "adverse report of a Board of Examination."

Born: 1807? Wales
Died: Sept. 7, 1874 Beverly, NJ
Other Wars: Mexican War (2 Lieutenant, Co. G, 1 PA Infantry)
Occupation: Druggist and physician
Miscellaneous: Resided Beverly, Burlington Co., NJ
Buried: Monument Cemetery, Beverly, NJ (Central Section, Lot 377, unmarked)
References: Randy W. Hackenburg. *Pennsylvania in the War with Mexico*. Shippensburg, PA, 1992. Military Service File, National Archives. Death notice, *Philadelphia Public Ledger*, Sept. 9, 1874. Letters Received, Volunteer Service Branch, Adjutant General's Office, File M211(VS)1862, National Archives. Death Records, New Jersey State Archives.

SAMUEL L. BUCK

Major, 2 NJ Infantry, May 22, 1861. Lieutenant Colonel, 2 NJ Infantry, Jan. 20, 1862. Colonel, 2 NJ Infantry, July 2, 1862. Commanded 1 Brigade, 1 Division, 6 Army Corps, Army of the Potomac, May 3–4, 1863. Accidentally injured Banks Ford, VA, May 4, 1863, shoulder dislocated by horse falling on him. Honorably discharged Feb. 17, 1864, on account of physical disability. Discharge revoked Feb. 24, 1864, "his services being needed as a member of a Court Martial now in session." Honorably mustered out, June 21, 1864.

Born: June 8, 1820 Bethel, VT
Died: Feb. 5, 1892 Newark, NJ

Occupation: Engaged in the express business for many years. Later employed as auditor of the New York and New Jersey Telegraph and Telephone Co.
Miscellaneous: Resided Newark, Essex Co., NJ
Buried: Fairmount Cemetery, Newark, NJ (Section 2, Lot 93)
References: Obituary, *Newark Daily Advertiser*, Feb. 6, 1892. Pension File, National Archives. Samuel Toombs. *New Jersey Troops in the Gettysburg Campaign*. Orange, NJ, 1888. Letters Received, Volunteer Service Branch, Adjutant General's Office, File T142(VS)1864, National Archives. *A History of the City of Newark, NJ*. New York and Chicago, 1913.

Samuel L. Buck
MASSACHUSETTS MOLLUS COLLECTION, USAMHI.

John Julius Cladek (right, as Lt. Col., 30th New Jersey) with Maj. Walter Camman
John W. Kuhl Collection.
Whitehurst Gallery, 434 Pennsylvania Avenue, Washington, DC.

JOHN JULIUS CLADEK

1 Lieutenant, Co. B, 3 NJ Militia, April 22, 1861. Honorably mustered out, July 31, 1861. Captain, Co. H, 5 NJ Infantry, Aug. 28, 1861. Resigned July 31, 1862, due to physical disability from miasmatic fever and diarrhea. Lieutenant Colonel, 30 NJ Infantry, Sept. 11, 1862. Colonel, 30 NJ Infantry, March 4, 1863. Honorably mustered out, June 27, 1863. Colonel, 35 NJ Infantry, Aug. 15, 1863. Dismissed Aug. 12, 1865, for "conduct to the prejudice of good order and military discipline" in allowing "one George H. Moore (citizen) to come within the limits of the camp . . . and take the pay rolls of Company G . . . and pay the men of the company thereon, and did knowingly allow the said George H. Moore to deduct and retain ten per cent from the amount of local or state pay or bounty due, . . . at the same time knowing that the regiment was to be paid by the regular paymaster within a few days, thereby permitting some of the men to be defrauded of a part of the money justly due them, . . . and did receive in consideration thereof the sum of $335."

Born: March 24, 1824 Hungary
Died: April 5, 1884 Rahway, NJ
Other Wars: Hungarian War of Independence, 1848–49. Severely wounded while serving as artillery officer in Austrian army.
Occupation: Wood carver and carpenter
Offices/Honors: Bvt. Brig. Gen., USV, March 13, 1865, for long, faithful and gallant services during the war. Upon his arrest and court martial, the War Department revoked his commission, which had not been confirmed by the Senate.
Miscellaneous: Resided Rahway, Union Co., NJ
Buried: Rahway Cemetery, Rahway, NJ
References: Pension File and Military Service File, National Archives. *Encyclopedia of American Biography*, Vol. 29. Letters Received, Volunteer Service Branch, Adjutant General's Office, File C1869(VS)1863, National Archives. Letters Received, Commission Branch, Adjutant General's Office, File C655(CB) 1865, National Archives.

MARK WILKS COLLET

Major, 3 NJ Infantry, May 28, 1861. Lieutenant Colonel, 3 NJ Infantry, May 15, 1862. Lieutenant Colonel, 1 NJ Infantry, Sept. 14, 1862. Colonel, 1 NJ Infantry, Nov. 29, 1862. GSW heart, Salem Church, VA, May 3, 1863.

John Julius Cladek
MICHAEL J. MCAFEE COLLECTION.

Born: June 2, 1826 Paterson, NJ
Died: May 3, 1863 KIA Salem Church, VA
Education: Attended US Military Academy, West Point, NY (Class of 1846). Graduated Jefferson Medical College, Philadelphia, PA, 1848.
Occupation: Physician
Miscellaneous: Resided Philadelphia, PA
Buried: Churchyard of St. James the Less, Philadelphia, PA (Lot 241)
References: Pension File and Military Service File, National Archives. US Military Academy Cadet Application Papers, National Archives. Camille Baquet. *History of the First Brigade, New Jersey Volunteers from 1861 to 1865*. Trenton, NJ, 1910.

Mark Wilks Collet
MASSACHUSETTS MOLLUS COLLECTION, USAMHI.

JOHN SISBY COX

Colonel, 23 NJ Infantry, Sept. 11, 1862. Described by Brig. Gen. Torbert as "totally incompetent" and facing court martial charges preferred by Brig. Gen. Gabriel Paul, he resigned Nov. 9, 1862.

Born: Aug. 6, 1817 near Jacobstown, NJ
Died: Oct. 9, 1888 Columbus, Burlington Co., NJ
Occupation: Carpenter and justice of the peace
Miscellaneous: Resided Philadelphia, PA; and Columbus, Burlington Co., NJ
Buried: St. Andrew's Episcopal Churchyard, Mount Holly, NJ
References: Henry M. Cox. *The Cox Family in America.* New York City, NY, 1912. Obituary, *Burlington Daily Enterprise,* Oct. 12, 1888. Military Service File, National Archives. *History of the Re-union Society of the 23rd Regiment New Jersey Volunteers.* Philadelphia, PA, 1890.

ABRAHAM GARRISON DEMAREST

Major, 22 NJ Infantry, Sept. 9, 1862. Colonel, 22 NJ Infantry, Jan. 26, 1863. Honorably mustered out, June 25, 1863.

Born: Nov. 16, 1830 Oakland, Bergen Co., NJ
Died: Oct. 12, 1900 Tenafly, NJ
Occupation: Grocer
Miscellaneous: Resided New York City, NY; and Tenafly, Bergen Co., NJ
Buried: Brookside Cemetery, Englewood, NJ (East Side, Lot 118)
References: *In Memory: Col. Abraham G. Demarest.* New York City, NY, 1900? Obituary Circular, Whole No. 670, New York MOLLUS. Pension File, National Archives. Mary A. and William H. S. Demarest. *The Demarest Family.* New Brunswick, NJ, 1938. Obituary, *New York Times,* Oct. 13, 1900.

Abraham Garrison Demarest
JOHN W. KUHL COLLECTION.

ANDREW DERROM

Colonel, 25 NJ Infantry, Sept. 24, 1862. Honorably mustered out, June 20, 1863.

Born: Nov. 30, 1817 England
Died: July 15, 1892 Paterson, NJ
Occupation: Construction engineer and architect
Miscellaneous: Resided Paterson, Passaic Co., NJ
Buried: Cedar Lawn Cemetery, Paterson, NJ (Section 8, Lot 196)
References: Obituary Circular, Whole No. 390, New York MOLLUS. Pension File, National Archives. W. W. Clayton, compiler. *History of Bergen and Passaic Counties, NJ*. Philadelphia, PA, 1882. Obituary, *Paterson Daily Press*, July 16, 1892.

ALEXANDER E. DONALDSON

Colonel, 30 NJ Infantry, Sept. 11, 1862. Resigned March 1, 1863, on account of continued disability due to "neuralgia and functional derangement of the heart."

Born: 1828? Charleston, SC
Died: July 5, 1871 Clarendon, AR
Other Wars: Mexican War (Private, Co. C, US Mounted Rifles)
Occupation: Printer and newspaper editor before war. US War Department clerk and printer after war.
Miscellaneous: Resided Somerville, Somerset Co., NJ; Washington, DC; and Clarendon, Monroe Co., AR
Buried: Probably Clarendon, AR, but there is no grave marker, and cemetery records no longer exist
References: Pension File and Military Service File, National Archives. Letters Received, Volunteer Service Branch, Adjutant General's Office, File D214(VS)1863, National Archives. Obituary, *Hunterdon Republican*, July 27, 1871. *Proceedings of the Annual Meeting, New Jersey Press Association*, 1928. Enlistment Papers, Regular Army, National Archives.

JAMES NICHOLSON DUFFY

Captain, Co. C, 2 NJ Infantry, May 27, 1861. Major, 2 NJ Infantry, July 1, 1862. Lieutenant Colonel, 3 NJ Infantry, Sept. 14, 1862. Acting AIG, 1 Division, 6 Army Corps, Army of the Potomac, Jan. 25, 1863–April 1864. *Colonel*, 4 NJ Infantry, Sept. 29, 1863. Never joined regiment, the reduced strength of regiment preventing his muster as colonel. Honorably mustered out, June 23, 1864.

Andrew Derrom
COURTESY OF HENRY POMERANTZ.

Born: Aug. 23, 1829 Ireland
Died: Oct. 18, 1901 Newport, KY
Occupation: Leather manufacturer
Miscellaneous: Resided Newark, Essex Co., NJ; Eldred, McKean Co., PA; and Newport, Kenton Co., KY
Buried: Holy Sepulchre Cemetery, East Orange, NJ (Section A, Lot 11, Grave 6)
References: Samuel Toombs. *New Jersey Troops in the Gettysburg Campaign*. Orange, NJ, 1888. Obituary, *Newark Evening News*, Oct. 19, 1901. Obituary, *Cincinnati Enquirer*, Oct. 19, 1901. Military Service File, National Archives.

James Nicholson Duffy
MASSACHUSETTS MOLLUS COLLECTION, USAMHI.

Cornelius Fornet
FROM *LIFE OF G. C. FORNET, COLONEL OF LINCOLN'S ARMY.*

CORNELIUS FORNET

Major, Engineers, Staff of Major Gen. John C. Fremont, Sept. 1, 1861. GSW left shoulder, Jefferson City, MO, Sept. 26, 1861. Appointed Colonel, 22 NJ Infantry, Sept. 9, 1862. When he failed to return within four months from an authorized five-week furlough to Hungary, his appointment was revoked.

Born: Aug. 20, 1818 Strazsa, Szepes, Hungary
Died: March 10, 1894 Vacz, Pest, Hungary
Education: Graduated Technical University, Budapest, Hungary, 1843
Other Wars: Hungarian War of Independence, 1848–49
Occupation: Civil engineer and accountant
Miscellaneous: Resided Mohacs, Baranya, Hungary, after war
Buried: Budapest, Hungary
References: Pension File, National Archives. Laszlo Fornet. *Life of G. C. Fornet, Colonel of Lincoln's Army.* Budapest, Hungary, 1946. Edmund Vasvary. *Lincoln's Hungarian Heroes.* Washington, DC, 1939. Eugene Pivany. *Hungarians in the American Civil War.* Cleveland, OH, 1913. Letters Received, Volunteer Service Branch, Adjutant General's Office, File F116(VS)1862, National Archives.

ENOS FOURAT

Captain, Co. F, 1 NJ Infantry, May 25, 1861. GSW head, Crampton's Pass, MD, Sept. 14, 1862. Major, 1 NJ Infantry, Nov. 29, 1862. *Lieutenant Colonel,* 4 NJ Infantry, July 21, 1863. Declined. Resigned July 29, 1863, in order to accept promotion. Lieutenant Colonel, 33 NJ Infantry, Sept. 4, 1863. *Colonel,* 10 NJ Infantry, March 31, 1865. Declined. Honorably mustered out, July 17, 1865. Bvt. Colonel, USV, March 13, 1865, for long, faithful, and distinguished services, and for conspicuous gallantry in every engagement of the Atlanta campaign.

Born: Sept. 19, 1827 Piscataway, NJ
Died: July 22, 1888 Milburn, NJ
Occupation: Railroad track master and section foreman until 1880. Policeman in later years.
Offices/Honors: New Brunswick Chief of Police, 1885–88
Miscellaneous: Resided New Brunswick, Middlesex Co., NJ; and Metuchen, Middlesex Co., NJ
Buried: Elmwood Cemetery, New Brunswick, NJ

Enos Fourat

Samuel Fowler

References: Pension File and Military Service File, National Archives. Obituary, *New Brunswick Daily Fredonian*, July 23, 1888. *Appletons' Annual Cyclopedia and Register of Important Events of the Year 1888.* New York City, NY, 1889. Letters Received, Volunteer Service Branch, Adjutant General's Office, File F487(VS)1865, National Archives. John G. Zinn. *The Mutinous Regiment: The 33rd New Jersey in the Civil War.* Jefferson, NC, 2005.

SAMUEL FOWLER

Colonel, 15 NJ Infantry, July 10, 1862. Resigned March 6, 1863, on account of "continued ill health and physical disability," due to "rheumatism and chronic diarrhea, the effects of a severe attack of typhoid fever."

Born: March 25, 1818 Ogdensburg, Sussex Co., NJ
Died: Jan. 14, 1865 Trenton, NJ
Education: Attended Lafayette College, Easton, PA
Occupation: Lawyer and mine operator
Offices/Honors: NJ Assembly, 1865

Miscellaneous: Resided Port Jervis, Orange Co., NY; and Franklin, Sussex Co., NJ
Buried: North Hardyston Cemetery, Franklin, NJ
References: *Biographical Encyclopedia of New Jersey of the Nineteenth Century.* Philadelphia, PA, 1877. Military Service File, National Archives. Obituary, *Sussex Register*, Jan. 20, 1865. Alanson A. Haines. *History of the 15th Regiment New Jersey Volunteers.* New York City, NY, 1883. Alanson A. Haines. *Hardyston Memorial: A History of the Township and the North Presbyterian Church.* N.p., 1888.

STEPHEN ROSE GILKYSON

Captain, Co. A, 6 NJ Infantry, Aug. 19, 1861. Major, 6 NJ Infantry, July 22, 1862. GSW left thigh, Groveton, VA, Aug. 29, 1862. Lieutenant Colonel, 6 NJ Infantry, Oct. 11, 1862. GSW right arm, Wilderness, VA, May 6, 1864. *Colonel*, 6 NJ Infantry, June 1, 1864. Honorably mustered out, Sept. 7, 1864. Lieutenant Colonel, 40 NJ Infantry, Feb. 18, 1865. Colonel, 40 NJ Infantry, March 7, 1865. Honorably mustered out, July 13, 1865.

Stephen Rose Gilkyson
ROGER D. HUNT COLLECTION, USAMHI.
GOOD & STOKES, PHOTOGRAPHERS,
No. 27 EAST STATE AND 36 GREENE STREETS, TRENTON, NJ.

Born: 1832? PA
Died: Dec. 31, 1892 Trenton, NJ
Occupation: Lumber merchant and coal company superintendent
Miscellaneous: Resided Hightstown, Mercer Co., NJ; Yardley, Bucks Co., PA; Doylestown, Bucks Co., PA; and Trenton, Mercer Co., NJ. Brother of Colonel James Gilkyson (17 PA Militia).
Buried: St. Andrews Episcopal Churchyard, Yardley, PA
References: Richard Wynkoop. *Wynkoop Genealogy in the United States of America*. New York City, NY, 1904. Obituary, *Trenton Daily True American*, Jan. 2, 1893. Pension File and Military Service File, National Archives. Letters Received, Volunteer Service Branch, Adjutant General's Office, File I600(VS)1862, National Archives. Obituary, *Doylestown Democrat*, Jan. 5, 1893. Edmund J. Raus, Jr. *A Generation on the March: The Union Army at Gettysburg*. Gettysburg, PA, 1996.

WILLIAM HALSTED

Colonel, 1 NJ Cavalry, Sept. 1, 1861. Discharged Feb. 18, 1862, upon "adverse report of a Board of Examination."

Born: June 4, 1794 Elizabeth, NJ
Died: March 4, 1878 Trenton, NJ
Education: Graduated Princeton (NJ) University, 1812
Occupation: Lawyer
Offices/Honors: US House of Representatives, 1837–39 and 1841–43. US District Attorney for NJ, 1849–53.
Miscellaneous: Resided Trenton, Mercer Co., NJ
Buried: Riverview Cemetery, Trenton, NJ (Section D, Lot 306)
References: William L. Halstead. *The Story of the Halsteads of the United States*. Ann Arbor, MI, 1934. Military Service File, National Archives. Obituary, *Trenton Daily State Gazette*, March 5–6, 1878. *Biographical Directory of the American Congress*. Thomas P. Lowry. *Tarnished Eagles: The Courts-Martial of Fifty Union Colonels and Lieutenant Colonels*. Mechanicsburg, PA, 1997. Evan M. Woodward. *History of Burlington and Mercer Counties, NJ*. Philadelphia, PA, 1883. Letters Received, Volunteer Service Branch, Adjutant General's Office, File

William Halsted
NEW JERSEY STATE ARCHIVES.
ANSON'S, 589 BROADWAY, NEW YORK.

H537(VS)1862, National Archives. Earl Schenck Miers, editor. *Ride to War: The History of the 1st New Jersey Cavalry*, by Henry R. Pyne. New Brunswick, NJ, 1961. Edward G. Longacre. *Jersey Cavaliers: A History of the 1st New Jersey Volunteer Cavalry, 1861–65*. Hightstown, NJ, 1992. Obituary, *New York Times*, March 5, 1878. Civil War Officer Memorials, Department of Defense, New Jersey Archives.

WILLIAM B. HATCH

1 Lieutenant, Adjutant, 4 NJ Militia, April 27, 1861. Honorably mustered out, July 31, 1861. Major, 4 NJ Infantry, Aug. 19, 1861. Lieutenant Colonel, 4 NJ Infantry, Sept. 9, 1861. Taken prisoner, Gaines' Mill, VA, June 27, 1862. Confined Libby Prison, Richmond, VA. Exchanged Aug. 12, 1862. Colonel, 4 NJ Infantry, Aug. 26, 1862. GSW right leg (amputated), Fredericksburg, VA, Dec. 13, 1862.

Born: July 30, 1838 Camden, NJ
Died: Dec. 18, 1862 DOW Falmouth, VA
Occupation: Having a great fondness for military pursuits, he spent some months in observation of the military systems in Europe, including the cavalry of the Russian Army.
Miscellaneous: Resided Camden, Camden Co., NJ. In the words of Brig. Gen. Philip Kearny: "Lieutenant Colonel Hatch is as elegant a gentleman as he is an exemplary and distinguished officer."
Buried: Evergreen Cemetery, Camden, NJ (Section D, Lot 118)
References: Pension File and Military Service File, National Archives. Obituary, *West Jersey Press*, Dec. 24, 1862. George R. Prowell. *History of Camden County, NJ*. Philadelphia, PA, 1886. Civil War Officer Memorials, Department of Defense, New Jersey Archives.

JAMES THOMAS HATFIELD

Colonel, 6 NJ Infantry, Sept. 2, 1861. Resigned April 27, 1862, on account of physical disability due to "protracted rheumatic affections."

Born: Jan. 7, 1819 New York City, NY
Died: May 1, 1893 New York City, NY
Occupation: Tailor, commission merchant and hammock manufacturer
Miscellaneous: Resided Hoboken, Hudson Co., NJ; and New York City, NY

William B. Hatch
MASSACHUSETTS MOLLUS COLLECTION, USAMHI.

James Thomas Hatfield
COURTESY OF GIL BARRETT.

Buried: Cypress Hills Cemetery, Brooklyn, NY (Section 3, Lot 82, family vault)
References: Abraham Hatfield. *The Hatfields of Westchester*. Rutland, VT, 1935. Pension File and Military Service File, National Archives.

WILLIAM HENRY, JR.

1 Lieutenant, Adjutant, 1 NJ Infantry, May 31, 1861. Major, 1 NJ Infantry, Aug. 12, 1862. GSW Bull Run Bridge, VA, Aug. 27, 1862. Lieutenant Colonel, 1 NJ Infantry, Nov. 29, 1862. *Colonel*, 1 NJ Infantry, March 11, 1864. GSW Cold Harbor, VA, June 1, 1864. Honorably mustered out, June 23, 1864.

Born: Dec. 15, 1830 Stroudsburg, PA
Died: March 16, 1889 Fort Worth, TX
Occupation: Engaged in the iron and coal business
Miscellaneous: Resided Scranton, Lackawanna Co., PA; Oxford, Warren Co., NJ; and Fort Worth, Tarrant Co., TX

William Henry, Jr.
ROGER D. HUNT COLLECTION, USAMHI.
DERMAN & HEERMANS (SUCCESSORS TO DEANS),
UNION PHOTOGRAPH GALLERY, SCRANTON, PA.

Buried: Belvidere Cemetery, Belvidere, NJ (Johnston Addition, Lot 186)
References: Obituary, *Hackettstown Gazette*, March 22, 1889. Obituary, *Stroudsburg Jeffersonian*, March 28, 1889. Death Notice, *Army and Navy Journal*, Vol. 26, No. 30 (March 23, 1889). James I. Robertson, Jr., editor. *The Civil War Letters of General Robert McAllister*. New Brunswick, NJ, 1965. Military Service File, National Archives. Samuel Toombs. *New Jersey Troops in the Gettysburg Campaign*. Orange, NJ, 1888.

HUGH HARTSHORNE JANEWAY

1 Lieutenant, Co. L, 1 NJ Cavalry, Sept. 9, 1861. GSW near Camp Custis, VA, Dec. 17, 1861. Captain, Co. L, 1 NJ Cavalry, Feb. 19, 1862. Major, 1 NJ Cavalry, Jan. 27, 1863. Acting ADC, Staff of Major Gen. John Sedgwick, May 1863. GSW Haw's Shop, VA, May 28, 1864. Lieutenant Colonel, 1 NJ Cavalry, July 6, 1864. GSW right index finger, Gravel Hill, VA, Aug. 14, 1864. Colonel, 1 NJ Cavalry, Oct. 11, 1864. Commanded 1 Brigade, 2 Division, Cavalry Corps, Army of the Potomac, Dec. 22, 1864–Jan. 12, 1865 and Jan. 25–March 27, 1865. GSW right leg, Hatcher's Run, VA, Feb. 6, 1865. GSW head, Amelia Springs, VA, April 5, 1865.

Born: Nov. 14, 1842 near Rahway, NJ
Died: April 5, 1865 KIA Amelia Springs, VA
Education: Attended Princeton (NJ) University
Miscellaneous: Resided New Brunswick, Middlesex Co., NJ
Buried: Elmwood Cemetery, New Brunswick, NJ (Section C, Lot 114)
References: *Biographical Encyclopedia of New Jersey of the Nineteenth Century*. Philadelphia, PA, 1877. Samuel Toombs. *New Jersey Troops in the Gettysburg Campaign*. Orange, NJ, 1888. Earl Schenck Miers, editor. *Ride to War: The History of the 1st New Jersey Cavalry*, by Henry R. Pyne. New Brunswick, NJ, 1961. Edward G. Longacre. *Jersey Cavaliers: A History of the 1st New Jersey Volunteer Cavalry, 1861–65*. Hightstown, NJ, 1992. Pension File and Military Service File, National Archives. Joseph T. Duryea. *An Oration Commemorative of the Restoration of the Union, with a Tribute to the Alumni and Under-Graduates of the College of New Jersey, Who Fell in the National Struggle*. Philadelphia, PA, 1866. Letters Received, Volunteer Service Branch, Adjutant General's Office, File P2531(VS)1864, National Archives.

Hugh Hartshorne Janeway

ADOLPHUS JAMES JOHNSON

Colonel, 1 NJ Militia, April 30, 1861. Honorably mustered out, July 31, 1861. Colonel, 8 NJ Infantry, Sept. 14, 1861. GSW entering left side abdomen and exiting right side, Williamsburg, VA, May 5, 1862. Resigned March 19, 1863, on account of disability arising from his wounds. Major, VRC, July 16, 1863. Colonel, 4 VRC, Sept. 28, 1863. Commanded Rock Island (IL) Prison, Jan. 1864–July 1865. Commanded Camp Butler, Springfield, IL, Nov. 1865–June 1866. Honorably mustered out, July 10, 1866.

Born: March 26, 1816 Newark, NJ
Died: May 29, 1893 Newark, NJ
Occupation: Barber and hatter before war. Warden of Essex Co. (NJ) Jail, 1866–88.

Miscellaneous: Resided Newark, Essex Co., NJ
Buried: Evergreen Cemetery, Hillside, NJ (Section O, Lot 15)

Adolphus James Johnson

References: Obituary, *Newark Daily Advertiser*, May 30, 1893. Pension File and Military Service File, National Archives. Benton McAdams. *Rebels at Rock Island*. DeKalb, IL, 2000. *Report Annual Reunion and Dinner of the Old Guard Association, 12th Regiment, N. G. S. N. Y.* New York City, NY, 1894. Letters Received, Volunteer Service Branch, Adjutant General's Office, File J115(VS)1862, National Archives.

Robert Carney Johnson
NATIONAL ARCHIVES.

ROBERT CARNEY JOHNSON

Major, 4 NJ Militia, April 27, 1861. Honorably mustered out, July 31, 1861. Colonel, 12 NJ Infantry, July 9, 1862. Commanded 2 Brigade, 3 Division, 2 Army Corps, Army of the Potomac, Dec. 20, 1862–Jan. 24, 1863. Discharged for disability, Feb. 27, 1863, due to "a weak and sore back, caused by a fall since entering the service."

Born: Sept. 29, 1811 Salem, NJ
Died: March 25, 1881 Salem, NJ
Occupation: Farmer
Offices/Honors: Mayor of Salem, NJ, 1860–66
Miscellaneous: Resided Salem, Salem Co., NJ
Buried: St. John's Episcopal Churchyard, Salem, NJ

References: Thomas Cushing and Charles E. Sheppard. *History of the Counties of Gloucester, Salem and Cumberland*. Philadelphia, PA, 1883. Military Service File, National Archives. Obituary, *Woodbury Constitution*, March 30, 1881. Edward G. Longacre. *To Gettysburg and Beyond: The 12th New Jersey Volunteer Infantry, II Corps, Army of the Potomac, 1862–65*. Hightstown, NJ, 1988. William P. Haines. *History of the Men of Co. F with Description of the Marches and Battles of the 12th New Jersey Volunteers*. Mickleton, NJ, 1897.

JOHN WOOD KESTER

2 Lieutenant, Commonwealth Artillery, PA Volunteers, April 24, 1861. Honorably mustered out, Aug. 5, 1861. Captain, Co. E, 1 NJ Cavalry, Aug. 9, 1861. Acting ACM, Staff of Brig. Gen. David M. Gregg, May 13–Nov. 2, 1863. Lieutenant Colonel, 1 NJ Cavalry, Sept. 21, 1863. Shell wound (contused), head and neck, Sulphur Springs, VA, Oct. 12, 1863. Colonel, 1 NJ Cavalry, July 6, 1864. Honorably mustered out, Sept. 25, 1864.

Born: 1842 Frankford, PA
Died: March 1, 1904 Philadelphia, PA
Education: Attended Allegheny College, Meadville, PA. Attended University of Pennsylvania, Philadelphia, PA (Class of 1863).
Occupation: Wholesale druggist before war. Engaged in numerous unprofitable business ventures after war as his mental capacity steadily decreased. Confined to insane asylum after 1882.
Miscellaneous: Resided Philadelphia, PA. Brother-in-law of Bvt. Brig. Gen. Cecil Clay.
Buried: St. Lukes Episcopal Churchyard, Germantown, Philadelphia Co., PA (Wyndham H. Stokes Vault)
References: Donald E. Kester. *Cavalryman in Blue: Colonel John Wood Kester of the 1st New Jersey Cavalry in the Civil War*. Hightstown, NJ, 1997. *University of Pennsylvania: Biographical Catalogue of the Matriculates of the College*. Philadelphia, PA, 1894. Edward G. Longacre. *Jersey Cavaliers: A History of the 1st New Jersey Volunteer Cavalry, 1861–65*. Hightstown, NJ, 1992. Earl Schenck Miers, editor. *Ride to War: The History of the 1st New Jersey Cavalry*, by Henry R. Pyne. New Brunswick, NJ, 1961. George B. Kinkead. "Gilbert Livingston and Some of his Descendants," *New York Genealogical and Biographical Record*, Vol. 87, No. 1 (Jan. 1956). Pension File and Military Service File, National Archives.

John Wood Kester
NEW JERSEY STATE ARCHIVES.
J. E. McCLEES, ARTIST, 910 CHESTNUT STREET, PHILADELPHIA, PA.

GEORGE WASHINGTON McLEAN

Colonel, 2 NJ Infantry, May 22, 1861. Facing charges of incompetency and unfitness for command, "by reason of an utter ignorance and disregard of the duties which attach to his position," he resigned Dec. 31, 1861, since "the peculiar position of my private business, bearing upon the comfort of my family and security of my property, renders it imperatively necessary that I should return home."

Born: April 9, 1801 NY
Died: Jan. 10, 1878 New York City, NY
Education: Attended Newburgh (NY) Academy. Attended US Military Academy, West Point, NY (Class of 1822).
Occupation: US Marine Corps (1 Lieutenant, resigned Feb. 7, 1839)
Miscellaneous: Resided Elizabeth, Union Co., NJ; and New York City, NY
Buried: Woodlawn Cemetery, New York City, NY (Section 52, Sycamore Plot, Lot 3324, family marker)
References: Military Service File, National Archives. US Military Academy Cadet Application Papers, National Archives. Obituary, *New York Times*, Jan. 12, 1878.

JAMES W. McNEELY

Private, Co. A, NJ National Guard, April 16, 1861. Honorably mustered out, July 16, 1861. 1 Lieutenant, Co. G, 10 NJ Infantry, April 17, 1862. Captain, Co. G, 10 NJ Infantry, June 20, 1863. Major, 10 NJ Infantry, April 5, 1865. Lieutenant Colonel, 2 NJ Infantry, June 26, 1865. *Colonel*, 2 NJ Infantry, July 10, 1865. Honorably mustered out, July 11, 1865.

Born: 1836 Trenton, NJ
Died: Dec. 9, 1903 Trenton, NJ
Occupation: Bank clerk. Later connected with the Mechanics National Bank in the capacity of messenger.
Miscellaneous: Resided Trenton, Mercer Co., NJ
Buried: Riverview Cemetery, Trenton, NJ (Section D, Lot 31)
References: Pension File and Military Service File, National Archives. Obituary, *Trenton Daily True American*, Dec. 10, 1903.

MATTHEW MILLER, JR.

Colonel, 4 NJ Militia, April 27, 1861. Honorably mustered out, July 31, 1861.

Born: 1817 Camden, NJ
Died: May 30, 1898 Camden, NJ
Occupation: Engaged in banking and hotel business early in life. Later engaged in the insurance business.
Miscellaneous: Resided Camden, Camden Co., NJ
Buried: Evergreen Cemetery, Camden, NJ
References: Pension File, National Archives. Obituary, *West Jersey Press*, June 1, 1898.

ANDREW JACKSON MORRISON

Colonel, 7 NY Cavalry, Nov. 6, 1861. Honorably mustered out, March 31, 1862. Volunteer ADC, Staff of Brig. Gen. Innis N. Palmer, May–Sept. 1862. GSW left hand, Oak Grove, VA, June 25, 1862. Colonel, 26 NJ Infantry, Sept. 16, 1862. Dismissed June 11, 1863, for "drunkenness on duty." Dismissal revoked, Feb. 6, 1864. Colonel, 3 NJ Cavalry, Nov. 4, 1863. Resigned Aug. 29, 1864, due to "reasons referring to the interests of the service and myself."

Born: Oct. 3, 1828 Argyle, Washington Co., NY
Died: Jan. 28, 1907 Troy, NY

Andrew Jackson Morrison
MASSACHUSETTS MOLLUS COLLECTION, USAMHI.

Other Wars: Mexican War (Volunteer ADC to Capt. John Butler, 3 US Dragoons). War for Italian Unification, 1860 (Major of cavalry under Gen. Garibaldi).

Occupation: Adventurer before war, participating in the abortive filibuster expeditions of Narciso Lopez and William Walker. Railway postal agent after war.

Miscellaneous: Resided West Troy, Albany Co., NY

Buried: Rural Cemetery, Albany, NY (Section 105, Lot 447)

References: Alan A. Siegel. *For the Glory of the Union: Myth, Reality, and the Media in Civil War New Jersey.* Rutherford, NJ, 1984. Pension File, National Archives. Obituary, *Albany Evening Journal,* Jan. 29, 1907. Letters Received, Volunteer Service Branch, Adjutant General's Office, File B118(VS)1864, National Archives. Civil War Officer Memorials, Department of Defense, New Jersey Archives. Joseph G. Bilby. "Through Hades with His Hat Off: The Strange Career of A.J. Morrison," *Military Images,* Vol. 11, No. 5 (March–April 1990).

WILLIAM ROBINSON MURPHY

Captain, Co. A, NJ National Guard, April 16, 1861. Honorably mustered out, July 16, 1861. Colonel, 10 NJ Infantry, Jan. 19, 1862. Resigned March 12, 1863, due to "motives . . . purely domestic but of such a nature as to render it imperative and vital." Captain, Co. A, NJ Militia, June 17, 1863. Honorably discharged, July 16, 1863.

Born: Nov. 27, 1809 Princeton, NJ
Died: Dec. 19, 1887 Bordentown, NJ
Occupation: Cabinetmaker and undertaker in early life. Inspector and collector of the Delaware & Raritan Canal after war.
Offices/Honors: Supervisor of NJ State Prison, 1869–1877
Miscellaneous: Resided Princeton, Mercer Co., NJ; Trenton, Mercer Co., NJ; and Bordentown, Burlington Co., NJ
Buried: Princeton Cemetery, Princeton, NJ (Map 2, Lot 614)

William Robinson Murphy
COURTESY OF DENNIS BABBITT.

References: *Biographical Encyclopedia of New Jersey of the Nineteenth Century.* Philadelphia, PA, 1877. Obituary, *Trenton Daily True American*, Dec. 20, 1887. Military Service File, National Archives.

WILLIAM NAPTON

Colonel, 3 NJ Militia, April 27, 1861. Honorably mustered out, July 31, 1861.

Born: Nov. 7, 1809 Trenton, NJ
Died: May 27, 1874 Trenton, NJ
Occupation: Real estate agent, auctioneer and Democratic politician
Offices/Honors: Mayor of Trenton, NJ, 1850–52, 1854–55, 1868–71. NJ Assembly, 1852. Sheriff of Mercer County, NJ, 1856–59.
Miscellaneous: Resided Trenton, Mercer Co., NJ
Buried: Riverview Cemetery, Trenton, NJ (Section L, Lot 399)
References: Obituary, *Trenton Daily True American*, May 28, 1874. Obituary, *Trenton Daily State Gazette*, May 28, 1874. Biography, *Trenton Sunday Times Advertiser*, Aug. 28, 1955.

HENRY AUGUSTUS PERRINE

Captain, Co. A, 4 NJ Militia, April 24, 1861. Honorably mustered out, July 31, 1861. Captain, Co. K, 10 NJ Infantry, Oct. 12, 1861. GSW lower jaw, Spotsylvania, VA, May 14, 1864. Major, 10 NJ Infantry, July 19, 1864. Discharged for disability, March 29, 1865, due to the effects of his wound. *Colonel*, 10 NJ Infantry, June 30, 1865.

Born: Feb. 5, 1828 Princeton, NJ
Died: Nov. 13, 1869 Jamesburg, NJ (killed in railroad accident)
Other Wars: Mexican War (2 Lieutenant, 10 US Infantry)
Occupation: Railroad agent
Miscellaneous: Resided Princeton, Mercer Co., NJ; and Jamesburg, Middlesex Co., NJ
Buried: Princeton Cemetery, Princeton, NJ (Map 2, Lot 717)
References: Howland D. Perrine. *Daniel Perrin, "The Huguenot," and His Descendants in America.* South Orange, NJ, 1910. Pension File and Military Service File, National Archives. Obituary, *Mount Holly Mirror*, Nov. 17, 1869.

Henry Augustus Perrine
NEW JERSEY STATE ARCHIVES.
ADDIS GALLERY, 308 PENNA. AVE., BETWEEN 9TH & 10TH STREETS, WASHINGTON, DC.

WILLIAM BOYD ROBERTSON

Colonel, 24 NJ Infantry, Sept. 16, 1862. Commanded 1 Brigade, 3 Division, 2 Army Corps, Army of the Potomac, Dec. 1862–Feb. 1863. Honorably mustered out, June 29, 1863.

Born: June 21, 1821 Glasgow, Scotland
Died: Aug. 10, 1889 Atlantic City, NJ
Occupation: Sergeant, US Marine Corps, 1837–45. Druggist before war. China merchant and mail contractor after war.
Offices/Honors: Postmaster, Salem, NJ, 1861–66 and 1867–74
Miscellaneous: Resided Salem, Salem Co., NJ; and Camden, Camden Co., NJ
Buried: Old Camden Cemetery, Camden, NJ
References: Pension File and Military Service File, National Archives. Obituary, *Bridgeton Evening News*, Aug. 13, 1889. Obituary, *Atlantic City Daily Union*, Aug. 12, 1889. Obituary, *Camden Democrat*, Aug. 17, 1889. James J. Reeves. *History of the 24th Regiment New Jersey Volunteers.* Camden, NJ, 1889. Benjamin Borton. *Awhile with the Blue.* Passaic, NJ, 1898.

Badge featuring a cameo portrait of
William B. Robertson
JOHN W. KUHL COLLECTION.

HENRY OGDEN RYERSON

Captain, Co. B, 2 NJ Infantry, May 27, 1861. Major, 2 NJ Infantry, Jan. 20, 1862. GSW both thighs, Gaines' Mill, VA, June 27, 1862. Taken prisoner, Gaines' Mill, VA, June 27, 1862. Confined Richmond, VA. Paroled July 17, 1862. Lieutenant Colonel, 2 NJ Infantry, July 1, 1862. Colonel, 23 NJ Infantry, Nov. 12, 1862. Colonel, 10 NJ Infantry, March 26, 1863. GSW head, Wilderness, VA, May 6, 1864.

Born: Jan. 10, 1826 Newton, NJ
Died: May 12, 1864 DOW Wilderness, VA
Occupation: Lawyer
Miscellaneous: Resided Newton, Sussex Co., NJ
Buried: Presbyterian Church Cemetery, Newton, NJ
References: James P. Snell, compiler. *History of Sussex and Warren Counties, NJ.* Philadelphia, PA, 1881. Albert W. Ryerson. *The Ryerson Genealogy.* Chicago, IL, 1916. *History of the Re-union Society of the 23rd Regiment New Jersey Volunteers.* Philadelphia, PA, 1890. Military Service File, National Archives. Letters Received, Volunteer Service Branch, Adjutant General's Office, File R458(VS)1862, National Archives.

Henry Ogden Ryerson
COURTESY OF STEVE MEADOW.
J. E. McCLEES, ARTIST, 910 CHESTNUT STREET, PHILADELPHIA, PA.

SAMUEL HENRY STARR

Captain, 2 US Cavalry, Aug. 3, 1861. Colonel, 5 NJ Infantry, Aug. 28, 1861. Commanded 3 Brigade, Hooker's Division, Army of the Potomac, Nov. 30, 1861–March 13, 1862. Commanded 3 Brigade, 2 Division, 3 Army Corps, Army of the Potomac, March 13–May 3, 1862. GSW face, Williamsburg, VA, May 5, 1862. "Mortified by perceiving that my services in this war pass unnoticed by my superiors; that officers, my juniors in rank, without any military experience save that gained in the present war, without any military education or knowledge except that imparted by my unceas-

Samuel Henry Starr
MASSACHUSETTS MOLLUS COLLECTION, USAMHI.

ing labors of the last winter and spring, without courage or capacity, are appointed and placed in command over me," he resigned volunteer commission, Oct. 20, 1862, no longer able to serve "in the volunteers with satisfaction to myself or without humiliation." Major, 6 US Cavalry, April 25, 1863. Commanded Reserve Brigade, 1 Division, Cavalry Corps, Army of the Potomac, June 9–28, 1863. Sabre wound side, Upperville, VA, June 21, 1863. GSW right arm (amputated), Fairfield, PA, July 3, 1863. Chief Mustering and Disbursing Officer, State of Ohio, Oct. 1863–Sept. 1864. Special Inspector of Cavalry, Army of the Potomac, Nov. 1864–Aug. 1865. Bvt. Colonel, USA, July 2, 1863, for gallant and meritorious services in the Gettysburg Campaign.

Born: July 31, 1810 Leyden, NY
Died: Nov. 23, 1891 Philadelphia, PA
Other Wars: Seminole War (Sergeant, Co. G, 4 US Artillery). Mexican War (Sergeant, Co. A, US Engineer Battalion).
Occupation: Regular Army (Colonel, 6 US Cavalry, retired Dec. 15, 1870)
Miscellaneous: Resided Philadelphia, PA
Buried: Arlington National Cemetery, Arlington, VA (Section 1, Lot 99-A)
References: *National Cyclopedia of American Biography.* Pension File, National Archives. *A Biographical Album of Prominent Pennsylvanians.* First Series. Philadelphia, PA, 1888. Obituary Circular, Whole No. 223, Pennsylvania MOLLUS. Letters Received, Volunteer Service Branch, Adjutant General's Office, File S1259(VS)1862, National Archives. Obituary, *Philadelphia Public Ledger*, Nov. 25, 1891.

WILLIAM REMSEN TAYLOR

Lieutenant Colonel, 29 NJ Infantry, Sept. 12, 1862. Colonel, 29 NJ Infantry, Jan. 27, 1863. Honorably mustered out June 30, 1863.

William Remsen Taylor (1860)
RUTGERS ALUMNI BIOGRAPHICAL FILE, SPECIAL COLLECTIONS AND UNIVERSITY ARCHIVES, RUTGERS UNIVERSITY LIBRARIES.

Born: Feb. 4, 1840 Middletown, NJ
Died: Oct. 2, 1896 Middletown, NJ
Education: Graduated Rutgers College, New Brunswick, NJ, 1860. Attended Bellevue Medical College, New York City, NY.
Occupation: Physician
Miscellaneous: Resided Astoria, Queens Co., NY
Buried: Hillside Cemetery, Scotch Plains, NJ (Section A, Division 4, Lot 139)
References: *Portrait and Biographical Record of Queens County, NY.* New York and Chicago, 1896. John H. Raven, compiler. *Catalogue of the Officers and Alumni of Rutgers College.* Trenton, NJ, 1916. Pension File and Military Service File, National Archives. Obituary, *Brooklyn Daily Eagle,* Oct. 3, 1896.

Isaac Miller Tucker
COURTESY OF STEVE MEADOW.
BRADY'S NATIONAL PHOTOGRAPHIC PORTRAIT GALLERIES,
352 PENNSYLVANIA AVE., WASHINGTON, DC.

ISAAC MILLER TUCKER

Lieutenant Colonel, 2 NJ Infantry, May 22, 1861. Colonel, 2 NJ Infantry, Jan. 20, 1862. GSW breast and heart, Gaines' Mill, VA, June 27, 1862.

Born: 1827? Springfield, Essex Co., NJ
Died: June 27, 1862 KIA Gaines' Mill, VA
Occupation: Lawyer
Miscellaneous: Resided Newark, Essex Co., NJ
Buried: Gaines' Mill, VA (Body never recovered). Cenotaph, Mount Pleasant Cemetery, Newark, NJ (Section H, Lot 21).
References: Pension File and Military Service File, National Archives. William H. Shaw, compiler. *History of Essex and Hudson Counties, NJ.* Philadelphia, PA, 1884. Obituary, *Newark Advertiser,* July 26, 1862. John Y. Foster. *New Jersey and the Rebellion.* Newark, NJ, 1868. *In Memoriam. Sermon and Oration: Sermon preached by E.R. Craven, D.D., in the Third Presbyterian Church, Newark, NJ, July 20, 1862, on occasion of the death of Col. I.M. Tucker . . . Oration delivered by Bro. John Y. Foster.* Newark, NJ, 1862. Camille Baquet. *History of the First Brigade, New Jersey Volunteers from 1861 to 1865.* Trenton, NJ, 1910. Joseph Atkinson. *The History of Newark, NJ.* Newark, NJ, 1878. *A History of the City of Newark, NJ.* New York and Chicago, 1913.

GILLIAM VAN HOUTEN

Colonel, 21 NJ Infantry, Sept. 6, 1862. GSW right leg, Salem Heights, VA, May 4, 1863. Taken prisoner, Salem Heights, VA, May 4, 1863.

Born: Aug. 13, 1819 Bloomingdale, NJ
Died: May 6, 1863 DOW near Banks' Ford, VA
Occupation: Engaged in cooperage business, manufacturing tubs, pails and churns
Miscellaneous: Resided Hoboken, Hudson Co., NJ; and Jersey City, Hudson Co., NJ
Buried: Van Houten Cemetery, Franklin Lakes, NJ
References: Alexander McLean. *History of Jersey City, NJ.* Jersey City, NJ, 1895. James M. Madden and Ronald P. McGovern. *In Memory of Colonel Gilliam Van Houten, July 27, 1991, Franklin Lakes, NJ.* New York City, NY, 1991. John Y. Foster. *New Jersey and the Rebellion.* Newark, NJ, 1868. Civil War Officer Memorials, Department of Defense, New Jersey Archives.

Gilliam Van Houten
ROGER D. HUNT COLLECTION, USAMHI.
J. GOOD, 36 GREENE STREET, OPPOSITE THE POST OFFICE,
TRENTON, NJ.

JOHN HOWARD WILLETS

Captain, Co. H, 7 NJ Infantry, Oct. 18, 1861. GSW breast, Williamsburg, VA, May 5, 1862. Lieutenant Colonel, 12 NJ Infantry, Aug. 8, 1862. Colonel, 12 NJ Infantry, Feb. 27, 1863. GSW left arm and right side of face, Chancellorsville, VA, May 3, 1863. Discharged for disability, Dec. 19, 1864, due to the lingering effects of his wounds.

John Howard Willets
MASSACHUSETTS MOLLUS COLLECTION, USAMHI.

Born: Nov. 18, 1834 Deas Creek, Cape May Co., NJ
Died: Jan. 22, 1926 Bridgeton, NJ
Education: Attended US Military Academy, West Point, NY (Class of 1856). Graduated Jefferson Medical College, Philadelphia, PA, 1858.
Occupation: Physician
Offices/Honors: NJ Assembly, 1872–73. NJ Senate, 1875–77.
Miscellaneous: Resided Port Elizabeth, Cumberland Co., NJ; and Bridgeton, Cumberland Co., NJ
Buried: Methodist Churchyard, Port Elizabeth, NJ

References: *Biographical Review of Cumberland County, NJ.* Boston, MA, 1896. *Biographical Encyclopedia of New Jersey of the Nineteenth Century.* Philadelphia, PA, 1877. Edward G. Longacre. *To Gettysburg and Beyond: The 12th New Jersey Volunteer Infantry, II Corps, Army of the Potomac, 1862–65.* Hightstown, NJ, 1988. William P. Haines. *History of the Men of Co. F with Description of the Marches and Battles of the 12th New Jersey Volunteers.* Mickleton, NJ, 1897. Military Service File, National Archives. Isaac T. Nichols. *Historic Days in Cumberland County, NJ, 1855–1865.* Bridgeton, NJ, 1907. Letters Received, Volunteer Service Branch, Adjutant General's Office, File W1251(VS)1864, National Archives.

Percy Wyndham
MASSACHUSETTS MOLLUS COLLECTION, USAMHI.
BRADY'S NATIONAL PHOTOGRAPHIC PORTRAIT GALLERIES,
BROADWAY AND TENTH STREETS, NEW YORK.

PERCY WYNDHAM

Colonel, 1 NJ Cavalry, Feb. 19, 1862. Taken prisoner, Harrisonburg, VA, June 6, 1862. Paroled Aug. 17, 1862. Commanded 1 Brigade, Bayard's Cavalry Division, Army of the Potomac, Oct. 11, 1862–Feb. 15, 1863. "Being placed under the command of an officer, who, in my opinion, is incompetent and for whom I cannot feel the proper respect," he resigned Feb. 16, 1863. Acceptance of resignation revoked, Feb. 28, 1863. Commanded 2 Brigade, 3 Division, Cavalry Corps, Army of the Potomac, Feb. 16–June 9, 1863. GSW right leg, Brandy Station, VA, June 9, 1863. Upon returning Oct. 2, 1863, from leave of absence, he was charged with "absence without leave," his leave having expired Sept. 5, 1863. He was relieved from "regimental command, or other military duty, and ordered to proceed to Washington, but not in arrest," Oct. 2, 1863, in response to the following mysterious order from Secretary of War Stanton to Maj. Gen. Meade, "Information received at this Department indicates that Colonel Percy Wyndham should not be permitted to have a command or come within the lines of your army at present." The information referred to may have been allegations that Wyndham was connected with a plot to kidnap Lincoln and his Cabinet. Having repeatedly applied for reinstatement, without effect, he returned to the army in April 1864 in a volunteer capacity, "rendering all the service in my power for the advancement and success of the Union cause." When Maj. Gen. George Meade learned that he was again with the army without proper authority, he ordered on June 26, 1864, that Wyndham "be sent by the Provost Marshal General to Washington, in charge of an officer, and reported to the Adjutant General." On July 2, 1864, Secretary of War Stanton ordered, "Col. Wyndham will be mustered out of service," and he was discharged effective, July 5, 1864.

Born: Sept. 22, 1833 Aboard the ship *Arab* in "the Downs"

Died: Jan. 25, 1879 Mandalay, Burma (killed in hot air balloon accident)

Other Wars: War for Italian Unification, 1860 (Lieutenant Colonel and brigade commander under Gen. Garibaldi)

Occupation: Professional soldier and adventurer, serving in the French navy, 1848–50; the English artillery, 1850–52; the Austrian lancers, 1852–60; and the Italian army, 1860–61. Operated military school, served in Italian army, 1866–67, engaged in petroleum refining, and speculated in lumber operations after war.

Offices/Honors: Knighted by King Victor Emanuel of Italy and appointed a Chevalier of the Military Order of Savoy

Miscellaneous: Resided New York City, NY; and many other cities world-wide

Buried: Burial place unknown

References: Samuel Toombs. *New Jersey Troops in the Gettysburg Campaign.* Orange, NJ, 1888. Edward G. Longacre. *Jersey Cavaliers: A History of the 1st New Jersey Volunteer Cavalry, 1861–65.* Hightstown, NJ, 1992. Earl Schenck Miers, editor. *Ride to War: The History of the 1st New Jersey Cavalry,* by Henry R. Pyne. New Brunswick, NJ, 1961. Military Service File, National Archives. Civil War Officer Memorials, Department of Defense, New Jersey Archives. Letters Received, Volunteer Service Branch, Adjutant General's Office, File P1836(VS)1864, National Archives. Correspondence from James O. Hall, citing an article in the July 29, 1867 issue of the *Philadelphia Inquirer.*

ABRAM ZABRISKIE

1 Lieutenant, Adjutant, 9 NJ Infantry, Oct. 8, 1861. Major, 9 NJ Infantry, Feb. 10, 1862. Lieutenant Colonel, 9 NJ Infantry, Dec. 22, 1862. Colonel, 9 NJ Infantry, Jan. 8, 1863. Commanded District of Beaufort, 18 Army Corps, Department of North Carolina, May 1863. GSW neck, Drewry's Bluff, VA, May 16, 1864

Born: Feb. 18, 1841 Hackensack, NJ

Died: May 24, 1864 DOW Fort Monroe, VA

Education: Graduated Princeton (NJ) University, 1859

Occupation: Law student

Miscellaneous: Resided Jersey City, Hudson Co., NJ

Buried: Green-Wood Cemetery, Brooklyn, NY (Section 32/33, Lots 14954–14956)

References: J. Madison Drake. *The History of the 9th New Jersey Veteran Vols.* Elizabeth, NJ, 1889. John Y. Foster. *New Jersey and the Rebellion.* Newark, NJ, 1868. *Memorial of Colonel Abram Zabriskie.* Jersey

Abram Zabriskie
ROGER D. HUNT COLLECTION, USAMHI.
BRADY'S NATIONAL PHOTOGRAPHIC PORTRAIT GALLERIES, BROADWAY AND TENTH STREETS, NEW YORK.

City, NJ, 1864. *Digest No. 1 of the Class of 1859, College of New Jersey, from 1859 to 1864.* Philadelphia, PA, 1864. W. Woodford Clayton, compiler. *History of Bergen and Passaic Counties, NJ.* Philadelphia, PA, 1882. Military Service File, National Archives. Civil War Officer Memorials, Department of Defense, New Jersey Archives. Joseph T. Duryea. *An Oration Commemorative of the Restoration of the Union, with a Tribute to the Alumni and Under-Graduates of the College of New Jersey, Who Fell in the National Struggle.* Philadelphia, PA, 1866.

MARYLAND

1st Cavalry

Andrew G. Miller	May 4, 1862	Resigned May 22, 1862
Eugene von Kielmansegge	Oct. 9, 1862	Dismissed May 14, 1863
Andrew W. Evans	April 15, 1864	Mustered out Aug. 8, 1865

1st Potomac Home Brigade Cavalry

Henry A. Cole	April 20, 1864	Mustered out June 28, 1865

3rd Cavalry

C. Carroll Tevis	Dec. 23, 1863	Discharged July 20, 1864, **Bvt. Brig. Gen.**

1st Infantry

John R. Kenly	June 11, 1861	Promoted **Brig. Gen., USV**, Aug. 22, 1862
Nathan T. Dushane	Aug. 22, 1862	KIA Aug. 21, 1864
John W. Wilson	Sept. 6, 1864	KIA Feb. 6, 1865
David L. Stanton	March 20, 1865	Mustered out July 2, 1865, **Bvt. Brig. Gen.**

1st Potomac Home Brigade Infantry

William P. Maulsby	Nov. 28, 1861	Resigned Aug. 25, 1864
Roger E. Cook	Feb. 24, 1865	To 13th MD Infantry, April 8, 1865

1st Eastern Shore Infantry

James Wallace	Aug. 16, 1861	Resigned Dec. 23, 1863
John R. Keene	March 10, 1864	Revoked May 30, 1864

2nd Infantry

John Sommer	Sept. 21, 1861	Resigned April 20, 1862
Thomas B. Allard	June 26, 1862	Resigned Jan. 19, 1864
Benjamin F. Taylor	July 10, 1865	Mustered July 17, 1865

2nd Potomac Home Brigade Infantry

Thomas Johns	Oct. 9, 1861	Resigned Dec. 31, 1861
Robert Bruce	Jan. 3, 1862	Mustered out Oct. 4, 1864

2nd Eastern Shore Infantry

Edward Wilkins	Dec. 25, 1861	Resigned Dec. 23, 1862
Robert S. Rodgers	Jan. 28, 1863	Mustered out Oct. 31, 1864

3rd Infantry

John C. McConnell	Aug. 5, 1861	Mustered out Feb. 18, 1862
David P. DeWitt	March 29, 1862	To 143rd NY Infantry, Oct. 8, 1862, **Bvt. Brig. Gen.**
Joseph M. Sudsburg	Oct. 24, 1862	Mustered out June 24, 1864

3rd Potomac Home Brigade Infantry

Stephen W. Downey	Sept. 8, 1862	Resigned Nov. 6, 1862
Charles Gilpin	April 14, 1864	Mustered out Jan. 2, 1865
Henry C. Rizer	May 6, 1865	Mustered out May 29, 1865

4th Infantry

William J. L. Nicodemus	Oct. 9, 1862	Resigned Nov. 17, 1862
Richard N. Bowerman	April 4, 1863	Mustered out May 31, 1865, **Bvt. Brig. Gen.**

5th Infantry

William Louis Schley	Sept. 4, 1861	Resigned Oct. 6, 1864
William W. Bamberger	May 1, 1865	Mustered out Sept. 1, 1865

6th Infantry

George R. Howard	Sept. 3, 1862	Resigned Feb. 5, 1863
John W. Horn	March 27, 1863	Discharged Feb. 4, 1865, **Bvt. Brig. Gen.**
Joseph C. Hill	April 25, 1865	Mustered out June 20, 1865

7th Infantry

Edwin H. Webster	Sept. 12, 1862	Resigned Nov. 6, 1863
Charles E. Phelps	April 13, 1864	Discharged Sept. 9, 1864, **Bvt. Brig. Gen.**

8th Infantry

Andrew W. Denison	Sept. 12, 1862	Mustered out May 31, 1865, **Bvt. Brig. Gen.**

9th Infantry

Benjamin L. Simpson	Aug. 17, 1863	Mustered out Feb. 24, 1864

10th Infantry

William H. Revere, Jr.	July 30, 1863	Mustered out Jan. 29, 1864, **Bvt. Brig. Gen.**

11th Infantry (100 Days)

William T. Landstreet	June 13, 1864	Mustered out Oct. 1, 1864

11th Infantry (One Year)

John G. Johannes	March 3, 1865	Mustered out June 15, 1865

13th Infantry

Roger E. Cook	April 8, 1865	Mustered out May 29, 1865

Purnell Legion Infantry

William H. Purnell	Nov. 1, 1861	Resigned Feb. 17, 1862
William J. Leonard	March 17, 1862	Resigned Nov. 26, 1862
Samuel A. Graham	Jan. 12, 1863	Mustered out Oct. 24, 1864

THOMAS B. ALLARD

Lieutenant Colonel, Baltimore Light Infantry, MD Volunteers, Feb. 8, 1862. Honorably mustered out, May 28, 1862. Colonel, 2 MD Infantry, June 26, 1862. Commanded 1 Brigade, 2 Division, 9 Army Corps, Army of the Potomac, Dec. 1862. Commanded Post of Frankfort, KY, April–Sept. 1863. Commanded 1 Brigade, 2 Division, 9 Army Corps, Army of the Ohio, Oct. 16–Nov. 16, 1863. Resigned Jan. 19, 1864.

Born: March 18, 1812 Shrewsbury, Shropshire, England
Died: Jan. 27, 1877 Baltimore, MD
Occupation: Carpenter and construction superintendent early in life. Dealer in provisions and produce and US Customs inspector after war.
Miscellaneous: Resided Baltimore, MD. Father-in-law of Colonel William W. Bamberger.
Buried: Green Mount Cemetery, Baltimore, MD (Area WW, Lot 81)
References: Obituary, *Baltimore Sun*, Jan. 29, 1877. Military Service File, National Archives. Thomas B. Allard Papers, Maryland Historical Society.

WILLIAM W. BAMBERGER

Captain, Co. B, 5 MD Infantry, Oct. 9, 1861. GSW both lungs, Antietam, MD, Sept. 17, 1862. Discharged for disability, March 9, 1863, due to wounds. Lieutenant Colonel, 5 MD Infantry, Nov. 22, 1864. Colonel, 5 MD Infantry, May 1, 1865. Honorably mustered out, Sept. 1, 1865.

Born: Aug. 27, 1839 Baltimore, MD
Died: Jan. 12, 1920 Reisterstown, MD
Occupation: Carpenter and letter carrier
Miscellaneous: Resided Baltimore, MD; and Reisterstown, Baltimore Co., MD. Son-in-law of Colonel Thomas B. Allard.
Buried: Green Mount Cemetery, Baltimore, MD (Area WW, Lot 81)
References: Pension File and Military Service File, National Archives.

ROBERT BRUCE

Lieutenant Colonel, 2 Potomac Home Brigade MD Infantry, Aug. 27, 1861. Colonel, 2 Potomac Home Brigade MD Infantry, Jan. 3, 1862. Commanded 3 Brigade, Railroad Division, 8 Army Corps, Middle Department, Nov. 17, 1862–Jan. 1863. Honorably mustered out, Oct. 4, 1864.

Born: March 26, 1805 Cumberland, MD
Died: June 14, 1890 Cumberland, MD
Occupation: Bank cashier and accountant
Offices/Honors: MD House of Delegates, 1836. Judge of Allegany County Orphans Court, 1874–90.
Miscellaneous: Resided Cumberland, Allegany Co., MD. Father-in-law of Brig. Gen. Benjamin F. Kelley.
Buried: Rose Hill Cemetery, Cumberland, MD (Section 8, Lot 11)
References: Pension File and Military Service File, National Archives. James W. Thomas and T. J. C. Williams. *History of Allegany County, MD.* N.p., 1923. Obituary, *Cumberland Civilian*, June 15, 1890. Keith O. Gary. *Answering the Call: The Organization and Recruiting of the Potomac Home Brigade Maryland Volunteers.* Bowie, MD, 1996.

HENRY ALEXANDER COLE

Captain, Co. A, 1 Potomac Home Brigade MD Cavalry, Aug. 10, 1861. Major, 1 Potomac Home Brigade MD Cavalry, Aug. 1, 1862. Lieutenant Colonel, 1 Potomac Home Brigade MD Cavalry, March 5, 1864. Colonel, 1 Potomac Home Brigade MD Cavalry, April 20, 1864. Commanded Post of Frederick, MD, Sept. 1864. Commanded Post of Martinsburg, WV, Feb. 1865. Commanded 1 Brigade, 3 Division, Department of West Virginia, March–May 1865. Honorably mustered out, June 28, 1865.

Born: July 25, 1834 Frederick, MD
Died: May 26, 1909 Baltimore, MD
Occupation: Carpenter and builder before war. Contractor and builder after war.
Offices/Honors: US Internal Revenue Storekeeper, 1881–90. US Internal Revenue Gauger, 1890–1909.
Miscellaneous: Resided Frederick, MD, to 1866; and Baltimore, MD, after 1866
Buried: Mount Olivet Cemetery, Frederick, MD (Section R, Lot 98)

References: *The Union Army.* Maryland/Washington, DC, Edition. Madison, WI, 1908. Pension File and Military Service File, National Archives. Obituary, *Frederick Daily News,* May 26, 1909. Letters Received, Volunteer Service Branch, Adjutant General's Office, File C648(VS)1863, National Archives. William H. Powell, editor. *Officers of the Army and Navy (Volunteer) Who Served in the Civil War.* Philadelphia, PA, 1893. C. Armour Newcomer. *Cole's Cavalry; or Three Years in the Saddle in the Shenandoah Valley.* Baltimore, MD, 1895. Obituary, *Baltimore Sun,* May 26, 1909. Daniel C. Toomey and Charles A. Earp. *Marylanders in Blue: The Artillery and the Cavalry.* Baltimore, MD, 1999.

Henry Alexander Cole
District of Columbia MOLLUS Collection, USAMHI.

ROGER ELLSWORTH COOK

Captain, Co. A, 1 Potomac Home Brigade MD Infantry, Aug. 15, 1861. Major, 1 Potomac Home Brigade MD Infantry, Feb. 6, 1863. Lieutenant Colonel, 1 Potomac Home Brigade MD Infantry, Sept. 1, 1863. Colonel, 1 Potomac Home Brigade MD Infantry, Feb. 24, 1865. Commanded 3 Brigade, 3 Division, Department of West Virginia, Feb.–March 1865. Colonel, 13 MD Infantry, April 8, 1865. Commanded 1 Brigade, 2 Division, Department of West Virginia, April 1865. Honorably mustered out, May 29, 1865.

Born: Nov. 23, 1809 Hartford, CT
Died: Nov. 12, 1893 Hagerstown, MD
Occupation: School teacher before war. Clerk and justice of the peace after war.
Miscellaneous: Resided Hagerstown, Washington Co., MD
Buried: Rose Hill Cemetery, Hagerstown, MD (Section B, Lot 87)
References: Obituary, *Hagerstown Mail,* Nov. 17, 1893. Pension File and Military Service File, National Archives.

STEPHEN WHEELER DOWNEY

Private, Co. C, 3 Potomac Home Brigade MD Infantry, Sept. 12, 1861. 1 Lieutenant, Co. C, 3 Potomac Home Brigade MD Infantry, Jan. 1, 1862. 1 Lieutenant, Adjutant, 3 Potomac Home Brigade MD Infantry, Jan. 26, 1862. Lieutenant Colonel, 3 Potomac Home Brigade MD Infantry, March 1, 1862. Colonel, 3 Potomac Home Brigade MD Infantry, Sept. 8, 1862. Taken prisoner, Harper's Ferry, WV, Sept. 15, 1862. Paroled Sept. 16, 1862. Resigned Nov. 6, 1862, "having for five months been in ill health, with little hope of improvement."

Born: July 25, 1839 Westernport, Allegany Co., MD
Died: Aug. 5, 1902 Denver, CO
Education: Attended Georgetown (DC) University
Occupation: Practiced law and speculated in land and mining enterprises
Offices/Honors: Treasurer, WY Territory, 1872–75. Auditor, WY Territory, 1877–79. US House of Representatives, 1879–81. WY House of Representatives, 1893–95.
Miscellaneous: Resided Cumberland, Allegany Co., MD; Washington, DC; and Laramie, Albany Co., WY, after 1869

Stephen Wheeler Downey

Buried: Green Hill Cemetery, Laramie, WY

References: Pension File and Military Service File, National Archives. I. S. Bartlett. *History of Wyoming.* Chicago, IL, 1918. Obituary, *Rocky Mountain News,* Aug. 6, 1902. *Biographical Directory of the American Congress.* Paul R. Teetor. *A Matter of Hours: Treason at Harper's Ferry.* Rutherford, NJ, 1982.

NATHAN THOMAS DUSHANE

Lieutenant Colonel, 1 MD Infantry, June 11, 1861. GSW Front Royal, VA, May 23, 1862. Taken prisoner, Front Royal, VA, May 23, 1862. Paroled Aug. 17, 1862. Colonel, 1 MD Infantry, Aug. 22, 1862. Commanded 3 Brigade, 3 Division, 1 Army Corps, Army of the Potomac, July 11–Dec. 28, 1863. Commanded 2 Brigade, 3 Division, 1 Army Corps, Jan. 20–March 24,

Nathan Thomas Dushane
NATIONAL ARCHIVES.

1864. Commanded 3 Brigade, 2 Division, 5 Army Corps, Army of the Potomac, March 24–April, 1864 and May 23–June 6, 1864. Commanded 2 Brigade, 2 Division, 5 Army Corps, June 6–Aug. 21, 1864. Shell wound, Weldon Railroad, VA, Aug. 21, 1864.

Born: Feb. 3, 1817 St. George's Hundred, New Castle Co., DE

Died: Aug. 21, 1864 KIA Weldon Railroad, VA

Occupation: Master builder, architect and real estate operator

Offices/Honors: MD House of Delegates, 1854–56

Miscellaneous: Resided Baltimore, MD

Buried: Western Cemetery, Baltimore, MD

References: James H. Dushane, compiler. *Genealogical Record of the Dushane Family, 1640–1942.* Baltimore, MD, 1942. Charles Camper and Joseph W. Kirkley. *Historical Record of the 1st Regiment Maryland Infantry.* Washington, DC, 1871. Obituary, *Baltimore Sun,* Aug. 23, 1864. Military Service File, National Archives.

Andrew Wallace Evans (left)
COURTESY OF GIL BARRETT.

ANDREW WALLACE EVANS

Captain, 3 US Cavalry, May 14, 1861. Captain, 6 US Cavalry, Aug. 3, 1861. Acting AIG and Commissary of Musters, Department of New Mexico, April 25, 1862–Sept. 26, 1863. Colonel, 1 MD Cavalry, April 15, 1864. Commanded 3 Brigade, Cavalry Division, Army of the James, Oct. 14, 1864–Feb. 5, 1865. Honorably mustered out of volunteer service, Aug. 8, 1865.

Born: July 6, 1829 Elkton, MD
Died: April 24, 1906 Elkton, MD

Education: Attended Harvard University, Cambridge, MA. Graduated US Military Academy, West Point, NY, 1852.
Occupation: Regular Army (Lieutenant Colonel, 7 US Cavalry, retired Sept. 22, 1883)
Offices/Honors: Bvt. Brig. Gen., USA, Feb. 27, 1890, for gallant services in action against Indians at Big Dry Wash, AZ, July 17, 1882
Miscellaneous: Resided Elkton, Cecil Co., MD
Buried: Presbyterian Cemetery, Elkton, MD
References: *Annual Reunion*, Association of the Graduates of the US Military Academy, 1906. George W.

Cullum. *Biographical Register of the Officers and Graduates of the US Military Academy.* Third Edition. Boston and New York, 1891. Constance Wynn Altshuler. *Cavalry Yellow & Infantry Blue.* Tucson, AZ, 1991. Pension File and Military Service File, National Archives. *Portrait and Biographical Record of Harford and Cecil Counties, MD.* New York and Chicago, 1897. Obituary, *The Cecil Whig*, April 28, 1906. Obituary, *Baltimore Sun*, April 25, 1906. Daniel C. Toomey and Charles A. Earp. *Marylanders in Blue: The Artillery and the Cavalry.* Baltimore, MD, 1999.

CHARLES GILPIN

Captain, Co. D, 3 Potomac Home Brigade MD Infantry, Jan. 30, 1862. Lieutenant Colonel, 3 Potomac Home Brigade MD Infantry, Sept. 8, 1862. Taken prisoner, Harper's Ferry, WV, Sept. 15, 1862. Paroled Sept. 16, 1862. Colonel, 3 Potomac Home Brigade MD Infantry, April 14, 1864. Honorably mustered out, Jan. 2, 1865.

Born: 1812 NY
Died: Feb. 27, 1889 Cumberland, MD (struck by locomotive while crossing railroad tracks)
Occupation: Engaged in the tanning and mercantile business
Offices/Honors: Surveyor of the Port of Baltimore, 1873–77. US Customs Inspector, 1881–88.
Miscellaneous: Resided Cumberland, Allegany Co., MD; and Baltimore, MD
Buried: Rose Hill Cemetery, Cumberland, MD (Section 24, Lot 19)
References: Obituary, *Cumberland Civilian*, March 3, 1889. Obituary, *Baltimore Sun*, Feb. 28, 1889. Pension File and Military Service File, National Archives.

SAMUEL ALEXANDER GRAHAM

Captain, Co. D, Purnell Legion MD Infantry, Sept. 15, 1861. Colonel, Purnell Legion MD Infantry, Jan. 12, 1863. Commanded 1 Separate Brigade, 8 Army Corps, Middle Department, Feb. 4–14, 1863 and Feb. 1864. Commanded 3 Separate Brigade, 8 Army Corps, Middle Department, July 12–Aug. 10, 1863. GSW hand, Petersburg, VA, July 30, 1864. Commanded 2 Brigade, 2 Division, 5 Army Corps, Army of the Potomac, Aug. 21–Oct. 24, 1864. Honorably mustered out, Oct. 24, 1864.

Born: Nov. 30, 1828 Tuscarora Valley, Juniata Co., PA
Died: Dec. 7, 1890 Salisbury, MD
Education: Graduated Dickinson College, Carlisle, PA, 1849
Occupation: School teacher and lawyer before war. Lawyer after war.
Offices/Honors: Prosecuting Attorney, Somerset Co., MD, 1859–61. Assessor of Internal Revenue, 1869–73.
Miscellaneous: Resided Salisbury, Wicomico Co., MD
Buried: Parsons Cemetery, Salisbury, MD
References: *The Biographical Cyclopedia of Representative Men of Maryland and District of Columbia.* Baltimore, MD, 1879. Obituary, *Baltimore Sun*, Dec. 9, 1890. George L. Reed, editor. *Alumni Record Dickinson College.* Carlisle, PA, 1905. Military Service File, National Archives.

Joseph C. Hill
COURTESY OF GIL BARRETT.
B. E. LODORE, ELKTON, MD.

Joseph C. Hill (left) after the war, with officers of the 6th Maryland:
Bvt. Brig. Gen. John W. Horn (center) and Lt. Col. William A. McKellip.

COURTESY OF GIL BARRETT.

JOSEPH C. HILL

2 Lieutenant, Co. B, 6 MD Infantry, Aug. 1, 1862. Captain, Co. B, 6 MD Infantry, Aug. 20, 1862. Major, 6 MD Infantry, March 27, 1863. Lieutenant Colonel, 6 MD Infantry, Nov. 24, 1863. GSW right thigh, Wilderness, VA, May 5, 1864. Honorably discharged July 5, 1864, on account of physical disability from wounds received in action. Lieutenant Colonel, 6 MD Infantry, Sept. 21, 1864. *Colonel*, 6 MD Infantry, April 25, 1865. Honorably mustered out, June 20, 1865.

Born: April 9, 1828 Chester Co., PA
Died: Dec. 30, 1896 Baltimore, MD
Occupation: Miller and US Customs Inspector
Miscellaneous: Resided Elkton, Cecil Co., MD; and Baltimore, MD
Buried: Loudon Park Cemetery, Baltimore, MD (Section N, Lot 115)

References: Pension File and Military Service File, National Archives. Obituary, *The Cecil Whig*, Jan. 2, 1897. Obituary, *Baltimore Sun*, Dec. 31, 1896. Jerre Garrett. *Muffled Drums and Mustard Spoons: Cecil County, Maryland, 1860–65*. Shippensburg, PA, 1996. Letters Received, Volunteer Service Branch, Adjutant General's Office, File H1271(VS)1864, National Archives.

GEORGE REYNOLDS HOWARD

Colonel, 6 MD Infantry, Sept. 3, 1862. Resigned Feb. 5, 1863, due to "a lack of physical vigor to endure the exposure consequent upon the performance of his duties."

Born: Feb. 4, 1801 Lancaster Co., PA
Died: Aug. 4, 1884 Elkton, MD
Occupation: Merchant and farmer

Offices/Honors: MD Senate, 1840–45. Register of Wills, Cecil Co., MD, 1845–50.
Miscellaneous: Resided Elkton, Cecil Co., MD
Buried: Presbyterian Cemetery, Elkton, MD
References: Obituary, *The Cecil Democrat*, Aug. 9, 1884. Obituary, *The Cecil Whig*, Aug. 9, 1884. Vertical File, Cecil County Historical Society. Military Service File, National Archives. *Portrait and Biographical Record of Harford and Cecil Counties, MD.* New York and Chicago, 1897.

JOHN G. JOHANNES

Lieutenant Colonel, Purnell Legion MD Infantry, Sept. 30, 1861. Resigned April 20, 1862, because "subalterns in the staff are incessantly undermining and subverting all my efforts to establish proper discipline." 2 Lieutenant, Co. D, 8 MD Infantry, Aug. 9, 1862. Captain, Co. D, 8 MD Infantry, Sept. 4, 1862. Lieutenant Colonel, 8 MD Infantry, Sept. 8, 1862. GSW left breast, Dabney's Mill, VA, Feb. 6, 1865. Discharged to accept promotion, Feb. 25, 1865. Colonel, 11 MD Infantry, March 3, 1865. Honorably mustered out, June 15, 1865.

Born: 1824 Baltimore, MD
Died: Jan. 27, 1904 Washington, DC
Occupation: Jewelry manufacturer
Miscellaneous: Resided Baltimore, MD; New York City, NY, 1865–68; Leavenworth, KS, 1868–75; and Washington, DC
Buried: Arlington National Cemetery, Arlington, VA (Section 3, Lot 1425)
References: Pension File and Military Service File, National Archives. Obituary, *Washington Post*, Jan. 29, 1904. Kevin C. Ruffner. *Maryland's Blue & Gray: A Border State's Union and Confederate Junior Officer Corps.* Baton Rouge, LA, 1997. Letters Received, Volunteer Service Branch, Adjutant General's Office, File J146(VS)1865, National Archives.

THOMAS JOHNS

Colonel, 2 Potomac Home Brigade MD Infantry, Oct. 9, 1861. Resigned Dec. 31, 1861, due to physical disability from "inflammation of the spinal column, in the lumbar region, attended with severe pain and inability to move without great pain."

Born: March 5, 1812 Georgetown, DC
Died: June 17, 1882 Cumberland, MD

Education: Graduated US Military Academy, West Point, NY, 1833
Occupation: Regular Army (1 Lieutenant, 8 US Infantry, resigned Aug. 31, 1841). Secretary of a coal and iron company and later a hardware merchant.
Miscellaneous: Resided Cumberland, Allegany Co., MD. Brother-in-law of Brig. Gen. George W. Getty.
Buried: Rose Hill Cemetery, Cumberland, MD (Section 10, Lot 2)
References: Matthew P. Andrews. *Tercentenary History of Maryland.* Chicago and Baltimore, 1925. Obituary, *Cumberland Civilian*, June 18, 1882. Military Service File, National Archives. James W. Thomas and T. J. C. Williams. *History of Allegany County, MD.* N.p., 1923. Letters Received, Volunteer Service Branch, Adjutant General's Office, File J31(VS)1861, National Archives. George W. Cullum. *Biographical Register of the Officers and Graduates of the US Military Academy.* Third Edition. Boston and New York, 1891. *Annual Reunion*, Association of the Graduates of the US Military Academy, 1883. Keith O. Gary. *Answering the Call: The Organization and Recruiting of the Potomac Home Brigade Maryland Volunteers.* Bowie, MD, 1996.

JOHN RICHARD KEENE

Captain, Co. C, 1 Eastern Shore MD Infantry, Oct. 31, 1861. Colonel, 1 Eastern Shore MD Infantry, March 10, 1864, "with the understanding that should the regiment not be reenlisted as veterans, the muster in will be revoked." Failing to accomplish the veteran reenlistment of the regiment, he was ordered, May 30, 1864, to fall back to his original position as captain with "pay as such during the time he has been colonel." Major, 1 Eastern Shore MD Infantry, June 9, 1864. Honorably mustered out, Feb. 23, 1865.

Born: 1836?
Died: Spring 1870. Place of death unknown.
Occupation: Farmer
Miscellaneous: Resided Church Creek, Dorchester Co., MD
Buried: Burial place unknown
References: Elias Jones. *History of Dorchester County, MD.* Baltimore, MD, 1902. Military Service File, National Archives. Elias Jones. *Keene Family History and Genealogy.* Baltimore, MD, 1923. Letters Received, Volunteer Service Branch, Adjutant General's Office, File M478(VS)1864, National Archives.

EUGENE VON KIELMANSEGGE

Captain, Co. C, Fremont Hussars, Sept. 4, 1861. Captain, Co. E, 4 MO Cavalry, Feb. 14, 1862. Major, 4 MO Cavalry, March 1, 1862. Being absent from his regiment without authority at the time of the special muster of Aug. 18, 1862, he was mustered out to take effect June 24, 1862. Colonel, 1 MD Cavalry, Oct. 9, 1862. Commanded 2 Brigade, 3 Division, Cavalry Corps, Army of the Potomac, Feb. 1863. Dismissed May 14, 1863, "having been discharged the service as major of the 4 MO Cavalry . . . for absence without leave, and no authority given for him to re-enter the service." Colonel, 1 FL Cavalry, March 29, 1864. Regiment not achieving full strength, he was mustered in as Major, 1 FL Cavalry, June 26, 1864. Lieutenant Colonel, 1 FL Cavalry, July 21, 1864. Disability resulting from dismissal removed, Oct. 4, 1864, and he was re-mustered as major and lieutenant colonel, Nov. 4, 1864. Discharged for disability, April 17, 1865, "on account of myopia contracted prior to his muster into service."

Born: 1830? Germany
Died: Sept. 3, 1868 St. Andrews Bay, Washington Co., FL
Occupation: Captain of Hussars in German army before war. US Customs inspector after war.
Offices/Honors: Postmaster, Apalachicola, FL, 1865–67
Miscellaneous: Resided New York City, NY; and Apalachicola, Franklin Co., FL
Buried: Burial place unknown
References: Pension File and Military Service File, National Archives. Letters Received, Volunteer Service Branch, Adjutant General's Office, File K232(VS)1863, National Archives. Daniel C. Toomey and Charles A. Earp. *Marylanders in Blue: The Artillery and the Cavalry.* Baltimore, MD, 1999.

WILLIAM T. LANDSTREET

Colonel, 11 MD Infantry, June 13, 1864. Honorably mustered out, Oct. 1, 1864.

Born: March 2, 1825 Baltimore, MD
Died: April 1, 1873 Baltimore, MD (accidental gunshot wound)
Occupation: Commission merchant
Miscellaneous: Resided Baltimore, MD

Buried: Loudon Park Cemetery, Baltimore, MD (Section P, Lot 225)
References: Obituary, *Baltimore Sun*, April 2, 1873. Pension File and Military Service File, National Archives. Letters Received, Volunteer Service Branch, Adjutant General's Office, File L618(VS)1864, National Archives.

WILLIAM JAMES LEONARD

Colonel, Purnell Legion MD Infantry, March 17, 1862. Taken prisoner, Catlett's Station, VA, Aug. 22, 1862. Confined at Libby Prison, Richmond, VA. Paroled Sept. 24, 1862. Resigned Nov. 26, 1862, due to "family affliction and private business requiring my attention." Provost Marshal, Eastern MD, Feb. 15, 1864. Appointment revoked, Sept. 15, 1864.

Born: Sept. 16, 1816 near Salisbury, MD
Died: Oct. 14, 1901 Salisbury, MD
Education: Attended Wesleyan University, Middletown, CT (Class of 1836)
Occupation: Engaged in grain, lumber and general merchandise business before war. Engaged in political affairs and agricultural pursuits after war.
Offices/Honors: MD House of Delegates, 1849–51, 1854–56 and 1874–76. MD State Comptroller, 1867–70. Wicomico County Commissioner, 1882–83.
Miscellaneous: Resided Salisbury, Wicomico Co., MD
Buried: Parsons Cemetery, Salisbury, MD
References: *The Biographical Cyclopedia of Representative Men of Maryland and District of Columbia.* Baltimore, MD, 1879. Pension File and Military Service File, National Archives. Obituary, *Salisbury Advertiser*, Oct. 19, 1901. *Alumni Record of Wesleyan University.* Third Edition. Hartford, CT, 1883.

WILLIAM PINKNEY MAULSBY

Colonel, 1 Potomac Home Brigade MD Infantry, Nov. 28, 1861. Taken prisoner and paroled, Harper's Ferry, WV, Sept. 15, 1862. Commanded 2 Brigade, Maryland Heights Division, Department of the Susquehanna, July 1863. Commanded 2 Brigade, Maryland Heights Division, Army of West Virginia, Aug. 3–Dec. 1863. Commanded 2 Brigade, 1 Division, Army of West Virginia, Dec. 1863–April 1864. Resigned Aug. 25, 1864, due to physical disability from "chronic bronchitis."

Born: July 10, 1815 Bel Air, MD

Died: Oct. 3, 1894 Westminster, MD

Education: Attended Bel Air (MD) Academy. Graduated Union College, Schenectady, NY, 1832.

Occupation: Lawyer and judge

Offices/Honors: MD Senate, 1838–43. MD Constitutional Convention, 1867. Judge, MD Court of Appeals, 1870–71.

Miscellaneous: Resided Frederick, Frederick Co., MD; and Westminster, Carroll Co., MD

Buried: Mount Olivet Cemetery, Frederick, MD (Section G, Lot 191)

References: Ella K. Barnard. *The Maulsby Family.* Baltimore, MD, 1909. Obituary, *Frederick Daily News,* Oct. 4, 1894. Military Service File, National Archives. Keith O. Gary. *Answering the Call: The Organization and Recruiting of the Potomac Home Brigade Maryland Volunteers.* Bowie, MD, 1996. J. Thomas Scharf. *History of Western Maryland.* Philadelphia, PA, 1882.

William Pinkney Maulsby
PORTRAIT PAINTING, HARFORD COUNTY COURT HOUSE, BEL AIR, MD.

William Pinkney Maulsby (postwar) with three of his great-granddaughters, Bessie Maulsby McLean, Rebekah McCormick McLean, and Emily Nelson Ritchie McLean.
COURTESY OF THE HISTORICAL SOCIETY OF FREDERICK COUNTY, MD.

JOHN C. McCONNELL

Captain, Co. A, 1 MD Infantry, May 10, 1861. Colonel, 3 MD Infantry, Aug. 5, 1861. Mustered out Feb. 18, 1862, by direction of Adjutant General Lorenzo Thomas, who explained, "The frequent disobedience of Col. McConnell of orders given him from this office has proved his unfitness for the position of colonel. He was improperly mustered into service upon six companies (the command of a Lieut. Colonel) without the knowledge or sanction of this office. Men were enlisted for him by his orders after the Secy. of War had revoked his authority to raise troops. Men were also enlisted by McConnell's orders for Engineer soldiers under false promises of increased pay and bounty."

Born: 1811? GA
Died: April 14, 1883 Pfeiffer Corners, MD
Other Wars: Mexican War (Private, Co. H, 1 GA Infantry)

Andrew Galbraith Miller
ROGER D. HUNT COLLECTION, USAMHI.

Occupation: Property agent (1860 Baltimore census) and merchant before war. Superintendent of the US Topographical Bureau and farmer after war.
Miscellaneous: Resided Baltimore, MD; and Pfeiffer Corners, Howard Co., MD
Buried: Trinity Chapel Cemetery, Pfeiffer Corners, Howard Co., MD (unmarked)
References: Obituary, *Baltimore Sun*, April 16, 1883. Obituary, *Baltimore American*, April 15, 1883. Kevin C. Ruffner. *Maryland's Blue & Gray: A Border State's Union and Confederate Junior Officer Corps.* Baton Rouge, LA, 1997. Letters Received, Volunteer Service Branch, Adjutant General's Office, File C89(VS)1862, National Archives. Pension File and Military Service File, National Archives.

ANDREW GALBRAITH MILLER

Lieutenant Colonel, 1 MD Cavalry, Dec. 20, 1861. Colonel, 1 MD Cavalry, May 4, 1862. Resigned May 22, 1862, since "the state of my health will not permit me to remain longer."

Born: Dec. 21, 1827 Gettysburg, PA
Died: Oct. 21, 1865 Milwaukee, WI
Education: Attended Gettysburg (PA) College. Graduated US Military Academy, West Point, NY, 1848.
Occupation: Regular Army (Captain, 1 US Infantry, resigned Oct. 31, 1857). Cashier of La Crosse and Milwaukee Railroad Co., 1857–61.
Miscellaneous: Resided Milwaukee, WI. Nephew of Brig. Gen. James Cooper.
Buried: Forest Home Cemetery, Milwaukee, WI (Section 32, Block 2, Lots 1–2)
References: Thompson P. Ege. *History and Genealogy of the Ege Family in the United States, 1738–1911.* Harrisburg, PA, 1911. Military Service File, National Archives. George W. Cullum. *Biographical Register of the Officers and Graduates of the US Military Academy.* Third Edition. Boston and New York, 1891. Obituary, *Milwaukee Daily Sentinel*, Oct. 23, 1865.

WILLIAM JOSEPH LEONARD NICODEMUS

1 Lieutenant, 11 US Infantry, May 14, 1861. Captain, 12 US Infantry, Oct. 24, 1861. Acting AAG, Department of New Mexico, Oct. 1861–June 1862. Colonel, 4 MD Infantry, Oct. 9, 1862. Resigned from volunteer service, Nov. 17, 1862, for reasons which "are strictly private and have no reference to the administration of the Government." Major, US Signal Corps, March 3, 1863.

*William Joseph Leonard Nicodemus
with his wife, Frances*

COURTESY OF GIL BARRETT.
BRADY'S NATIONAL PHOTOGRAPHIC PORTRAIT GALLERIES,
352 PENNSYLVANIA AVE., WASHINGTON, DC

Chief Signal Officer, Nov. 10, 1863–Dec. 26, 1864. Lieutenant Colonel, US Signal Corps, June 30, 1864. Dismissed Dec. 26, 1864 for "irregular and improper conduct" in publishing without authority "the annual report of the Signal Corps, which contains information useful to the enemy and prejudicial to the service of the United States." Reinstated March 31, 1865. Inspector, US Signal Corps, March 31–Aug. 23, 1865. Honorably mustered out of Signal Corps, Aug. 23, 1865.

Born: Aug. 21, 1834 near Hagerstown, MD
Died: Jan. 6, 1879 Madison, WI
Education: Graduated US Military Academy, West Point, NY, 1858

Occupation: Regular Army (Captain, 12 US Infantry, honorably mustered out Dec. 29, 1870). Professor of Military Science and Civil and Mechanical Engineering, University of Wisconsin, 1871–79. Topographical Assistant, Wisconsin State Geological Commission, 1875–79.
Miscellaneous: Resided Hagerstown, Washington Co., MD; and Madison, Dane Co., WI
Buried: Resurrection Catholic Cemetery, Madison, WI (Section 3, Block 21, Lot 1.1)
References: *History of Dane County, WI.* Chicago, IL, 1880. J. Willard Brown. *The Signal Corps, USA, in the War of the Rebellion.* Boston, MA, 1896. George W. Cullum. *Biographical Register of the Officers and Graduates of the US Military Academy.* Third Edition. Boston and New York, 1891. Obituary, *Wisconsin State Journal*, Jan. 7, 1879. Pension File and Military Service File, National Archives. *Annual Reunion*, Association of the Graduates of the US Military Academy, 1879. Ivan J. Nicodemus. *Nicodemus Notes in America.* N.p., 1995.

WILLIAM HENRY PURNELL

Colonel, Purnell Legion MD Infantry, Nov. 1, 1861. Resigned Feb. 17, 1862, to resume his duties as Postmaster. Major Gen. John A. Dix endorsed his resignation, "Col. Purnell is the Postmaster of the City of Baltimore and cannot perform the duties of both offices."

Born: Feb. 3, 1826 Worcester Co., MD
Died: March 30, 1902 Atlantic City, NJ
Education: Graduated Delaware College, Newark, DE, 1846
Occupation: Lawyer
Offices/Honors: MD State Comptroller, 1856–61. Postmaster, Baltimore, MD, 1861–66. President of Delaware College, Newark, DE, 1870–85.
Miscellaneous: Resided Snow Hill, Worcester Co., MD; Annapolis, Anne Arundel Co., MD; Baltimore, MD; and Newark, New Castle Co., DE
Buried: St. Annes Cemetery, Annapolis, MD
References: *Dictionary of American Biography.* Obituary, *Baltimore Sun*, April 1, 1902. Military Service File, National Archives. Letters Received, Volunteer Service Branch, Adjutant General's Office, File P71(VS)1862, National Archives. John A. Munroe. *The University of Delaware: A History.* Newark, DE, 1986.

William Henry Purnell (postwar)
COURTESY OF THE UNIVERSITY OF DELAWARE ARCHIVES.

HENRY CLAY RIZER

1 Sergeant, Co. C, 3 Potomac Home Brigade MD Infantry, Sept. 16, 1861. 1 Lieutenant, Co. C, 3 Potomac Home Brigade MD Infantry, Jan. 30, 1862. Captain, Co. C, 3 Potomac Home Brigade MD Infantry, March 1, 1862. Taken prisoner and paroled, Harper's Ferry, WV, Sept. 15, 1862. Major, 3 Potomac Home Brigade MD Infantry, April 14, 1864. Lieutenant Colonel, 3 Potomac Home Brigade MD Infantry, Jan. 18, 1865. Colonel, 3 Potomac Home Brigade MD Infantry, May 6, 1865. Honorably mustered out, May 29, 1865.

Born: Feb. 1, 1844 Cumberland, MD
Died: July 21, 1938 Washington, DC
Occupation: Lawyer, newspaper editor and disbursing agent
Offices/Honors: Chief Clerk, US Geological Survey, 1891–1925
Miscellaneous: Resided Cumberland, Allegany Co., MD; Ellicott City, Howard Co., MD, 1865–67; Hagerstown, Washington Co., MD, 1867–70; Eureka, Greenwood Co., KS, 1870–83; Topeka, Shawnee Co., KS, 1883–91; and Washington, DC, 1891–1938

Henry Clay Rizer
FROM *THE UNION ARMY.*

Buried: Arlington National Cemetery, Arlington, VA (Section 3, Lot 2008)
References: Obituary, *Washington Post*, July 22, 1938. Pension File and Military Service File, National Archives. *The Union Army.* Maryland/Washington, DC, Edition. Madison, WI, 1908. Letters Received, Volunteer Service Branch, Adjutant General's Office, File R1153(VS)1863, National Archives. Martha N. McLeod. *Brother Warriors, The Reminiscences of Union and Confederate Veterans.* Washington, DC, 1940. Kathleen L. Rizer. *Rizer Research.* Feb.–May 1990.

ROBERT SMITH RODGERS

Major, 2 Eastern Shore MD Infantry, Dec. 24, 1861. Colonel, 2 Eastern Shore MD Infantry, Jan. 28, 1863. Commanded 3 Brigade, 1 Division, Army of West Virginia, Dec. 1863–April 1864. Honorably mustered out, Oct. 31, 1864.

Born: Jan. 17, 1809 Sion Hill, near Havre de Grace, MD

Died: July 10, 1891 Sion Hill, near Havre de Grace, MD

Education: Attended Norwich Military Academy, Middletown, CT

Occupation: Civil engineer and farmer

Miscellaneous: Resided near Havre de Grace, Harford Co., MD; and Washington, DC. Son of Commodore John Rodgers (1770–1838) and brother of Admiral John Rodgers (1812–1882). Son-in-law of Commodore Matthew C. Perry.

Buried: Rock Creek Cemetery, Washington, DC (Section E, Lot 4)

References: Obituary, *Bel Air Aegis and Intelligencer*, July 17, 1891. Military Service File, National Archives. Frederick L. Cobourn. *A Short Biography of Those Whose Portraits Adorn the Walls of the Court House, Bel Air, MD.* Bel Air, MD, 1942. Robert S. Rodgers Papers, Duke University, Durham, NC. Obituary, *Harford Democrat*, July 17, 1891.

Robert Smith Rodgers
PORTRAIT PAINTING, HARFORD COUNTY COURT HOUSE, BEL AIR, MD.

WILLIAM LOUIS SCHLEY

Colonel, 5 MD Infantry, Sept. 4, 1861. On Sept. 28, 1864 he was relieved from his command and ordered to appear before a Board of Examination. Feeling "the sting and injury of this examination," which "has worked much wrong and injustice to myself, and from no act or fault of mine," he resigned Oct. 6, 1864.

Born: Aug. 26, 1823 Frederick, MD

Died: Dec. 15, 1898 Baltimore, MD

Education: Attended Marshall College, Mercersburg, PA

Other Wars: Mexican War (Sergeant Major, 3 US Dragoons)

Occupation: Lawyer

Miscellaneous: Resided Baltimore, MD. First cousin of Admiral Winfield Scott Schley.

Buried: Loudon Park Cemetery, Baltimore, MD (Section Q, Lot 310)

References: Obituary, *Baltimore Sun*, Dec. 16, 1898. Pension File and Military Service File, National Archives. Letters Received, Volunteer Service Branch, Adjutant General's Office, File S387(VS)1862, National Archives. Calvin E. Schildknecht. *Emigrants Thomas and Margaret Schley and Some of Their Descendants.* Gettysburg, PA, 1993.

William Louis Schley
ROGER D. HUNT COLLECTION, USAMHI.

Benjamin Louis Simpson (left) with an unidentified officer
THE MARYLAND HISTORICAL SOCIETY, BALTIMORE, MD.

BENJAMIN LOUIS SIMPSON

Captain, Co. A, Purnell Legion MD Infantry, Aug. 24, 1861. Major, Purnell Legion MD Infantry, April 9, 1862. Lieutenant Colonel, Purnell Legion MD Infantry, July 23, 1862. Resigned Dec. 5, 1862, due to "serious pecuniary loss" and "the feeble condition of the health of my family." In accepting his resignation, Brig. Gen. Nathaniel J. Jackson commented, "I consider this officer inefficient and incompetent for the position he occupies." Lieutenant Colonel, 9 MD Infantry, June 29, 1863. Colonel, 9 MD Infantry, Aug. 17, 1863. Honorably mustered out, Feb. 24, 1864.

Born: July 15, 1818 Baltimore, MD
Died: Feb. 27, 1888 Washington, DC
Occupation: Ship carpenter by trade. Foreman at the Washington Navy Yard after war.
Miscellaneous: Resided Baltimore, MD, to 1870; and Washington, DC, after 1870

Buried: Congressional Cemetery, Washington, DC (Range 95, Site 330)
References: Pension File and Military Service File, National Archives. Obituary, *Baltimore Sun*, Feb. 28, 1888. Letters Received, Volunteer Service Branch, Adjutant General's Office, File H33(VS)1863, National Archives.

JOHN SOMMER

Colonel, 2 MD Infantry, Sept. 21, 1861. Arrested and placed in confinement by Brig. Gen. Jesse L. Reno for alleged disobedience of orders, he resigned April 20, 1862. Captain, Co. E, 2 MD Cavalry, July 29, 1863. Honorably mustered out, Jan. 31, 1864.

Born: Sept. 15, 1816 Lancaster, PA
Died: Dec. 10, 1892 Baltimore, MD
Other Wars: Mexican War (service alleged but not confirmed)
Occupation: Coach painter before war. US Customs inspector after war.
Miscellaneous: Resided Towson, Baltimore Co., MD; and Baltimore, MD
Buried: Baltimore Cemetery, Baltimore, MD (Area II, Walk 4, Lot 8, South Side)
References: Obituary, *Baltimore Sun*, Dec. 12, 1892. Pension File and Military Service File, National Archives. Letters Received, Volunteer Service Branch, Adjutant General's Office, File P268(VS)1862, National Archives.

John Sommer
ROGER D. HUNT COLLECTION, USAMHI.

JOSEPH M. SUDSBURG

Captain, Co. K, 2 MD Infantry, Sept. 18, 1861. Lieutenant Colonel, 3 MD Infantry, May 7, 1862. Colonel, 3 MD Infantry, Oct. 24, 1862. Commanded 2 Brigade, 2 Division, 12 Army Corps, Army of the Potomac, Dec. 1862. Commanded 2 Brigade, 1 Division, 9 Army Corps, Army of the Potomac, May 31–June 4, 1864. Honorably mustered out, June 24, 1864, by reason of consolidation of regiment into battalion of four companies.

Born: March 17, 1827 Nymphenburg, Bavaria
Died: April 8, 1901 Baltimore, MD
Other Wars: Hungarian War of Independence, 1848–49
Occupation: Wood carver and designer
Miscellaneous: Resided Baltimore, MD
Buried: Loudon Park National Cemetery, Baltimore, MD (Officer Section, Site 18)

Joseph M. Sudsburg
COURTESY OF GIL BARRETT.
W. J. MILLER, 256 W. PRATT STREET,
BETWEEN HANOVER AND SHARP, BALTIMORE, MD.

References: Pension File and Military Service File, National Archives. *The Biographical Cyclopedia of Representative Men of Maryland and District of Columbia.* Baltimore, MD, 1879. Obituary, *Baltimore Sun*, April 9, 1901.

BENJAMIN FRANKLIN TAYLOR

Private, Co. B, 2 MD Infantry, June 30, 1861. Sergeant Major, 2 MD Infantry, Sept. 30, 1861. 2 Lieutenant, Co. B, 2 MD Infantry, April 23, 1862. Captain, Co. B, 2 MD Infantry, Sept. 23, 1862. Acting ADC, 1 Brigade, 2 Division, 9 Army Corps, Army of the Ohio, Nov.–Dec. 1863. Acting AIG, 2 Brigade, 2 Division, 9 Army Corps, Jan.–March 1864. GSW left shoulder, Petersburg, VA, June 25, 1864. Lieutenant Colonel, 2 MD Infantry, Oct. 6, 1864. Shell wound left heel and ankle, Petersburg, VA, April 2, 1865. *Colonel*, 2 MD Infantry, July 10, 1865. Honorably mustered out, July 17, 1865. Bvt. Colonel, USV, April 2, 1865, for conspicuous gallantry in the assault before Petersburg, VA.

Born: Nov. 13, 1840 Baltimore, MD
Died: Feb. 25, 1919 Baltimore, MD
Education: Graduated St. Timothy's Hall, Catonsville, MD, 1859. Attended Maryland Agricultural College, College Park, MD.
Occupation: Farmer
Offices/Honors: Superintendent, Loudon Park National Cemetery, Baltimore, MD, at his death
Miscellaneous: Resided Baltimore, MD; and Kingsville, Baltimore Co., MD
Buried: St. Johns Episcopal Churchyard, Kingsville, MD
References: *Genealogical and Biographical Record of the Leading Families of the City of Baltimore and Baltimore County, MD.* New York and Chicago, 1897. Pension File and Military Service File, National Archives. Obituary, *Baltimore Sun*, Feb. 28, 1919. Benjamin F. Taylor Collection, Maryland Historical Society.

Benjamin F. Taylor
THE MARYLAND HISTORICAL SOCIETY, BALTIMORE, MD.

JAMES WALLACE

Colonel, 1 Eastern Shore MD Infantry, Aug. 16, 1861. Resigned Dec. 23, 1863, due to "embarrassing and afflicting circumstances" affecting his family and others and requiring his presence to resolve. "My professional income is gone, the revenue from my lands has ceased and other sources have failed. The labor and toil of years have been swept away, and ruin is staring me in the face."

Born: March 14, 1818 Dorchester Co., MD
Died: Feb. 12, 1887 Baltimore, MD
Education: Graduated Dickinson College, Carlisle, PA, 1840

Occupation: Lawyer, farmer and fruit grower
Offices/Honors: MD House of Delegates, 1854–56. MD Senate, 1856–60.
Miscellaneous: Resided Cambridge, Dorchester Co., MD
Buried: City Cemetery, Cambridge, MD
References: *The Biographical Cyclopedia of Representative Men of Maryland and District of Columbia*. Baltimore, MD, 1879. Elias Jones. *Revised History of Dorchester County, MD*. Baltimore, MD, 1925. Military Service File, National Archives. Obituary, *Baltimore Sun*, Feb. 14, 1887. Oliver S. Phelps. *The Phelps Family of America*. Pittsfield, MA, 1899.

EDWIN HANSON WEBSTER

Colonel, 7 MD Infantry, Sept. 12, 1862. Resigned Nov. 6, 1863, having "recently been elected a member of the House of Representatives."

Born: March 31, 1829 near Churchville, MD
Died: April 24, 1893 Bel Air, MD
Education: Graduated Dickinson College, Carlisle, PA, 1847
Occupation: Lawyer
Offices/Honors: MD Senate, 1856–59 (Senate President, 1858–59). US House of Representatives, 1859–65. US Collector of Customs, Baltimore, MD, 1865–69, 1882–86.
Miscellaneous: Resided Bel Air, Harford Co., MD; and Baltimore, MD
Buried: Calvary Methodist Cemetery, Churchville, MD

Edwin Hanson Webster
COLLECTION OF THE NEW-YORK HISTORICAL SOCIETY.
PUBLISHED BY E. ANTHONY, 501 BROADWAY, NEW YORK,
FROM PHOTOGRAPHIC NEGATIVE IN
BRADY'S NATIONAL PORTRAIT GALLERY.

References: *The Biographical Cyclopedia of Representative Men of Maryland and District of Columbia*. Baltimore, MD, 1879. Military Service File, National Archives. Obituary, *Bel Air Aegis and Intelligencer*, April 28, 1893. Obituary, *Baltimore Sun*, April 25, 1893. *Biographical Directory of the American Congress*. Frederick L. Cobourn. *A Short Biography of Those Whose Portraits Adorn the Walls of the Court House, Bel Air, MD*. Bel Air, MD, 1942.

EDWARD WILKINS

Colonel, 2 Eastern Shore MD Infantry, Dec. 25, 1861. Resigned Dec. 23, 1862, due to "the impaired state of my health resulting from a serious and protracted illness."

Born: Oct. 6, 1813 Kent Co., MD
Died: Dec. 28, 1878 near Chestertown, MD

Edward Wilkins (postwar)
FROM *THE BIOGRAPHICAL CYCLOPEDIA OF REPRESENTATIVE MEN
OF MARYLAND AND DISTRICT OF COLUMBIA.*

Occupation: Farmer and fruit grower
Offices/Honors: MD Senate, 1856–60. US Collector of
Customs, Baltimore, MD, 1876–77.
Miscellaneous: Resided Chestertown, Kent Co., MD
Buried: Chester Cemetery, Chestertown, MD
References: *The Biographical Cyclopedia of Representative
Men of Maryland and District of Columbia.* Baltimore,
MD, 1879. *Portrait and Biographical Record of the
Eastern Shore of Maryland.* New York and Chicago,
1898. Military Service File, National Archives.
Obituary, *Baltimore Sun,* Dec. 30, 1878.

JOHN W. WILSON

Captain, Co. G, 1 MD Infantry, May 27, 1861. Major, 1
MD Infantry, Feb. 1, 1862. Taken prisoner, Front Royal,
VA, May 23, 1862, but escaped. Lieutenant Colonel, 1
MD Infantry, Aug. 27, 1862. Colonel, 1 MD Infantry,
Sept. 6, 1864. GSW head, Dabney's Mill, VA, Feb. 6,
1865.

Born: Feb. 2, 1828 Lancaster Co., PA
Died: Feb. 6, 1865 KIA Dabney's Mill, VA
Other Wars: Mexican War (Private, Co. G, Maryland
and DC Infantry)

John W. Wilson
COURTESY OF GIL BARRETT.
RICHARD WALZL, 103 W. BALTIMORE STREET, BALTIMORE, MD.

Occupation: Farmer
Miscellaneous: Resided Chestnut Grove, Baltimore Co.,
MD
Buried: Chestnut Grove Cemetery, Jacksonville, MD
References: Charles Camper and Joseph W. Kirkley.
*Historical Record of the 1st Regiment Maryland
Infantry.* Washington, DC, 1871. Kevin C. Ruffner.
*Maryland's Blue & Gray: A Border State's Union and
Confederate Junior Officer Corps.* Baton Rouge, LA,
1997. Pension File and Military Service File,
National Archives. Obituary, *Baltimore Sun,* Feb. 11,
1865. Letters Received, Volunteer Service Branch,
Adjutant General's Office, File W2945(VS)1864,
National Archives.

DELAWARE

1st Cavalry

George P. Fisher	Oct. 13, 1862	Resigned March 21, 1863
Edwin Wilmer	Dec. 9, 1864	Not mustered

1st Infantry (3 months)

Henry H. Lockwood	May 25, 1861	Promoted **Brig. Gen., USV**, Aug. 8, 1861

1st Infantry (3 years)

John W. Andrews	Sept. 17, 1861	Resigned Feb. 7, 1863
Thomas A. Smyth	Feb. 7, 1863	Promoted **Brig. Gen., USV**, Oct. 1, 1864
Daniel Woodall	Dec. 23, 1864	Mustered out July 12, 1865, **Bvt. Brig. Gen.**

2nd Infantry

Henry W. Wharton	July 13, 1861	Resigned Oct. 6, 1862
William P. Baily	Oct. 6, 1862	Resigned May 16, 1864

3rd Infantry

William O. Redden	May 15, 1862	Resigned Dec. 6, 1862
Samuel H. Jenkins	Feb. 5, 1863	Discharged Feb. 26, 1864

4th Infantry

Arthur H. Grimshaw	June 7, 1862	Resigned Dec. 9, 1864

5th Infantry

Henry S. McComb	Nov. 26, 1862	Mustered out Aug. 12, 1863

6th Infantry

Edwin Wilmer	June 27, 1863	Mustered out Aug. 22, 1863

7th Infantry

Edgar Hounsfield	July 28, 1864	Mustered out Aug. 12, 1864

JOHN WILLIAMS ANDREWS

Colonel, 1 DE Infantry, Sept. 17, 1861. Commanded 3 Brigade, 3 Division, 2 Army Corps, Army of the Potomac, Sept. 17–Dec. 13, 1862. Shell wound Fredericksburg, VA, Dec. 13, 1862. Resigned Feb. 7, 1863, due to physical disability from hemorrhoids and chronic rheumatism.

Born: June 4, 1814 Bordeaux, France
Died: Aug. 24, 1881 near Wilmington, DE
Education: Attended University of Pennsylvania, Philadelphia, PA
Occupation: Gentleman farmer
Miscellaneous: Resided Wilmington, New Castle Co., DE. Father-in-law of Major Gen. James Harrison Wilson.

William P. Baily
FROM *A BRIEF ACCOUNT OF THE SERVICES RENDERED
BY THE 2ND REGIMENT DELAWARE VOLUNTEERS
IN THE WAR OF THE REBELLION.*

Buried: Old Swedes Churchyard, Wilmington, DE
References: Obituary, *Wilmington Every Evening*, Aug. 25, 1881. *Colonial and Revolutionary Lineages of America*, Vol. 8. New York City, NY, 1941. Military Service File, National Archives. William P. Seville. *History of the 1st Regiment Delaware Volunteers.* Wilmington, DE, 1884.

WILLIAM P. BAILY

Corporal, Co. C, 7 NY State Militia, April 26, 1861. Lieutenant Colonel, 2 DE Infantry, July 16, 1861. Colonel, 2 DE Infantry, Aug. 22, 1862. Shell wound left breast, Fredericksburg, VA, Dec. 13, 1862. Commanded 4 Brigade, 1 Division, 2 Army Corps, Army of the Potomac, May 20–June 12, 1863 and Dec. 29, 1863–Jan. 10, 1864. His "immediate and unconditional" resignation was accepted May 16, 1864. In recommending acceptance of the resignation, brigade commander Col. John R. Brooke added the underlined comment, "for the good of the service."

Born: Dec. 5, 1825 Wilmington, DE
Died: Feb. 1, 1883 Plainfield, NJ
Occupation: Merchant engaged in importing business
Miscellaneous: Resided New York City, NY; and North Plainfield, Somerset Co., NJ
Buried: Hillside Cemetery, Scotch Plains, NJ (Section A, Division 2, Lot 21)
References: Obituary, *Plainfield Constitutionalist*, Feb. 9, 1883. Pension File and Military Service File, National Archives. Robert G. Smith. *A Brief Account of the Services Rendered by the 2nd Regiment Delaware Volunteers in the War of the Rebellion.* Wilmington, DE, 1909. Letters Received, Volunteer Service Branch, Adjutant General's Office, File D777(VS)1864, National Archives.

GEORGE PURNELL FISHER

Colonel, 1 DE Cavalry, Oct. 13, 1862. Resigned March 21, 1863, "having been nominated by the President . . . for the position of Associate Justice of the Supreme Court of the District of Columbia."

Born: Oct. 13, 1817 Milford, DE
Died: Feb. 10, 1899 Washington, DC
Education: Graduated Dickinson College, Carlisle, PA, 1838

George Purnell Fisher
NATIONAL ARCHIVES.

Arthur Harper Grimshaw
COURTESY OF STEVE MEADOW.
A. GAWTHROP & CO., PHOTOGRAPHERS,
NO. 415 MARKET STREET, WILMINGTON, DE.

Occupation: Lawyer and judge

Offices/Honors: DE House of Representatives, 1844. Secretary of State of Delaware, 1846–47. Attorney General of Delaware, 1855–60. US House of Representatives, 1861–63. Associate Justice, DC Supreme Court, 1863–70. First Auditor, US Treasury, 1889–93.

Miscellaneous: Resided Dover, Kent Co., DE; and Washington, DC. Presided at the trial of John H. Surratt in connection with the assassination of President Lincoln.

Buried: Christ Episcopal Churchyard, Dover, DE

References: *Dictionary of American Biography.* Charles B. Lore. *The Life and Character of George P. Fisher.* Wilmington, DE, 1902. *Historical and Biographical Encyclopedia of Delaware.* Wilmington, DE, 1882. Henry C. Conrad. *History of the State of Delaware.* Wilmington, DE, 1908. J. Thomas Scharf. *History of Delaware, 1609–1888.* Philadelphia, PA, 1888. Pension File and Military Service File, National Archives. Obituary, *Washington Evening Star,* Feb. 11, 1899.

ARTHUR HARPER GRIMSHAW

Colonel, 4 DE Infantry, June 7, 1862. Commanded 3 Brigade, Casey's Division, Defenses of Washington, Nov. 1862. Commanded 1 Brigade, Tyler's Division, 22 Army Corps, Department of Washington, Jan.–March 1864 and April–May 1864. GSW right arm, Petersburg, VA, June 18, 1864. Commanded 3 Brigade, 2 Division, 5 Army Corps, Army of the Potomac, Sept. 14–Nov. 1, 1864 and Nov. 17–21, 1864. "Being again relieved from command of a brigade, and placed under his junior officer, a Brevet Brig. Gen., and in view of the fact that the 4th regt. Del. Vols. has three field officers, . . . and is reduced to the number of 217 men present for duty," he resigned Dec. 9, 1864.

Born: Jan. 16, 1824 Philadelphia, PA
Died: May 17, 1891 Wilmington, DE
Education: M.D., University of Pennsylvania Medical School, Philadelphia, PA, 1845

Occupation: Physician
Offices/Honors: Postmaster, Wilmington, DE, 1861–66
Miscellaneous: Resided Wilmington, New Castle Co., DE
Buried: Wilmington and Brandywine Cemetery, Wilmington, DE (Section I, Lots 21–22)
References: *Historical and Biographical Encyclopedia of Delaware.* Wilmington, DE, 1882. Obituary, *Wilmington Every Evening*, May 18, 1891. Pension File and Military Service File, National Archives. Charles A. Foster. *History of the Grand Army of the Republic and of Delaware, and Its Auxiliaries, Union Veteran Legion and National Guard of Delaware.* N.p., 1893. Letters Received, Volunteer Service Branch, Adjutant General's Office, File R718(VS)1864, National Archives.

EDGAR HOUNSFIELD

Captain, Co. E, 5 DE Infantry, Oct. 25, 1862. Major, 5 DE Infantry, Nov. 26, 1862. Honorably mustered out, Aug. 12, 1863. Lieutenant Colonel, 7 DE Infantry, July 12, 1864. Colonel, 7 DE Infantry, July 28, 1864. Honorably mustered out, Aug. 12, 1864.

Henry Simpson McComb
COURTESY OF THE HISTORICAL SOCIETY OF DELAWARE.
F. GUTEKUNST, PHOTOGRAPHER,
704 & 706 ARCH STREET, PHILADELPHIA.

Born: 1836? Wilmington, DE
Died: Dec. 9, 1911 Dansville, NY
Occupation: Merchant and paper mill operator
Miscellaneous: Resided Wilmington, New Castle Co., DE; and Louisville, Jefferson Co., KY
Buried: Cave Hill Cemetery, Louisville, KY (Section 1, Lot 28)
References: Obituary, *Louisville Courier Journal*, Dec. 11, 1911. Military Service File, National Archives.

SAMUEL HOWELL JENKINS

Captain, Co. H, 1 DE Infantry, May 4, 1861. Honorably mustered out, Aug. 16, 1861. Lieutenant Colonel, 3 DE Infantry, Nov. 1, 1861. Colonel, 3 DE Infantry, Feb. 5, 1863. Honorably discharged, Feb. 26, 1864, upon "adverse report of a Board of Examination," which found him "deficient in Capacity, wholly deficient in Qualifications, and unquestionably deficient in Efficiency."

Born: 1837? Camden, DE
Died: June 24, 1892 Glenolden, Delaware Co., PA
Occupation: Hardware merchant and broker
Miscellaneous: Resided Camden, Kent Co., DE; Philadelphia, PA; and Woodbury, Camden Co., NJ
Buried: Camden Friends Meeting House Cemetery, Camden, DE
References: Pension File and Military Service File, National Archives. Letters Received, Volunteer Service Branch, Adjutant General's Office, Files R832(VS)1863 and J41(VS)1864, National Archives.

HENRY SIMPSON McCOMB

Colonel, 5 DE Infantry, Nov. 26, 1862. Honorably mustered out, Aug. 12, 1863.

Born: July 28, 1825 Wilmington, DE
Died: Dec. 30, 1881 Philadelphia, PA
Occupation: Leather goods manufacturer and railroad president
Miscellaneous: Resided Wilmington, New Castle Co., DE
Buried: Wilmington and Brandywine Cemetery, Wilmington, DE (Section A, Lot 29)
References: *Historical and Biographical Encyclopedia of Delaware.* Wilmington, DE, 1882. J. Thomas Scharf. *History of Delaware, 1609–1888.* Philadelphia, PA, 1888. Obituary, *Wilmington Every Evening*, Dec. 31, 1881. Military Service File, National Archives.

WILLIAM O. REDDEN

Colonel, 3 DE Infantry, May 15, 1862. Commanded 3 Brigade, 2 Division, 12 Army Corps, Army of the Potomac, Sept.–Oct. 1862. Having been cited to appear before a Board of Examination, he resigned Dec. 6, 1862, "feeling incompetent, through physical disability, to stand a thorough examination." His request for reinstatement was denied, Dec. 29, 1862, since "you voluntarily resigned to escape examination by a Military Board . . . and you are considered by Brigade, Division, and Corps commanders utterly incompetent."

Born: Aug. 11, 1806 Sussex Co., DE
Died: July 18, 1877 Eldorado, KS
Occupation: Farmer before war. Clerk in the US Post Office Department after war.
Offices/Honors: Sheriff, Sussex Co., DE, 1838–40. DE House of Representatives (Speaker), 1842–44.
Miscellaneous: Resided Bridgeville, Sussex Co., DE; Washington, DC; and Eldorado, Butler Co., KS
Buried: Bridgeville Cemetery, Bridgeville, DE
References: Pension File and Military Service File, National Archives. Letters Received, Volunteer Service Branch, Adjutant General's Office, File R883(VS)1862, National Archives. Henry C. Conrad. *History of the State of Delaware*. Wilmington, DE, 1908.

HENRY WILLIAMS WHARTON

Captain, 6 US Infantry, Feb. 16, 1847. Colonel, 2 DE Infantry, July 13, 1861. Major, 9 US Infantry, Sept. 9, 1861. Resigned volunteer commission, Oct. 6, 1862, on account of "extreme debility consequent upon a severe attack of malarial fever and dysentery." Commissary of Musters, 8 Army Corps, Middle Department, March 23, 1863–Aug. 1, 1865.

Born: Sept. 16, 1811 Washington, DC
Died: March 23, 1868 Baltimore, MD
Occupation: Regular Army (Major, 9 US Infantry, retired Dec. 1, 1863)
Miscellaneous: Resided Philadelphia, PA; and Baltimore, MD
Buried: St. John's Episcopal Churchyard, Norristown, PA

References: Anne H. Wharton. *Genealogy of the Wharton Family of Philadelphia*. Philadelphia, PA, 1880. Pension File and Military Service File, National Archives. Obituary, *Baltimore American & Commercial Advertiser*, March 24, 1868. Letters Received, Volunteer Service Branch, Adjutant General's Office, File W764(VS)1862, National Archives. Jerre Garrett. *Muffled Drums and Mustard Spoons: Cecil County, Maryland, 1860–65*. Shippensburg, PA, 1996.

EDWIN WILMER

Captain, Co. A, 6 DE Infantry, Oct. 25, 1862. Provost Marshal, District of Delaware, May 1, 1863. Colonel, 6 DE Infantry, June 27, 1863. Honorably mustered out as colonel, Aug. 22, 1863. *Colonel*, 1 DE Cavalry, Dec. 9, 1864. Not mustered due to reduced strength of regiment. Dismissed as provost marshal, June 15, 1865.

Edwin Wilmer
COURTESY OF ANDY MCKAY.
OIL PAINTING BY DAVID A. WOODWARD.
DELAWARE BUREAU OF MUSEUMS & HISTORIC PROPERTIES.

Born: Sept. 10, 1819 Smyrna, DE
Died: Jan. 27, 1888 Govanstown, Baltimore Co., MD
Education: Attended Dickinson College, Carlisle, PA
Occupation: Merchant and granite contractor before war. Brick manufacturer after war.
Miscellaneous: Resided Port Deposit, Cecil Co., MD, to 1857; Elkton, Cecil Co., MD, 1857–60; Smyrna, Kent Co., DE, 1860–65; New York City, NY, 1865–69; and Baltimore, MD, 1869–88
Buried: Hopewell United Methodist Churchyard, near Woodlawn, Cecil Co., MD

References: *The Biographical Cyclopedia of Representative Men of Maryland and District of Columbia.* Baltimore, MD, 1879. Pension File and Military Service File, National Archives. Obituary, *The Cecil Whig*, Feb. 4, 1888. Obituary, *Baltimore American*, Jan. 28, 1888. Robert C. Moon. *The Morris Family of Philadelphia.* Philadelphia, PA, 1898. Letters Received, Volunteer Service Branch, Adjutant General's Office, Files J650(VS)1863 and D1538(VS)1864, National Archives. George L. Reed, editor. *Alumni Record Dickinson College.* Carlisle, PA, 1905.

DISTRICT OF COLUMBIA

1st Cavalry

Lafayette C. Baker | May 5, 1863 | Promoted **Brig. Gen., USV**, April 26, 1865

1st Infantry

James A. Tait | July 23, 1861 | Discharged July 31, 1863

2nd Infantry

Isaac A. Peck	Feb. 26, 1862	Resigned June 7, 1862
Charles M. Alexander	June 12, 1862	Mustered out Feb. 16, 1865
William M. Graham	April 7, 1865	Mustered out Sept. 12, 1865, **Bvt. Brig. Gen.**

5th Battalion Militia Infantry

William H. Philip | April 1, 1862 | Mustered out July 15, 1862

Charles Madison Alexander
Massachusetts MOLLUS Collection, USAMHI.

CHARLES MADISON ALEXANDER

Major, 2 DC Infantry, Feb. 7, 1862. Colonel, 2 DC Infantry, June 12, 1862. Commanded Tyler's Division, 22 Army Corps, Department of Washington, Dec. 1863–Jan. 1864. Commanded 1 Brigade, Tyler's Division, 22 Army Corps, Department of Washington, March–April, 1864. Commanded Hardin's Division, 22 Army Corps, Department of Washington, July 1864. Honorably mustered out, Feb. 16, 1865.

Born: Nov. 7, 1832 Woodford Co., KY
Died: Jan. 27, 1891 Washington, DC
Education: Graduated Marietta (OH) College, 1852
Occupation: Patent attorney
Offices/Honors:: Postmaster, Washington, DC, 1868–69
Miscellaneous: Resided Washington, DC

Buried: Oak Hill Cemetery, Washington, DC (Lot 952)
References: George J. Blazier. *Marietta College: Biographical Record of the Officers and Alumni.* Marietta, OH, 1928. Pension File and Military Service File, National Archives. Madison Davis. "A History of the City Post Office," *Records of the Columbia Historical Society,* Vol. 6 (1903). Obituary, *Washington Evening Star,* Jan. 28, 1891. William T. Lewis. *Genealogy of the Lewis Family in America.* Louisville, KY, 1893. *Marietta College Alumni Memorial No. 7.* Marietta, OH, 1895.

ISAAC AUGUSTUS PECK

Colonel, 2 DC Infantry, Feb. 26, 1862. Resigned June 7, 1862.

Born: April 9, 1828 Catskill, NY
Died: Feb. 4, 1893 Redden, DE
Occupation: Carriage manufacturer before war. Lumber manufacturer and farmer after war.
Miscellaneous: Resided Rahway, Union Co., NJ; Washington, DC; Wilmington, New Hanover Co., NC; and Redden, Sussex Co., DE
Buried: Union Cemetery, Georgetown, Sussex Co., DE (Section G, Lot 46, unmarked)
References: J. M. Runk. *Biographical and Genealogical Encyclopedia of the State of Delaware.* Chambersburg, PA, 1899. *Historical and Biographical Encyclopedia of Delaware.* Wilmington, DE, 1882. Pension File and Military Service File, National Archives. Letters Received, Volunteer Service Branch, Adjutant General's Office, File P118(VS)1863, National Archives.

WILLIAM HENRY PHILIP

Colonel, 5 Battalion DC Militia Infantry, April 1, 1862. Acting ADC, Staff of Major Gen. William B. Franklin, May 23, 1862. Honorably mustered out, July 15, 1862.

Born: Sept. 6, 1824 Claverack, NY
Died: May 7, 1881 New York City, NY
Education: Graduated Williams College, Williamstown, MA, 1846
Occupation: Lawyer
Miscellaneous: Resided Claverack, Columbia Co., NY; and Washington, DC
Buried: Oak Hill Cemetery, Washington, DC (Van Ness Mausoleum, Lot 173 East)

William Henry Philip
USAMHI.
MCCLEES, NO. 308 PENN. AV., WASHINGTON,
AND 910 CHESTNUT ST., PHILADELPHIA.

References: Leila Philip. *A Family Place: A Hudson Valley Farm, Three Centuries, Five Wars, One Family.* New York City, NY, 2001. Obituary, *Hudson Evening Register*, May 9, 1881. Military Service File, National Archives. Obituary, *Washington Evening Star*, May 8, 1881. *A Biographical Record of the Kappa Alpha Society in Williams College, 1833–1881.* New York City, NY, 1881. Eugene A. Hoffman. *Genealogy of the Hoffman Family.* New York City, NY, 1899.

JAMES A. TAIT

Lieutenant Colonel, 6 Battalion DC Militia Infantry, May 1, 1861. Colonel, 1 DC Infantry, July 23, 1861. Commanded 2 Brigade, 2 Division, 2 Army Corps, Army of Virginia, July 1–10, 1862. Commanded 3 Brigade, 2 Division, 2 Army Corps, Army of Virginia, Aug. 9–Sept. 12, 1862. Appointed Provost Marshal General, Defenses South of the Potomac, Nov. 13, 1862.

James A. Tait (postwar)
FROM *WASHINGTON EVENING STAR*, MAY 15, 1895.

Although acquitted by a Court Martial on charges of "neglect of duty" and "disobedience of orders," connected with the passage of contraband goods (including 4,000 packs of playing cards) through Alexandria, VA, to the Confederate lines, he was dismissed Sept. 21, 1863, the reviewing officer (Maj. Gen. Heintzelman) disapproving the acquittal since "the evidence adduced shows each charge and specification conclusively proved." Since he had already been honorably discharged, July 31, 1863, upon consolidation of the regiment, his dismissal was revoked, Jan. 4, 1864.

Born: 1811? Scotland
Died: May 15, 1895 Washington, DC
Occupation: Stone mason and public works contractor before war. Real estate agent and insurance agent after war.
Miscellaneous: Resided Washington, DC
Buried: Congressional Cemetery, Washington, DC (Range 55, Site 220)
References: Obituary, *Washington Evening Star*, May 15, 1895. Military Service File, National Archives. Letters Received, Volunteer Service Branch, Adjutant General's Office, File T584(VS)1863, National Archives.

INDEX